T0269923

Winston Churchill

ALSO AVAILABLE FROM VERSO BY TARIQ ALI

{NON-FICTION}
Can Pakistan Survive? The Death of a State
The Clash of Fundamentalisms: Crusades, Jihads and Modernity
Bush in Babylon
Street-fighting Years: An Autobiography of the Sixties
Pirates of the Caribbean: Axis of Hope
Rough Music: Blair, Baghdad, London, Terror
The Duel
The Protocols of the Elders of Sodom: Essays
The Obama Syndrome
The Extreme Centre: A Warning
The Dilemmas of Lenin
The Forty-Year War in Afghanistan

{FICTION}
Fear of Mirrors

THE ISLAM QUINTET
Shadows of the Pomegranate Tree
The Book of Saladin
The Stone Woman
A Sultan in Palermo
Night of the Golden Butterfly

Winston Churchill

His Times, His Crimes

Tariq Ali

VERSO

London • New York

First published by Verso 2022
© Tariq Ali 2022

1 3 5 7 9 10 8 6 4 2

Verso
UK: 6 Meard Street, London W1F 0EG
US: 20 Jay Street, Suite 1010, Brooklyn, NY 11201
versobooks.com

Verso is the imprint of New Left Books

ISBN-13: 978-1-78873-577-3
ISBN-13: 978-1-78873-578-0 (UK EBK)
ISBN-13: 978-1-78873-579-7 (US EBK)

British Library Cataloguing in Publication Data
A catalogue record for this book is available from the British Library

Library of Congress Cataloging-in-Publication Data
Names: Ali, Tariq, author.
Title: Winston Churchill : his times, his crimes / Tariq Ali.
Description: London ; New York : Verso Books, 2022. | Includes
    bibliographical references and index.
Identifiers: LCCN 2021050568 (print) | LCCN 2021050569 (ebook) | ISBN
    9781788735773 (hardback) | ISBN 9781788735797 (ebk)
Subjects: LCSH: Churchill, Winston, 1874–1965 – Influence. | Great
    Britain – Colonies – History – 20th century. | Great Britain – Foreign
    relations – 20th century. | Great Britain – Politics and government – 20th
    century. | Historiography – Great Britain – History – 20th century. | Prime
    ministers – Great Britain – Biography.
Classification: LCC DA566.9.C5 A45 2022 (print) | LCC DA566.9.C5 (ebook)
    | DDC 941.084092 [B] – dc23/eng/20211020
LC record available at https://lccn.loc.gov/2021050568
LC ebook record available at https://lccn.loc.gov/2021050569

Typeset in Sabon LT by Hewer Text UK Ltd, Edinburgh
Printed and bound by CPI Group (UK) Ltd, Croydon CR0 4YY

For Garth Fawkes, who will be twenty-three when the centenary of the Second World War is marked. I hope much of this book will be redundant by then, but fear it won't.

Chronology

Winston Churchill: Servant of Empire

1874	Born at Blenheim Palace, Oxfordshire, son of Tory MP Randolph Churchill and American heiress Jennie Jerome
1876	Family moves to Dublin when Randolph Churchill becomes private secretary to the viceroy of Ireland, his father John Spencer-Churchill
1888–95	Educated at Harrow School and Royal Military Academy, Sandhurst
1895–99	Commissioned as second lieutenant in the 4th Queen's Hussars; skirmishes in Cuba, India, Sudan furnish material for early journalistic interventions
1899–1901	Resigns from the regiment to launch career in politics; free-booting military and journalistic engagements in South Africa
1901–04	Enters Parliament as Conservative MP for Oldham
1904	Defects to the Liberal Party
1906–08	Undersecretary of state for the Colonial Office in Campbell-Bannerman government
1908–10	Enters Asquith's Cabinet as president of Board of Trade
1910–11	Asquith's home secretary
1911–15	First lord of the admiralty; from 1914, member of Asquith's War Council
1915–16	Forced to resign as first lord of the admiralty as condition of Conservatives joining Asquith's National Government; rejoins Army but swiftly secures permission to leave active service after a few months on the Western Front
1917–19	Minister of Munitions in Lloyd George's Cabinet
1919–21	Lloyd George's secretary of state for war
1921–22	Secretary of state for the colonies; loses parliamentary seat in 1922 election
1924–29	Defects to the Conservative Party; chancellor of the Exchequer in Baldwin's Cabinet
1929–39	Resigns from Shadow Cabinet in protest against Dominion Status for India; excluded from the Cabinet 1931–39; writes pot-boiling histories
1939	First lord of the admiralty in Chamberlain's Cabinet
1939–45	Prime minister
1945–51	Leader of the opposition
1951–55	Prime minister
1955–65	In retirement. Dies in London, 1965, aged ninety

CONTENTS

CONTENTS

PREFACE

Is another book on Churchill necessary? I've asked myself this question more than once, but it seems very few others have. Most people I spoke to, including many who do not share my political opinions, argued strongly in favour of this project. Their motivation was simple. The Churchill cult was drowning all serious debate. An alternative was badly needed and instead of moaning I should get on with it. This is not to suggest that all historians who focus on Churchill are uncritical. There are some fine books out there, and I refer to them later in these pages. It's not now simply a question of providing an alternative, but of defending the right to do so. Churchill himself, whatever his shortcomings, relished a political duel and gave as good as he got. His epigones feel less intellectually/politically secure and regard any serious criticism as *lèse-majesté*. Not to be tolerated. This is unacceptable.

Participants in an anti-capitalist demonstration in 2000 sprayed Churchill's statue in Parliament Square with paint and gave him a turf Mohican. The prime minister at the time, Tony Blair, was livid. According to his spin doctor's diary, he 'went a bit over the top saying "This sort of thing must never be allowed to happen again" and suggesting that such demonstrations should be kept out of London'. The spraying continued at irregular intervals over the following years, reaching a peak in 2020 when Black Lives Matter activists painted 'Churchill Was a Racist' on the plinth.

This is one of the mildest criticisms of Churchill that can be made, but it caused a furore. More was to follow. In February 2021, as I was engaged in completing this book, I received a Zoom invitation to attend a virtual conference organised in Churchill College, Cambridge to discuss the politics of its namesake. Two of the panel members were academics of South Asian origin. One of them, Priya Gopal, was and remains a Fellow of the College. Unsurprisingly, the tone was critical since the discussion centred on the colonisation of India and its aftermath, especially the Bengal Famine.

It was a sober discussion, but a hullabaloo followed, orchestrated by the Tory press. The *Daily Telegraph* headlined its 11 February report: 'Churchill College panel claims wartime PM was a white racist and "worse than the Nazis"'. In fact nobody had said that, but it was enough to push Sir Nicholas Soames (Churchill's grandson) to become the standard bearer for the outrage. As any regular reader of *Private Eye* over the years will be aware, intellectual weight is not one of Soames's attributes, and his interventions on this occasion only confirmed the fact. But he was a descendant and made himself available to be used to crush dissenting voices.

Donors threatened to withdraw funding, the family was displeased, and the College hurriedly disbanded its working group on 'Churchill, Race and Empire', which had organised the offending conference. To protest this capitulation, that same night local Extinction Rebellion (XR) activists neatly daubed 'Churchill Was a Racist' on one of the brick walls of Churchill College.

Soames had characterised the panel discussion as marking a 'new low in the current vogue for the denigration in general of British history and of Sir Winston Churchill's memory in particular', and threatened the College by wondering aloud and in public whether it should be allowed to benefit from the Churchill name after permitting such an appalling event. In fact, both sides of the debate could come up with better names: Wellesley or Curzon for the glorifiers of empire, and Gandhi or Mandela for the other side. Meanwhile, the rapid response unit of XR Cambridge replied to Soames:

> Across this city, there are so many institutions whose money comes from exploitation and colonialism. We are not going to let Cambridge colleges censor the truth about their harmful historical

and modern connections. As a city and a country, we desperately need to face up to the legacy of the British Empire, which did so much damage around the world and is still causing harm today. It is increasingly evident that there is a deep connection between global, racial, social and climate justice. The idea that those with money, power and military strength have the right to exploit the earth and its people is responsible both for colonialism and the climate and ecological emergency. We have learned so much from anti-racist activists – we won't let Britain's racist history be swept under the rug.

The debate continues. This little book is another pebble in the pond. It does not concentrate exclusively on Churchill and is not a biography in the traditional sense. It situates Churchill within the ruling class that fought against workers and dissidents at home and built a huge empire abroad. It was this combination that enabled defeats of working-class organisations in Britain and the colonisation of large tracts of Asia and Africa. Without understanding the histories of those who resisted at home and abroad it is not easy to understand the hostility towards Churchill that still exists in this country.

Half a century ago I was enjoying a meal in Phnom Penh with Lawrence Daly, the Scottish miner's leader. The conversation was wide-ranging. The noise of the bombs dropping on Vietnam resounded throughout the region. Daly was an auto-didact, an organic intellectual and attached to no political party. The discussion turned to Britain. How did he explain the British electorate voting Churchill out in 1945? What had happened to the projected images of the great war leader? Daly paused for a moment and then said: 'It's not a mystery. Thanks to the Tories, the country was neck-deep in shit. People felt that if they elected Churchill, he would force them to do sit-ups.'

After one hundred and fifty years of continuous growth, as Eric Hobsbawm pointed out in *Industry and Empire*, the British economy was in trouble and mass unemployment was threatening social peace. Churchill wished to reverse the process by any means necessary. His favourite method was the use of force. On this he would never change, falter or repent. He never fully understood that American and German successes owed a great deal to scientific research and technological development. British universities were left untouched, continuing their normal pursuits, till it was too late to catch up with the US and Germany. A complacent ruling class in Britain, fed on the fruits of empire, was not capable of making up the ground. Despite what is hallowed as Churchill's 'finest hour', the 1945 victory was a huge defeat for the British Empire.

It took Churchill and his Labour mimics, Attlee and Bevin, some time to understand the full implications of this. Churchill accepted the role of second fiddle as long as he could pretend he was the first, issuing Cold War proclamations that generally amused and occasionally annoyed the new masters of the Western world. The US leaders humoured him, while getting on with their own business of taking over the European and Japanese colonies, with varying degrees of success.

Churchill's genetic racism never disappeared, trickling down homewards as labour shortages necessitated the import of colonial workers from the West Indies and South Asia. During his last weeks in Downing Street he was intransigent. His defence minister Harold Macmillan (later to be prime minister) recorded in his diary on 20 January 1955: 'More discussion [in Cabinet] about the West Indian immigrants. A Bill is being drafted – but it's not an easy problem. P.M. [Winston Churchill] thinks "Keep England White" a good slogan.'[1] A decade or so later, confronting a bout of heckling from racists at a public meeting, I shouted back: 'We're here because you were there. And we've got another century and a half to go.' They shut up temporarily, but I don't think they fully grasped the dialectic. Nor did Churchill.

This is what I explain in this book, accompanying Churchill's political life-line with a political and historical analysis that runs counter to his views and those of his many epigones. In highlighting the story of a defiant opposition (weak or strong), the book engages with a working-class history and colonial rebellions in a dialectical relation with the worshipful texts.

1 David Kynaston, *Family Britain, 1951–1957*, London, 2009, p. 453.

The emergence of an anti-colonial movement on campuses in different parts of the world a few years ago was an added inducement to writing about Churchill. The fact that Barack Obama and, more recently, Joe Biden, removed the Churchill bust from the Oval Office was another push (before 9/11 and George W. Bush's war on Afghanistan and Iraq, few were even aware that the bust existed). They did so because of British atrocities in Kenya and Churchill's record on Ireland, two of the imperial crimes he is charged with in this book. Their removal of the bust, however, was largely symbolic. Obama and Biden spoke as re-colonisers, as the modern heirs of Churchill and Curzon, Leopold and Salazar. The country over which they preside is the only real empire today, in a position much stronger than that of the British Empire even at its peak, and with a record of war crimes second to none.

The decolonisers in Britain and the anti-racists in the United States have torn down or demanded the removal of statues of slave owners and scoundrels such as Rhodes (greatly admired by Churchill). Churchill's statue has merely been daubed with red paint, to mark a Remembrance Day for the victims of empire. I'm not in favour of destroying his statue or that of most other imperial warlords or underlings. That would be a wrong-headed attempt to wipe out three hundred years of British history. A similar process in the United States would entail destroying the statues of most of the Founding Fathers on the grounds that they were slaveholders.

Far better to demand or implement the right to install plaques that challenge the official view, so that visitors to the site can read both sides of the argument and make their own decisions. And, of course, to demand new statues of those who were on the other side. This book is written in that spirit – an irruption, I hope, into a historical-political order that appears hegemonic but remains vulnerable. And with it, history remains the roiling, contradictory, conflict-ridden, international human story that it has always been.

ACKNOWLEDGEMENTS

It is necessary to start by stressing that nobody who helped is responsible for my arguments or conclusions. It was Mike Davis, longstanding comrade on the West Coast and a great historian, who insisted almost a decade ago that such a book needed writing. I hope he isn't too disappointed. Thanks go first and foremost to my editors JoAnn Wypijewski in Buffalo, NY and Leo Hollis in lockdown London. Leo, of course, is well used to my eccentricities and tends to remove them from the page. His insistence on combining some chapters and restructuring others has been very valuable. JoAnn is an old friend and a very stern editor. The combination worked.

For early research that included a lengthy reading list I must thank Pablo Bradbury, who was then a Verso intern. For reading three books on the Irish and Indian famines, as well as Churchill's novel, and writing reports on all of them, I must thank my grandson Jordan Beaumont, who had taken a gap year that coincided with the lockdown. His brother Aleem saved the manuscript from a computer disaster and demanded a tenner. Sebastian Budgen was helpful as usual, forwarding useful documentation from many quarters.

For sharing personal and political material relevant to the chapter on Greece I am very grateful to Gella Skouras, a Greek friend since 1967, and to Jane Gabriel, who produced (with Gella's help), the Channel 4 documentary on the Greek Civil War that shook the British establishment. Daniel Finn, a colleague at the *New Left Review*, read through the chapter on Ireland, pointing out some errors and suggesting some additions and deletions but giving me the green light at the end. David Harvey shared a revealing personal episode.

As the mess in my study mounted, a local craftsman and Corbyn supporter, John Purcell, who had come to check on something else, constructed a revolving bookshelf within a week – a transformative and comradely act that I will not forget.

On the Verso production side, Mark Martin in Brooklyn and Bob Bhamra in London supervised quality control. Tim Clark, a veteran now, did the final copy edit.

To all of them and many others, my warm thanks.

Tariq Ali
London, 20 September 2021

INTRODUCTION

The Cult of Churchill

Unhappy the land that needs a hero.

Brecht, *Galileo*

Do not impute past disorders to the nature of the men, but to the times which, being changed, give reasonable ground to hope that, with better government, our city will have better fortune in the future.

Machiavelli, *Florentine Histories*

On 30 May 1945, a month after Hitler's suicide and the liberation of Berlin by the Red Army commanders Georgy Zhukov and Ivan Konev, twenty-one days after the German surrender ended the Second World War in Europe, the country's most respected liberal historian, G.M. Trevelyan, delivered a lecture to a packed Conway Hall in Red Lion Square, central London. Neither the Allied victory nor Winston Churchill was mentioned in his talk. Not once.

Instead, Trevelyan stuck doggedly to the agreed theme, 'History and the Reader'. Having made his name by rejecting the notion of history as a science, he proposed an alternative to what he called 'dryasdust' historians, stressing the importance of history both as a rendering of past facts, collected through as diligent a search as possible, and as literature. But he could not resist a nod in the direction of recent events, nor indulging in some English self-puffery. Britain, he said, had a balanced approach to history. If only others could emulate it, the world might be better educated.

His tone was lofty, his posture that of a sage. 'Some nations', he declaimed, 'like the Irish, are *too* historically minded, in the sense that they cannot get out of the past at all.' 'The Germans themselves', he noted, 'have been brought up on one-sided, ultra-patriotic versions of things past. The harm that one-sided history has done in the modern world is immense. When history is used as a branch of propaganda it is a very deadly weapon.' The only alternative was 'history as it is now taught and written in England. It is rather the ignorance of history than the misuse of it, from which we suffer in this island now.'

That last sentence still applies. English history itself cannot be understood without recognising the interlacing histories of other peoples. Trevelyan felt no need to explain why, for instance, the Irish nation became over-historicised. Perhaps he should have considered the words of his fellow believer: 'What do they know of England', groaned Kipling, 'who only England know?'

Trevelyan then elaborated on how cultural prejudice and historical ignorance might consign old civilisations (outside Greece and Rome) to the dustbin. This was something that even the finest historians had fallen foul of. From his lighthouse perch as Regius Professor of History at Cambridge, he shone the lamp on Carlyle and Macaulay (his great-uncle), and warned that they too had been hampered. How? Using the language of a shop-steward of the official historian's union, Trevelyan judged that they 'would have been better historians if they had been through an academic course of history such as they could have got if they had lived at the end of the nineteenth century instead of at the beginning'.

Trevelyan then retreated to the eighteenth century for his paradigm of the scholar-historian: 'In Gibbon the perfection both of the science and of the art of history was reached, and has never since been surpassed.' This was certainly not, however, the prevailing view when *The Decline and Fall of the Roman Empire* first appeared, between 1776 and 1789. Gibbon's six volumes were intellectually emancipatory, his fearless assault on Christianity for its role in bringing Rome low leading to both widespread adulation and condemnation. Establishment bishops went on the warpath, while dissenting William Blake cursed Gibbon's mockery. Clearly he was doing something right.

A critical Gibbonesque history with the British Empire as its subject is still needed. Among much else, Christianity would figure, as would Islam. (Gibbon speculates, without a trace of prejudice, that if the Prophet's followers had not lost a key battle or two, Notre-Dame might have been a fetching mosque, and the sonorous Arabic of the Koran might have replaced vespers in Oxford.) Had such a history been written in the late nineteenth or early twentieth century, it would have made for a provocative debate on the Empire and compelled later historians (M.M. Kaye comes to mind) to be a bit more cautious in their assumptions. It would also have made for better educated school children and university graduates.

What, you might ask, has this to do with Winston Churchill?

Just as we have never faced up to the truths of empire, there has been a failure to reckon with our most faithful household gods. An honest reckoning with History has been avoided thus far. Trevelyan virtually ignored Churchill in his 900-page *History of England*. There are only three references to him: firstly as a staunch Free Trader in Balfour's Cabinet; secondly as a member of the Liberal Party 'looking around for a kingdom'; and lastly, in 1940, when 'England', facing 'supreme danger with her old courage', 'found the symbol in Winston Churchill'. The fact that the symbol was totally absent in Trevelyan's Conway Hall speech helps to put things somewhat in perspective.

Rather than a subject of intense historical scrutiny, Churchill has become a burnished icon whose cult has long been out of control. Interestingly, during the five phases of his life – adventures abroad, the First World War, the twenty-year truce in the European civil war, the Second World War and his last period in office – it was a relatively low-profile cult. Even at the height of the Blitz it was nothing like what it would later become in the hands of Tory politicians and a layer of conservative and liberal historians.

A brace of movies in 2017 was preceded by numerous biographies. There are currently more than 1,600 books on Churchill. Several shelves are devoted to him in the biography section of the London Library – even more in the British Library – and that is excluding his own prolific output. The biographies include the eight-volume tombstone whose erection was the life work of the late Sir Martin Gilbert, but whose foundation was laid by Churchill's son, Randolph; a conservative version by Andrew Roberts; a shorter one by Robert Blake before him; and a stylish, lucid, 1,000-page offering by the well-read Liberal politician Roy Jenkins. There is much else in between, most of it published during and after the 1980s. The most objective biography is that written by Clive Ponting, sadly out of print. Among the latest products is an offering ('a number one bestseller' no less) from Boris Johnson, currently the prime minister of the United Kingdom.

Johnson's is a revealing book on many levels. Whereas some conservative historians have been annoyed by Churchill's apparent fluidity in switching parties – Robert Rhodes James stresses that Churchill's erratic pre-1939 career was rightly criticised by his contemporaries – Johnson makes it clear that Churchill spent much of his political life as an outsider, waiting for the moment of glory. This, in common myth, arrived in 1939. But even here the historians cannot agree. Churchill, we are told, stood steadfastly against the appeasers and saved the day. In contrast, John Charmley, in his 1993 book *The End of Glory*, argued that Churchill's self-serving career shifts led to numerous errors. By refusing to negotiate a peace treaty with Hitler in 1940 and instead turning to the United States, Churchill precipitated the end of the British Empire.

In an unpublished entry in his diaries, Chips Channon recalls an unhappy club lunch with fellow Tory appeasers the day Churchill went to kiss hands at the Palace. He quotes Rab Butler as saying: 'We have a half-breed as our Prime Minister.' A day or so later, the chairman of the Tory backbenchers' 1922 Committee reported that 'three-quarters of his members were willing to give Churchill the heave-ho' and restore Neville Chamberlain, architect of the Munich Agreement with Hitler. In *The Churchill Factor*, Boris Johnson revels in the hatred towards Churchill exhibited by swathes of Tory MPs, and identifies strongly with his subject: 'To lead his country in war, Churchill had to command not just the long-faced men of Munich – Halifax and Chamberlain

– but hundreds of Tories who had been conditioned to think of him as an opportunist, a turncoat, a blowhard, an egotist, a rotter, a bounder, a cad, and on several well-attested occasions a downright drunk.' He goes on to quote a letter from Nancy Dugdale to her husband, Tommy, a pro-Chamberlain MP serving in the armed forces. She reports on the mood inside the Conservative Party:

> WC they regard with complete distrust, as you know, and they hate his boasting broadcasts. WC really is the counterpart of Goering in England, full of the desire for blood, Blitzkrieg, and bloated with ego and over-feeding, the same treachery running through his veins, punctuated by heroics and hot air. I can't tell you how depressed I feel about it.[1]

Who and what was Churchill? Was he anything more than a plump carp happy to swim in the foulest of ponds as long as his own career and the needs of the Empire (in his own mind there was no difference between the two) were fulfilled? A little more, perhaps, but not too much. What accounts, then, for his elevation to a cult figure?

The cult proper, with all its excesses, long post-dates the Second World War. Anthony Barnett, in his sharp polemic against the Falklands/Malvinas war waged by Margaret Thatcher in 1982, suggested that the birth of 'Churchillism' was linked to the propaganda need to secure acceptance of that conflict. It was eagerly and embarrassingly promoted by Michael Foot, the Labour leader at the time. As Barnett writes:

> Churchill*ism* is like the warp of British political culture through which all the main tendencies weave their different colours. Although drawn from the symbol of the wartime persona, Churchillism is quite distinct from the man himself. Indeed, the real Churchill was reluctantly and uneasily conscripted to the compact of policies and parties which he seemed to embody. Yet the fact that

---

1   Boris Johnson, *The Churchill Factor*, London, 2014, pp. 38–9.

the ideology is so much more than the emanation of the man is part of the secret of its power and durability.[2]

One could add that the manufactured love for Churchill, and the uses made of him, came to embody the nostalgia for an Empire that was long gone, but that had been supported by all three political parties and the large trade unions.[3] The 'glory days' of the past have become embedded in the historical subconscious of the British. And when it was needed – such as in 1982, when the reality that the United Kingdom was little more than a few North European islands was difficult to accept – his name was invoked. Thatcher's successful war gave her another term of office and projected her as the leaderene. She even began referring to Churchill as 'Winston', as if to suggest she had known him personally.

The social historian Paul Addison concurred with Barnett on the importance of the Falklands conflict in re-launching Churchill. Reviewing four new books in the 1980s, he argued that the cultural and political regression could be traced to the failure of Harold Wilson and Edward Heath to modernise the country in the 1960s and '70s. 'In spirit at least, Churchill has outlived them, taking his place again in British politics as one of the household gods of Mrs Thatcher.' Nevertheless, Addison further argues that those same decades had brought with them a refreshing breeze to clear the cobwebs: 'The patriotic epic, except in the debased and self-destructive form of the Bond films, was an offence to the spirit of the age. The old military-imperial spectaculars were acceptable

2 Anthony Barnett, 'Iron Britannia', Special Issue, *New Left Review* I/134, July–August 1982.

3 I have yet to find a single meaningful act of solidarity by the British Labour movement with any anti-British colonial struggle, leaving apart a tiny minority: William Morris and his newspaper *Commonweal* in the nineteenth century; the early British Communist Party and the ILP, as well as their intellectual fellow travellers, in the twentieth century. Valiant figures, no doubt, but not representative of the big battalions. The soldiers, conscripted or volunteer, despatched to police the Empire were not unlike the poor whites who fought to maintain slavery in the United States.

only when infused with anti-war feeling and social satire, as in Tony Richardson's *The Charge of the Light Brigade*.'[4]

When, in 1974, Howard Brenton's *The Churchill Play* opened under Richard Eyre's direction at the Nottingham Playhouse, it was warmly applauded by audiences and welcomed by most critics. The staid, respected Harold Hobson, reviewing the play in *The Sunday Times*, was surprised by the sharp tone but found it stimulating nonetheless: 'The haunting and alarming suggestion made in Mr Brenton's powerful play is that the man England found [in 1940] was the wrong man ...'

The play opens at Churchill's funeral. The uniformed men carrying the coffin hear rumblings from inside the catafalque. They look at one another in horror:

MARINE: He'll come out, he'll come out. I do believe that of him. Capable of anything that one. [*Fiercely*] To bugger working people. [*He coughs. Recovers. Fiercely*] We've never forgiven him in Wales. He sent soldiers against us, the bloody man. Sent soldiers against Welsh mining men in 1910 ... He was our enemy. We hated his gut. The fat English upper-class gut of the man. When they had the collection, for the statue in front of Parliament ... All over Wales town and county councils would not collect ...

PRIVATE: But 'e won the war. 'E did that, 'E did that.

MARINE: People won the war. He just got pissed with Stalin ...

CHURCHILL [*From within his coffin*]: England! Y' stupid old woman. Clapped out. Undeserving, Unthankful. After all I did for you, you bloody tramp!

CHURCHILL *bursts out of his coffin, swirling the Union Jack. The Churchill actor must assume an exact replica. His face is a mask. He holds an unlit cigar. The* SERVICEMEN *turn round and back away, rifles at the ready.*

In the United States the success of the Churchill industry, which has promoted the man as the 'Yankee Marlborough', has been relative to shifting priorities on the academic and cultural fronts.

---

4 Paul Addison, 'Buggering On', *London Review of Books*, 21 July 1983. Some, myself included, saw the early Bond movies as low comedy.

In the mid-1980s, the Thatcher–Reagan economic consensus required a political and cultural remodelling and a psychological reconditioning in tune with the start of a new world order. New stories were needed for a global Anglophone marketplace. As a result, numerous British documentaries, serials and films were geared for adoption by the larger market. As far as the British culture industry was concerned, what the US public wanted to watch were Jane Austen adaptations, each one cruder and more dumbed down than the last, and costumed soaps glorifying the pre-1945 ruling classes. Churchill became the daily fibre for this staple diet. The British actor Robert Hardy even played him in three separate movies: *Churchill: The Wilderness Years*, *War and Remembrance* and *Churchill: 100 Days That Saved Britain*.

Like Trevelyan, the living Churchill always understood the importance of history and, not least, his own part in it. His witty boast that 'I have not always been wrong. History will bear me out, particularly as I shall write that history myself', was only half a joke. That is what he did from his early years, producing further self-justificatory accounts across the succeeding decades.

Now, early in the twenty-first century, Churchill's deification as the imperial warlord par excellence is being challenged by a small but effective minority of decolonisers. Nothing too unusual there, if one takes the long view. As the historian of the ancient world, Mary Beard, pointed out in her regular *TLS* blog, 'A Don's Life', this was the fate of not a few Roman Emperors during the existence of that empire. It was a tradition emulated in later European empires. One of the worst criminals Europe ever produced was Leopold of Belgium, whose ownership of and brutalities in the Congo led to the deaths of several million Africans. His statues in Belgium fell in the spring of 2020, during protests triggered by the Black Lives Matter movement in the United States. Whether the toppling of statues is just a spasm, and things will return, as they so often do, to post-imperial conformity, remains to be seen.

Despite his enormous talent as a self-publicist, a source of much irritation to his liberal and conservative colleagues, Churchill did not in the end need to 'write the history myself'. He would have been delighted not only by the diligence of his epigones in burnishing his image, but also by the weightless attacks of his few critics. With a keen eye on book sales, he did not particularly mind a little negative publicity if it helped shift a few copies. Money was always in short supply.

This tolerance, however, would perhaps not have stretched to encompass assaults on the British imperial mission, whether levelled against him in critiques by colonial subjects in the past, or launched on his statue by protesters on English campuses today. Imperialism was Churchill's true religion. He was never ashamed of it. Even before he became its High Priest, he worshipped at its altar. The British Empire, then possessor of the largest chunk of colonies the world had ever seen, was for him an awe-inspiring achievement.

With this view came a belief in and promotion of racial and civilisational superiority. But the maintenance and defence of the Empire was the prism through which Churchill viewed this and almost everything else at home and abroad. Race faded into the background when the enemies of the British Empire were white and part of the same 'civilisation'. Churchill admired the fierceness demonstrated by the Boers in southern Africa, but not that of the Pashtun tribes resisting the British on the northwest frontier of India; he appreciated the Gurkhas' capacity to fight as mercenaries, but only because they had been trained by the British as imperial auxiliaries. The Third Reich might be awful, but it was not as unacceptable as the hateful Japanese, who became hateful only after they attacked British colonies in Asia.

Empire so dominated Churchill's political thought that no adventure was too risky, no crime too costly, no war unnecessary, if British possessions, global hegemony and trade interests were at stake. Domestic upheavals and conflicts that threatened the status quo would also be dealt with harshly. Churchill might have changed political parties at will to enhance his own career, but this rarely affected his politics.

Virtually any reactionary cause that emerged could rely on him for support. He may not have been opposed to middle- and upper-class women bicycling or playing tennis, or, in the case of married women, having their own bank accounts or slashing their evening skirts. What he strongly objected to was the extension of democracy. Women's suffrage, he argued, 'is contrary to natural law and the practice of civilized states ... only the most undesirable class of women are eager for the right – those who discharge their duty to state – viz marrying & giving birth to children are adequately represented by their husbands ... I shall unswervingly oppose this ridiculous movement.'[5]

The militant suffragette movement, in particular, angered him. He assumed, like many other men and women, that granting women the right to vote would double the electoral strength of the working class. Votes for women challenged the male monopoly of politics and a great deal else. His views on this were never hidden, during either his Liberal or his Conservative days, as his clash with Sylvia Pankhurst demonstrates:

In the midst of the vast Liberal Party rally just before the 1906 general election, the suffragette waited to ask her question, steeling herself for the violent ejection that invariably followed. The speaker was Winston Churchill, well known for his particularly 'insulting attitude' towards women's suffrage. When the suffragette stood up and asked her question, 'Will the Liberal Government give women the vote?', he just ignored her, but when some of the men in the audience demanded an answer the chairman invited the suffragette to ask her question from the platform. After doing so, Churchill took her roughly by the arm and forced her into a seat on the platform saying, 'No, you must wait here till you have heard what I have to say,' and told the audience, 'Nothing would induce me to vote for giving women the franchise.' Suddenly all the men on the platform stood up, blocking the suffragette from view, while others pushed her into a back room. One man went to find a key to lock her in, while another, standing against the door, 'began to use the most violent language and, calling her a cat, gesticulated as though he would scratch her face with his hands'. She ran to the barred

---

5 Quoted in Clive Ponting, *Churchill*, London, 1994, pp. 24–5.

window and called out to the people in the street. The threatening man left and the crowd pointed out a window with some bars missing which the suffragette climbed through and then, at the crowd's request, delivered an impromptu speech of her own.[6]

In many ancient religions, there were sacred figures who performed specific functions. The most important of these was the role of binders: almost everything was bound to and linked through them. Politically, Winston Churchill never played such a role during his lifetime, except for a limited period at the height of the war. Even then, critics who defied or challenged him were rarely silenced. 'Idolatry is a sin in a democracy', Aneurin Bevan, the left-wing Labour MP, had shouted when the flattery became too intense.

In style, Churchill was often impulsive, always discursive, sometimes chaotic but also possessed of a peculiar dynamism that made him, despite his class, quite down-to-earth. He was equally at home at Blenheim Palace as in the murky corridors of the political underworld. He became prime minister at a time when Britain faced an existential crisis, with the country's elite and its citizens seriously divided on the dangers posed by the Third Reich. Till then, he had been little more than a clever politician engaged in career building and desperate to climb as high as he could. To which end he was prepared to get his hands dirty. Very dirty. This aspect of him was aired in the popular BBC drama, *Peaky Blinders*, where Churchill is portrayed giving support to a Special Branch officer tasked with killing Sinn Féin supporters in the Midlands.

His pre-war career – glorifying colonial atrocities abroad, suppressing working-class revolts at home – dwelt in the memory of his opponents among the populace. In 'A Safe Job', a short story published in *The New Reasoner* in the late 1950s, Peter Barnes brought back to life a Labour activist in London's East End, where mainly Jewish and a sprinkling of non-Jewish migrant workers had given the area a strong reputation for radical politics. The opening paragraph conveys a flavour of the times:

6 Katherine Connelly, *Sylvia Pankhurst: Suffragette, Socialist and Scourge of Empire*, London, 2013, p. 1.

My Uncle Nathaniel was the man who threw a brick at Churchill in 1929. He always regretted that he had missed. It happened when Churchill was making a campaign speech in the East End. The crowd got out of hand and tried to charge him. Beating a hasty retreat to a waiting car, the politician was helped on his way by jeers, catcalls and a badly aimed brick. My Uncle threw it. He had been an active Socialist all his life. This story was one of his favourites . . .

Stories of this nature were not uncommon, even amid the great dangers of the war years. The eminent geographer David Harvey recalls:

My grandma would only shop at the co-op and when I was 8 or 9 (in 1943–4) I often spent Saturdays with her. One time we went somewhere to get her 'divvy' and we ended up in some queue where she pontificated rather loudly to the effect that Churchill was a rotten bugger, enemy of the working people. I was banned from using such language at home so I probably remember it because it was quite shocking to hear her going on in that vein in a public setting. Quite a few people were getting upset and defended him for leading the fight against Hitler to which my grandma replied that Hitler was a rotten bugger too and maybe it would take one rotten bugger to get rid of another rotten bugger but after this war was over we would get rid of all the rotten buggers, every one of them . . . I told this anecdote to a colleague when at Oxford and he told me around the same period he went to picture shows on Saturday mornings and they always showed Pathé[tic] News and when a certain person appeared on screen the whole audience would hiss and boo. He thought it was Hitler for a while, but it turned out to be Churchill.

Another episode: a *New York Times* writer in the 1970s was taken aback while interviewing Richard Burton after his success playing Churchill in a TV dramatisation called *Walk With Destiny*. The actor, asked for his own views on the great man, replied: 'I hate Churchill and all his kind . . . a bad man . . . a vindictive toy soldier child.' Burton had grown up in the Welsh valleys.

And most recently, a 2021 memoir by the historian Jeffrey Weeks, *Between Worlds: A Queer Boy from the Valleys*, includes an account of how hatred of Churchill was still very much alive when the author was growing up in the Rhondda. Tonypandy, where Churchill had sent troops against the miners, was never forgotten: 'As a young boy in the 1950s I vividly remember cinema audiences still erupting in loud boos whenever Churchill, by then in his second term as prime minister, appeared in a newsreel.'

Why this degree of hatred? Churchill was not the only reactionary politician in modern British history. His arrogance is often cited as a factor, and perhaps what angered people was that he was a boaster. He enjoyed his triumphs too well. The British do not mind forthright leaders – Canning, Peel, Disraeli – Lloyd George, Keir Hardy, Nye Bevan – but they do not like British noses being rubbed in British dust. And on too many occasions – at Tonypandy in 1910, during the 1926 General Strike, in 1919 in Scotland – Churchill treated his own citizens as enemies. How can this ever be universally popular?

Nevertheless, History is unpredictable. It picks an actor, bedecks them with fine costumes, and pushes them to play a particular role to such an extent that the part melds with reality. When the curtain comes down, it dismisses them and picks up new actors, raw but eager to learn, and throws them into battle. Churchill was one such actor formed by his times.

This did not make him a cult figure at the time, in fact the opposite. He was accepted as a war leader, but the ambiguities never disappeared. By the time he became prime minister at the head of a National Government, with Attlee as deputy prime minister, people realised they had nothing else with which to fight a war that had to be fought. So they supported him till the first opportunity arose to get rid of him, which they promptly did, without many regrets, in July of 1945.

But even during the war the support was always contingent. It needs to be remembered, despite the dramatics of the widely applauded film *Darkest Hour*, that when Churchill delivered his famous 'we shall never surrender' speech, the defeat at Dunkirk had traumatised the nation. It was obvious then that the herd mentality exhibited during the early years of the First World War would not be at work again. The men fleeing Dunkirk knew how unprepared and badly armed they were, and that the governing class had no idea of why this had happened. Even semi-defeats raise questions in the minds of those taught to obey their superior officers at all times.

Dunkirk caused a serious loss of self-confidence in ruling-class circles. The Tory gang running the country was not at all sure whether Britain could survive. They had won the propaganda war, but the much-touted 'spirit of Dunkirk' was little more than a victory mask concealing a dejected and fearful face. On 1 July 1940, *The Times* published a remarkable editorial that is still more or less applicable today, but could not be written by any employee of Murdoch or, for that matter, any liberal media outlet in the Western world:

> If we speak of democracy, we do not mean a democracy which maintains the right to vote but forgets the right to work and the right to live. If we speak of freedom, we do not mean a rugged individualism which excludes social organisation and economic planning. If we speak of equality we do not mean a political equality nullified by social and economic privilege. If we speak of economic reconstruction we think less of maximum production (though this too will be required) than of equitable distribution ... The European house cannot be put in order unless we put our own house in order first. The new order cannot be based on the preservation of privilege, whether the privilege be that of a country, of a class, or of an individual.

Angus Calder's ground-breaking works, *The People's War* (1969) and *The Myth of the Blitz* (1991), record this seismic shift well in the aftermath of Dunkirk. In the first book, Calder explained how British Labour and other progressive forces in the country understood very rapidly that the new war was not a repeat of the previous disaster, that fascism had to be defeated, and that a temporary alliance with anyone (including even Churchill) to achieve this goal was necessary. The national mood was one of united defiance.

However, by the time he came to write the second volume on the Blitz, Calder had clearly changed his mind. In the second book, he exposes the myths of British pluck in the face of German bombing, revealing a darker scene. Crime levels rose throughout the country. Anti-Semitism was rife. The propaganda machine attempted to disguise a shattered people with hearty cheer and the deification of young, dead pilots. Here, the national mood emerges as one of division and paranoia.

Calder is scathing on the tit-for-tat bombing raids carried out by Britain and Germany with the sole purpose of demoralising civilian populations by targeting private homes and other civilian targets. He explains how the head of Bomber Command, 'Bomber Harris', fully backed by Churchill, decided to carry out an experimental raid on the ancient German city of Lubeck. The bombs created a firestorm that destroyed half the city and killed thousands of civilians.

The Luftwaffe responded in kind by launching the 'Baedeker' raids against old English cities of historic and cultural importance: Bath, Norwich, York, Canterbury. A lot of damage was done. People were killed. But citizens in both countries held firm. There was no serious demoralisation, not even when Harris unleashed the 'Thousand bombers' assault on Cologne and boasted that over 6,500 British airmen dispersed in 868 crews had reached their target, unloading some 1,500 tons of bombs in total, 60 per cent of which were incendiaries. The city was engulfed in fire.

Churchill was fulsome in his praise, exhilarated by the destruction. Yet none of this had any dramatic impact on German morale. Within a fortnight Cologne was functioning normally.

By 1942, however, discontent with Churchill's leadership was widespread among the governing elite. Singapore had fallen to Japan. Gandhi and Nehru had launched a Quit India movement that was bound to affect the morale of the tens of thousands of Indians serving as cannon fodder. The ultra-nationalist Subhas Chandra Bose had decided to create an Indian National Army, recruited from Indian POWs captured by the Japanese, tasked with fighting the British in India.

At home, the failure to achieve production targets had affected supplies in Britain and on the frontlines. A Gallup poll revealed that only one-third of the population expressed satisfaction with the war cabinet, i.e. Churchill. The diarist Harold Nicolson recorded that several centre politicians had told him 'Churchill had to be brought down', despite his protests that such a move would shock the country. Cecil Beaton, another friend of Conservative politicians, reported that they freely discussed Churchill's faults and weaknesses. When asked who might replace him, they replied: 'Sir Stafford Cripps'. Not Attlee, not Bevin, but Cripps, a name rarely conjured with today as the greatest leader we never had.

Discontent in the military too was evident. The now-forgotten 'Forces Parliament' took place in Cairo between 1943 and 1944. Organised by soldiers and junior officers to discuss the future of Britain after the war, the 'Cairo Parliament' was inspired by the Putney debates between the Levellers and Oliver Cromwell. It discussed nationalisation, land and banking reform, inheritance and work. In the mock elections Labour obtained a thumping majority. The Tories came last. Inevitably the exercise was swiftly shut down.

Ahead of the 1945 general election it was widely assumed that a Tory victory was inevitable, given Churchill's prestige in the war. But *The Times* leader-writer had been prophetic. Anti-Churchill feelings, especially in working-class communities, had remained strong throughout the war, contrary to the propaganda. Labour swept to victory on a social-democratic programme that used a much milder version of *The Times* editorial as its mantra.

On Churchill's death in 1965, tributes and eulogies from all sides were not in short supply. Richard Crossman, a Labour Party intellectual and senior member of Harold Wilson's Cabinet, grumbled publicly about being forced to attend, and later wrote that 'it felt like an end of an epoch, possibly even the end of a nation'. How wrong he was. Many others too.

At that time it did appear that the post-war settlement, the gradual decolonisation abroad and the creation of a welfare state with its comforting, happy-families atmosphere had seen off the iniquities of the past and laid the foundations of a post-Churchill modernism. The Conservative leader Edward Heath was an ardent European; Wilson, the prime minister, a more reluctant convert to the idea. Europe, geographically little more than a cape attached to the giant Asian continent, would become for post-war politicians the embodiment of hope and the repository of Western civilisation. Its crimes at home and abroad, its wars, imperial, civil and religious, were virtually forgotten, with the single exception of the Judeocide.

Most of the obituaries lauded Churchill's role as wartime prime minister. On other subjects, opinion in the country was much more divided. The morale-boosting propaganda that Churchill had both created and participated in spoke to collective endurance. On this score he had been a masterful rhetorical tactician. What his eulogists forgot was that the history of that endurance ran far deeper, and was far more lasting, than the heroic appeals of a moment.

Many of those who had suffered the mass unemployment of the 1920s and '30s had not yet passed away. It was not uncommon to hear remarks such as 'My family (or my father) hated Churchill.' Many of the soldiers who had greeted him with cheers during the war had also voted against him when it was all but won. Memories were longer in those days.

Even when Churchill was not directly involved, he typified the more adventurist wing of the British ruling class: its violence, its arrogance, its complacency and its incubation of white supremacy. His military-aristocratic heritage was useful to him, but not a great recommendation for many others. As Roy Jenkins and others have pointed out, Churchill's ancestors in the dukedom of Marlborough, after the founding duke died, produced nobody of significance apart from Winston and his father, Randolph. A trend, one could add, that has continued to this day. Soames is little more than a minor character in P. G. Wodehouse.

Unlike many of his peers, Churchill was not satisfied with being a backroom boy or a passive Member of Parliament. He was, above all, an imperial activist. He wanted to fight, to kill and, if necessary, to die for the cause always uppermost in his mind: the British Empire. Death to all its enemies at home and abroad. And where whites were forced to kill other whites (Boers, the Irish, the

Germans, the post-1917 Russians), ideologies complementary to white supremacy could be brought into play without too much difficulty.

The boom in Churchilliana began four decades ago. Since then Churchill's history has surreptitiously become that of Britain (or at least England) as a whole. It is easy to forget how it was in 1965. Back then, satirists, filmmakers and others staunchly opposed imperial wars. Joan Littlewood's mocking *Oh! What a Lovely War*, a savage assault on the first World War, packed Stratford's Theatre Royal. Richardson's *Charge of the Light Brigade* laid bare the worship of the Imperial Great Game. It would have been hard to predict then the rise of Margaret Thatcher, the Falklands war, the instrumentalisation of Churchill, now elevated to the status of a national icon, courtesy of Thatcher, Blair and Johnson. And the legend has grown on both sides of the Atlantic.

A cloying scent of incense surrounds most of the paper shrines that commemorate Churchill and his wars, small and big. Together with the celluloid versions, their effectiveness cannot be denied. What the student decolonisers and their allies have made indisputable, however, is that a new conversation has been broached.

1

A World of Empires

Now, this is the faith that the White Men hold
When they build their homes afar –
'Freedom for ourselves and freedom for our sons
And failing freedom, War.'

Kipling, 'A Song of the White Men' (1899)

'I was a child of the Victorian era,' wrote Churchill in *My Early Life*, 'when the structure of our country seemed firmly set, when its position in trade and on our seas was unrivalled, and when the realisation of the greatness of our Empire and of our duty to preserve it was ever growing stronger.' In 1874, when Churchill was born, Britain was the dominant empire, its global reach surpassing that of its rivals. It had lost its American colonies but retained a boot-hold in Canada. The American losses were more than recompensed by the conquest of India. Africa was divided according to an agreement reached by the European powers.

Most Europeans of all classes viewed their respective colonies in a similar fashion. None could match, whatever else may be thought of it, the Iberian seizure and possession for three centuries of a vast continent beyond a perilous ocean. That was a feat unparalleled in history. Yet even today the majority of Churchill's biographers cling to the view that while the Spanish Empire and others were cruel, indeed barbarous, the British Empire was more benign and, for this reason, more appreciated by those it colonised.

As a result, the British Empire has become a staple of the heritage industry. The Thatcher governments of the 1980s (and their Blairite successors) did not simply assault the hallowed domains of the welfare state or destroy trade union militancy, they also sought to reverse anti-colonial trends in the public sphere that rubbished or were sharply critical of Britain's imperial past. The response to this shift has come from many sources. In Britain, most recently, the cosmetic version of colonisation has been effectively demolished by the English historian Richard Gott in his masterly study of resistance to the British Empire. He encapsulates the problem neatly:

> [I]t is often suggested that the British Empire was something of a model experience, unlike that of the French, the Dutch, the Germans, the Spaniards, the Portuguese – or, of course, the Americans. There is a widespread opinion that the British Empire was obtained and maintained with a minimum degree of force and with maximum co-operation from a grateful indigenous population. This benign, biscuit-tin view of the past is not an understanding of their history that young people in the territories that once made up the Empire would now recognize.[1]

It is through this lens that we need to see the young imperialist, Winston Churchill. A particular kind of Victorian-era child, he spent his early formative years in a colonial setting, living in Dublin where his grandfather was viceroy of Ireland. As a boy neglected by his parents, he found solace in toy soldiers and oft-repeated tales of his great military forebear, the first Duke of Marlborough. Stories of the duke's tactical prowess on international battlefields – not to mention his political cunning, beginning with the Glorious Revolution – only enhanced the young Churchill's desire to be a soldier.

The parental neglect continued when he was sent away to school at Harrow. There he found comfort in the school cadet corps and began to prepare himself for the military academy at Sandhurst,

1 Richard Gott, *Britain's Empire: Repression, Resistance and Revolt*, London, 2011, p. 3.

where competition for a place was stiff. His father, Lord Randolph Churchill, by then a Tory MP, was not keen on the idea, preferring that his son might join a financial firm in the City (Rothschild was a friend) and make some money. Winston, both scared and in awe of his striving, reckless and bad-tempered father, persisted nonetheless, and after two failed attempts finally got into Sandhurst.

His marks being insufficient to join the infantry (which in those days prized intellect highly), Churchill was, like many other upperclass men, assigned to the more glamorous but less demanding cavalry. That same year, 1893, to celebrate his elevation to cadet, he went on a skiing holiday in Switzerland. His enjoyment was cut short by a stern missive from his father, a man whose mental stability was impaired by syphilis and who had hitherto given no personal attention to his son:

> Never have I received a really good report of your conduct in your work from any master or tutor you had from time to time to do with. Always behind-hand, never advancing in your class, incessant complaints of total want of application . . . [W]ith all the efforts that have been made to make your life easy and agreeable and your work neither oppressive nor distasteful, this is the grand result that you come up among the 2nd rate and 3rd rate class who are only good for commissions in a cavalry regiment . . . I shall not write again on these matters and you need not trouble to write any answer to this part of my letter because I no longer attach the slightest weight to anything you may say about your own acquirements and exploits. Make this position indelibly impressed on your mind, that if your conduct and action at Sandhurst is similar to what it has been in the other establishments in which it has sought vainly to impart to you some education. Then that my responsibility for you is over.'

It is not difficult to imagine the psychological impact such a letter might have had on a nineteen-year-old boy (though it should be pointed out that language of this sort deployed by an upper-class father to his son was not unfamiliar at the time or later). On a psychological level, from this moment on, proving his father wrong became part of Winston's life work.

His American heiress mother, Jennie Jerome, was only marginally better as a parent. She was fond of Winston in absentia. As he grew up, she was not averse to sleeping with the highest figures in the realm to help his career and re-fill her own purse, emptied after an economic collapse in the United States wrecked her family's fortune. She did the rounds of the SW1 squares (even, according to some reports, sleeping with the king), a process that had begun while her husband was dying of syphilis and continued apace after his death.

There was a possibility at one stage that Churchill might succeed to the dukedom, since his cousin Sunny, in direct line, was unmarried. The duchess insisted that 'it would be intolerable if that little upstart Winston ever became duke', and summoned the monied cavalry in the US to mount a rescue. Eventually, Consuelo Vanderbilt was persuaded to marry the wastrel Sunny. Accompanying the heiress was a lump sum donation of $2.5 million and an annuity of $30,000, a useful contribution to the family coffers. In due course, a child was produced. No chance now of Churchill moving to Blenheim. Winston would have to make his own fortune.

Could the young cadet at Sandhurst graduate to the status of an imperial warlord? No doubt he would have loved that, but it was not to be. A few adventures observing and participating in wars was all fate assigned to him. But he never had any doubts regarding the efficacy of imperial rule. Proud of his glorious ancestor, founder of the Marlborough/Churchill dynasty, he was determined to play his part in defending the Empire in both theory and practice. War was an elixir, a cure-all for boredom and ennui, and more exciting than hunting since the targets were usually 'savages'. Whatever language they spoke, however 'primitive' they might be, they were human rivals. What other adventure could beat this one? War was, in Churchill's own words, a most 'desirable commodity'.

At twenty-one, however, newly enlisted with the 4th Hussars, Winston was to be disappointed. It was 1895 and there was no British colonial war in sight. He was bored at home and 'all [his] money had been spent on polo ponies'. How then to find the 'swift road to distinction' and the 'glittering gateway' to fame? After a few inquiries, his gaze crossed the Atlantic. As he later recalled, since

> [I] could not afford to hunt, I searched the world for some scene of adventure or excitement. The general peace in which mankind had for so many years languished was broken only in one quarter of the globe. The long-drawn guerrilla war between the Spaniards and the Cuban rebels was said to be entering upon its most serious phase.[2]

The Spanish Empire was in a state of collapse. It had been attempting to suppress two liberation movements simultaneously for years, in Cuba and the Philippines. The political-intellectual leadership of these movements was provided by José Martí in Cuba and José Rizal in the Philippines: the first a poet and essayist, the second a novelist of the highest rank. Both lives were tragically truncated, Martí in a military skirmish, Rizal executed by a Spanish firing squad.

Cuba and Puerto Rico were the last remaining Spanish possessions in the Americas and among the least developed colonies. The discovery of gold and silver on the mainland and the relative lack of either men or minerals to exploit in Cuba relegated the island to a minor, mainly military and administrative, role in the imperial system. Between 1720 and 1762, the Cuban economy was so undeveloped that its entire European trade was carried by an average of only five or six merchant ships each year. The plantation system, dependent on the large-scale slavery of kidnapped Africans, began late, and only escalated after the Haitian Revolution. The drive for independence was delayed too. By 1825, the whole of the Spanish American mainland had been liberated, but in Cuba Spanish rule lasted until 1898. In 1895, as Churchill weighed his options, Spain was waging a vicious last-ditch assault against the Cuban patriots.

Churchill was never slow to exploit an opportunity, and this one was perfect. He obtained leave from his regiment to become a

---

2 Churchill, *My Early Life*, p. 84.

military observer and witness a colonial war first-hand. Having been left a skimpy inheritance by his father, who had died at the start of that year, he struck on journalism as a means both to promote himself and earn some money. He sought and obtained a newspaper commission to cover the Spanish–Cuban war. Together with a fellow officer, he set off for the Caribbean via the United States.

Churchill did not need to know too much about his chosen war zone. Instinctively, he sided with the Spanish. The reason was simple: an imperial power was attempting to drown a native rebellion in blood.

He arrived in Havana in November 1895. Typhus, smallpox and cholera stalked the island. Famine was widespread, and any journalist who travelled a bit could not have failed to witness the immense suffering of the Cubans. Nevertheless, Churchill underplayed these horrors, themselves a direct result of the colonial war. In an early despatch home – getting almost everything wrong, not unlike journalists reporting from five-star hotels in more recent colonial wars – he wrote:

> [Havana] shows no sign of the insurrection, and business proceeds everywhere as usual. Passports are, however, strictly examined, and all baggage is searched with a view to discovering pistols or other arms. During the passage from Tampa on the boat the most violent reports of the condition of Havana were rife. Yellow fever was said to be prevalent, and the garrison was reported to have over 400 cases. As a matter of fact, there is really not much sickness, and what there is is confined to the lower part of the town.[3]

Even when Churchill could no longer ignore what was taking place, and realised that the Cuban Revolutionary Party had the overwhelming support of the people, he could not bring himself to examine let alone appreciate the perspective of its fighters. The Spanish he understood only too well. For them, Cuba was what Ireland was for the British.

---

3 'The Insurrection in Cuba. Letters from the Front – 1', *Daily Graphic*, 13 December 1895.

José Martí does not rate a single mention in Churchill's reports or in *My Early Life*. Martí had written to the British foreign secretary in April 1895, pleading that Britain stay out of the conflict. Three weeks later, he was dead, shot by the Spanish in an unnecessary encounter. The result was an avoidable tragedy. These events, involving Cuba's most prominent nationalist leader, were still fresh when Churchill arrived, but he could think only of how much luckier Cuba might have been had the British not exchanged Havana for Florida in 1763 after an eleven-month occupation:

> It may be that as the pages of history are turned brighter fortunes and better times will come to Cuba. It may be that future years will see the island as it would be now, had England never lost it – a Cuba free and prosperous, under just laws and a patriotic administration, throwing open her ports to the commerce of the world, sending her ponies to Hurlingham and her Cricketers to Lords, exchanging the cigars of Havana for the cottons of Lancashire, and the sugars of Matanzas for the cutlery of Sheffield.

Churchill was only too aware of what imperialism entailed. Could he have been unaware that it was during the brief period of British occupation in 1762 that 10,000 more slaves had been imported into Cuba to sustain a thriving plantation economy?[4]

In December 1954, about to enter his final decade, Churchill listened to tales of woe told by a visiting white settler from Kenya, who explained why the atrocities against the Mau Mau rebellion were necessary. Churchill was worried mainly by how these might affect Britain's standing in the world. He recalled his own 1907 trip to the African colony, when the Kikuyu tribe was such 'a happy, naked and charming people'. But now, he wrote, public

---

4 Over two centuries later, when socialist Cuba despatched an army to Angola to help the liberation movement stave off an attack by a rival group backed by apartheid South Africa, Fidel Castro informed his people that most of the slaves sent to Cuba had come from Angola and nearby regions. Cuba was paying off a 'blood debt'. It was the country's' internationalist duty to help the Angolans against the white regime.

opinion would watch 'the power of a modern nation being used to kill savages. It's pretty terrible. Savages, savages? Not savages. They're savages armed with ideas, much more difficult to deal with.'[5]

There were plenty of 'savages' in Cuba too. In 1895 and 1896, as the rebels gained more support, Generals Antonio Maceo and Máximo Gómez had the island virtually under their control and Havana under siege. Maceo, an Afro-Cuban, was without doubt the most outstanding guerrilla leader of the nineteenth century. Spain and its supporters went into panic mode. Churchill described the rebels as 'an undisciplined rabble' consisting 'to a large extent of coloured men'. If the revolution succeeded, he worried, 'Cuba will be a black republic', registering no connection to the slaves Britain had brought in to increase the enslaved population Spain had already accumulated over the previous two centuries.[6]

Self-induced amnesia has always been a characteristic of imperial leaders and their ideologues. Fears of another Haiti in the region were ever present in the thinking of the United States as well. Grover Flint, a US journalist who had attached himself to Gómez's army, wrote in his despatches that 'half of the enlisted men were negroes' while other sinister types were also present: 'Chinamen (survivors of the Macau coolie traffic) . . . shifty, sharp-eyed Mongols, with none of the placid laundry look about them'.[7]

The Spanish had agreed to the abolition of slavery in Cuba in 1886, but, fearful of the very notion of a majoritarian black republic, they encouraged mass migration from the peninsula to the island. Between 1882 and 1894 a quarter of a million Spaniards emigrated to Cuba, whose population was then under two million.

---

5 Quoted in Richard Toye, *Churchill's Empire*, London, 2010, p. xi. The British atrocities in Kenya, under both Conservative and Labour governments, underplayed by most British historians, will be discussed in Chapter 15.

6 Churchill quoted in Richard Gott, *Cuba: A New History*, New Haven, 2004, p. 92.

7 Ibid.

They included the Catalan anarchist Enrique Roig, who wasted little time in linking up with Martí. The flood of white immigrants did not prove sufficient from the Spanish point of view. Two-thirds of the new migrants were illiterate. Most were peasants and workers, with Catalans composing a majority. Many veered automatically in the direction of Martí and Maceo. As Benedict Anderson noted:

> This demographic transformation, combined with the unalarming, gradual end of slavery, made it possible for Martí to recast the revolutionary enterprise in a nationalist style, which transcended, or appeared to transcend, the discourse of race. So to speak, white and black Cuban males would (metaphorically or on the battlefield) embrace each other as equals in the fight against imperial rule. The gradual disappearance of 'Haiti' and the collapse of the sugar 'aristocracy' left Madrid with fewer and fewer fanatical supporters. Rizal-style general nationalism thus spread rapidly after 1888 in almost all sectors.[8]

On the verge of a catastrophic defeat in 1896, the Spanish sent out a new Captain-General to regain the upper hand. Chosen for his ruthlessness, General Valeriano Weyler was known in Madrid for preferring animals to humans. He was a mixture of both. He had funded a care home for horses in Madrid, where they were well treated and provided regularly with oats. In Cuba he created a network of concentration camps to isolate the guerrillas from the people. The consequences were catastrophic: not only were families torn apart and women and girls forced into prostitution, but in some Cuban towns up to 50 per cent of those in the camps died. Altogether, at least 170,000 'concentrated' civilians died, mostly of disease and hunger, representing about 10 per cent of the total Cuban population of the time.

Weyler had served as a military attaché at the Spanish embassy in Washington during the US Civil War, and was a great admirer of

---

8   Benedict Anderson, *The Age of Globalization: Anarchists and the Anti-Colonial Imagination*, London, 2005, pp. 143–4.

General Sherman's scorched-earth tactics en route to Atlanta. He now envisaged a similar policy for Cuba and proceeded to carry it out. It did not succeed as he had hoped and a stalemate of sorts was reached. Major political and military leaders on both sides were dead: Maceo in Cuba, and the warmongering Spanish prime minister, Antonio Cánovas, in Spain.

The latter was assassinated in June 1897 by Michele Angiolillo, a Barcelona-based Italian anarchist, as revenge for the execution of anarchists in Barcelona. He had originally planned to bump off a Spanish royal, but was talked out of it by a black Puerto Rican supporter of the Cuban struggle, who convinced Angiolillo that Cánovas would be a better target. The prime minister's departure would be genuinely helpful to the Cubans, he argued, and provided 500 francs as an inducement. The 'three bullets' Angiolillo fired, wrote Richard Gott, 'did as much for the Cuban independence movement as three years of combat'.⁹ Regime change in Madrid led to a reforming administration that promised Cuba home rule. By then, the United States had declared war against the Spanish Empire and invaded the Philippines; its armed intervention in Cuba in 1898 ended the Spanish–Cuban war.

Ironically, Cuba's rise as a sugar and coffee producer (and hence its delayed independence) was the result of the 1790 Haitian Revolution, which had eliminated the largest such producer from the world market. The black republic of Haiti was the spectre now being invoked endlessly in the US imperial imagination and in the crude propaganda of its leaders. One of the first things the United States did after entering Cuba was to disarm and dissolve the Cuban Revolutionary Army. Armed black insurgents so close to the US mainland had to be neutralised before their example became infectious. A suitable regime was established before the United States withdrew its forces, except from Guantánamo Bay, where it maintained de facto control in the form of a naval base: an infernal, continuing presence.

---

9   Gott, *Cuba: A New History*, p. 96.

Churchill's sojourn in Cuba – where his adventure-seeking sometimes strayed from journalism into military moonlighting on behalf of Spain – lasted only a few months. He did not witness the disarming of the revolutionary army, but there is not the slightest doubt he would have supported this outcome. The obsession with race came into play once again. On his return home he wrote: 'The Cuban rebels give themselves the names of heroes and only are boastful and braggarts', insisting contrary to most other reports that the insurgents 'neither fight bravely nor do they use their weapons effectively'.[10]

On his return from Cuba in 1896, the young adventurer was keen to depart immediately for the African continent, which had by now been fully colonised by the Europeans. Wars were brewing, and easy career gains might be made without too much effort. Instead, his senior commanders decided he should go with his regiment on a tour of duty to India. Churchill protested and used his titled friends and relations to try to have the decision changed, but to no avail. He was desperate to switch to the 9th Lancers, due to be sent to Matabeleland in South Africa. 'This we will talk over on Friday,' he wrote to his mother, 'but my dear Mamma you cannot think how I would like to sail in a few days to scenes of adventure and excitement – to places where I could gain experience and derive advantage – rather than to the tedious land of India, where I shall be equally out of the pleasures of peace and the chances of war.'

Going to India with his 'unfortunate regiment' ... was an 'utterly unattractive' prospect. Not to go to the war in Matabeleland was to let 'the golden opportunity' go by. By failing in that, 'I feel that I am guilty of an indolent folly that I shall regret all my life.' A few months in Matabeleland would earn him the South Africa Medal and 'in all probability' the British South Africa Company's Star.[11]

---

10   Quoted in Hugh Thomas, *Cuba: A History*, Harmondsworth, 1971, pp. 187–8.

11   Martin Gilbert, *Churchill: A Life*, 2nd edition, London, 2000, p. 62.

~

Kipling, 'A Song of the White Men' (1899)

Now, this is the cup that White Men drink
　　When they go to right a wrong,
And that is the cup of the old world's hate –
　　Cruel and strained and strong.
We have drunk that cup – and a bitter, bitter, cup –
　　And tossed the dregs away.
But well for the world when the White Men drink
　　To the dawn of the White Man's day! . . .

Now, this is the faith that the White Men hold
　　When they build their homes afar –
'Freedom for ourselves and freedom for our sons
　　And failing freedom, War.'
We have proved our faith – bear witness to our faith,
　　Dear souls of freemen slain!
Oh, well for the world when the White Men join
　　To prove their faith again.

~

~

Brecht, 'The Caledonian Market' (1934)

'Oh, East is East and West is West!'
Their hireling minstrel cried.
But I observed with interest
Bridges across the great divide
And huge guns trundling East I've seen
And cheerful troops keeping them clean.
Meanwhile, from East to West, back rolled
Tea soaked in blood, war wounded, gold.

And the Widow at Windsor, all dressed in black
Grins, takes the money, stuffs it in her pocket
And gives the wounded a pat on the back
And sends them down to the Caledonian Market.
Their walk may have lost its spring, but they try
To hobble around the stalls and buy
A second-hand wooden leg instead
To match their equally wooden head.

~

The Jewel in the Crown

Churchill's India obsession was many things, but it was not irrational. No other modern empire had succeeded in grabbing so much land and so many people in Asia as had the British. This posed some problems in India because there were too many people, making even a partial extermination difficult. Nor could they be confined in reservations or concentration camps. The advantages, however, vastly outweighed the problems.

Churchill never liked India. His first armed encounter was not a pleasant affair. He wrote of his shock at encountering the subcontinent, and was relieved to be put on active duty on the Afghan border. In a despatch to the *Daily Telegraph* on 6 November 1897 he wrote:

> The rising of 1897 is the most successful attempt hitherto made to combine the frontier tribes. It will not be the last. The simultaneous revolt of distant tribes is an evidence of secret workings ... Civilization is face to face with militant Mohammedanism. When we reflect on the moral and material forces arrayed, there need be no fear of the ultimate issue, but the longer the policy of half-measures is adhered to the more distant the end of the struggle will be.
>
> An interference more galling than complete control, a timidity more rash than reckless, a clemency more cruel than the utmost severity, mark our present dealings with the frontier tribes. To terminate this sorry state of affairs it is necessary to carry a recognized and admitted policy to its logical and inevitable conclusion.

A month or so earlier he had been shaken by the sight of thirty-six dead bodies, hurriedly buried by the British, that had been discovered and mutilated by Pashtun tribesmen. But this was no more unedifying than the violence meted out regularly by the British Army. Civilisation and barbarism are Siamese twins. Churchill confided to his diary:

> The tribesmen are among the most miserable and brutal creatures on earth. Their intelligence only enables them to be more cruel,

more dangerous, more destructible than the wild beasts . . . I find it impossible to come to any other conclusion than that, in proportion that these valleys are purged from the pernicious vermin that infest them, so will the happiness of humanity be increased, and the progress of mankind accelerated.

No word to explain why the British were under attack. The Empire had already lost wars against Afghanistan. The first ended in January 1842, with the defeat of a large British-led force under the command of General Elphinstone. The Governor-General of India, Lord Auckland, was so shaken by the news that it gave him a stroke from which he never recovered. In April the same year, General Pollock led a 'Force of Retribution' that destroyed the old sixteenth-century bazaar in Kabul and other old buildings. Having carried out their revenge, the British left Afghanistan and resolved never to attempt a take-over again.

However, in 1893 the Empire insisted on drawing a formal border between Afghanistan and India, and a civil servant, Sir Mortimer Durand, was despatched to do the job. He drew a line to establish a 1,640-mile border that divided the Pashtun tribes and was often ignored by the local people. It was against this purely arbitrary division that the 'wild beasts' were up in arms again.

Late one night in 1897, a Pashtun tribe (with whom the British wrongly assumed they were not in dispute) launched a stealth attack on the British encampment. Churchill, an eager twenty-something subaltern on his first visit to the turbulent northwest frontier, was outraged by the 'treachery'. The guerrilla attack cost the British Indian army forty officers and men as well as many horses and pack animals. To the young Churchill's delight, the commander of the operation, Sir Bindon Blood ordered an immediate retaliation. The new recruit joined General Jeffreys in the punitive expedition to 'chastise the truculent assailants'. The exciting encounter between the flashing swords of the Pashtuns and English rifles was all in a day's work, as Churchill later wrote in *My Early Life*, but what afforded young Winston the greatest pleasure was the disciplined accomplishment of a colonial mission: 'The chastisement was to take the form of marching up their valley, which is a *cul de sac*, to its extreme point, destroying all the crops, breaking the reservoirs of water, blowing up as many forts as time permitted, and shooting anyone who obstructed the process.' Who can blame the Afghans in subsequent centuries for believing that in the second and third intrusions they were once again seeing the first in a new guise? What has changed is the technology and the rhetoric: helicopter gunships and drones instead of bayoneted rifles; 'humanitarian' explanations and lies instead of Churchill's straightforwardness.

The merciless Pashtun campaign was depicted thus in Kipling's poem 'The Young British Soldier':

When you're wounded and left on Afghanistan's plains,
And the women come out to cut up what remains,
Jest roll to your rifle and blow out your brains
 An' go to your Gawd like a soldier.
 Go, go, go like a soldier,
 Go, go, go like a soldier,
 Go, go, go like a soldier,
 So-oldier of the Queen!

An earlier poem, 'Das Trauerspiel von Afghanistan' (The Tragedy of Afghanistan) by the German poet Theodor Fontane, then living in London, struck a different note. Sombre and melancholic, it was a more accurate reflection of the magnitude of the 1842 defeat, as this extract reveals:

The snow falls quietly from the sky,
A lone, snow-clad rider stops in front of Jalalabad,
'Who's there!' – 'A British horseman,
I bring a message from Afghanistan.'

Afghanistan! He spoke it so weakly;
Half the city is crowded around the rider,
Sir Robert Sale, the commander,
Lifts him off the horse with his own arms.

They lead him to the stone watch house,
They put him down by the fireplace
How does the fire warm him, how does the light feed him
He breathes deeply and thanks and speaks:

'Thirteen thousand we started From Kabul city, beast and man,
Soldiers, leaders, child and maid,
Frozen, slain, and betrayed.
Our army wrecked . . .'

And what of the victors? No poetry for them. Just stories of heroism and courage and the crimes committed by the foreigner, tales
handed down orally from one generation of Pashtuns to another
as the invasions kept coming. But what if you were a Pashtun
fighter, captured by British-Indian soldiers and slowly roasted to
death in an earth oven? Churchill described this too, without any
trace of emotion or civilisational remonstrations. Imperial domination invariably leads to crimes against those who resist.

Carving Up Africa

In the latter decades of the nineteenth century, with slavery abolished, the white imperialist powers went in search of substitutes. If
the taking of people was no longer permitted, then by the impeccable logic of Empire the next question was 'Why not take the
land?' Africa beckoned, the continent that had spawned humanity,
given birth to ancient civilisations and, most importantly, was full
of riches: diamonds, minerals and, later, oil. Tribal divisions and
localised conflicts had weakened black Africa. Those countries
with a recognisable political structure were a diverse and scattered
group.

The oldest of these was Abyssinia, later Ethiopia, a region that
formed part of the Amharic Empire. As European vultures divided
the continent, it stood alone. Its independence had not yet been
violated. The British had provoked a conflict in 1868 and built an
imperial base at Zula, south of Massawa on the Red Sea, from
which they successfully assaulted the ruler's mountain city of

Magdala. Britain was trying out its new weaponry (Snider breech-loaders in this case), developed after the Crimean War. The weapons alone may not have been enough, had the British not also won over the effective ruler of the Tigre Province, who had his own problems with the Abyssinian king. Italy, too, had turned its gaze to the region.

European incursions throughout the nineteenth century had marked out Africa as a continent that could be taken. Provided the white empires did not succumb to fits of uncontrolled greed and turn on one another, there was enough for all. That was the thinking of the new German state and of its architect and first chancellor, Otto von Bismarck. Unified Germany was a country without colonial possessions. It wanted to play catch-up in Africa. That is why Bismarck convened an imperialist summit in Berlin in 1884–85. It lasted three months. The real agenda consisted of a single item: how best to divide Africa. The seizure, rape and occupation that followed was the responsibility of 'civilisation', elder brother of the 'humanitarian interventions' of the late twentieth and twenty-first centuries.

The only absentee at the conference was the United States. It had agreed to attend, but then had a last-minute change of mind. Every other imperial power or aspirant was present. Africa was divided into fifty different colonised countries, regardless of ethnicity or geography, a brutal exercise that left its mark on black Africa for the next century and a half. The effects of this are still experienced today, with the national borders drawn on the map remaining largely the same. At the time the conference took place, France occupied Algeria and Tunisia and shared Morocco with Spain. Britain dominated Egypt and the Sudan, though the latter was in continuous rebellion. The French and Spanish were left in control of their Maghrebian possessions, and Britain's sphere of influence was not challenged. Indeed, by the end of the proceedings, the lion's share had been formally awarded to Britain, which extended its presence in the continent to East and South Africa as well as Nigeria and Ghana. France got most of West Africa. Italy obtained Somalia and some parts of Ethiopia. Portugal retained Angola and Mozambique. Germany was awarded southwest Africa (Namibia) and Tanganyika (Tanzania).

The Belgian King Leopold II was given Congo as a personal fiefdom, an event unique in the annals of imperialism. This was the only occasion in modern times that an entire territory had been formally, internationally recognised as the personal possession of a single human being. The Congo kept this remarkable status for a quarter of a century. Although Congo had become his life-obsession, and was also the source of his enormous wealth, Leopold never bothered to visit his property (he was scared of being infected by 'African diseases'), making him the most notorious absentee landlord in the history of modern imperialism.

The horror inflicted on the Congolese people was on a scale, and of a level of sadistic brutality, that surpassed anything else that went on during the colonisation of Africa. The conquerors of the Congo, principally the Belgians, but also some others, were after ivory and rubber. Bonuses were paid to soldiers and administrators on how much ivory and rubber they could force villagers to collect. If a village did not turn over enough, its adult males – and sometimes women and children too – were killed. To prove that they had killed the necessary number of people without wasting bullets, soldiers cut off the hands of their victims while they were still alive. Sometimes feet, heads and breasts were added to the gruesome collection sent back to Brussels. To prevent decay the hands were often smoked, while heads and breasts were put in jars of spirit to preserve them.

Leopold declared himself satisfied. It was necessary, he argued, as did other colonial leaders, to be strict and to stop Arab traders from kidnapping Africans and selling them in the black market. But as the photographs of the horrors began to trickle back to Europe there were many expressions of outrage, most commonly from British writers, relieved in some cases by the fact that these crimes were being committed by a non-British empire.

Leopold's soldiers and settlers killed half the population of the Congo. Figures vary, but it is generally agreed that the dead totalled between eight and ten million. In size and scale the closest equivalent crime by a European state was the Judeocide of the Second World War, carried out in most of Europe by Germany and its quislings. The indirect victims of that crime are still being counted in Palestine every single week.

'Satan! I tell you that man is Satan!' declared Cecil Rhodes – no angel himself – after meeting Leopold II. The American poet Vachel Lindsay wrote a poem entitled 'The Congo':

> Listen to the yell of Leopold's ghost
> Burning in Hell for his hand-maimed host,
> Hear how the demons chuckle and yell
> Cutting his hands off, down in Hell

In 1904, E.D. Morel and Roger Casement set up the Congo Reform Association to publicise Leopold's crimes, the first such act of solidarity with a colonised people. Arthur Conan Doyle met with the group, was enraged by what he heard, and did his own research; after studying in detail all the reports of the Belgian atrocities, he sat down and produced a book in nine days. *The Crime of the Congo*, written in cold anger, sold more than half a million copies in its first three months. Conrad's *Heart of Darkness* had a similar impact when its readers realised that the darkness he was characterising as a horror was not the black-skinned African but the white oppressor in their midst. However else they might be described, the events in the Congo could not be characterised as a 'jolly little war against barbarous peoples'. I have yet to come across a single mention of the Congolese genocide in any of Churchill's books or papers.

Imperialist politicians tended not to denounce one another unless they were engaged in conflict among themselves, but the silence on the Congo throughout the chanceries of Europe is not surprising, indicating as it does the deep and ingrained hostility towards black people that had developed over centuries. The three wise monkeys – Britain, France and Germany – simply averted their eyes. The rulers of 'plucky little Belgium', as the country became known in the two world wars that lay ahead, were adepts at mass murder. (Against armed opponents of the same skin colour they capitulated without a struggle.) Nor did plucky little Belgium lose its taste for murder. After the Second World War, it was only too pleased to work with the US, the new hegemonic imperial power, to undermine Congolese independence, resulting in the killing of Patrice Lumumba in 1961, regime change, and finally the installation of the puppet ruler

Colonel Mobuto. Lumumba's assassination shocked black America and the post-colonial world. In Moscow, a Lumumba University was set up to provide free education in every field (including medicine) for African and Asian students who would otherwise not have had any further education at all. The African-American poet Langston Hughes penned these lines in 1961:

> They buried Lumumba
> In an unmarked grave.
> But he needs no marker –
> For air is his grave.
>
> Sun is his grave,
> Moon is, stars are,
> Space is his grave.
>
> My heart's his grave,
> And it's marked there.
> Tomorrow will mark
> It everywhere.

Sixty years later, as the campaign against statuaries gained momentum after the Black Lives Matter movement erupted once again in the United States, a Belgian writer, commenting on Leopold's statues in her own country, evoked the words of Adrienne Rich in 'What Kind of Times Are These':

> . . . this is not somewhere else but here,
> our country moving closer to its own truth and dread,
> its own ways of making people disappear.

~

The colonisation of Africa did not proceed without resistance. In quite a few cases the continent's people and their leaders fought back. European barbarism reacted as barbarism is wont to do: bribe, steal, exterminate.

Britain was establishing its power on the west coast of the continent and then slowly moving inland. It encountered fierce resistance from the Ashanti, whose rulers had enhanced their power by controlling the inland trades routes and utilising their superiority in arms. The Ashanti were effective bush guerrillas, and in their first test of strength against the British, in 1824, the latter lost the battle as well as their commanding officer, Sir Charles MacCarthy. It took more than seventy years before Britain defeated the Ashanti and imposed its rule. Both sides had hired Hausa contingents, but more than mere numbers, the British had the latest weapons too.

In 1896, the Hova kingdom in Madagascar fell to the French after a prolonged resistance. Four years previously the French had taken on the kingdom of Dahomey. Dahomey was ruled by men and women who were trying to mould their country into an ethnically mixed nation-state. The travel writer Richard Burton had mocked King Glele for his celibate female battalions that formed an important segment of his army. (The writer was more scathing about the male soldiers, who, through no fault of their own, were neither well armed nor well trained.) However, this same army inflicted serious losses on the approaching French column in 1892. Though they lost the battle to save their capital, the Dahomean men and women, much to the annoyance of the French, carried on guerrilla warfare in the years that followed. In revenge, the defeated women soldiers were exhibited in Paris in the late 1890s.

Across the continent, in Somalia at the turn of the century, the British faced the toughest resistance in a zone they occupied as a result of the carving-up exercise conducted by the European powers at the Berlin conference. In Mohammed Abdullah Hassan they faced a political-religious leader and poet with strong proto-nationalist views and a gift for military strategy. He was the most capable guerrilla commander that Africa produced in its long battle against European intrusion.

Christened the 'Mad Mullah' by the British occupiers, and mostly described as such in the British press, he became a hate figure like others before and after him. Churchill had utilised the 'Mad Mullah' soubriquet to describe Britain's Pashtun opponents in Malakand. How could anyone who resisted the benevolent and well-meaning Empire be anything but mad? Mohammed Abdullah Hassan is regarded today as the founding father of the Somali state. His wife and other women were military commanders as well, a fact that must have shocked the occupiers.

Two of the British officers who fought in the Somalian war later served under Churchill in another war. One of them was Hastings Ismay, who served as Churchill's chief military consiglieri during the Second World War and was afterwards appointed the first Secretary-General of NATO, the creation of the American Empire. Initially he was reluctant, seeing the outfit as designer-made to 'keep the Soviet Union out, the Americans in, and the Germans down'. Churchill persuaded him to accept the position. Ismay, always a loyal member of the top echelons of the politico-military imperial bureaucracy, fell into line and accepted hard facts. Britain's global 'responsibilities' had to be handed over to Washington. There was no other form of dissolution.

The Sudanese War: Defeat and Revenge

Churchill would have his chance to fight in Africa, after all, but first the context. In Sudan, the proto-nationalists who began contesting outside rule in the late 1800s were led by a religious leader, Mohammed Ahmed bin Abdullah, who referred to himself as the Mahdi – the saviour, whose arrival had been predicted in Shi'ite Islam. For mainstream Sunnis, the very idea constituted heresy, since there could be no other Prophet except *the* Prophet.

Mohammed Ahmed had started the Sudanese war by attempting to wrest the country away from Egyptian and Ottoman control. In order to do so he needed a title that would trump the Sultan-Caliph in Istanbul and his underlings in the region. His army of volunteers accepted him as the Mahdi. Contrary to British accounts describing his fierce fighting force as crazed dervishes blinded by prejudice, the Mahdi was not a literalist like the anti-Ottoman Wahhabis in the Arab Peninsula. He was a reformer who wanted changes in the religion, a proponent of social justice who castigated local and Egyptian notables for collaborating first with the Ottomans and later, from around 1882, the British.

The Sudanese war was a major event in imperialist politics. Britain was divided. The prime minister, W. E. Gladstone, was not keen on war and in 1884 despatched General Charles Gordon, a former imperial consul in Egypt, to evacuate Egyptian and British troops from Khartoum. Gordon settled in, contrary to his orders, and was besieged. In an exchange of letters with the Mahdi, he insisted that 'God is on our side'.

The Mahdi offered safe passage to the general and his soldiers – they would not be harmed if they left the city peacefully. Gordon in his imperial arrogance rejected the offer. Gladstone was not convinced that an army should be sent to try to relieve the general, but he caved in under pressure. The expedition did not succeed, and in 1885 Gordon was martyred by the Mahdi's soldiers when they took Khartoum.

Professor Mekki Shibeika, a respected Sudanese historian, sums up the Gordon affair this way: 'The Mahdi warned that in front of his army marched the Prophet Himself, behind Him the Angel Azrael, Peace be upon Him, holding a luminous banner, and around him the four Khalifas and all the dignitaries of Islam both dead and alive, and that the Prophet had presented him with The Sword of Victory. So no one could conquer him.' That the Mahdi's armies had taken control of large parts of their own country, defeated the British, taken Khartoum, and were acquiring a reputation for invincibility was a source of pride to the rest of the region. This was politically and militarily intolerable to London, even after the Mahdi himself died of typhus in 1885.

After the failure to rescue Gordon, another imperial warlord, General Herbert Kitchener, built up support, with the help of the right-wing press, for a jingoist campaign to return and punish the Sudanese patriots. Kitchener, the principal guest at many a banquet, was received by Queen Victoria and became a popular celebrity, sometimes cheered in the streets by veterans and the populace.

A decade after Gordon's death, the River War of 1896–99 commenced, attracting Churchill's attention like a moth to a lamp. He had been watching events in Africa from afar. His tour of duty in India near the Afghan frontier had been remarkable mainly for a novelistic Henty-style report he had written on Malakand. Now his principal preoccupation was how to get into action as soon as possible. In this endeavour he was repeatedly thwarted by Kitchener. There was no dispute on principle between the two men. Both were Empire-loyalists. However, for both, fame was the spur. Kitchener had a bloody global record: he had served in Egypt, Sudan, India, South Africa and Australia. He simply regarded the young Churchill as a spoilt brat.

Churchill pressed his mother to use her charms to secure him a posting. She failed. Invited to tea at Downing Street by the prime minister, Lord Salisbury, who had liked his Malakand report, Churchill hinted strongly how much he would like to serve in Africa. He later sought and obtained a meeting with Sir Schomberg Kerr McDonnell, a close friend of and adviser to Salisbury, 'whom I had seen and met in social circles since I was a child'. He pressed his plea for favouritism still further. Kerr McDonnell's response was friendly but non-committal. 'I am sure he [Salisbury] will do his best', he informed Churchill. 'He is very pleased with you, but he won't go beyond a certain point. He may be willing to ask the question in such a way as to indicate what he would like the answer to be. You must not expect him to press it if the answer is unfavourable.' It was.

Churchill refused to give up. Finally, after enlisting the help of more family friends in the War Office, he circumvented Kitchener and was informed that he had been 'attached as a supernumerary Lieutenant to the 21st Lancers for the Soudan Campaign . . . report at once to the Abassiyeh Barracks, Cairo to the Regimental Headquarters. You will proceed at your own expense and . . . in the event of your being killed or wounded . . . no charge of any kind will fall on British army funds.'[12] He was now both a freelance journalist and a freelance soldier.

He had won, but the feud with Kitchener had been debilitating. An entire chapter, self-pitying and self-justificatory, is devoted to it in *My Early Years*, Churchill's first and best memoir, published in 1930. He had discovered that 'there were many ill-informed and ill-disposed people who did not take a favourable

---

12   Churchill, *My Early Life*, pp. 46–51.

view of my activities'. The numbers of such people would multi-
ply with the passing of the years. The motive ascribed to them by
their target was jealousy. But Churchill's own account of their
comments suggests otherwise. What was resented was the blatant
cronyism. He was not the only young man who took advantage
of his social and class privileges, but no subaltern in a similar
position boasted of them more than Churchill did. He was upset
at the abuse he suffered, but the terms his detractors used for
him, such as 'Medal-hunter' and 'Self-advertiser', seem mild even
for the times.

Kitchener himself was not innocent of self-puffery. By dint of
hard work, clever self-placement in key imperial hotspots, and a
friendly London press, he had promoted himself as the heroic
symbol of Empire. Napoleon he wasn't. His hostility to Churchill
appears to have been motivated by the fact that the young inter-
loper, with his grander background, was trying to do much the
same thing. The young man in a hurry had to be slowed down.

But Churchill's feelings of 'mistreatment' rankled. In his 1897
novel, *Savrola*, dedicated to 'The Officers of the 4th (Queen's Own)
Hussars', the eponymous hero, after describing the obloquy –
hankering after titles and honours, cringing before power, etc. –
being hurled at him by all sides, reflects:

> Savrola read these criticisms with disdain. He had recognised the
> fact that such things would be said and had deliberately exposed
> himself to them. He knew he had been unwise to go ... and yet
> somehow, he did not regret his mistake ... He would never resign
> his right to go where he pleased. In this case he had followed his
> own inclination, and the odium which had been cast upon him was
> the price he was prepared to pay ... The damage, however, must be
> repaired.

On his way from Cairo to the Sudanese war zone, Churchill was
trying to look on the brighter side. He was delighted by 'the excellent arrangements made for our comfort and convenience'. The
scenery on the 400-mile train journey was stunning and 'the excitement and thoughtless gaiety with which everyone looked forward

to the certainly approaching battle . . . all combined to make the experience pleasant'.

Could there be a problem? There could but it was not the large number of Sudanese about to be exterminated that worried him: 'I was pursued and haunted by a profound, unrelenting fear. I had not heard a word in Cairo of how Sir Herbert Kitchener had received the overriding by the War Office of his wishes upon my appointment.' In fact, as Churchill admitted, on being informed that the brat was on his way, Kitchener 'had simply shrugged his shoulders and passed on to what were after all matters of greater concern'.

Churchill arrived in the Sudan in late summer, 1898. The Battle of Omdurman took place on 2 September. A British flotilla was in position on the Nile. A British Army numbering 25,000 men (of which 8,000 were white) faced 15,000 Sudanese. Given the numerical and technological imbalance, the outcome was hardly a surprise: a British victory. Churchill's description is characteristic: 'It was the last link in the long chain of those spectacular conflicts whose vivid and majestic splendour has done so much to invest war with glamour', and so on.

It is instructive to compare Churchill's war orgasms with the strictures that emanated from William Morris and his fellow socialists gathered in the Socialist League. Morris's newspaper, the *Common Weal*, regularly attacked the jingoism of *The Times*, the *Pall Mall Gazette* and their friends. Steadfast anti-imperialists, Morris and his circle denounced the wanton wars of aggression considered necessary to construct a global empire.

A statement released in 1885 by the 'Provisional Council of the Socialist League', signed by Morris, Eleanor Marx, Ernest Belfort Bax and a few dozen others, challenged the official views justifying the Sudanese war. They pointed out, correctly, that Mohammed Ahmed (the Mahdi) had been prepared to negotiate an organised withdrawal of British garrisons. Wilfrid Scawen Blunt, an intermediary accepted by both sides, had even informed the British that he could assist in having Gordon released, but the brigands in London wanted to teach the natives a lesson. They failed.

Morris poured scorn on the foul streams of 'hypocrisy and

fraud' that characterised British foreign policy. He referred to Gordon and his ilk as 'Khartoum-stealers and spreaders of shoddy civilization'. The statement by the Provisional Council retains a certain freshness:

> The expedition is despatched. British cut-throats slaughter a few thousand Arabs amid the jubilation of the press, when – oh horror! – Khartoum is fallen: and fallen, too, into the hands of the Sudanese themselves. Gordon, no more! In Fleet Street a cry is heard; lamentation and weeping and great mourning. Never was the dust of a hero so watered by the gush of newspaper before. Nowadays, however, we produce emotion like other things – primarily for profit – and only secondarily for use ... Now the factory system and the division of labour supersede individual emotion: it is distilled for us by the journalist, and we buy it ready-made from the great vats in Fleet Street and Printinghouse Square. The result is that the public sometimes have emotion forced upon them when it suits the purveyor, for other reasons than the greatness of the departed ... Anyway, from the well-watered dust of Gordon rises up for *The Times*, *Pall Mall* and their clients, the fair prospect of British Protectorate at Khartoum, railway from Sukian to Berber, new markets, fresh colonial posts.

In the full flush of victory at Atbara in the spring of 1898, Kitchener had ordered the defeated Muslim leader, Emir Mahmud Ahmed, bound in chains and whipped behind the triumphal victory procession. After Omdurman, he ordered the execution of wounded Muslim prisoners. This was followed by desecration of the Mahdi's tomb. His bones were thrown into the Nile; his skull retained by Kitchener as a ghoulish souvenir. This bloody prologue to the full-scale colonisation of Sudan supposedly shocked Queen Victoria. Churchill, too, despite his own gung-ho approach, expressed regret that the Mahdi's body was being desecrated. In the first edition of his book *The River War*, he changed his attitude towards the enemy he had formerly traduced as a 'savage', a 'barbarian' and a 'ruthless fanatic'. The obituary was more refined:

Whatever misfortunes the life of Mohammed Ahmed may have caused, he was a man of considerable nobility of character, a priest, a soldier, and a patriot. He won great battles; he stimulated and revived religion. He founded an empire. To some extent he reformed the public morals. Indirectly, by making slaves into soldiers, he diminished slavery.

By 1931, the praise flowed as generously as had the blood in 1898. In an introduction to *The Mahdi of Allah*, by the German author Richard Bermann, Churchill wrote in even more exaggerated vein:

> The life of the Mahdi is a romance in miniature and wonderful as that of Mohammed himself. The rebellion of the Sudan was the last great outburst of the blood-red flower of Islam ... The black banner of the Mahdi swept the Sudan to the booming of the war trombone made of elephant tusk. The rule of the Saints was established ... The Mahdi was a mystic and a visionary ... The Mahdi raised himself to dazzling heights by the virtue of poverty and the Holy War ... [He was] the ascetic and the Sufi, the Twelfth Imam that was to come, who came and conquered, and wisely went again before he was conquered himself.

After hearing that the Queen was displeased and had compared the outrage upon the tomb as a deed worthy of the Middle Ages, especially since the Mahdi had been a 'man of certain importance', General Kitchener responded that he was going to donate the skull to the Royal College of Surgeons.

How could Churchill not have been more than slightly pleased at the discomfiture of his (pardon the expression) bête noire? As a soldier Churchill was a dilettante, keen on glory and a few medals to help his future political and journalistic career. Kitchener was a sadistic brute. Whenever he was compelled to confront an enemy equal in size or skill he was a disastrous failure. During the Boer War he was trounced and mocked at the battle of Paardeburg. During the First World War, his dictatorial conduct in military direction led to bloody chaos, and it was with sighs of secret relief that his Cabinet colleagues received the news that the North Sea had claimed him.

Kitchener is remembered today, if at all, as a symbol of imperial kitsch. His image on the famous recruiting poster for the First World War, 'Your Country Needs YOU', was cruelly satirised in Carnaby Street in sixties London, with waxed moustaches for sale along with the peaked cap. His figure going down with the ship, the SS Hampshire, off Orkney in 1916, has been depicted 'standing bolt upright, still saluting, as the waters close around him and his hat floats away, like the admiral in Kind Hearts and Coronets'.[13] Flippancy aside, the poster had a huge impact elsewhere. An early Soviet version was produced during the civil war.

Premature death always helps to enhance the image.[14] But Kitchener's career raises some questions in relation to waging colonial wars, questions that were valid then and remain so to this day. They apply even more strongly to Churchill and more than a few of his underlings. Does not the practice of war and the strict code of military discipline (obey orders or be executed) lead to an automatic dehumanisation? The native enemy is always sub-human. The relative decencies observed at home (though not in the case of the US treatment of the indigenous population or the slaves and their descendants) are discarded. The sight of different coloured skins and the vastness and untapped riches in the territories to be occupied loosens all restraints. Human fellow feeling ceases to exist. An animal ferocity comes into play.

Kitchener was the supreme practitioner in this field. His

---

13   John Campbell, 'Triumphalism', London Review of Books, 19 December 1985. Kind Hearts and Coronets (1949) is a comic masterpiece of English cinema, starring Alec Guinness.

14   It's worth stressing that attitudes to Kitchener (as to Churchill himself) registered a sharp shift after the Falklands/Malvinas war. As John Campbell (ibid.) noted, the biographies produced by Trevor Royle and Philip Warner in 1985 were apologist in tone and content, in contrast to that by Philip Magnus, published in 1958, two years after the Suez debacle had set the seal on glorifying the imperial past and the era of decolonisation had begun. Despite that, Magnus is too forgiving of his subject's crimes.

desperation to be appointed viceroy of India was well known. The suggestion was vetoed by John Morley as Secretary of State for India in the Liberal Cabinet. He knew well that, whatever else was required, autocratic sadism was not what British India needed at the time. Despite the media-promoted adulation and official junketing, Morley and fifty other MPs were still willing to stand up and oppose the cash prize granted to Kitchener on his return from the Sudan.

Similarly, throughout his life Churchill was motivated by the necessity of preserving, expanding and defending the British Empire whatever the military or moral cost. As he saw it, and said as much, it was to the benefit of mankind that civilisation was being taken to the savages and inferior peoples. How could they not benefit? Decades later, when asked by an American journalist what he thought of Western civilisation, Gandhi famously replied: 'It would be a good idea.'

Kitchener was cruder in his approach than Churchill, but the project was the same. The victory at Omdurman, he said, had opened the Nile Valley 'to the civilising influence of commercial enterprise'. Kitchener was not an ideologue but a useful technician. His ambition took the form of colonial conquest and bathing in glory, even if the bath was full of blood. In this aspect he was more ruthless than, but not so different from, other members of the imperial military caste. Churchill was all these things and more. But it was his vainglory that made him even more dangerous.

White on White

The last nineteenth-century war on the African continent was fought in South Africa, between the British and the Boers, descendants of the Dutch who had arrived in the Cape in the seventeenth century to build an outpost for the Dutch East India Company, and whose numbers had swelled with Huguenot refugees from France after the revocation of the Edict of Nantes. From then on, a power seesaw in Europe affected the Cape Colony, with Britain taking over and the Dutch returning, a pattern that was repeated till British hegemony became unchallengeable.

But the number of Dutch settlers and the spread of the language meant there were regions where the latter were dominant. Jan Smuts, of Dutch heritage but ultra-Anglophile (later prime minister of South Africa and a close friend of Churchill), proposed a compromise whereby Cecil Rhodes became the effective ruler and presided over a mixed European government. The Boers were not interested. They wanted to govern themselves, keep hold of their own mines and wealth, and not pay taxes to London.

Settlers, as history reveals, tend to be the most vicious, diehard representatives of their respective cultures. The English Puritans in North America, the Spanish Catholics in South America, the French settlers in Algeria and Morocco, the English again in Central Africa, the Portuguese in Goa and East Timor, the Brooklyn Jews in occupied Palestine, etc. The Boers were no different. In December 1880, at the start of the first Boer War, they had declared independence for Transvaal and started to surround the British garrisons in the region. Peace was declared in 1881 but tensions continued with sporadic violent eruptions. By 1899, the two sides once again faced each other. Churchill ensured that he had a ring-side seat.

Gold mines on African (now Boer) lands were the *casus belli*. British officers – Kitchener once again in the lead, with Churchill reprising the role of the journalist forever on his heels – arrived in 1899 fully equipped with valets, grooms and hampers packed with delicacies from Fortnum & Mason (which had proudly, and absurdly, boasted since the Crimean War that it catered to 'soldiers and officers alike'). Arrogant and drunk on their own successes, the British thought it would be an easy victory. What took them by surprise was that this was not a 'gentlemanly war'.

There was another problem, as 'Looker-On' warned in the November 1899 issue of *Blackwood's Magazine*: 'There is no denying that war between white people in presence of black has always been deprecated as a sort of treachery to a common bond.' Up to a point. The war between the British and American colonists was fought predominantly by whites in the presence of slaves and indigenous tribes. The latter were used by both sides when the occasion demanded, and, as we shall see in a subsequent chapter, black and brown colonial soldiers were used in the two world wars by all the combatants. But the fear was real in South Africa. Two white minority groups were battling for control in a country where both were collectively outnumbered by the black inhabitants. What if the restless natives launched uprisings of their own? To avoid any such calamity, an unwritten protocol agreed by Brit and Boer specified that neither side would use black troops in the conflict. Imperial minds now feared that putting guns in the hands of black people was a prelude to dangerous ideas entering black heads.

The war itself pitted a conventional British Army in red tunics and pith helmets against Boer guerrilla units of twenty-five or so men travelling on ox wagons, who became experts at harassing British columns and evading capture. The Boers knew the territory well, while British intelligence, it was commonly agreed, was poor. Kitchener was lucky to survive the conflict with his reputation intact.

His first incursion led to 1,200 British casualties, the highest of the war. Many senior officers were removed from their commands. Too many of them, it was felt, had surrendered out of sheer cowardice. Somerset Maugham reported that 'it was not till some were shot and more cashiered that the majority nerved themselves to a stouter courage'.[15] All in all, some 3,700 British officers were killed. The imperial yeomanry, hurriedly recruited with the inducement of five shillings a day, suffered three times that number. The losses led to desperation, and desperation led to war crimes. At home, the Liberal leader Henry Campbell Bannerman denounced what British troops were doing as 'barbarous'. He was strongly backed by the *Guardian*, whose correspondent, the Liberal thinker J.A. Hobson, interviewed Olive Schreiner and the Transvaal leader Paul Kruger to provide an alternative view. The war had been promoted by the scoundrel Rhodes after a previous 'informal' attempt had failed. It was Rhodes, backed by South African capital, who had egged Kitchener on. Hobson referred to 'Jewish financiers', an anti-Semitic codeword for capitalists, but his principal aim was to reflect on and conceptualise the transition from national capitalism to imperialism. His classic work *Imperialism* grew out of this endeavour.

---

15 W. Somerset Maugham, *A Writer's Notebook*, London, 1949.

That Churchill was present in the region while Hobson was reflecting on what all of this meant was fortuitous, and symbolic. Churchill, of course, had very different journalistic and political objectives. Another jolly little war had begun, so why not participate and report on it as best he could? His gung-ho articles in the *Morning Post* were widely read, and the recounting of his own little adventure was par for the course. The reporting certainly improved his knowledge of geography, but also demonstrated that whites sometimes had to kill other whites in order to safeguard the interests of the British Empire.

He became embroiled in an incident during the relief of Mafeking, when a train came under attack by the Boers. L. S. Amery, *The Times* correspondent, reported:

> We found twelve men ... who had escaped from the disaster and we pieced the story together. We heard how Mr Churchill had walked round and round the wreckage while the bullets were spitting against the iron walls and had called for volunteers to free the engine and how he had said, 'This will be good for my paper.'

As the Boers moved in, Churchill surrendered immediately. As with most episodes connected to him, this account (apart from his surrender) was questioned. Whatever the exact truth, as a career-enhancer it was perfect.

Interestingly, if coincidentally, Churchill had now had occasion to observe on two continents similar methods of what later became known as 'counter-insurgency' measures. The Spanish concentration camps in Cuba were being mimicked in the South African *veldt*. Locking up whites in camps was justified by many bishops, but the reports were not pleasing to Liberal ears. Opposition to the war at home began to mount. In a *Guardian* editorial of 27 September 1901, headed 'The Mortality in Concentration Camps', the anonymous leader-writer informed readers:

> Two thousand three hundred and forty-five persons – men, women and children – died during August in what the Government, with grim humour, calls the 'Camps of Refuge' in South Africa. One

thousand eight hundred and seventy-eight were white, and of these more than fifteen hundred were children. The remainder, 467, were natives, whose promised career of happiness under British care has thus sadly been cut short. They are ugly figures . . . People have not hesitated to heap insult on injury by accusing the Boer mothers of neglect and incompetence . . . The concentration policy may or may not have contributed to the success of our arms, but let us at least be candid and recognise what it has meant and still means in human suffering.

Churchill doesn't mention the concentration camps in his account of the Boer War, which focuses mainly on his own adventures. He came to South Africa to cover the war and, as an 'embedded journalist' par excellence, successfully managed to embroil himself in the conflict itself, much to the irritation of the British generals, including Kitchener and Haig. His surrender to a Boer is justified with a banal quote from 'the great Napoleon'. His escape is described in vainglorious terms. As the long-awaited British triumph neared, Churchill provided his readers with these words of wisdom:

The Boers were the most humane people where white men were concerned. Kaffirs [a derogatory term for blacks] were a different story, but to the Boer mind the destruction of a white man's life, even in war, was a lamentable and shocking event. They were the most good-hearted enemy I have ever fought against in the four continents in which it has been my fortune to see active service.

2

Skirmishes on the Home Front

Those gilded flies
That, basking in the sunshine of a court,
Fatten on its corruption! – what are they?
– The drones of the community; they feed
On the mechanic's labour: the starved hind
For them compels the stubborn glebe to yield
Its unshared harvests; and yon squalid form,
Leaner than fleshless misery, that wastes
A sunless life in the unwholesome mine,
Drags out in labour a protracted death,
To glut their grandeur; many faint with toil
That few may know the cares and woe of sloth.

Shelley, *Queen Mab* (1813)

For almost a century (1819–1914), the politically conscious segments of a British working-class-in-formation had fought hard and sacrificed lives to win basic social and political rights for themselves. They met with strong resistance from the owners of property and their political backers, buttressed by church, police, judiciary and, when necessary, military force. The regular outbreaks of political unrest for most of the nineteenth and early twentieth centuries had created the combined and uneven development of consciousness that assisted the formation both of the young workers and radical movements of those times and of the governing class. Each side preserved a historical memory. Hopeful in one case, fearful in the other.

Churchill entered politics in 1900, taking a seat as a Conservative in Parliament the following year, in a period of political mutability and uneasiness among the ruling class. In 1885, the Liberal Party leader Joseph Chamberlain had railed against the new rich, the magnates grown wealthy in towns and on the seas, busy building their grand mansions in the country-side. He was not opposed to their accretion of wealth, but felt they should pay a price. As he launched a campaign for an early version of the welfare state, Chamberlain posed a question that sought to democratise *noblesse oblige*: 'I ask what ransom will property pay for the security which it enjoys?' Attacked for the use of the word 'ransom', he subsequently regretted his rashness and substituted the less offensive 'insurance', but the message was clear. The monied class was nervous.

On the face of it, this seems irrational. But those with long memories were aware of the dangers posed, even in apparent periods of calm, by those at the losing end of the industrial revolution.

The radical century in Britain had followed the arc of the French Revolution of 1789–1815. In London in 1794, at the height of the revolution across the Channel, large crowds picketed and attacked army recruitment centres in Holborn, the City, Clerkenwell and Shoreditch, finally burning them to the ground after three days of rioting. After 1815, the rulers' hope that the defeat of Napoleon at Waterloo and his incarceration on Saint Helena might drastically reduce the radical temperature at home was only partially fulfilled. Followers of Tom Paine clustered in several cities, co-existing with even more radical currents. There was strong resistance among the non-privileged classes to the creation and presence of a police force, first established as a consolidated public body to discipline labour on the docks of the Thames in 1800.[1] Even reformers who accepted that localised, preventive police units might be necessary

---

1 See 'Sugar and Police' in Peter Linebaugh's *The London Hanged: Crime and Civil Society in the Eighteenth Century* (London, 1991), on the criminalisation of customary takings and the wide-ranging significance of Patrick Colquhoun's Marine Police Force.

to safeguard homes and shops were not prepared to tolerate any centralised police force, since its greater powers would lead to 'a system of tyranny; an organised army of spies and informers, for the destruction of all public liberty, and the disturbance of all private happiness. Every other system of police is the curse of despotism.'[2]

Discontent was not confined to apprentices and workers. Many middle-class liberals and small traders were enraged by the August 1819 Peterloo massacre in Manchester, immortalised by Shelley in 'The Masque of Anarchy', written in the immediate wake of Peterloo though not published until 1832. The poet had read the details of the atrocity against democratic Reformers in radical journals – 'Slash, and stab, and maim and hew; / What they like, that let them do' – and had relied on the razor-sharp despatches of Richard Carlile.

In the absence of political parties, the radical culture of the period played a huge role in fuelling discussion groups. Thomas Wooler's the *Black Dwarf*, established in 1819, became the largest circulation radical weekly. Wooler, a Sheffield printer, was a courageous editor. The publication's satire may have been heavy-handed on occasion, but always for a good cause. Wooler often set his articles directly on stone, and encouraged contributors to express themselves in whatever style they found most natural. This led to letters to the editor sometimes in the form of verse. In the 10 February 1819 issue, Wooler had denounced the imposition of the window tax, a levy that further punished the poor: 'The Window tax! – that execrable enemy of health – that blasphemous attempt to shut from the poor, the common inheritance of light and air.' Messages of support poured in, including a letter-poem, 'On the Candle and Window Tax':

---

2   Quoted in E. P. Thompson, *The Making of the English Working Class*, London 1968, p. 89. Over two centuries later, activists on the streets of the United States are demanding the dissolution of the police force for its consistent racism and incarceration and killing of black people.

Jove said, 'Let there be Light' and lo
It instant was, and freely given
To every creature under heaven.
Says Pitt – 'I will not have it so'
'Darkness much better suits my views,
'Let Darkness o'er the land diffuse:
'Henceforth I will that all shall pay
'For every light by night or day.'
He spoke – and as he'd been a God,
The venal herd obeyed his nod.
A wretched crew who right or wrong,
Would sell their country for a song.[3]

The use of cavalry bayonets against the Reformers at Peterloo is the best-known episode of class war in industrialising Britain, largely because of Shelley's poem, but the rally itself wasn't exactly a thunderbolt from a pristine blue sky. Much has been written about it in monographs, and most recently there's been an immensely educative film (a rarity these days) by Mike Leigh. The vicious satires produced at the time by Messrs Hone and Cruikshank, compiled in *The Political House that Jack Built*, sold in the region of 100,000 copies. Since most pamphlets, magazines, etc., were shared and passed around in taverns and other meeting places, the actual number of readers should, at the very least, be quadrupled. For contextualisation, Edward Thompson's *The Making of the English Working Class* remains unmatched. His account of Peterloo is enriched by descriptions of the various brands of radicalism that existed at the time, without which the huge gathering in Manchester would not have been possible.

The tens of thousands converging on St Peter's Field ('Peterloo' was a satirical coinage that stuck) were there to demand universal male adult franchise. This may seem trifling now, but at the time it was regarded as ultra-radical by the governing classes, who equated even a partial democracy with revolution. Thomas Davison, a radical bookseller in Smithfield, headlined one of his editorials

---

3   *Black Dwarf*, 10 March 1819, p. 152.

'The Blowing Up of the Present System', and mordantly advised readers of his magazine, *Medusa, Or, Penny Politician*, that 'there were trees, lamp-posts, and halters everywhere, if summary justice is required, to make examples of any hardened or incorrigible villain, or any *great* or little plunderer of property'. If the many got the vote, how would the few prosper?

Both sides got this one a bit wrong. It would take another century for women to get the vote, a demand that had not occurred to the radical Reformers or *Medusa*. Likewise, class oppression rather than gender equality was the central theme of *The Manchester Female Reformers' Address to the Wives, Mothers, Sisters and Daughters of the Higher and Middling Classes of Society*. Written a month before Peterloo, and signed by Susannah Saxton 'by Order of the Committee', it painted a grim picture of everyday working-class life and explained why people were at the end of their tether:

DEAR SISTERS OF THE EARTH,

It is with a spirit of peaceful consideration and due respect that we are induced to address you, upon the causes that have compelled us to associate together in aid of our suffering children, our dying parents, and the miserable partners of our woes ... Our minds are filled with horror and despair, fearful on each returning morn, the light of heaven should present to us the corpse of some of our famished offspring, or nearest kindred, which the more kind hand of death had released from the grasp of the oppressor ... Every succeeding night brings with it new terrors, so that we are sick of life and weary of the world, where poverty, wretchedness, tyranny and injustice, have so long been permitted to reign amongst men ...

From the very nature and deliberate consideration, we are thoroughly convinced, that under the present system, the day is near at hand, when nothing will be found in our unhappy country, but luxury, idleness, dissipation, and tyranny on the one hand; and abject poverty, slavery, wretchedness, misery and death on the other ...[4]

4 *Black Dwarf*, 4 August 1819, pp. 508–10.

Nothing much had changed by the end of the century, and similar descriptions would later be found in Thomas Hardy's novels, especially *Jude the Obscure*. What is particularly fascinating in the appeal of the Female Reformers – an appeal that fell mostly on deaf ears – was its linkage of oppression at home to reactionary policies abroad. Had there been a democratic Parliament, argued Saxton, 'the English nation would not have been stamped with the indelible disgrace of having been engaged in the late unjust, unnecessary, and destructive war against the liberties of France, that closed its dreadful career on the crimson plains of Waterloo'. The only function of that exercise was to place a dreadful dreg on the French throne, someone who had been parasiting from one end of Britain to another 'in cowardly and vagabond slothfulness and contempt'. Apart from the lives lost, 'the widows and orphans left destitute and unprotected', the war 'has tended to raise landed property threefold' and created 'an insurmountable burden of taxation' that was now dragging 'our merchants and manufacturers to poverty and degradation'.

All of the Reformers acknowledged Peterloo as a serious setback. But while moderates hastily retreated – a few weeks after the massacre, Manchester's Methodist Sunday Schools excluded all children wearing the Reformers' white hats and/or radical badges (an early version of Prevent strategy being used against young Muslims in Britain today) – the radical Reformers went on the offensive. They refused to accept the mealy-mouthed denials from government spokesmen that the decision to attack had been taken at the top. They rejected the government's conclusions, which scapegoated the magistrates and Yeomanry of Manchester. (Although the Yeomanry, little more than the local bourgeoisie and their henchmen on horseback, had been more vicious than the Hussars.) Thomas Wooler's editorial, 'Hints to the Reformers of the British Empire, as to the Real Authors of the Manchester Massacre', struck a sombre note, but there was no retreat. His tone was intransigent:

As the sword has been drawn against reform, and the only answer to our prayers has been brutal force, or shameful insults ... We must collect and unite our scattered forces; and endeavour to marshal our strength, to be prepared for any result. There is no hope for us, but in our own exertions ... Now it is evident that those who oppress us, are determined to continue their oppression, until we can strike the faulchion out of their hands and protect ourselves against the threatened slaughter. It is probable that in no other place than Manchester could be found brutes of so ferocious a description; but the same principles will produce effects elsewhere, if not quite so atrocious, yet equally destructive of the rights and liberties of the people ... While soldiers will fire upon, and bayonet the advocates of reform, there will be no want of monsters to give them the orders to do so.

The system that disgraced Ireland during the reign of Castlereagh and his colleagues will be introduced into England, if the temper of the times will bear it. The bloody tragedy has commenced in Lancashire, and the first scene has been performed with the same voracious appetite for blood, for which the tortures of Ireland were famed, in that detestable era.[5]

Wooler went on to accuse the government and the state of having authorised the use of force and the moves by magistrates, who 'were the cause of the slaughter, by acting in an illegal manner'. Like the Female Reformers, he linked the atrocities at home to butchery abroad. When it came down to it, the same methods were used, and would continue to be used.[6] A century after Peterloo, the British General Reginald Dyer would order his troops to seal off Jallianwala Bagh in Amritsar, India, where thousands had gathered to demand an end to colonial repression. There, as in Peterloo,

5   *The Black Dwarf*, 8 September 1819.
6   The continuities in ruling-class violence against workers of every sort refuse to disappear. Compare the attitudes prevailing in the early nineteenth century with Margaret Thatcher's ideological assault on the miners as the 'enemy within' and ordering of the use of physical force by combined units of the constabulary to crush them. For a forensic survey of the scene, Seumas Milne's classic account, *The Enemy Within: Thatcher's Secret War Against the Miners* (London, 1994), has yet to be equalled or seriously rebutted.

women and children were present. Instead of sabres, troops had machine-guns. Their orders were to intimidate the population. After continuous firing, at least 500 people were killed and more than 1,000 wounded.

For some radical groups in this nineteenth-century pre-socialist environment, Peterloo raised important questions of strategy and tactics. How should the violence of the state be combated? Should the many arm themselves with pikes, hammers, swords and butcher's knives? Was an insurrection to topple the existing order possible?

As models to help furnish an answer there were two revolutions, the English and the French. By the nineteenth century the impact of the latter was much greater, though references to 'levelling' and the 'good old cause' never completely disappeared from the political culture of radicals and, later, socialists. French Jacobinism was a major inspiration for radical groups in the nineteenth century, though a significant number of the Reformers were influenced by various currents within Methodism. All the groups, radical and less radical, would be united in a mass campaign demanding justice, with 300,000 people on the streets of London a month after the massacre. Later, in 1838, they would be united more systematically by the Chartists, in the first serious attempt to organise dissident forces throughout the country and create an extra-parliamentary opposition movement whose principal aim was the representation of the disenfranchised masses (their male section) in the House of Commons.

Long before Chartism, though, radicals were considering localised civil wars against the gentrified businessmen who stalked the land. The more ambitious were convinced that an insurrection could be triggered by an act of daring. Such as? Such as assassinating Prime Minister Lord Liverpool and his Cabinet while they were sitting to sup at Lord Harrowby's mansion in Grosvenor Square. The 1820 'Cato Street conspiracy' was foiled, but this fantasy of exterminating the whole Cabinet had gripped a not insignificant number of radical minds at the time. Nor were their terrorist intentions a huge secret.

Liverpool's predecessor at Downing Street, Spencer Perceval, had been shot dead in the lobby of the House of Commons in

1812. A pious and deeply reactionary prosecutor, Perceval had, as a junior, helped to indict Tom Paine and the radical John Horne Tooke. He was the principal prosecutor when Colonel Edward Despard (1751–1803) was tried and hanged for high treason. Perceval alleged that Despard was plotting the seizure of the Tower of London and the Bank of England, and the assassination of George III.

Despard, who hailed from an Irish landowning family, was a significant figure in the Jacobin underground. In his younger days he had been highly regarded as an officer, and Lord Nelson himself appeared in court to give evidence for the defence: 'no man could have shown more zealous attachment to his Sovereign and his Country than Colonel Despard'. But that was all some time prior. The colonel's consciousness had shifted dramatically. A convergence of forces – his Irish origins; his experiences in Jamaica and the colonies of Central America; his wife Catherine, an Afro-Caribbean actively hostile to slavery; his links with the Irish Republican Robert Emmet and, according to some, with British and Irish Jacobin groups in France – had radicalised him. He became a fervent opponent of enclosure and a believer in Irish independence, and began to work with the clandestine groups of the United Irishmen based in England, as well as with the radical reform group the London Corresponding Society. Despard's aim was to construct a revolutionary army that could fight to free both Ireland and Britain. He recruited a significant number of soldiers, including a Grenadier Guard who had named his son 'Bonaparte'.[7] His trial judge denounced him for advocating 'the wild and Levelling principle of Universal Equality', and Despard became a radical martyr after his execution, much admired by the poor.

---

7   E. P. Thompson, *The Making of the English Working Class*, Chapter 14, 'An Army of Redressers': 'Fifteen years later Oliver the Spy reported on a conversation with a key conspirator, Charles Pendrill: "He admitted that the soldiers were very deeply implicated, and very staunch."' Peter Linebaugh has written extensively on Despard, most recently in *Red Round Globe Hot Burning: A Tale at the Crossroads of Commons and Closure, of Love and Terror, of Race and Class, and of Kate and Ned Despard* (Berkeley, 2019).

But it was not one of Despard's followers who despatched Perceval to the nether regions. It was a seriously disgruntled businessman. The result, as the official UK government website admits, was large-scale rejoicing in London and elsewhere. The businessman, John Bellingham, was hurriedly tried and executed within a week, but in that one week he was the toast of radicals and reformers (and not just them) across the land.[8] Perceval's conduct of the war against Napoleon had made him unpopular with merchants and traders. They had felt the impact of his notorious 'orders in council' forbidding neutral states to trade with France and threatening trade and military sanctions. Napoleon had responded in kind, and an angry United States threatened a war against Britain which might have led to Canada's integration into the United States. Mercantile and manufacturing capital, as well as shopkeepers and workers, were hostile to Perceval's policies and his sanctimonious utterances. His unremitting assault on radicals and 'subversives' had made him a hated figure in those circles, while the Prince Regent was livid when Perceval objected on religious grounds to the Prince's intention of divorcing his wife, Caroline. It was as if the Reformation had never taken place. Perceval was on his way to the Commons to answer angry MPs, who wanted him to rescind his orders in council, when he was shot down. Few conservative historians have expressed much sympathy for the only British prime minister ever to be assassinated.

Before Peterloo, Lord Liverpool had suspended habeas corpus in England and Ireland. Afterwards, his Parliament passed the repressive Six Acts, which restricted free speech and assembly, with severe punishments decreed for those who defied the new laws. It also imposed a special tax on radical papers and pamphlets to try to put them out of business. Home Office spies were darting to and fro, penetrating one group of radicals, quietly watching another, provoking them into extreme acts in order to get rid of them for eternity. Others were busy manufacturing fake news (and pamphlets)

---

8 The assassin's direct descendant, Sir Henry Bellingham, a former Tory MP, was ennobled in Boris Johnson's much-criticised jokey honours list in July 2020.

to discredit the radicals. There was a serious concern that some groups might want revenge for the massacre, and the sooner they could be identified and jailed or hanged the safer it would be for the rulers. A month after Peterloo a clerical magistrate, combining the pieties of the faith with the objectivity of the legal system, informed a prisoner in the dock: 'I believe you are a downright blackguard reformer. Some of you reformers ought to be hanged, and some of you are sure to be hanged – the rope is already round your necks.'[9]

The Prince Regent, opening the next session of Parliament, concluded thus:

> Upon the loyalty of the great body of the people I have the most confident reliance; but it will require your utmost vigilance and exertion, collectively and individually, to check the dissemination of the doctrines of treason and impiety, and to impress upon the minds of all classes of his Majesty's subjects, that it is from the cultivation of the principles of religion, and from a just subordination to lawful authority, that we can alone expect the continuance of that divine favour and protection which have hitherto been so signally experienced by this kingdom.

William Hone, aided by Cruikshank's caricatures, composed a satirical response:

> 'Tis pity that these cursed State Affairs
> Should take you from your pheasants and your hares
> Just now:
> But lo!
> CONSPIRACY and TREASON are abroad!

---

9   *The Times*, 27 September 1819. Quoted in E. P. Thompson, *The Making of the English Working Class*, p. 752. Among other God-fearing supporters of the suspension of habeas corpus and the military charge at Peterloo was William Wilberforce. His sympathy for black slaves and advocacy for abolition of the trade did not extend, alas, to wage-slavery at home. Together with his friend William Pitt, he had defended the Combination Acts of 1799 and 1800, which made all combinations, hence trade unions, illegal.

Those imps of darkness, gender'd in the wombs
Of spinning-jennies, winding-wheels, and looms,
In Lunashire –
Oh, Lord!
My L – ds and G – tl – n, we've much to fear!

Reform, Reform, the swinish rabble cry –
Meaning, of course, rebellion, blood, and riot –
Audacious rascals! you, my Lords, and I,
Know 'tis their duty to be starved in quiet:
But they have grumbling habits, incompatible
With the repose of our august community –
They see that good things are with us come-at-ible,
And therefore slyly watch their opportunity
To get a share:
Yes, they declare
That we are not God's favorites alone –
That they have rights to food, and clothes, and air,
As well as you, the Brilliants of a throne!
Oh! indications foul of revolution –
The villains would destroy the Constitution!

The plot against Lord Liverpool seemed a suitable riposte to
Peterloo. It began with a group of Spencean radicals. Thomas
Spence, a schoolteacher from Newcastle, impressed by the French
Revolution and inspired by Tom Paine, had moved to London in
1792 and became a street bookseller, radical songster and
pamphleteer, and an advocate for common lands as against private
property, before being arrested for treason. On his release he established a bookshop in Chancery Lane and launched a magazine
intriguingly titled *Pig's Meat*, the first issue of which proclaimed:

Awake! Arise! Arm yourselves with truth, justice, reason. Lay siege
to corruption. Claim as your inalienable right, universal suffrage
and annual parliaments. And whenever you have the gratification
to choose a representative, let him be from among the lower orders
of men, and he will know how to sympathize with you.

Spence moved leftwards till his death in 1814, preaching the necessity of a revolution as in France, and of a Franco-British union to liberate the world. He was laid to rest by 'forty disciples', but his spirit remained restless. Five years later his followers were still meeting in rooms at various public houses.[10] One of their number, John Thistlewood, a former soldier, was reported by a Home Office spy to have uttered the following words: 'High Treason was committed against the people at Manchester. I resolved that the lives of the instigators of massacre should atone for the souls of murdered innocents.'

Six Home Office spies were assigned to the Spenceans. One of them, George Edwards, was the principal provocateur. It was he who suggested they wipe out the Cabinet; he who found the rooms at 1a Cato Street, off the Edgware Road in the Marylebone district of London, where they plotted; he who provided the false information that Lord Harrowby, the Lord President of the Council in the government, had invited the Cabinet, including Wellington, the victor of Waterloo, for supper. At the first meeting in Cato Street (so chosen because of its proximity to the venue for the supposed dinner in Grosvenor Square) there was only one item on the agenda: how best to assassinate Liverpool and his Cabinet as they sat down to dine. The Spenceans' aim was serious. They wanted to foment a revolution. A pro-government account based on evidence from the Home Office spies was presented at trial and was not denied by the defendants, though one of them, James Ings, shouted, 'The Attorney General knew all the plans for two months before I was acquainted with them', and said George Edwards had suggested some of the more gruesome acts.

It was to start with one of the party knocking on the door, purporting to have a parcel for Lord Harrowby, to allow the gang to burst in. One group would bind – or in the event of resistance, kill – the servants and occupy all quarters of the building, while a

---

10 These included The Mulberry Tree in Moorfields, The Carlisle in Shoreditch, The Cock in Soho, The Pineapple in Lambeth, The White Lion in Camden, The Horse and Groom in Marylebone and The Nag's Head in Carnaby Market.

second select group, led by Thistlewood, would proceed to the dining room. There, hand grenades would pave the way for an indiscriminate attack on the assembled ministers with guns and knives. Once the entire Cabinet had been murdered, the plan was to use the bodies for a gruesome *pièce de théâtre*. Thistlewood's right-hand man, the former butcher James Ings, would cut off all their heads and take away two of them, those of the particularly reviled Lord Castlereagh and the home secretary, Lord Sidmouth, to be displayed for public edification on spikes on Westminster Bridge.

Thistlewood and his cohorts then planned to seize the King Street Barracks, the Bishop of London's house, the Light House Barracks in Gray's Inn Lane, the Bank of England and Mansion House (which would house their provisional government). They were convinced from all their soundings that the country was on the verge of revolt, and that their act would trigger a mass uprising against the decapitated government. They believed disaffected Londoners would spontaneously flock to support a new Committee of Public Safety, while thousands of working men from Newcastle, Glasgow and Leeds would join the revolution. Thistlewood had even approached the leading Radical, John Cam Hobhouse, soon to be MP for Westminster, to head the new government. The coup leader was determined this would be Britain's 'Bastille moment'.

Something nagged Inglewood, a key conspirator. One of his trusted men was sent to Grosvenor Square on the morning of the supposed dinner to chat up the servants and get more details. A servant told him there was no dinner, and that Lord Harrowby was not even in London. Inglewood was convinced this was a lie. That same afternoon Cato Street was raided by armed police. One constable was killed in the clash. Eleven men were arrested. Thistlewood, Davidson, Ings, Tidd and Brunt were found guilty of high treason and hanged. None of them repented. Davidson reminded the court of the English Revolution:

> It is an ancient custom to resist tyranny . . . And our history goes on
> further to say, that when another of their Majesties the Kings of
> England tried to infringe upon those rights, the people armed, and

told him that if he did not give them the privileges of Englishmen, they would compel him by the point of the sword ... Would you not rather govern a country of spirited men, than cowards? I can die but once in this world, and the only regret left is that I have a large family of small children, and when I think of that, it unmans me.

The Chartist Rebellion

Much has been written about the Chartist rebellion that gripped Britain from 1832 to the early 1860s. Looking back, it is difficult to dispute that this was the most impressive organisation ever created by the British working class. A movement, rather than a party, it established a close link between its supporters and its leaders, however defined. The only real agreement was on the Charter itself. Its language seems moderate now – the aim was reform, not revolution – though talk of radical upheaval was always in the air. The Chartists were confronted with problems within their own ranks. In Manchester, for instance, there was initially a hostility towards Irish immigrants. Radicals on both sides brought the two groups together under the Chartist banners. In Liverpool, a city whose wealth had been created during the slave trade and where Irish immigrants had initially been greeted by locals with chants of 'green niggers', a similar process was in motion.

Virtually all were agreed on the six demands in the Charter, the implication of which was clear. Male adult franchise without any restrictions would transform Parliament and end oppression, corruption, the stranglehold of the Tory oligarchy, and the unfettered rule of property owners:

1. A vote for every man twenty-one years of age, of sound mind, and not undergoing punishment for a crime.
2. The secret ballot to protect the elector in the exercise of his vote.
3. No property qualification for Members of Parliament, to allow the constituencies to return the man of their choice.
4. Payment of Members, enabling tradesmen, working men or other persons of modest means to leave or interrupt their livelihood to attend to the interests of the nation.

5. Equal constituencies, securing the same amount of representation for the same number of electors, instead of allowing less populous constituencies to have as much or more weight than larger ones.

6. Annual parliamentary elections, thus presenting the most effectual check to bribery and intimidation, since no purse could buy a constituency under a system of universal manhood suffrage in every twelve month.

How these demands were to be fought for was the prerogative of towns and regions. As historians such as John Saville, Dorothy Thompson and John Foster have stressed, this was a defining feature of the movement. Foster's striking analysis and description of the movement in Oldham remains a vital point of reference, demonstrating in some detail how specific local conditions and socio-economic structures helped determine the degree of radicalism evinced. Petitions, large assemblies and sharp rhetoric were common, but although many torchlight marches revealed men carrying pikes, there was no general agreement on defensive or offensive violence against an arbitrary, undemocratic and deaf state, with a new layer of property owners determined to maintain their high levels of profits, backed by the Combination Acts which disallowed trade unions. The industrialists chose the landowners as their allies against the 'enemy within'. Deference to both coloured the attitudes of the burgeoning middle classes, who might sympathise with 'the poor' but not with Chartist activists. The landed gentry, with a monarch decorating the top of the pyramid, controlled the levers of power: Parliament, judiciary, army and navy. How different was this from the previous century? As pithily characterised by Edward Thompson, the 'British state, all eighteenth-century legislators agreed, existed to preserve the property and, incidentally, the lives and liberties, of the propertied'.[11]

In the nineteenth century, despite the growing movement for radical reforms, few concessions were made. The constitutional demands of Chartism were interpreted as little short of revolution

---

11 E. P. Thompson, *Whigs and Hunters: The Origin of the Black Act*, New York, 1975.

by the powers of the time as well as by Whig historians. Were their fears justified?

The Charter itself, on paper, was a generally moderate document. That the language of political manifestos is often an extension of a central and at least potentially unifying demand can be forgotten in any ensuing hubbub. The Chartists spelt out what it would mean if the bulk of the male population was accurately represented in Parliament. They did not include, for instance, the abolition of the House of Lords or the monarchy, two major achievements of the seventeenth-century English Revolution, let alone any form of social or economic levelling. Those absences, however, should not be taken to indicate the non-existence of such ideas in the minds of many of the individuals who collectively led the Chartists and the radical Jacobin groups that preceded them.

Spies often reported 'treasonous talk' overheard in taverns and meeting places. Had a civil war erupted, there is no way of telling how political consciousness would or would not have been altered. Total reliance on what is written on paper or said in court may be partially justified during peace time, but in the clash between classes or between nations, nothing is predictable. The Chartists agreed to restrict their demands to issues on which there was total agreement, and for the publication of which they could not be prosecuted and imprisoned or charged with high treason and hanged. Any other decision would have been irresponsible. As a result, they said yes to male liberty and fraternity, but kept equality (social, economic, gender) at bay.

For the ultra-radicals it was a question of stages. First, the right of all men to vote in annual parliamentary elections (which was a genuinely radical demand); then, a challenge to other forms of the existing structures. Class consciousness is not linear, but when radicalised it is never static, as virtually all histories of rebellions, uprisings and revolutions, whether successful or not, have taught us.[12]

---

12 Fluctuating consciousness was witnessed in Tsarist Russia between February and October 1917, Japanese-occupied China in 1936–49, French and US-occupied Vietnam in 1945–75, and in Cuba

Also, as we've seen on every continent at some stage or another, the demand for freedom and democracy under a domestic or imperial dictatorship, coupled with actions designed to achieve those aims, does have revolutionary implications regardless of what rebels, reformers or revolutionaries have written on paper.[13] This is evident in the *actions* of the more radical Chartist groups in Lancashire, South and mid-Wales and Scotland.

The 1839 Newport uprising, for instance, seriously worried the governing classes, despite the Charter's relatively benign expressions. In this case, John Frost and several thousand Chartists armed with pikes, staves, hammers, sickles and muskets marched towards the Westgate Hotel to free their comrades who were being held there after demanding that a popular Chartist leader be released from prison. In the ensuing clashes, with women particularly active on the Chartist side, thirty activists were killed and dozens more wounded. Frost was sentenced to death. Fearing more armed unrest, the government commuted the sentence, and Frost was

---

from Fidel Castro's assault on Moncada to the Second Declaration of Havana. The written programme of the Chinese and Vietnamese communist parties laid huge stress on national-democratic demands and expulsion of the colonisers. In practice, land reforms were introduced in liberated zones in both countries. Here we have a case of 'moderate' manifestos, radical actions and socialist revolutions with a much wider popular base (in both countryside and town) than that achieved by the Russians in October 1917. An equally illustrative model, reminiscent of Chartism in some ways, has been the eruption of the Black Lives Matter movement in the United States, with flanking solidarity actions of varying strength throughout Western Europe. Virtually nobody imagined that the killing of George Floyd would unleash such a response at a time of social distancing necessitated by the Covid-19 pandemic.

13 In his essay, 'Rethinking Chartism', published in *Languages of Class* (Cambridge, 1982), Gareth Stedman-Jones raised some important and thought-provoking questions that challenged both Whig and some Marxist assertions (often along similar lines) about what Chartism represented. The eruption of the *gilets jaunes* in France, two centuries after the Chartists, prompted reflections along similar lines to Stedman-Jones. See, for instance, Stathis Kouvelakis, 'The French Insurgency', *New Left Review*, 116/117, March–June 2019.

deported to Australia, where he spent the rest of his life as a school-teacher in Tasmania.

Four years later, in 1843, Daniel M'Naghten, a Scottish wood-turner from Glasgow, made a serious attempt to assassinate Prime Minister Robert Peel. He had stalked Peel for some days, but on the planned day he mistook Edward Drummond, Peel's private secretary, for the prime minister. He walked behind him from Charing Cross to Downing Street, crept up close and shot him. Drummond died five days later. At his trial, M'Naghten's clever barrister, Alexander Cockburn, argued that he was insane at the time the crime was committed and got him acquitted – thus estab-lishing 'criminal insanity' as a precedent in English law.

Committed to the Bedlam asylum, the prisoner played the part. The admission papers state: 'Imagines the Tories are his enemies. Shy and retiring in his manner.' After his transfer to Broadmoor, the files describe him as 'an intelligent man', who when asked if he was insane responded: 'Such was the verdict, the opinion of the Jury after hearing the evidence.' The twentieth-century mystery writer Sarah Cockburn, a barrister herself, wrote a play about M'Naghten titled *The Madman's Advocate*. During a conversation in the early 1990s, she told me her researches suggested that the jury's verdict did not displease the Crown. Why? 'Because', she replied as she puffed her pipe, 'Daniel was a Chartist and completely sane. Had that become known he would have become yet another Chartist sent to the gallows. Had he bumped off Peel he would have pleaded guilty. His mistake angered him, but he did not want to die for it.'

For the governors of the UK, universal democracy was consid-ered unthinkable and subversive, but they realised that some reforms were necessary. The Reform Act of 1832 had enlarged the male franchise somewhat and gave greater representation to large cities in the House of Commons. Yet the limited character of the suffrage reforms, after the hopes that had been raised, only served to fuel the Chartist agitation.

By 1848, the Chartists' democratic aspirations and demands were both heightened and quickly dashed by revolutionary move-ments on the Continent. What came to the fore in France on 24 February, with the toppling of King Louis Philippe and the establishment of the Second Republic, led to immediate tremors in Italy, Germany, Austria/Hungary and Bohemia. Distant echoes were felt in Switzerland, Denmark, Rumania, Poland and, of course, Ireland. It would take several years before those movements were defeated, while the failure of the huge Chartist rally on Kennington Common in April marked the end of any possibility of a centralised rebellion in Britain. Once again, though, Chartist groups in cities and villages saw this not as a defeat but as a setback. Some decades later, their political heirs would create trade unions, then the Independent Labour Party and, finally, the Labour Party. All three would, in time, both partially reflect and largely confiscate the aspirations of the masses.

Although the 1848 wave of revolutions, uprisings and rebellions was eventually crushed, for the most part denting rather than destroying the old regimes and their foundations, the kings and queens of Europe were shaken and would remain so for some time afterwards. In a private letter, Leopold I, the founding monarch of Belgium (created in 1830), confided to his niece Queen Victoria that he was sick with fear: 'I am very unwell in consequence of the *awful* events in Paris . . . What will become of us God alone knows; great efforts will be made to revolutionise this country; as there are poor and wicked people in all countries, it may succeed.' Some months later Victoria responded:

Since 24th February I feel an uncertainty in everything existing, which one never felt before. When one thinks of one's children, their education, their future – and prays for them – I always think and say to myself, 'Let them grow up fit for *whatever situation* they may be placed in – *high or low.*' This one never thought of before, but I do always now . . .

She underestimated the strong instinct for self-preservation that characterised her class. Her consort, Prince Albert, a liberal-conservative and a highly cultured German intellectual, sent his own private letter to the prime minister, Lord John Russell, on the day of the Chartist Assembly at Kennington Common. His advice was to make the government's response a show rather than a test of strength: 'I don't feel doubtful for a moment who will be found the stronger, but should be exceedingly mortified if anything like a commotion was to take place.' Albert's advice went beyond the tactics for the day. For him the Chartists were the most radical sections of the working class, and he even recommended a palliative: 'I find, to my great regret, that the number of workmen of all trades out of employment is *very* large, and that it has been increased by the reduction of all the works under governments, owing to the clamour for economy in the House of Commons . . . Surely this is not the moment for the taxpayers to economise upon the working classes.' In this Albert took a position somewhat to the left of every British government from Thatcher onwards.

A Weak Bourgeoisie, a Strong Ruling Class

Unlike on the Continent, there was no such thing as an enlightened liberal bourgeoise (let alone a revolutionary segment) in industrialising Britain. Tom Nairn and Perry Anderson outlined the reasons in their pathbreaking essays in the *New Left Review*, summarised recently by Anderson:

A highly successful agrarian capitalism, controlled by large landowners, long preceded the arrival of industrial capitalism in Britain, installing by the 1690s an aristocratic ruling class, flanked by mercantile capital, at the head of a state shaped in their image, which went on to acquire the largest empire in the world well before the emergence of a manufacturing class of any political consequence. The industrial revolution of the 19th century generated just such a bourgeoisie. But in not having to break feudal fetters in its path, nor possessing either the wealth or political experience of the agrarian aristocracy, the manufacturing class settled for a subordinate position in the ruling bloc, sealed by the reform of 1832, generating no hegemonic ambition or ideology of its own. Ideologically speaking, classical political economy was perfectly palatable to the landowning class, leaving only utilitarianism as a shrunken worldview of distinctively bourgeois stamp. A further powerful motivation for this abdication was fear of the world's first industrial proletariat, which for some three decades rose in a sequence of mutinies against both the bourgeoisie and the landowner state.[14]

Within the ruling class there were individuals, of course, who understood the Chartists and were, broadly, sympathetic to their demands if not their actions. Prince Albert was one. Disraeli, too, was astute in this regard. He understood the basic moderation of many Chartists. His very readable state-of-the-nation novel *Sibyl* portrays one such as a hero. Years after Engels wrote the first serious sociological study of the English working class, in 1845, some progressive Liberals spoke clearly in favour of improving working-class lives and conditions. When would this new class of labourers, apprentices and workers speak for itself?

As the events described up to this point, and far more unmentioned here, have shown, the labouring classes had been in rebellion against 'the Furies of private interest' almost continuously since the enclosures of the 1700s separated them from the land. In an essay, lyrical and elegiac, Tom Nairn summarised the evolution of the English industrial working class:

It was born in conditions of the utmost violence, harshly estranged from all traditional and tolerable conditions of existence and thrown into the alien, inchoate world of the first industrial revolution. Formed in this alienation by the blind energies of the new capitalist order, its sufferings were made more hopeless by the severest political and ideological persecution. From the outset it inspired fear by its very existence. In the time of general fear produced by the French Revolution, such dread and hostility became chronic, affecting the old ruling class and the new industrial bourgeoisie alike, and creating a climate of total repression. What was possible but revolt, in the face of this? Humanity, pulverised and recast in this grim mould, had to rebel in order to live, to assert itself as more than a mere object of history, as more than an economic instrument. The early history of the English working class

---

14 Perry Anderson, 'Ukania Perpetua', *New Left Review*, 125, September–October 2020.

is therefore a history of revolt, covering more than half a century, from the period of the French Revolution to the climax of Chartism in the 1840s.

And yet, what became of this revolt? The great English working class, this titanic social force which seemed to be unchained by the rapid development of English capitalism in the first half of the century, did not finally emerge to dominate and remake English society. It could not break the mould and fashion another.[15]

The pattern of trade union formation in Britain was not dissimilar to the structures of Chartism. It was uneven, with some areas stauncher than others. In the early decades of the nineteenth century strikes took place in Scotland, Tyne and Wear and London (*The Times* compositors in 1810, coachmakers in 1819). In Glasgow, on 1 April 1820, 60,000 workers came out in a political general strike. A clash between a small group of weavers and the 10th Hussars had been encouraged by Home Office agents, who described the strike as a prelude to insurrection. So many preludes, so few insurrections. In Wales, the trade union leader Dick Penderyn organised the ironworkers in a defensive guerrilla war against yeomanry and regular troops. He was captured, tried and executed in 1831. Lancashire was a stronghold of resistance before and after 1819. It was here that trade unionists from all over the country gathered at the Mechanics Institute in 1868 and inaugurated the first Trades Union Congress. A resolution – 'that it is highly desirable that the trades of the United Kingdom should hold an annual congress, for the purpose of bringing the trades into closer alliance, and to take action in all Parliamentary matters pertaining to the general interests of the working classes' – was unanimously approved.

'Parliamentary matters' was a reference to the Liberal Party, an alliance of Whigs, a few Peelites and, more important for the TUC, the radical Reformers. It was to the latter, if not exclusively, that the TUC turned both to offer and demand help. In

15 Tom Nairn, 'The English Working Class', *New Left Review*, I/24, March–April 1964.

pursuit of direct labour representation, the TUC set up the Labour Party as a pressure group in 1900. It won twenty-nine seats in the 1906 election which, amid rising food prices, public anger and a split among the Tories, produced a Liberal landslide.

Churchill had been a free-trader throughout his political life. He had voted with sixty other Conservatives against their own government's abandonment of the principle. Unlike the others, Churchill left the Conservatives and joined the Liberals. His colleagues never forgave this 'treachery'. For the divide between the two parties was not essentially on free trade. Each represented different forces. The Tories (and Churchill) were the party of land-lords, church and monarch, of ultra-patriotism and Empire. The Liberals supported Irish Home Rule and non-conformist religion, and provided an umbrella for radical republicans and atheists. Churchill was accused by most of the political class of 'self-advancement'. When he was returned as a Liberal MP for North-West Manchester in 1906, and given a government post, the Tories reserved their special abuse for him. The right-wing *National Review* commented:

> Mr Winston Churchill is rewarded for his active apostasy by the Under-Secretaryship at the Colonies, an appointment causing unmitigated disgust throughout the Empire, which has formed a much sounder estimate of this pushful soldier of fortune, whose sword is ever at the service of the highest bidder, than the Fleet Street friends, who he so assiduously cultivates and who repay his attentions by advertising his vulgar speeches.[16]

As a Liberal member of the Cabinet, Churchill was first at the Admiralty and later appointed home secretary. How would he fare in the war at home? Liberal and Tory at the same time, Churchill's aggression against a working class attempting desperately to organise itself against a brutish ruling class left a permanent blot

---

16 Quoted in Paul Addison, *Churchill: The Unexpected Hero*, Oxford, 2005, p. 36.

on his political reputation, and for good reason. He was extremely hostile to the rise of Labourism, seeing it as a dangerous intrusion by aliens into the hitherto safe spaces of British politics. He feared its growth and that of those who had begun to abandon the Liberals and move towards Labour: organised workers and the unemployed. This trend alarmed Churchill and the leaderships of both the dominant political parties. Neither realised that repression would only accelerate the process.

In 1910, South Wales had experienced a concatenation of strikes, street battles, severe hardships for mining families, mass picketing and looting of local shops, etc. An impression had been created by the conservative press that the region was the epicentre of confrontation and class struggle. The newspapers waged a campaign of fear, based on the possible 'collapse of law and order'. The fact that this had been provoked by the obduracy of the mine owners was rarely mentioned. In September 1910, 950 miners were locked out. They were accused by management of engaging in a 'go-slow' on a new seam in the Ely Pit. The response was immediate. A strike enveloped all the pits across the Cambrian Combine, the cartel of mining companies in South Wales. On 7 November, thousands of miners assembled outside the only working pit. There were fierce clashes and hand-to-hand fighting, but the constabulary, after a succession of baton charges, succeeded in pushing the miners back to Tonypandy Square, where strikers and their families smashed some shop windows and confronted mounted police hurriedly summoned from Cardiff. Both sides reported injuries.

The *Manchester Guardian*'s special correspondent recounted the extended battle: 'Strikers and policemen were in furious conflict, stones were thrown in showers, truncheons were drawn and vigorously used, colliery property was smashed, and more than a hundred strikers and six or seven policemen were injured.' This description was followed by an astonishing sentence: 'What set the bad spirit abroad cannot be known.' Militant miners, fighting against an employer's lockout and the use of scabs (a mixture of under-managers and non-miner employees), were later described as 'distempered minds'. The correspondent's sympathies were with the police: as the miners hurled stones at them from a path above, 'it was appalling to think of [the policemen] enduring that merciless, invisible hail'. The casualty figures he had cited contradicted his own language. (The newspaper then, as later, was rarely neutral in reporting the class struggle.)

The chief constable, Lionel Lindsay – much hated by local people – requested military intervention. The Liberal government was faced with a choice. Either put serious pressure on the mine owners to make meaningful concessions, or call in the troops. With Churchill in command at the Home Office, few were surprised when the latter option was chosen.

But what actually happened? Accounts have differed. Initially, Churchill stopped the troops from proceeding and instructed the military command to keep them in reserve at Swindon and Cardiff. When the chief constable insisted that unless troops were sent onto the streets there was a danger of anarchy, Churchill gave permission for the soldiers to be despatched. For weeks they were active in the Tonypandy region. No account suggests that the troops killed anyone, but their intervention ensured that the strike would ultimately fail. The trauma experienced by the mining communities ran deep. Churchill became a hated figure in South Wales. Even during the Second World War, people in local cinemas heckled *Pathé News* images of him. He was never allowed to forget the episode and could never understand why he was vilified for simply doing what was all in a day's work. During the 1950 election campaign, worried that chants of 'Tonypandy' or worse might be hurled at him, he attempted to clarify the matter in a private letter to the Lord Mayor of Cardiff:

I see that one of the Labour men referred to Tonypandy as a great crime I had committed in the past. I am having the facts looked up and will write to you again on the subject. According to my recollection the action I took at Tonypandy was to stop the troops being sent to control the strikers for fear of shooting, and I was much attacked by the Conservative opposition for this 'weakness'. Instead I sent Metropolitan Police who charged with their rolled mackintoshes and no one was hurt. The Metropolitan Police played football with the strikers at the weekend.[17]

Anthony Mòr O'Brien shows how the Blue Book – the official Home Office papers and records – were tampered with on Churchill's instructions. Thus the story constantly repeated, most recently by Boris Johnson, that 'rolled up umbrellas' rather than truncheons were the only 'weapons' carried by the constabulary, is manufactured. Churchill's instructions to the military commander, General Nevil Macready of Boer War fame, were expressed verbally as well as on paper. There is no way of knowing what was said in those conversations, but Macready made official reports.

The references to 'police charges' and 'vigorous baton charges' that were excised from the Blue Book speak for themselves. The senior civil servant at the Home Office, Sir Edward Troup, was still nervous, since it was 'impossible to say that even with the omissions suggested there are not many points on which troublesome questions might be asked or a debate raised in the House'. If Churchill still insisted on a version, then he should agree at the very least 'that General Macready's reports might now be omitted'. Troup was worried not only that they would trigger awkward questions, but that including them 'would create a precedent for the publication of official reports made to the Home Office by an officer who is carrying out the Secretary of State's directions'.

Churchill agreed that the general's reports should be truncated, and anything damaging redacted, a judgement with which Macready readily concurred. In his memoir, *Annals of an Active Life*, Sir Nevil Macready gives us a hint or two as to what might

---

17 Anthony Mòr O'Brien, 'Churchill and the Tonypandy Riots', *Welsh History Review*, Vol. 17, No. 1, 1994, pp. 67–99. This is probably the best-researched text on Tonypandy, research for which I am very grateful, especially since all the conservative histories accept Churchill's view without criticism. Roy Jenkins is equivocal on the subject. He comes down on Churchill's side on Tonypandy, but is critical of how Newport and Liverpool were handled. O'Brien contextualises the events to provide a picture of what was happening in all the South Wales coalfields and beyond.

have been written in the disappeared files. Bayonets to prod miners along were clearly much more effective than rolled-up umbrellas:

> During the rioting that occurred on 21 November throughout the Tonypandy valley, the Metropolitan police while driving the mob before them along the main road were heavily stoned from the side tracks, and suffered severe casualties. In order to counter these tactics on the part of the strikers on the next occasion when trouble was afoot, small bodies of infantry on the higher ground, keeping level with the police on the main road, moved slowly down the side tracks, and by a little gentle persuasion with the bayonet drove the stone throwers into the arms of the police on the lower road. The effect was excellent; no casualties were reported, though it was rumoured that many young men in the valley found that sitting down was accompanied with a certain amount of discomfort for several days. As a general instruction the soldiers have been warned that if obliged to use their bayonets they should only be applied to the portion of the body traditionally held by trainers of youth to be reserved for punishment.[18]

How they must have roared at the Carlton and Reform clubs when he regaled them with more spiced-up versions of how his troops had bayoneted Welsh bums at Tonypandy. The folk memories of South Walians were pretty much accurate, if exaggerated a little.

Seven weeks after Tonypandy, Churchill embroiled himself in what these days would be referred to as a minor 'terrorist episode'. The Siege of Sidney Street, also known as the Battle of Stepney, was a confrontation between two Latvian Jewish radicals and the Metropolitan Police. From the Huguenots onwards, the East End of London had been a haven for those fleeing persecution in their own countries. Jewish asylum seekers and refugees had been victim to vicious pogroms in Tsarist Russia and its Baltic possessions.

The Latvian Jews were raising money for the anti-Tsarist movements at home, and they saw no need to change their targets simply because they were in a new and partially democratic country. A

---

18   Quoted in O'Brien, 'Churchill and the Tonypandy Riots'.

fortnight or so before the confrontation in Stepney, a group of recently arrived Latvian immigrants busy digging a tunnel into a jeweller's shop in Houndsditch were surprised by police, who were unarmed. In the ensuing clash, the armed Latvians killed two policemen and wounded another before escaping.

Newspaper coverage of radical Jewish activities in the East End in those times – anti-Semitic, xenophobic and tarring all residents of the district with the same brush – was little different from what is written about Muslims or immigrants today.[19] The police were, unsurprisingly, determined to arrest the ones who got away. Two of them were spied entering a building in Sidney Street. Churchill was in his bath when he was informed. Instead of telling them to get on with it and arrest the men, he saw it as an opportunity.

What was he thinking as he got out of the bath and dried himself? Was he going to play Marlborough or Napoleon in the East End? What fantasies stirred his mind? Dressed to kill, the home secretary arrived promptly at the scene, which was being covered by Pathé News in its first colour broadcast, as well as by other news organisations. He struck a pose. Afterwards, the Tory leader, Arthur Balfour, mocked him in the House of Commons: 'I understand what the photographer was doing, but what was the Right Honourable gentleman doing?' To capture two armed men, police reinforcements were not considered to be enough. Churchill ordered in troops, artillery in this case, and took effective command.

The building, 100 Sidney Street, was soon on fire. Churchill personally ordered the Fire Brigade to let it burn. Two charred bodies were later found. What might have been a tiny footnote in London's turbulent history was never to be forgotten because of Churchill's involvement. A plaque in the street commemorates 'Peter the Painter', as one of the Latvian revolutionaries was

---

19 The Aliens Act of 1904 was designed to restrict Jewish immigration and subsequent acts strengthened these measures, which were in force when the Third Reich came into existence. There was a strict quota on the number of Jewish refugees fleeing fascist Germany who were permitted to enter the country. From a single acorn ...

known. No stray bullet ever pierced Churchill's top hat, as was reported. That was simply 'colour' added to enhance his role.

The class struggles unleashed in South Wales and elsewhere continued for another four years. With a dock strike looming in the summer of 1911 in Liverpool, and a national railway strike threatened, the Liberal government played soft cop, hard cop, with the chancellor, Lloyd George, and Churchill assuming the two parts. The former, with his matchless demagogy, offered reforms; the latter, out of conviction, issued threats and made no attempt to conceal that he was on the warpath. A cable from George V was all the support he needed. The monarch advised that all caution should now be abandoned: 'Accounts from Liverpool show that the situation there more like revolution than a strike.' The Lord Mayor of Liverpool and his equivalent in Birkenhead wanted troops and a warship to be moored in the Mersey. Churchill agreed to both requests.

With a railway strike on the way, Churchill ordered troops to be kept ready for action; Hyde Park in London as well as Manchester Railway Station took on the appearance of armed encampments. This proved to be a step too far for the *Manchester Guardian*; its founding editor, C. P. Scott, broke with Churchill, whom he had hitherto supported. The newspaper's breach with Churchill, a Liberal home secretary, was painful, but considered necessary. The interests of the Liberal Party and government had to come before any individual politician and his war-lust.

Only too aware of the social and political unrest that had marked the eighteenth and nineteenth centuries, the post-1906 Liberal governments realised that for things to fundamentally remain the same, some things had to change. Although the Labour Party was little more than a sidecar attached to the roaring Liberal motorbike from 1906 to 1914, the cleverer Liberal leaders recognised the new party as a potential menace. Mystagogues of the calibre of Lloyd George were determined to preserve and dominate the anti-Tory political space. It was hoped that a series of reforms might do the trick:

1906: Meals for schoolchildren in need
1907: Medical inspection of schoolchildren

1908: The first old-age pensions
1909: The first Trade Boards Act and establishment of a minimum wage in selected industries
1911: The beginnings of national health and unemployment insurance

Serious reforms, as these were, have a dialectic of their own. They both appease and excite the social layers for whom they are intended. Some are satisfied and espouse gradualism; others feel that the reforms are not enough and want more. While most of the Parliamentary Labour Party supported the 1911 measures, the left of the party, represented by George Lansbury, Philip Snowden, Keir Hardie and a few others, voted against them on the basic principle that social reforms *must at all times* be paid for by those best able to bear the burden. Snowden accused the government of side-stepping the issue of serious wealth redistribution by putting some of the financial burden back on the poor.

Any reforming government operates within these parameters, as do its extra-parliamentary opponents. It is worth stressing that during this period no political concessions were made to women. Patriarchy ruled the roost. But the battle for women's suffrage was beginning to take ultra-radical forms. Women finally got the vote because they fought on the streets, in prison, on the racecourses, and as a consequence of the First World War.

As for Churchill, he supported some of the reformist programme, but his enthusiasms lay elsewhere. In Parliament, defending his actions on the industrial battlefields, he painted a lurid picture of the political conjuncture: 'in that great quadrilateral of industrialism, from Liverpool and Manchester on the west to Hull and Grimsby on the east, from Newcastle down to Birmingham and Coventry in the south ... it is practically certain that a continuance of the railway strike would have produced a swift and certain degeneration of all the means, of all the structure, social and economic, on which the life of the people depend.'[20] This was

20 Parliamentary debate on Labour Disputes, 22 August 1911, quoted in Roy Jenkins, *Churchill: A Biography*, London, 2001, p. 201. Jenkins describes Churchill's speech as 'flaming hyperbole' that deserved to be satirised.

grotesque but based on a tiny element of reality. A rising working class confronted the ruling class. Violence, for Churchill, had always been a tonic.

In the meantime, tensions were developing between the European powers that had agreed to divide up Africa. The prime minister, H.H. Asquith, felt that the Home Office needed a calmer hand in charge. Churchill, convinced that a new war might start soon, was perfectly happy to be demoted to First Lord of the Admiralty. The navy, for a long time, had been a particular passion. Without the navy there would have been no empire. Churchill was convinced of his abilities as a war leader, regardless if the enemy was at home or abroad. The Welsh miners, the Jewish radicals, were little more than a bagatelle. In a letter to his mother written two years prior to those skirmishes, he had confessed:

Do you know I would greatly like to have some practice in the handling of large forces. I have much confidence in my judgment on things, when I see clearly, but on nothing do I seem to *feel* the truth more than in tactical combinations . . . I am sure I have the root of the matter in me – but never I fear in this state of existence will it have a chance of flowering – in bright red blossom.

3

The 'Great' War

And when the war reached its final spring
With no hint of a pause for breath
The soldier did the logical thing
And died a hero's death.

Bertolt Brecht, 'The Legend of the Dead Soldier' (May 1918)[1]

Eight hundred and eighty-eight thousand, two hundred and forty-six ceramic poppies, representing the number of British and colonial dead from the First World War, spilled from the Tower of London into its moat in 2014. It was an art installation seen by millions, most of whom will never have read a single critical monograph on the war. History as image. As with the deification of Churchill that began in earnest during the post-Falklands phase of the Thatcher government, so too with the enhanced memorialisation and glorification of 'the Great War' on its centenary.[2]

Did the images promoted by the state provoke any critical questions? A few readings from the war poets at literary festivals that year were far more stimulating than the official spectacle. The history lesson provided by David Cameron and his government,

---

1 This poem was cited by the Nazis as a reason for depriving Brecht of his German citizenship in 1935.
2 Very different in tone and style were events on the fiftieth anniversary, in 1964, when many veterans were still alive, and both they and the political culture were averse to prettifying the conflict.

meanwhile, reverted to the explanation given during the war itself, but considered unfit for use in ensuing decades: Britain went to war, they said, to defend gallant little Belgium. Alternatively, the ghost of the dreaded Hun stalked the linked corridors of Whitehall and the BBC, with Murdoch's papers fanning chauvinism, as younger generations were informed that the war was all Germany's fault. To leave this nonsense unchallenged in the twenty-first century, as the bulk of the mainstream media did, was a disgrace.

The prime cause of the war was imperial greed. The British elite could not stay out of the war, since they occupied or controlled the largest number of colonies and economic strongholds on the globe. They were not prepared to share anything with the Germans. The headquarters of all the empires involved, partially barring the Ottoman and the Japanese, were in Europe. It was the European nation-states that had divided the world into colonies and ruled them. Germany and Italy, the two late arrivals to nation-statedom, were keen to fight within the pack of wolves for a larger share of the planet.

It was this competition that triggered the conflict. Sides in the war were chosen purely on the basis of national interest, whether in terms of expanding or merely clinging on to colonies. It had little to do with democracy. The two imperialist gangs were ranged accordingly. The Triple Entente was led by the British, French and Russians, together with their colonies. They subsequently attracted Serbia, Portugal, Japan, Romania, China, Italy (which switched sides in 1915), Brazil, Peru and, decisively in 1917, the United States, after the February Revolution in Russia had toppled the Tsar and destabilised the Eastern Front. The Central Powers were led by Germany and Austria-Hungary, and were joined by the Ottoman Empire.

There was a clear-cut pattern to the war's lead-up. From the very first decade of the twentieth century, a *definitive* movement of history – a tremor before the earthquake – was recognised both by those who were preparing to wage war and by the European working-class and socialist parties who opposed them. A diverse group of individuals – the Liberal historian Hobson, the Russian Bolshevik Lenin, the English socialists Brailsford, Keir Hardie and

Ramsay MacDonald, the German Social Democrats, Luxemburg, Liebknecht and Kautsky, and others – had already taken note of the clash between competing European empires. In 1912, socialists of the Second International were so sure that war was looming they unanimously approved an anti-war resolution drafted by Lenin and Luxemburg, with an attached proviso that, when the conflict came, they would organise a Europe-wide strike to paralyse the war machine. Workers would not die for capital and empire.

In Britain, the Liberal government under Asquith contained three key players: Lloyd George at the Exchequer, Winston Churchill at the Admiralty and Sir Edward Grey at the Foreign Ministry. Churchill had supported the Liberals' social welfare reforms introduced after the 1906 election, and also backed Lloyd George during the 1911 constitutional crisis when the House of Lords, with the support of the king, tried to block the reforms. Two years prior, he had joined Lloyd George in rejecting the naval estimates, only to recant soon afterwards. The visit of a German naval vessel to the Moroccan port of Agadir in July 1911 signalled what was becoming increasingly clear to all. Berlin wished to provoke and send a message to the French, who had sent troops into the heart of the Arab state. Rather than challenging French expansionism, the German leaders were demanding some territory for their own fledgling empire.

This was enough to jolt Churchill into action: Germany was clearly on manoeuvres. He pressed Lloyd George to insert a passage in his Mansion House address that year, delivered to the assembled ranks of financiers and their friends, a gathering that also included the merchants of death, the makers of munitions who grew richer with every new war. The chancellor obliged. After making the ritual obeisance to peace, he went on to say:

> But if a situation were to be forced upon us in which peace could only be preserved by the surrender of the great and beneficent position Britain has won by centuries of heroism and achievement, by allowing Britain to be treated where her interests were vitally affected as if she were of no account in the Cabinet of nations, then

I say emphatically that peace at that price would be a humiliation intolerable for a great country like ours to endure.

No direct British interests were invested in the Maghreb, but a growing trade and naval rivalry with Germany was causing concern. Furthermore, Britain was determined to block all German efforts to trade with British colonies and semi-colonies dotted over the globe. Despite this, the Germans were extending their own territorial reach by thrusts into south-eastern Europe, the Balkans and the by now very sick Ottoman Empire. Franco-German economic rivalry was symbolised by the huge iron deposits in France and the massive coal deposits in Germany's Ruhr Valley. The uniting of coal and iron was a dream of industrialists and their favoured politicians on both sides. On this question, British sympathies were with the French.

The figures told the story. Britain as the 'workshop of the world' had no desire to be replaced by anyone, and certainly not the upstart Germany, but while it still boasted a huge advantage in terms of colonial railways (spread over an area four times larger than Germany's colonies), on the industrial front proper the Germans had overtaken the British. In 1892, as Lenin never failed to stress, German output of pig iron stood at 4.9 million tons, while Britain was ahead with 6.8 million tons. By 1912 the situation was reversed by a much wider margin: Germany produced 17.6 million tons, Britain 9 million. German superiority was undeniable. Lenin inquired politely: 'is there *under capitalism* any means of remedying the disparity between the development of *production* and the accumulation of capital on one side, and the division of colonies and "spheres of influence" by finance capital on the other side – other than by resorting to war?'

Given the economic structures of the capitalist system, war and conquest were the only possible ways of uniting minerals under one flag. France and Germany were equally bellicose, and it was their mutual hostility that determined the nature of the alliances that were shaping up for the long (1914–45) European civil war that lay ahead. Tsarist objectives included control of the straits linking the Black Sea to the Mediterranean, and removing Austrian influence in the Balkans, in the cause of Slav nationalism.

These rivalries were responsible for the crises that punctuated the five years before the outbreak of war in 1914. The world was already divided into lender and borrower states. The British maintained their hegemony in Africa and Asia through a combination of direct colonies and semi-colonies. Where loans had been given – to China, Egypt, Argentina – the British navy was the bailiff of last resort. However, continued access to those countries was vital to British trade. Were Germany to become the dominant European power, all this would, sooner or later, come under challenge.

It would have been entirely possible for the leaders of the British Empire to remain neutral. As always, and like all other empires, Britain put its own interests first, regardless of methods used or negative outcomes. The nature of life and death in the colonies was rarely challenged anywhere in the dominant imperial political discourse in London. The Liberal Party, and later the Parliamentary Labour Party, went along with empire. Dissenting voices were few, and at key moments most of those, too, fell silent.

On the priority of British interests, Churchill, in or out of power, whether on the Liberal front bench or resting on a Tory berth, was the supreme political exponent. And the spectre of impending war galvanised his energies. Churchill, his old friend Viscount Haldane at the War Office and Foreign Secretary Edward Grey – backed by the sly Asquith and the less strident Lloyd George – were determined on conflict. Grey, whose fame rests on the phrase 'the lights are going out all over Europe', was himself a snuffer of lamps and a foaming imperialist. Churchill never got on with him on a personal level, but had no doubt about where he stood on what Britain had to do next.

The extent of the differences within Asquith's Cabinet were brought to light in Douglas Newton's valuable history of Britain's July 1914 days, published on the centenary. Cabinet ministers in favour of some form of neutrality threatened to go public and resign if the government blindly committed itself to giving guarantees to its Entente allies. On 27 July, Lewis Harcourt, the colonial secretary, boasted that eleven out of nineteen members of the government shared this conviction, constituting a 'Peace Party which if necessary shall break up the Cabinet in the interest of our abstention'.[3]

Over the next seven days this was revealed to be nothing more than hot air. Britain declared war. The Cabinet remained unbroken. How did this happen? Newton provides the startling timeline that led to Britain's involvement in the carnage about to sweep the Continent. Asquith's three bloodhounds – Churchill in the lead, backed by Haldane and Grey – were busy sniffing out the best possible routes to a war not yet approved by the Cabinet.

It is a story of subterfuge and pre-emptive decision-making. Churchill, for instance, put the navy on alert with a 'stand-fast order' on 26 July, announced it to the media the following morning, and presented the Cabinet with a fait accompli. He ordered the Royal Navy to battle stations, once again doing so without consulting the Cabinet – lest they, as he put it, mistake it for 'a provocative action'.

Simultaneously, the crisis between the four powers in Europe – France, Germany, Russia and Austria – was reaching the point of no return. On 29 July the Austrian Empire declared war on Serbia. Tsarist Russia ordered a general mobilisation, which had, in fact, been secretly begun four days earlier, with the total backing of France. The Germans were allied with Austria. They now confronted a war on two fronts. They had prepared to do battle with France. The German high command envisaged a swift advance to Paris via Belgium. But Russia presented a problem, both geopolitically and militarily.

The German chancellor Theobald von Bethmann Hollweg – a highly intelligent civil servant, born in a family of scholars, and a senior adviser to the Kaiser – suggested concessions to Britain to keep it neutral. An offer was sent: if Britain remained neutral and France was defeated, the Germans would not proceed to annex

---

3   Douglas Newton, *The Darkest Days: The Truth Behind Britain's Rush to War, 1914*, London, 2014, p. 45. See also an appreciative, critical review by Alexander Zevin, 'The Snuffer of Lamps', *New Left Review*, 94, July–August 2015.

any territory in Europe. Belgium would remain untouched, but Germany would take over all French overseas colonies. The offer was peremptorily rejected by Asquith and Grey, who felt no need to trouble the Cabinet on such a minor detail. The offer was 'dishonourable', and there was no more to be said.

But Grey was slightly apprehensive that the Cabinet's radicals might kick up an unseemly fuss that would be unfortunate on the eve of a war. On 31 July, without consulting his colleagues, he despatched cables to Paris and Berlin demanding pledges from both that in the event of war Belgian neutrality would not be violated. The German ambassador in London met Grey and posed an awkward question: if Germany pledged to respect Belgian neutrality *and* not violate the territorial integrity of either France or its colonies – that is, if it were to fight only on the Eastern Front – would Britain stay out of the war?

The snuffer of lamps responded bluntly. Britain would not remain neutral even if Germany kept out of Belgium and France. 'In this way', Douglas Newton wrote, 'Berlin was told of Britain's inflexible position: a German decision to respect Belgian neutrality would win it neither credit nor advantage. Britain would still probably rush to the assistance of France and Russia if it came to war.'[4] A day later, Grey backtracked, informing the Germans that Britain might remain neutral if there was no conflict between Germany and France, and the war was effectively fought out in the east. The French were livid. Their position on Serbia was often more hawkish than that of the Russians. George V was outraged. Grey was summoned to the palace, given a severe dressing down and instructed to retract the message, which he proceeded to do.

Meanwhile that same evening, Churchill, after a convivial dinner with Asquith and the Tsar's ambassador at Downing Street, fully mobilised the naval reserves, leaving little doubt that Britain was preparing for war. A 'complicit' look from Asquith at the dinner had been interpreted (rightly) as approval. This went against an earlier decision by the Cabinet to reject such an action. But with both monarch and prime minister strongly in favour of war, why

---

4 Newton, *The Darkest Days*, p. 142.

should a parliamentary democracy bother with the ministers or Parliament? Much has been written about the exclusiveness of the German ruling group that imposed a form of institutional rigidity on the country's political system. This was true, but the British system, while more elastic in appearance, was also governed by a group that took key decisions without consulting the supposed source of democratic political power, the House of Commons.

A couple of days later, Grey informed the Commons that Britain had no option but to intervene if Belgian neutrality was violated. The momentous entry into the war had not been decided by any Cabinet meeting or parliamentary vote. Most ministers never had even the briefest glimpse of the ultimatum that was sent to Germany on 4 August, after its troops had crossed the Belgian frontier. Likewise, they had no say in the official declaration of war that followed. It was a decision taken under cover of darkness in the Privy Council, composed of three peers and the monarch. So much for parliamentary democracy.

These diplomatic games and feints are underplayed by most British historians. That such deceptions were necessary speaks to the case that opposition to the war within the Cabinet was not an imagined roadblock. The war party was convinced that resignations would bring down the government, leading to political chaos if the opposition decided to go on a countrywide political tour to make their case. Yet, as Alexander Zevin asks, how deep was this opposition within the Liberal government?

[T]he fact remains that of the eleven ministers Harcourt claimed were firmly opposed to intervention, all but four accepted it; of the quartet who did resign, two returned within twenty-four hours after tearful exchanges with Asquith; and the other two – Gladstone's biographer Morley, and Burns, the only workingman in the government – uttered not a squeak of objection in public. Their actions had nothing to do with the German invasion of Belgium. All four resignations, whether retracted or maintained, were in protest at British backing of the Entente, set in motion on 2 August, when Grey secured from his colleagues a pledge of naval support for France should the German fleet enter the Channel – a decision, said

Burns, 'tantamount to a declaration that we take part in this war'. But once war was declared, opposition to it collapsed overnight. A handful of backbench Radical MPs criticized the government, but none opposed War Credits for it.[5]

So the war had little, if anything, to do with the defence of plucky Belgium. The dismemberment of this 'gallant' country actually would have been a tremendous service to central Africa and humanity. By 1914 there was no reason for anyone in Britain to be unaware of Belgians' barbarity in the Congo. But then none of the powers lining up for war, on either side, had denounced the genocidal Leopold II. Not even the Belgian social democrats, who had turned a blind eye to empire except when atrocities became incompatible with the claim to the mantle of European civilisation.

A more serious, though still wrongheaded, argument justifying the conflict was that German militarism was a threat to that civilisation. More dangerous and reckless than the other European powers, Germany had to be curbed. This was a war for democracy: Parliament versus Kaiser-rule. Neither Britain nor Germany were democratic – the franchise was limited in both – but if one were to compare differences in political culture and intellectual diversity, the conclusion is obvious: Germany was ahead on both counts.

The German Social Democratic Party (SPD) was founded in 1875, four years after universal male suffrage had been granted by Bismarck. The Labour Party in Britain was founded in 1900, and adult male suffrage without restriction would not be conceded until 1918. By 1914, the German SPD had just over a million members. Labour was yet to become a mass party, and a majority of workers would still vote Liberal or Tory for some decades after the 'Great War'.[6] Already by 1890, the SPD had become the largest party in Germany, winning 110 seats in the Reichstag. Those successes led to the SPD model, its propaganda and its leaders,

5   Zevin, 'The Snuffer of Lamps'.
6   Donald Sassoon, *One Hundred Years of Socialism: The West European Left in the Twentieth Century*, London, 1996.

Karl Kautsky and August Bebel in particular, being revered throughout the Continent, including by both wings of Russian social democracy. Britain was cut off from these progressive developments.

And yet, advanced or delayed, in neither case were social democrats able to prevent the rush to war. The stage was set for mass killings on the fields of Western Europe. In 1961, Alan Clark, who would go on to become a Conservative MP, produced a biting indictment of the war party in his book *The Donkeys*. The title was inspired by the following exchange between two German generals:

> Ludendorff: The English fight like lions.
> Hoffman: But don't we know they are lions led by donkeys.

Clark spelt out the scale of disaster: the industrialised slaughter of the British Army at Neuve Chapelle, Loos and '2nd Ypres' in 1915. In the first two hours of Loos alone more British soldiers died than the total number of casualties on both sides on D-Day, 1944. Clark accused the donkeys – and in particular the Donkey-in-Chief, General Douglas Haig, commander on the Western Front – of criminal misconduct.

After the first wave of jingoism had swept the whole of Europe in August 1914, an eerie calm returned. Casualties mounted, mutinies were reported, bungling generals made the situation worse. Wounded soldiers on furlough informed their families of the realities on the battlefield, and slowly the virus of national chauvinism began to abate. An anti-war mood in the trenches spread to the major cities of Britain, France and Germany. The politicians who had engineered the war developed the most diabolical propaganda machines, with Britain in the lead. The German propaganda *Führer* in the next war (Goebbels) admitted that many of his ideas for spreading fake news had been inspired by the example set by the British in the previous war. By contrast, Kipling's wretched doggerel in *The Times* a month into the war was relatively moderate:

> For all we have and are,
> For all our children's fate,
> Stand up and take the war,
> The Hun is at the gate!

This war, both as it was being fought and after it was over, became known to many from all sides of the class, national and political divides as a 'bad war'. Even Kipling, who regarded the Germans as subhuman, was shaken to the core when his son died. The bard of empire had pulled strings to ensure that his son, despite his poor eyesight, was enlisted. In the end only his spectacles were discovered on the battlefield at Loos, his body lost forever in an unmarked grave. Fate had dealt the poet a cruel blow: '*If any question why we died, tell them, because our fathers lied.*' Were those words purely personal, or did they have a political intent as well?

The war poets were for the most part scathing about the war in which they participated. Siegfried Sassoon spoke for many veterans in his poem 'Base Details':

> If I were fierce, and bald, and short of breath,
>   I'd live with scarlet Majors at the Base,
> And speed glum heroes up the line to death.
>   You'd see me with my puffy petulant face,
> Guzzling and gulping in the best hotel,
>   Reading the Roll of Honour. 'Poor young chap,'
> I'd say – 'I used to know his father well;
>   Yes, we've lost heavily in this last scrap.'
> And when the war is done and youth stone dead,
> I'd toddle safely home and die – in bed.

The Dreaded Dardanelles

The first four months of the war alone cost Britain and France a million casualties. The stalemate in the trenches compelled Churchill to ask Asquith: 'Are there not other alternatives than sending our armies to chew barbed wire in Flanders?' With no satisfactory answer forthcoming, Churchill began to dream. His desire to excel at military strategy was well known, and either openly mocked or treated with polite condescension by the military caste. He now accepted that his previous idea of invading and occupying Germany via a naval assault from the Baltic Sea was unrealistic, but he had a new plan. He began to lobby Cabinet colleagues for a navy-led drive several hundred miles to the east.

The plan was simple and simplistic. The navy would, eel-like, wriggle its way through the Dardanelles, the narrow and strategically vital thirty-eight-mile strait that connects the Mediterranean to the Sea of Marmara, the Bosporus and the Black Sea, the geographical boundary between Asia and Europe. They would then capture Constantinople. This would force the Ottomans out of the war, which they had entered only reluctantly in October 1914.

A version of this plan had been considered prior to the Ottomans' decision to join the Central Powers. The new version, replete with Churchillian flourishes, sounded better. Victories on maps are just as unreliable as rehearsal room laughter before the show opens. Despite some opposition from military leaders, the Cabinet backed the plan. The opening salvoes would target Gallipoli. Churchill had no illusions but that 'the price to be paid in taking Gallipoli would no doubt be heavy', but he argued that the gains would far outweigh the sacrifice of troops. In his opinion, 50,000 soldiers and his beloved sea lions would see off the 'Turkish menace'.

The War Office bluntly refused to despatch the soldiers. Churchill sent in the warships regardless, and battle (i.e. long-distance bombardment) commenced on 19 February 1915. The weather was bad, the Turks were ready, and Entente minesweepers were endlessly shelled by Ottoman artillery. The British naval commanders counselled a rapid pullback. Churchill insisted they continue.

The chief operational commander, Admiral Sackville Carden, shocked by Churchill's irrational stubbornness, had a nervous breakdown. It took a month for British and French battleships to enter the straits. Ottoman mines sank three ships and damaged five others. Half the fleet was now out of action. Carden's replacement did not seek permission from London. He ordered a withdrawal and informed Churchill he would wait for military reinforcements. Whatever advantage had been imagined was now impossible.

When the troops did arrive a whole month later, consisting disproportionately of cannon fodder from Australia and New Zealand mustered in the ANZAC, they were pinned down on the beaches. The Turkish Army had used the four weeks to prepare an almost impregnable defence, and the Ottoman soldiers fought fiercely. The Entente suffered serious losses: 45,000 soldiers dead. Almost 10,000 were ANZAC, and just under 2,000 Indians. The Turkish figures were higher: 65,000 corpses to be buried. Yet the Entente finally withdrew, in January 1916.

The Battle of Gallipoli, the one major initiative undertaken by Churchill throughout the war, ended as a humiliating defeat, a disaster that was never forgotten. It revealed that avoiding the barbed wire in Flanders by opting for new battlefronts did not work either. A setback of such magnitude meant that heads had to roll. Asquith was replaced by Lloyd George, and before joining a coalition government, the Tories demanded that Churchill be sacked.

In high dudgeon, he loped off to participate in the war for a few months as a soldier. On his return he was offered a lowly job as minister for munitions. He displayed no regret about Gallipoli, despite the disaster haunting him for the rest of his political life. Hecklers at political meetings for years after would shout, 'Have you forgotten the Dardanelles?' His response: 'The Dardanelles might have saved millions of lives. Don't imagine I am running away from the Dardanelles. I glory in it.' This was sheer bravado.

The ghosts of Gallipoli never disappeared. Churchill thought of them again on the eve of D-Day in the Second World War, scared at the thought that the Normandy landing might be a repeat performance – not such a far-fetched thought at the time. It is difficult to disagree with the verdict on Gallipoli pronounced by Roy Jenkins:

Churchill's later summing up was that the concept was overwhelmingly right . . . had he been Prime Minister . . . he would have won a great victory, substantially shortened the war and saved many hundreds of thousands of lives. But it is difficult to find a serious military historian who agrees ... The third of Churchill's mistakes was to get himself into a position in which 'everyone is out of step but Winston'. All were on his side at some stage, but eventually everyone let him down. This is always a position in which some self-doubt is called for, but self-doubt was never one of Churchill's attributes.[7]

A young French officer of right-wing cast, observing the war first-hand before being taken prisoner by the Germans, was enraged by what he'd seen. Charles de Gaulle wrote in a letter home: 'Today, so as not to admit they are donkeys, they leave in Salonika 20,000 fine troops and millions of shells that I continue to believe serve no purpose at all and will not kill a single German ... As no valid strategic reason can be found to throw so many young men and so many shells down the drain, they try to console themselves by saying that this will, at least, cause the enemy some problems!!! I do not believe a word of it.'[8]

The ultimate defeat of the Ottoman Empire would make its colonies available to the Western powers, who would divide the Middle East. But the birth of nationalism weakened traditional modes of rule in the Islamic world. The effective Turkish military commander at Gallipoli was Mustafa Kemal (Ataturk), who, unlike Churchill, won his political spurs in that conflict, and went on to play a central role in modelling post-war and post-Ottoman Turkey, introducing modernist reforms that took the new country forward on a number of levels. The successes of the Turkish nationalists gave them confidence. They would make this very clear during post-war discussions: the status of Istanbul was not negotiable, and if the Entente were inclined to do something foolish, they should remember Gallipoli.

---

7 Roy Jenkins, *Churchill: A Biography*, London, 2001, pp. 260–5.
8 Quoted in Julian Jackson, *A Certain Idea of France: The Life of Charles de Gaulle*, London, 2018, pp. 37–8.

Mutinies and Demobilisation

During the war, Britain had for the most part avoided significant mutinies, but not completely. Soldiers had exploded in rage for a week in 1917 at Étaples, the largest supply camp in British military history, part of a huge network of bases in France that spread southwards from Dunkirk and employed nearly a million men. Wilfred Owen, on his way to the front, had witnessed the mood there:

> A vast, dreadful encampment. It seemed neither France nor England, but a kind of paddock where the beasts are kept a few days before the shambles . . . Chiefly I thought of the very strange look on all the faces in that camp; an incomprehensible look, which a man will never see in England; nor can it be seen in any battle, but only in Étaples. It was not despair, or terror, it was more terrible than terror, for it was a blindfold look, and without expression, like a dead rabbit's.

A serving soldier at the time later recalled: 'Discipline was strict at Étaples. That does not mean discipline was good: it merely means that what the Army calls "crime" was extensively manufactured and severely punished. There was always somebody tied to a gunwheel.'[9] The 1917 mutiny was triggered by the arbitrary arrest of a gunner, after which military police fired on rebellious troops, many from New Zealand and Australia. At least 4,000 soldiers witnessed the violence. Following the rebellion, Churchill would have liked many of the mutineers shot, but the Australian Imperial Force did not permit capital punishment within it ranks.

The soldiers' feelings of resentment only escalated as the war drew to a close. By 1919 they were impatient to get back home, triggering a wave of small but effective mutinies. When Churchill boasted in Parliament that the armed forces were citizen-soldiers,

---

9 Quoted in Douglas Gill and Gloden Dallas, *The Unknown Army: Mutinies in the British Army in World War I*, London, 1985, pp. 66–7.

his remark was greeted with hollow laughs in the trenches and the camps. There was also some anger that German prisoners of war were receiving better treatment than the British and colonial soldiers. One action of the mutineers was to release German and Turkish POWs.

After the war, troops complained about the countless delays following the promises made regarding rapid demobilisation, wherever they were still mustered. Colonial troops had been returned to the colonies; some British troops had been despatched to Russia and others to the Middle East. Battered and at least semi-traumatised by their experiences on the front – or suffering from 'the Spanish flu', initially diagnosed as a 'minor infection', which started in 1916 and ended up claiming 50 million lives globally – the soldiers were seriously angry. Their demands were mainly economic, insisting on better living conditions or immediate demobilisation.

Churchill was only too well aware that unless dealt with rapidly this mood might develop in a more political, perhaps insurrection-ary, direction. The men involved, after all, had been taught to use arms and to kill. Most of the soldiers were workers who were badly needed back home in the mines and factories. Miners were the first to be demobbed in large numbers – moving, as it would turn out, from one war zone to another.

In the post-war encampments in Folkestone and Dover, soldiers openly defied military authority as they left the camps and marched through the cities singing rude but effective anti-war, anti-officer songs. A strong pacifist mood had gripped Britain after the indus-trialised slaughter on the Western Front. Abroad, the soldiers were even more disturbed. A campaign to address grievances under-taken by the Soldiers, Sailors and Airmens' Union, and launched by the *Daily Herald*, exercised a particularly strong influence among British troops in Egypt and Palestine.

Snippets from the official records in May 1919, six months after the Armistice was signed in France, reveal that General Allenby had asked Churchill that 'every pledge may be fulfilled by the War Office as there is a dangerous and growing unrest'. And a few days later: 'We inform War Office that the reinforcements they are sending for Supply, HT and MT are absolutely inadequate & at the rate they are sending them it will take 1 year to demob them & a dangerous situation will arise.'

It was already too late. The huge Egyptian Expeditionary Force base in Kantara on the Suez Canal, which sustained half a million men and 160,000 animals (mainly camels, horses and mules), witnessed the first signs of dissent on the night the Armistice was agreed, in November 1918. The mood was not celebratory but riotous. Worried officers readied the Rifle Brigade for action against British troops in their effort to seal off the 'wild outburst of pent-up anger against ruthless conditions'. It was 'an insurrection of the rank and file that set the officers quaking with fright. The canteens were raided wholesale and the piano of a sergeants' mess was pitched into the Suez Canal.'[10] Veterans shell-shocked from the horrors of Gallipoli had been waiting three years to be sent back home. For them and others like them, Kantara was little more than a penal settlement in the desert, with limited rations and facilities for the soldiers. Officers and NCOs, like prison warders and governors, enjoyed a much better regime.

After their demobilisation had been postponed yet again, the soldiers at Kantara began to organise themselves and take charge of the encampments. Such camp occupations by rank-and-file soldiers began to spread to other parts of the region. This meant that day-to-day control was effectively taken out of the hands of officers, and sergeants and elected committees ran the show. They determined the size of the guard, insisted on equitable food rations, cancelled military routines and stultifying parades, which had no practical function whatsoever, and, regarding the officers as untrustworthy and hostile, they made sure commanding officers and adjutants were interrogated by the appropriate committee before they left camp.

A similar situation was developing in colonial India, where a rash of mutinies spread. The causes were the same. Broken promises, delayed demobilisation, food shortages, sickness, resentment over payoffs to appease soldiers who would be detained for

---

10 Ibid., pp. 123–6.

extended deployment, etc. In a letter published by the *Bombay Chronicle*, a soldier pleaded for action: 'If we do strike what action can the Military authorities take? . . . Are we to be completely crushed beneath the heel of Militarism or are we to assert our rights as Englishmen?'

In Poona in the autumn of 1919 there was open mutiny. An articulate and radical NCO, Sgt Bowker, became a hero for many soldiers, including many too scared to take part in the action. A delegation of senior officers was hastily organised to negotiate with the rank-and-file committees of the camp's various sections.

Bowker's own account, as recorded during the negotiations in Simla, is riveting:

> Discontent had been spreading from the beginning of this year and it had gradually grown worse until in the end the sore appeared on the surface at Poona. That was not to say that there was no discontent anywhere else. That delegation had been . . . to some extent a safety valve. While they were reasonable creatures themselves there were others who were not. Speaking for the Signal Service Depot, one man went down from their committee because he considered their views were not strong enough. He was for violence out and out, plundering, looting and burning. At the same time they must be prepared to admit that that man had certain feelings, and if nothing was done . . . that man might get out of hand . . . He read a resolution passed at a meeting of the NCOs and Men of the Signal Service Depot which stated:
>
> > That this meeting of the NCOs and men . . . expresses its strongest disapproval and disgust at the evasive nature of the reply . . . The reply does not differ in any way from other vague statements of the military authorities, and confirms our worst fears that the authorities have no intention of releasing men from India until such time as it suits their purpose . . . this meeting demands that it be allowed to send a deputation to Simla immediately to state its case and its dissatisfaction at the continued scandal and the persistent detention of men in India . . . It therefore instructs the delegates to communicate immediately with

the General Officer Commanding Poona Division to arrange for this deputation to Simla and demands *the arrangements be made forthwith. In the event of the above been* [sic] *refused, it is urged that a mass meeting of all troops in and around Kirkee be held at the racecourse on Tuesday at 6pm to decide on extreme action being taken.*

... whilst the delegation were at Simla, the men had given their loyal promise that they would keep quiet, but it behooved the Authorities to press forward the matter. It might be thought strange that men who had conformed to the rules of the military for so long should now at last decide to protest. They knew they were pawns in the game, but it must be remembered, as in Chess, pawns were a very powerful combination when working together. They were not, as in Chess, mere pawns of wood. They were human, sensitive creatures, and as such they had at least a love of home and kindred, which in the beginning of the war led them to great heights of patriotism, but if this love was going to be prevented from getting back to its object then it was likely to turn into a very bitter hatred towards those responsible for their detention ... From the beginning of the year they had had certain excuses put before them as to why they could not go home. The shipping excuse was first, yet during the years of war shipping had been found, and it was considered that shipping could not be found for demobilisation and the men began to wonder. After that, the hot weather excuse was brought along. Reliefs were not forthcoming was the next excuse whilst demobilisation was proceeding very rapidly in England ... Later on, 1 July was given as the date for the recommencement of demobilisation. By 30 June they were told that the reliefs would be coming out. These did not materialise until well into August.[11]

Bowker's indictment was extensive and stinging. Churchill, nervous that the mutinies might spread to Indian soldiers, made concessions, and officers were instructed to plead to the British soldiers'

---

11 Bowker quoted in Julian Putkowski, 'Mutiny in India in 1919', at marxists.org.

sense of imperial patriotism and get them to refrain from contacts with their non-white counterparts. This they did.

Reports of insurrection and calls for violence had Churchill worried, though. How might this inchoate, instinctive Bolshiness within the army work itself out once the men returned home? The British General Strike of 1926 was years in the future, and when it came it would not have the soldiers' radicalism. Nevertheless, Churchill would still fight the organised workers as if he were waging war.

'The British government', Lenin wrote in 1919, 'is the purest form of the executive Committee of the bourgeoisie.' He could have added that a figure like Churchill, whatever his actual post on this Committee, would always be the politician whose life and career, enhanced by wars of all sorts, would follow Bismarck's 1862 motto *in extremis*: 'Not by speeches and the will of the majority are the great questions of the time decided ... but by blood and iron.'

4

The Irish Dimension

If you had the luck of the Irish
You'd be sorry and wish you were dead
You should have the luck of the Irish
And you'd wish you was English instead

A thousand years of torture and hunger
Drove the people away from their land,
A land full of beauty and wonder
Was raped by the British brigands. (Goddamn, Goddamn.)

John Lennon, 'The Luck of the Irish' (1972)

Although Churchill was born at Blenheim Palace in Oxfordshire, his family moved to Phoenix Park in Dublin when he was three years old. His grandfather, John Churchill, the seventh Duke of Marlborough, had been appointed Lord Lieutenant in Ireland by Benjamin Disraeli in 1877. His father, Lord Randolph Churchill (MP for Woodstock since 1873), was appointed as Disraeli's private secretary. The move was Winston's first trip aboard, and it left its mark.

Ireland was gripped at the time by yet another famine, and the Catholic, nationalist Fenians were in open revolt. Childhood impressions can stoke adult prejudices, which can last a long time. Winston later confirmed this:

My nurse, Mrs. Everest, was nervous about the Fenians. I gathered these were wicked people and there was no end to what they would do if they had their way. On one occasion when I was out riding on my donkey, we thought we saw a long dark procession of Fenians approaching. I am sure now it must have been the Rifle Brigade out for a route march. But we were all very much alarmed, particularly the donkey, who expressed his anxiety by kicking. I was thrown off and had concussion of the brain. This was my first introduction to Irish politics.[1]

At the 1880 general election, Disraeli and the Tories were replaced by the Liberals. In Ireland, however, the unrest only heightened. Lord Randolph, who had supported extending the Irish franchise, reversed his position, sided with landlords confronting agitation by the Land League (led by Charles Stewart Parnell), and opposed Gladstone's 1881 Land Act as 'communist'. In fact, the Liberal prime minister's modest reform (which reduced Irish rents by 20 per cent) was accompanied by a bout of harsh repression, as more than 1,000 Land League activists, including Parnell, were arrested.

Disraeli's loss at the election forced the Churchill family's return to England. Young Churchill had his own take on the situation:

In 1880 we were all thrown out of office by Mr. Gladstone. Mr. Gladstone was a very dangerous man who went about rousing people up, lashing them into fury so that they voted against the Conservatives and turned my grandfather out of his place as Lord Lieutenant of Ireland. He liked this place much less than his old office of Lord President of the Council, which he had held in Lord Beaconsfield's previous Government. When he was Lord Lieutenant he had to spend all his money on giving entertainments to the Irish in Dublin; and my grandmother had also got up a great subscription called 'The Famine Fund'. However, it was borne in upon me that the Irish were a very ungrateful people: they did not say so much as 'Thank you' for the entertainments, nor even for 'The Famine Fund'.[2]

The involvement of the Churchill family in Ireland has been romanticised by Unionist, pro-Empire historians (with Lord Bew

---

1 Churchill, *My Early Life*, p. 10.
2 Ibid., pp. 15–16.

the last in the queue), as if their residence at Phoenix Park provided a special and sympathetic understanding of the needs and demands of the colony. This is questionable. When Churchill was a member of the Liberal government just prior to the outbreak of the First World War, key conferences were convened to discuss Home Rule, but were deliberately not minuted, suggesting murky dealings that needed to be kept off the record. In his own day, Lord Randolph had defended the Ulster Unionists in their total hostility to Home Rule and, by advocating a permanent Protestant base for the Empire, encouraged Ulster to fight.

Did Winston Churchill agree completely with his father? On Ireland as with most things, he promoted the strategic line that he thought best strengthened the British Empire. He would have preferred a united Ireland on the model of Canada, New Zealand and Australia, but the three stooges of empire were not destined to become a quartet.

Irish history, the country's geographical location, its rebellions and famines, made such a possibility impossible without genocide, and on a much larger scale than occurred under Cromwell. Instead, the British were to utilise a tried and tested colonial tactic: divide and rule. If they could not control the whole of Ireland, they would make sure that the nationalists could not do so either. Churchill played a key role in the later stages of this tormented history.

On the eve of the First World War, he was concerned by talk of mutiny in the army barracks at Curragh, where fifty-eight officers had declared they would not accept Home Rule and threatened to resign rather than be compelled to enforce it upon Irish Unionists. The facts regarding this period and Irish nationalism in general have been widely disputed, and a debate among Irish historians erupted during Margaret Thatcher's tenure as prime minister. A summary of that debate is necessary before returning to the role played by Churchill.

As 'revisionist history' – largely the work of Irish historians tenured in British universities and later in the House of Lords – gathered strength in the 1980s, a number of commentators in Ireland mounted a critique. Desmond Fennell saw this trend as 'a retelling of Irish history which seeks to show that British rule of Ireland was not, as we have believed, a bad thing, but a mixture of necessity, good intentions and bungling; and that Irish resistance to it was not, as we have believed, a good thing, but a mixture of wrong-headed idealism and unnecessary, often cruel violence'. Perry Curtis used a medical metaphor: 'In sum, rather like cholesterol, there is good and bad revisionism, and we have had too much of the latter in recent years.' He could have extended the metaphor, since medical researchers are regularly changing bad to good. A more unexpected intervention, and for that reason more effective, came from the non-nationalist Irish novelist and essayist Colm Tóibín in the *London Review of Books*, while reviewing a collection of Roy Foster's essays:

> This revisionism is precisely what our state needed once the North blew up and we joined the EC, in order to isolate Northern Ireland from us and our history, in order to improve relations with Britain, in order to make us concentrate on a European future. Foster and his fellow historians' work became useful, not for its purity, or its truth, but its politics. It can be argued that many of these historians did not 'seek to show' anything, they merely and dispassionately showed it, and the implications of what they showed happen to coincide with public policy. But this cannot be argued with much conviction.[3]

The history debates have continued. Two Irish historians, Ronan Fanning and Diarmaid Ferriter, have mounted a calm, considered and meticulously researched challenge to the England-based revisionism, a challenge that should (but probably won't) bring matters to a conclusion. Their books – *Fatal Path: British Government and Irish Revolution 1910–1922* and *A Nation and Not a Rabble: The Irish Revolution 1913–1923*, respectively – are damning rebuttals, written without a trace of bombast or swagger.

Irish history is a blend of continuity and discontinuity. What makes the former more important is the colonial aspect of Irish social and political development. Even the ostrich-historians who underplay or defend the British colonial role cannot deny its

---

3   Colm Tóibín, 'New Ways of Killing Your Father', *London Review of Books*, 18 November 1993.

existence. At best they can prettify it; at worst they can blame the victims for the famine and for the violence against the anti-imperialist resistance over the last four centuries. There were, of course, discontinuities in the form that resistance took, but the desire expressed in different ways by the Irish people for independence, as a dominion or a republic, remained constant.

There is a line in that compendium of idiocy *1066 And All That* to the effect that 'whenever the English looked to have solved the Irish question, the Irish changed the question'. This is the exact opposite of the truth, which makes one wonder whether it might originally have been one of Churchill's 'witticisms'. It was the Irish national movement that, every time it looked to be within sight of its goal, saw the goalposts being moved by London.

All the evidence for this has now been marshalled by Fanning, who tracks British policy towards Ireland from the Home Rule crises of the late nineteenth century to the partition of Ireland in the early twentieth. Irish nationalists had been waiting for two decades for the Home Rule promised by Gladstone, a pledge that he could never deliver. Frustrated by British democracy, sooner or later they would be forced to embark on a different path.

Not that this hadn't been tried before. In the wake of the French Revolution, the United Irishmen uprising of 1798 had challenged British power. Its leader, Theobald Wolfe Tone, a Protestant, had eight years earlier written a sharp and thoughtful pamphlet, radical if not revolutionary, demanding structural changes in his country. Its title was unusual: *An Argument on Behalf of the Catholics of Ireland in which the Present Political State of that Country and the Necessity of a Parliamentary Reform are Considered. Addressed to the People, and Particularly to the Protestants of Ireland*. It was dated 1 August 1791, and signed 'By a Northern Whig'. Tone was twenty-eight years old when he wrote this, and together with other texts it made him the key political inspiration of the 1798 uprising.

Tone had no time for sentimentality. He was critical of some nationalist myths, like the exaggerated importance given to 'Grattan's Parliament' as a supposedly independent Irish Parliament. 'What is our Government?', he began, and answered thus:

It is a phenomenon in politics, contravening all received and established opinions: It is a Government derived from another country, whose interest, so far from being the same with that of the people, directly crosses it at right angles. Does any man think that our rulers here recommend themselves to their creators in England, by promoting the interests of Ireland? . . . But how is this foreign government maintained? Look to your court calendar, to your pension list, to your concordatum, and you will find the answer written *in letters of gold*: This unnatural influence must be supported by profligate means, and hence corruption is the only medium of the Government in Ireland. The people is utterly disregarded and defied: Divided and distracted as they are, and distrustful of each other, they fall an easy prey to English rulers, or their Irish subalterns.

His anger rising, Tone denounced the 'Peerage prostituted', the venality and 'peculation' that characterises the ruling class of the country. In an obvious reference to the American and French revolutions he continued: 'We see all this at the very hour, when everywhere but in Ireland reform is going forward, and levelling ancient abuses in the dust.'

Within a few years, the United Irishmen had established contact with the French Revolutionary Army. The French were convinced by Tone that Ireland, once free of the British, might become a new beacon for liberty in Europe and, more to the point, a strong base against the British Empire. The French agreed to despatch a fleet and an expeditionary force to help the insurgents defeat the British.

Had bad weather not wrecked the Armada near Bantry Bay in 1796, the outcome might well have been different, with unforeseeable consequences. The armed rebellion lasted three years – 1798 marking the single most important uprising in Irish history. Another French fleet did reach Ireland, but too late. The carnage was horrific and, principally, the responsibility of the British troops and their Irish allies. The Catholic Church, true to form, was staunchly opposed to the United Irishmen because of their radical liberalism and alliance with the new France, where the 'dechristianising' of the country had created panic in the Vatican and its satellites.

The United Irishmen rebellion was fought on behalf of the Irish nation and its oppressed Catholic majority. Irish Protestants fought in large numbers, and dissident sects like the Presbyterians fought courageously to free their country, as did some from the Protestant Ascendancy. Nobody observing the battles could have seen Ireland as two nations. In the north, the regions of Derry and Tyrone as well as Belfast were hotbeds of rebellion. Spies sent by the English authorities at Dublin Castle confirmed official reports that in various counties between half and three-quarters of the population supported the United Irishmen, and that insurrection was being plotted throughout the land.[4]

In the last issue before (like its predecessors) it was banned, the United Irishmen's publication *Press* published an incendiary unsigned letter to Lord Clare, the Lord Chancellor. It was composed by one of the founders of the United Irishmen, Thomas Russell, from his prison cell in Newgate, where he had been confined for some time after being charged with high treason:

> I know, my lord, you plume yourself on the imaginary safety of your situation. But pride not yourself any longer on that circumstance: deceive yourselves no more; I tell you, you are in danger: think not to screen yourself behind the shield of parliamentary support; repose not on your delusive promises of military protection; they will avail you nothing in the dread moment of national retribution, and amid the confusion of revolutionary vengeance . . . There will be no necessity for suborned testimony or intoxicated jurymen to procure your condemnation. Ireland can afford the clearest evidence of your crimes; the unanimous voice of its inhabitants will pronounce you guilty; on such an occasion our disgust against the duty of the executioner will be suspended, and men will contend for the honour of terminating so destructive an existence.

---

4 Nancy J. Curtin's study of this movement, *The United Irishmen: Popular Politics in Ulster and Dublin 1791–1798*, Oxford, 1994, is detailed and scholarly, providing the best portrait yet of the rebellion, its social composition, its ideology, its poetry and songs.

The memory of the rebellion refuses to die, as Colm Tóibín noted with reference to his own family, who were there at Vinegar Hill in 1798, when 13,000 English soldiers charged at the camp of the Wexford United Irishmen. Approximately a thousand Irishmen were killed:

> The Rising was important for us: from our housing estate we could see Vinegar Hill where 'our side', the rebels, had made their last stand. From early childhood I knew certain things (I hesitate to say 'facts') about the Rising: how the English had muskets whereas we just had pikes, how the English poured boiling tar on the scalps of the Irish and then, when the tar had dried, peeled it off. The names of the towns and villages around us were in all the songs about 1798 – the places where battles had been fought, or atrocities committed.[5]

Tóibín mentions that 'our side' committed atrocities too. This is true, and the same is the case in most national struggles and wars. Ugly occupations have yet to produce a pretty resistance, and an attractive occupation is a contradiction in terms.

Five months after Vinegar Hill, the fight was lost. Having refused to seek exile in France, Wolfe Tone was captured during a naval skirmish and dragged to Dublin where he was court martialled and died on the eve of his execution under dubious circumstances. He was buried in the prison graveyard. To this day the Irish republican movement commemorates his legacy at graveside gatherings around the anniversary of his birth.

With the defeat of the armed rebellion and the forced incorporation of Ireland into the United Kingdom in 1801, the focus shifted in the second half of the century to parliamentary struggles for Home Rule. Wolfe Tone's successor in this field was Charles Stewart Parnell. Also a Protestant, Parnell, as leader of the Irish Parliamentary Party at Westminster, became known as the 'the uncrowned king of Ireland'. He was uncompromising as far as the goal of Irish freedom was concerned, and prepared to do anything to get rid of the colonisers. A few decades prior to the outbreak of

---

5 Tóibín, 'New Ways of Killing Your Father'.

the First World War, the possibility of another insurrection was not discounted by either side in the conflict.

This was the backdrop for Gladstone and his inner circle's determination to push the Irish Home Rule bills through Parliament. Parnell harboured no illusions regarding Gladstone or any other English politician, but he saw no other force on the horizon that could deliver Home Rule. James Joyce described Parnell as 'another Moses', who 'led a turbulent and unstable people from the house of shame to the verge of the Promised Land'. But verges can be dangerous places. The British establishment and its spies, once again in league with the Catholic Church, conspired to bring down Parnell.

Joyce's essay 'The Shade of Parnell', written for an Italian paper in 1912, is intellectually sharper than the work of most historians. 'The influence exerted on the Irish people by Parnell defies critical analysis', wrote Joyce:

> He had a speech defect and a delicate physique; he was ignorant of the history of his native land; his short and fragmentary speeches lacked eloquence, poetry and humour; his cold and formal bearing separated him from his own colleagues; he was a Protestant, a descendant of an aristocratic family, and, as a crowning disgrace, he spoke with a distinct English accent ... The applause and anger of the crowd, the abuse and praise of the press, the denunciations and defence of the British ministers never disturbed the melancholy serenity of his character.

The British state, angered by Parnell's arrogance, his unbreachable integrity and his success in Parliament, tried to discredit him, embroiling him in a murder case with a forged letter, which was made public. A Royal Commission set up to investigate the charges found him innocent. The forger by the name of Piggott committed suicide in Madrid. Joyce describes how, when Parnell entered the parliamentary chamber after all this, 'the House of Commons, without regard to party, greeted Parnell's entrance with an ovation that remains without precedent in the annals of the British parliament'. Joyce asks: 'Is it necessary to say that Parnell made no response to the ovation with a smile or a bow or a gesture, but merely passed to his place beyond the aisle and sat down?' Gladstone was probably thinking of this incident when he called the Irish leader 'an intellectual phenomenon'.

Joyce is scathing of Gladstone and his Liberals. They were self-seeking politicians. When he got his chance, Gladstone would accept nothing less than a crucifixion of Parnell. Parnell had fallen in love with a married woman, and her husband insisted on a divorce. (Many said the man was bribed into it by the then equivalent of the security services.) Gladstone refused to negotiate with a 'sinner'. The Catholic bishops, frightened of being seen as more liberal than a British Protestant, threw their support behind the vilification and called on the Irish parliamentarians to get rid of him.

Parnell refused to resign, but his fate was sealed. The Irish MPs capitulated. The dual pressure of the British Empire and the Catholic Church proved too much for them: twenty-six voted for retaining him as leader, forty-four against. Joyce provided his own epitaph for the fallen prince: 'In his final desperate appeal to his countrymen, he begged them not to throw him as a sop to the English wolves howling around them. It redounds to their honour that they did not fail this appeal. They did not throw him to the English wolves: they tore him to pieces themselves'. In *The Dubliners*, a young Joyce (he was nine when Parnell died, aged forty-five) recalls hearing his father and friends speak of the dead leader with love and reverence. In Joyce's *Portrait of the Artist*, Stephen D. recalls from his childhood a bitter row over dinner between a Parnell loyalist and a Church loyalist, culminating in the cry 'no God for Ireland!' Ireland never produced another Parnell.

The Easter Uprising

With the declaration of the First World War, the British government postponed Home Rule for Ireland indefinitely. Unionists enrolled to fight in large numbers. Nationalists were more divided. John Redmond, the collaborationist Irish Parliamentary Party leader, became – like Gandhi on another continent – a recruiting agent for the war. A total of 200,000 Irishmen joined up. Redmond famously declared that 'the government may withdraw every one of their troops from Ireland and rely that the coast of Ireland will be defended from foreign invasion by her armed sons'.

His Home Defence initiative had considerable support, but a sizeable minority within the nationalist Irish Volunteers remained strongly opposed, and organised clandestine resistance to recruitment was widely acclaimed. On the unabashed pro-imperialist side of the divide, the Unionist MP Edward Carson urged Protestant workers to do their duty, and launched the Ulster Volunteers. Redmond felt pressured to do more. On 24 September 1914, addressing a bevy of Irish Volunteers in Woodenbridge, County Wicklow, he spoke passionately in favour of enlistment to support the Entente:

> The interests of Ireland – of the whole of Ireland – are at stake in this war. This war is undertaken in the defence of the highest principles of religion and morality and right, and it would be a disgrace for ever to our country and a reproach to her manhood and a denial of the lessons of her history if young Ireland confined their efforts to remaining at home to defend the shores of Ireland from an unlikely invasion, and to shrinking from the duty of proving on the field of battle that gallantry and courage which has distinguished our race all through its history. I say to you, therefore, your duty is twofold. I am glad to see such magnificent material for soldiers around me, and I say to you: Go on drilling and make yourself efficient for the Work, and then account yourselves as men, not only for Ireland itself, but wherever the fighting line extends, in defence of right, of freedom, and religion in this war. It would be a disgrace forever to our country otherwise.

He was backed by the Catholic Church and its insistence that Belgium was a Catholic country. (Even though the Pope maintained the Vatican's formal neutrality throughout the war.) A delighted Churchill twisted his father's slogan, informing his cousin Clare Sheridan: 'Ireland will fight, and Ireland will be right.'

In his monograph *Churchill and Ireland*, Paul Bew recounts how reassured Foreign Minister Edward Grey had been after meeting with Carson and Redmond, later calming fears in the House of

Commons: 'One thing I would say, the one bright spot in the very dreadful situation, is Ireland. The position in Ireland ... is not a consideration among the things that we have to take into account now.' One can almost visualise the neocon Bew wiping away a tear himself as he writes: 'Carson saw tears trickling down the cheeks of Winston Churchill as Grey spoke. Carson went up to him as they passed behind the Speaker's chair and silently shook hands.'[6] Both men, and many others, could now get on with the killings in Europe.

The short-sightedness of bourgeois politicians and their tame ideologues never ceases to amaze. Centuries-old Irish anger and rebellions against British domination had passed them by. The war would solve it all, they assumed. Irish bodies on the barbed wire in Flanders would be added to the British imperial stew. Yet, as the war proceeded and wounded soldiers returned home to Ireland, describing what they had experienced, bitterness grew. Faith in the British Parliament to deliver anything began to disappear. John Redmond's toadying at the outbreak of war marked the beginning, middle and end of the post-Parnell collaborationist phase of nationalist politics.

Taking advantage of the British involvement in the war, a group of determined Irish men and women, fed up with years of public and private grievances, decided to launch an uprising whose aim was Irish independence. 'Irishmen and Irishwomen,' they declared, 'in the name of God and of the dead generations from which she receives her old tradition of nationhood, Ireland, through us, summons her children to her flag and strikes for her freedom ... the Irish republic is entitled to, and hereby claims, the allegiance of every Irishman and Irishwoman.'

This Irish national movement combined armed and parliamentary struggle. The Easter Rising of 1916, denounced by revisionists in our own time as a 'putsch' carried out by a 'death squad', was never seen as such by the national movement, or even by those who disagreed with the tactic or the timing.

Its outcome, undoubtedly, was a defeat. But setbacks of this magnitude can have two possible effects. They can leave a

---

6 Paul Bew, *Churchill and Ireland*, Oxford, 2016, p. 83.

population sullen, demoralised and politically apathetic for decades; or they can leave people angry, embittered, determined to reverse what has taken place and ready for more combat within a few years. The latter is what happened in this case, leaving a deep mark on Irish consciousness. It was hardly a secret that the Irish Volunteers who had pledged to join the uprising were pulled back at the last moment by their commanders. Despite this, the minuscule Irish Citizens Army and their allies fought. Dublin witnessed intense street battles. In the aftermath, the execution of the known leaders shocked the population for years to come, as did the arrest and execution of Roger Casement for high treason.

Yeats, much maligned for his wonderful poem 'Easter, 1916', was more in tune with the people than his detractors then and now:

> I have met them at close of day
> Coming with vivid faces
> From counter or desk among grey
> Eighteenth-century houses.
> I have passed with a nod of the head
> Or polite meaningless words,
> Or have lingered awhile and said
> Polite meaningless words,
> And thought before I had done
> Of a mocking tale or a gibe
> To please a companion
> Around the fire at the club,
> Being certain that they and I
> But lived where motley is worn:
> All changed, changed utterly:
> A terrible beauty is born.
>
> That woman's days were spent
> In ignorant good-will,
> Her nights in argument
> Until her voice grew shrill.

What voice more sweet than hers
When, young and beautiful,
She rode to harriers?
This man had kept a school
And rode our wingèd horse;
This other his helper and friend
Was coming into his force;
He might have won fame in the end,
So sensitive his nature seemed,
So daring and sweet his thought.
This other man I had dreamed
A drunken, vainglorious lout.
He had done most bitter wrong
To some who are near my heart,
Yet I number him in the song;
He, too, has resigned his part
In the casual comedy;
He, too, has been changed in his turn,
Transformed utterly:
A terrible beauty is born.

Hearts with one purpose alone
Through summer and winter seem
Enchanted to a stone
To trouble the living stream.
The horse that comes from the road,
The rider, the birds that range
From cloud to tumbling cloud,
Minute by minute they change;
A shadow of cloud on the stream
Changes minute by minute;
A horse-hoof slides on the brim,
And a horse plashes within it;
The long-legged moor-hens dive,
And hens to moor-cocks call;
Minute by minute they live:
The stone's in the midst of all.

Too long a sacrifice
Can make a stone of the heart.
O when may it suffice?
That is Heaven's part, our part
To murmur name upon name,
As a mother names her child
When sleep at last has come
On limbs that had run wild.
What is it but nightfall?
No, no, not night but death;
Was it needless death after all?
For England may keep faith
For all that is done and said.
We know their dream; enough
To know they dreamed and are dead;
And what if excess of love
Bewildered them till they died?
I write it out in a verse –
MacDonagh and MacBride
And Connolly and Pearse
Now and in time to be,
Wherever green is worn,
Are changed, changed utterly:
A terrible beauty is born.

Neither Churchill nor the war cabinet understood the scale and character of the new Irish republicanism after the Easter events of 1916. They could not perceive that the Irish revolution was not the work of 'thugs and fanatics' but a war for independence and a severing of ties with the British crown and state. British colonial policy was often characterised by the view that, if you nip the bad-uns in the bud, all will be well. This reflected an overdetermination of the role of individuals. Hence the execution of the Irish leaders in 1916. But what was happening in Ireland was part of a wave of radicalism during and after the First World War, which would soon sweep through colonies and the defeated empires.

The Rise of Sinn Féin

Two years after the Easter Rising, a general strike against conscription united the Irish nation, and in the October 1918 election Sinn Féin destroyed the remnants of the party that had sent Parnell to an early grave. Sinn Féin won 73 out of 105 Irish seats. Henceforth the independence struggle was fought on dual fronts. Daniel Finn's sprightly critical history of the Irish Republican Army recounts how, on 21 January 1919, Sinn Féin MPs 'gathered in Dublin's Mansion House to inaugurate a new assembly, Dail Eireann, and declare Irish Independence':

> On the same day, a group of Irish Volunteers began the War of Independence with an attack on the Royal Irish Constabulary in Tipperary. By now, the reorganised Irish Volunteers were generally known as the Irish Republican Army. The maxim of their new campaign might have been drawn from words attributed to John MacBride, one of those executed in 1916: 'If it ever happens again, take my advice and don't get inside four walls.'[7]

As the Irish Volunteers morphed into the IRA, the British state sponsored the creation of an Ulster Protestant equivalent.

Churchill's position on Ireland was the same as towards any other colony. His mistakes and crimes derived from his ardent, semi-religious belief in empire. Regarding Ireland, from early on he sympathised with his father, the Unionist position and the necessity to play the 'Orange card' to foil Home Rule. In 1897, three years after a venereal disease felled his father, young Churchill had denounced the 'great Liberal Party' for weighing itself down with Irish Home Rule. Two years later, in his first election address as a Conservative candidate, he stated that 'all true Unionists must be prepared to greet the reappearance of that odious measure [Irish Home Rule] with the most strenuous opposition'.

---

7 Daniel Finn, *One Man's Terrorist: A Political History of the IRA*, London, 2019, pp. 16–17.

By 1908, now a Liberal after changing parties because of differences on tariff reform, he was somewhat more expedient. Having been appointed to a post in Asquith's Cabinet he was obliged to submit to re-election in his Manchester North West seat. Aware of the size of the local Irish vote, he explained to his electorate: 'My opinion on the Irish question has ripened during the last two years.' He had been re-educated by 'the inner councils of Liberalism' and as a result had 'become convinced that a national settlement of the Irish difficulty on broad and generous lines is indispensable to any harmonious conception of Liberalism ... the Liberal Party should claim full authority and a free hand to deal with the problem of Irish self-government'.

But the 'Irish difficulty' could not so easily be appeased at home. Churchill lost the Manchester by-election by 429 votes. His Tory opponents had fought a vicious campaign against their 'renegade', but the renegade himself blamed 'those sulky Irish Catholics changing sides at the last moment under priestly pressure'. As Ronan Fanning points out, Churchill's hostility to Catholicism was essentially motivated by his imperialist cast of mind. He knew full well that the Church in Ireland was conservative on most important issues and would probably remain so. What bothered him was the fact that the Irish population was largely Catholic, and priests played an important cultural role.

He had reflected on this while in India in 1899: 'Superstitious faith in nations rarely promotes their industry', he wrote, and Catholicism was 'a delicious narcotic that checks our growth and saps our strength ... The Catholic Church has ruined every country where it has been supreme and worked the downfall of every dynasty that ruled in its name.' It had perhaps become a phobia. He preferred to ignore the fact that superstitions in Ireland faded away. In 1911 he wrote a letter to his wife on the same subject and in the same tone, published half a century later by his obnoxious and talentless son, with a helpful heading for illiterates: 'The Curse of Catholocism'.[8]

---

8 Quoted in Ronan Fanning, *Fatal Path: British Government and Irish Revolution 1910–1922*, London, 2013, pp. 35–8.

It was not the first or the last time that imperialist leaders have blamed the political resilience and obstinacy of an occupied population on its religion. Churchill and Lloyd George's loathing of Catholicism was premised on the fact that the Church helped create the post-Parnell identity of Irish nationalism. Catholic peasants had been brutalised, starved to death or forced to emigrate for centuries. They refused to discard their identity.

The hierarchy of the Church itself, however, played surprisingly little role in the nationalist movement proper. No Catholic commissars were attached to the IRA. The petty clergy were obviously sympathetic to the national cause, but they never rebelled openly against the cardinals and bishops, who remained staunchly collaborationist and loyal to English rule. The Jansenist ideology of this Church (which Joyce and others despised) was unlike Catholicism in the Mediterranean region, which had supplied the Vatican with quite a few libertine Popes.

The moral puritanism, dour and unforgiving, imposed on the republic after independence had finally been achieved was not a natural progression. It was a political choice, an ideology that suited Éamon de Valera's Fianna Fáil party and the rival Fine Gael the better to control their own intra-class parties and supporters. It became hegemonic because the working class was not strong, and Ireland had weak socialist or Marxist traditions and no radical Jewish intelligentsia, which played a huge role elsewhere in Europe. Even in the Catholic world, Ireland was isolated. Its social climate was far removed from Italy, Austria, France and even Spain, where strong radical currents – socialists, anarchists, communists – kept the Church at bay. Was Ireland's Jansenist puritanism the outcome of something else, closer to home? A reflection of the religious and ethical ideologies derived from the English Reformation?

The formation of the IRA effectively created a situation of dual power in Ireland. Clashes between IRA guerrillas and British soldiers and police units became more frequent. Churchill, rehabilitated after his demotion following the Dardanelles disaster, was Secretary of State for War during the Irish War of Independence (1919–21). As in the previous bloodletting, he made a decision that would only embolden his adversaries. On 25 March 1920, he despatched the notorious 'Black and Tans', paramilitaries attached to the Royal Irish Constabulary (RIC), who served as a torture and death squad.

Some months earlier, in October 1919, Churchill had denounced the IRA in strong language. It was 'a gang of squalid murderers', a criminal band that had till now avoided capture. He praised unreservedly the police and troops compelled to fight enemies 'who could not be easily identified because they could blend into the population without a trace' – always a problem for imperial states confronting a popular resistance. He was especially angered by the leniency shown to hunger strikers, who 'might get out of prison simply for refusing to take their food'. Only one response was possible: England must do what it takes to 'break up this murder gang'. Before too long, he was sitting opposite IRA leader Michael Collins negotiating a truncated version of Irish independence.

As has often been the case – in Algeria, Vietnam, Cyprus, Kenya, India, etc. – accelerated repression has the opposite effect to what was intended. It creates a huge reservoir of sympathy and support from which the resistance recruits new fighters. The Black and Tans and the Auxiliaries, another death squad, also damaged Britain's reputation in the United States. Countless Irish-Americans were brought up on stories of the Black and Tans' atrocities in Ireland during the War of Independence. Joe Biden, by his own account (which, for that reason, might not be totally reliable), was among those who grew up, sentimentally at least, supporting the IRA.

It should not, however, be forgotten that one-fifth of those who served in the various police and military outfits were Irish – another feature common to colonised countries. If anything symbolises this period it is an episode linked to the instructions given by a thirty-four-year-old British officer, Lt. Col. Gerald Smyth, to the new recruits of the RIC. Smyth was a veteran of the recent world war (as were many of the Black and Tans, so named for their uniforms, which were a mixture of RIC black and British khaki). The loss of an arm – and the experience of the war itself – had slightly unhinged him; alcohol was a permanent palliative. One of the constables present reported him as saying:

Should the order 'Hands Up' not be immediately obeyed, shoot and shoot with effect. If the persons approaching a patrol carry their hands in their pockets, or are in any way suspicious looking, shoot them down. You may make mistakes occasionally and innocent persons may be shot, but that cannot be helped, and you are bound to get the right parties some time.

The more you shoot, the better I will like you, and I assure you no policeman will get into trouble for shooting any man . . . hunger-strikers will be allowed to die in jail, the more the merrier. Some of them have died already and a damn bad job they were not all allowed to die.

As a matter of fact, some of them have already been dealt with in a manner their friends will never hear about. An emigrant ship left an Irish port for a foreign port lately with lots of Sinn Feiners on board. I assure you, men, it will never land. That is nearly all I have to say to you. General Tudor and myself want your assistance in carrying out this scheme and wiping out Sinn Fein. Any man who is prepared to be a hindrance, rather than a help to us, had better leave the job at once.

To which Constable Jeremiah Mee retorted: 'By your accent I take it you are an Englishman and, in your ignorance, forget that you are addressing Irishmen.'

Mee then proceeded to shed parts of his uniform, laying his gun and bayonet neatly on a table, saying, 'These too are English, take them as a present from me and to hell with you; you are a murderer.' Mee was from County Sligo. When Smyth ordered the others to arrest him, nobody moved. 'The room would run with blood', they said, if Mee were touched. Thirteen other constables resigned. The 'Listowel mutiny' was the first sign of the resistance within.

One of the constables present delivered a copy of Smyth's remarks to Michael Collins, who sent it to Irish Republican Brotherhoods throughout the land. Collins' own response? 'Justice should be swift.' Smyth lasted less than a month. He was in the smoking room of an Anglo-Irish club in Cork on 17 July 1920, when an IRA unit entered. Dan O'Donovan looked him in the eye and said: 'Colonel, were not your orders to shoot on sight? You're in sight now, so prepare.' Smyth was executed without further ado. Corporal Mee joined the IRA in Sligo.

Tensions rose to a level not seen since the rebellion of the United Irishmen. In December of that same year, the paramilitaries responded to an IRA ambush by burning Cork, causing massive damage, estimated at £2 million, and the loss of 2,000 jobs.

And so it continued. The IRA became adepts at clandestine guerrilla warfare. As Diarmaid Ferriter writes: 'What cannot be contested was the formidable achievement of Michael Collins, a masterful organiser, in cultivating contacts throughout the government, but also turning some of the opposing players against their own side, and in killing detectives and intelligence officers and their agents in order to protect his own intelligence network.'[9]

The damage, physical and psychological, done to civilians in Ireland should never be underestimated. Everyday life was war. Digging trenches for the IRA one day, filling them up again at gunpoint for the Black and Tans the next. Anti-Catholic pogroms in Ulster became a regular occurrence. Ultimately, however, the British government realised that it could not win the war.

Having privately agreed to partition the country, the British called a conference in London. Sinn Féin and the IRA – only too aware of the tragic dimensions of the conflict as far as their own people were concerned, and knowing that it was extremely difficult to defeat the British militarily – agreed to attend, with Collins, their most popular warlord, the effective leader of the delegation. The official leader was the weak-kneed founder of Sinn Féin, Arthur Griffiths, who was completely taken in by Prime Minister Lloyd George, leading the British delegation.

De Valera, soon to be president of the Irish republic, had refused to take part in the conference. He felt that an extra-large egg (himself) should be kept out of the basket in case the treaty needed to be rejected. Others whose presence would have been intellectually formidable, such as Roger Casement and James Connolly, had been executed by the British in 1916. It was, in political terms, a

---

9 Diarmaid Ferriter, *A Nation and Not a Rabble: The Irish Revolution 1913–1923*, London, 2015, p. 198.

B-team from Ireland confronting the British imperial state, determined to partition the island for sound imperialist reasons. Nobody should have been surprised by the result.

In Fanning's powerful account of the twists and turns of the negotiations, at which Churchill was always present, one fact above all becomes clear. The whole basis of the conference was dictated by the British, in their 'Gairloch Formula', whereby a fully sovereign Irish republic, demanded by de Valera, was deemed unacceptable. The only discussion possible was to ascertain 'how the association of Ireland with the community of nations known as the British Empire may best be reconciled with Irish national aspirations'.

As Collins correctly pointed out, the compromise was contained in the terms laid down by the colonial power. He complained bitterly to a friend that 'it was an unheard-of thing that a soldier who had fought in the field should be elected to carry out negotiations. It was de Valera's job, not his.' This was certainly the case. Even on partition there was a strong argument for detaching two and possibly three Catholic-majority counties from the Orange statelet. At the very least those counties should have been permitted a referendum.

But the Irish delegation, apart from demanding an all-Union parliament in which Ulster should be included, was not too interested in the nitty-gritty details of the partition. By contrast, as early as 1911, Lloyd George, together with Churchill, had determined that there could be no Home Rule without partition. As the conference dragged on, Lloyd George resorted to wizardry: 'The theatricality and melodrama of Lloyd George's behaviour – his affected rage, his waving of papers in the air, his threats of war, his talk of Belfast deadlines and of trains and destroyers – occasioned much subsequent but essentially meaningless debate on whether he was bluffing.'[10] Bluff or not, the British laughed to themselves. It had worked and they had got what they wanted. Churchill was confident that all would now be well.

---

10 Ronan Fanning, *Fatal Path: British Government and Irish Revolution 1910–1922*, London, 2015, pp. 277–311.

Surprisingly, there is no mention in Churchill's writings of a remarkable event that divided the British imperial army abroad, shortly after his decision to despatch the Black and Tans to Ireland in 1920. As a knock-on effect, that decision created havoc in India, 'the Jewel in the Crown' of the Empire, where the Connaught Rangers mutinied. It was the first such incident in the annals of imperial history.

The Connaught Rangers were an old Irish regiment, used to great effect in previous imperial conflicts. Wellington (another Irishman) had utilised them in the Peninsula War, remarking that while he did not know whether they would strike fear in the ranks of the enemy, they certainly scared the living daylights out of him. Their nickname, for good reason, was The Devil's Own. But letters that the Rangers were receiving from their families, coupled with news reports in British papers describing the atrocities back home, began to pose awkward questions for some.

On the evening of 27 June 1920, five soldiers stationed at Jullundur in the Punjab, one of whom had experienced the brutality of the Tans first hand, met in the Wet Canteen, so called for its liberal mix of human sweat and beer. (Temperatures at that time of the year averaged 100 degrees Fahrenheit in the cities of the Punjab.) The canteen was a place where, in the evening, letters from Ireland and old newspapers were passed around. It was a social network in which dissenting views were whispered.

On this night, for the first time ever according to some participants, the soldiers openly discussed their own role in India. None of them had been involved in the 1919 massacre in Jallianwala Bagh in nearby Amritsar, but Corporal Joe Hawes pointed out that the Connaught Rangers in India were carrying out the same functions as English regiments in Ireland. He calmly informed the other four soldiers that he would no longer serve the English crown in any capacity till all British forces had been withdrawn from Ireland. The others agreed. They would report their decision to the officer on duty and prepare to be imprisoned and sentenced. Only too aware that they could face summary execution, they told close friends in the barracks to inform their families in case they were disappeared.

To the sergeant outside the guardroom, Hawes declared: 'In protest against British atrocities in Ireland, we refuse to soldier any longer in the service of the king.' The astonished sergeant cursed them as 'Bolshies' and locked them up. The news spread rapidly throughout the regiment, some of whose detachments were on duty in nearby hill stations. On their return, Private Tommy Moran from Athlone offered himself to be imprisoned, like his colleagues, 'for Ireland's cause'. As he was led to the guardroom he turned around: twenty-nine other soldiers were following him, with four others not far behind.

While under arrest they began singing rebel songs – 'The Boys of Wexford', 'The Wearin' o' the Green' and others – punctuated by chants of 'Up the Republic', etc. The battalion commander, Colonel Deacon, apprised of the seriousness of the situation, ordered them out of the prison and issued a stern warning, while recalling the regiment's past glories in the Peninsula War, the Crimea, South Africa and, more recently, Flanders. Were they going to destroy the fine reputation of an old regiment with an absurd mutiny? There was silence for a moment, then Hawes responded: 'Colonel, all these honours on Connaught's flag were for England. Not one of them was for poor old Ireland. But there's hoping to be one added today, and it'll be the greatest honour of them all.'

This was the spirit that won over most of the Irish soldiers and a few officers. The armed rebellion lasted several weeks. A soldiers' committee was elected and took charge of the barracks. The Irish officers gave up on all attempts to exercise control. Threats from English officers that the Indians might come and kill them all received another response from Hawes: 'If we're going to be killed, I would rather it was by Indians than the English.' Rebels were despatched to the bazaar to buy cloth for the tricolour and armbands. The Union Jack fluttering over the barracks was taken down and replaced with the Irish flag.

Similar events were taking place in the nearby camp at Solon, in the foothills of the Himalayas, where soldiers obeyed the orders of Private Jim Daly rather than the officers. Courts martial and dismissals came later. When the barracks were surrounded by tanks and truckloads of English soldiers, the Rangers wisely opted against armed resistance. They were taken to Dagshai prison, tried and sentenced. Thirteen were sentenced to death, but behind-the-scenes arguments that this would provoke more trouble prevailed. Still, an example had to be made. The British picked out one of the most gifted and intelligent leaders: Jim Daly's life was brutally truncated. The rest were put in leg irons and shipped out of the country, ending up in Maidstone prison. In his last letter to his mother before he was executed, Daly wrote:

> My Dear Mother, I take this opportunity to let you know the dreadful news that I am to be shot on Tuesday morning, the 2nd November. But what harm, it is all for Ireland. I am not afraid to die; it is only thinking of you. If you will be happy on earth, I will be happy in heaven. I am ready to meet my doom . . . Out of sixty-two of us, I am the only one to be put out of this world. I am ready to meet it.[11]

Partition and Civil War

In 1921, at the conclusion of the conference in London, Collins returned to Dublin with few illusions. He knew that in reluctantly signing the treaty he had signed his own death warrant, and that of many others on both sides. The treaty divided Ireland. Sinn Féin was split. After an acrimonious debate, the Dáil approved the treaty by 64 votes to 57, and the Irish Free State came into existence. De Valera's decision to oppose the treaty had made it a narrow majority.

Collins, who knew his comrades well, realised there would be trouble. A civil war commenced, and the British provided arms and ammunition to the Free Staters. Collins was assassinated. The Free State government executed seventy-seven republican prisoners (more than the British had after 1916), in addition to committing numerous extrajudicial killings. The War of Independence had coincided with land and labour agitation, and both the Church and Irish conservative opinion wanted a firm government in place. They got one.

---

11 Sam Pollock, *Mutiny for the Cause*, London, 1969.

Just before the civil war began, James Connolly's son Roddy went to Moscow in search of assistance for Ireland's fledgling communist movement. The Bolshevik leader Mikhail Borodin told him that the treaty's opponents would soon be crushed: 'It is really laughable to fight the Free State on a sentimental plea. They want a Republic. What the hell do they want a Republic *for*?'[12]

The old Bolsheviks were hard-headed realists. Borodin's question would be answered by Irish history. The Irish civil war was one of the saddest and most unnecessary events in the country's history. The defeated wing of Sinn Féin should have fought back politically, as they were ultimately forced to do, voting through a break with the crown, and declaring a republic and total sovereignty, as they did later. But it is easy to write that in retrospect. 'Take it down from the mast, Irish traitors' was a powerful song at the time.[13]

De Valera had obviously worried that if the anti-treaty republicans were left leaderless, they might shift too far away from the original aims of the movement; no doubt he believed that his presence would be conducive to unity in the very near future. But the civil war left a permanent mark on the politics of the republic.

The power-sharing arrangement that emerged was a duck-billed platypus, embodied in two parties, not unlike the Democrats and Republicans across the Atlantic, and the Dáil, modelled on the House of Commons. The fact that both parties bent the knee before a Church that represented the most retrograde faction of Catholicism in Europe (if not the world) kept Ireland apart from the Western European norm. Its combination of nationalism and Catholicism made it difficult for other parties to find political space. No Conservative, Liberal, Socialist or Communist Party fertilised Irish soil. The civil war had helped to create this

---

12 Finn, *One Man's Terrorist*, p. 21. Borodin, a Comintern specialist, soon left Moscow for China, where he played a significant part in helping to found the Chinese Communist Party.

13 The war has been fought on celluloid as well: in Neil Jordan's hagiographical account, with Liam Neeson playing Collins; and in Ken Loach's *The Wind That Shakes the Barley*, reflecting the tragedies and dilemmas of the anti-treaty republicans. To each their own.

cultural-ideological vacuum. The Protestant Ascendancy did the job in the Six Counties, an extension of British power with self-rule at Stormont. Here, massive discrimination against the Catholic minority was institutionalised on every level, buttressed by force (the hated B-Specials in particular). This was the price paid by the pro-treaty politicians at the conference.

The republic turned out to be an astonishingly stable parliamentary democracy from the beginning. The political order – constitutionalism – was a strong element in nationalist politics, and once independence was achieved and the civil war ended, the resort to violence became completely subsidiary. James Joyce had written that the two enemies of the Irish people were the British Empire and the Catholic Church. The first came to an end after wars and peace negotiations. The erosion of clericalism (while not yet completed) required another three-quarters of a century. Mass mobilisations by women and the younger generations, aided by numerous child abuse scandals involving Catholic priests and bishops from Dublin to Sydney via Boston, has created an implosion.

And yet the partition supported by Churchill *père et fils*, and pushed through by Lloyd George and Bonar Law, remains a destabilising factor in Irish politics. Churchill was dead by the time 'The Troubles' erupted again, in the late 1960s. In his last years, speaking with friends, he expressed regrets over some imperial mistakes. The partitions imposed by his beloved Empire on three continents were not among them. Old prejudices ran deep within the British establishment. (It would be a sweet irony were Brexit to lead to a voluntarily united Ireland).

5

The Wind That Shook the World

Above the rhythmic snoring of the camp,
over the noise, the creak, the rustling sounds,
the Internationale's great chorus
engulfs the night-time steppe
and in the night a bright red star
gleams on a soldier's cap.
'... Who once was nothing
Will now be all ...'

Velimir Khlebnikov, 'Night in the Trenches' (1919)

The February Revolution erupted in Petrograd in 1917. The First World War had been going on for over two years. The Western Front was a bloody stalemate; on the Eastern Front, the German-led alliance was in a more commanding position, which would be strengthened by the revolution in Russia. Up to this point, a truce and a negotiated peace had appeared the only serious option, unless one of the empires collapsed or the United States entered the war. From the outset, the weakest link in the chain of Entente powers was Tsarist Russia. On paper its armed strength appeared formidable, but the Japanese had already made short work of the Tsarist navy and army in 1905, triggering a revolutionary uprising in Moscow and St Petersburg the same year.

That was a dress rehearsal, though it was not viewed as such at the time, except by the Bolsheviks, left-wing Mensheviks and one or two astute conservative intellectuals. Churchill never managed to grasp the essence of the Tsarist state, and assumed that with a few modifications it could last for a long time. After the February 1917 revolution broke out, the Tsar surrendered and a provisional government was formed. Russian absolutism was in its death throes. Churchill was horrified. For him and the Entente chanceries there was only one question: Would the new government keep Russia in the war and, if so, for how long?

If the Eastern Front collapsed, the Germans might win the war. The provisional government dithered, but finally decided to carry on fighting. This was the shortest route to political suicide. Lenin's return from exile galvanised the Bolshevik Party. They demanded an immediate end to the war. Desertions had already begun, and the Tsarist army was in a state of collapse. By the time the Bolsheviks took power in October and declared a unilateral truce, a large proportion of the soldiers were on their side.[1]

The two revolutions in Russia unnerved the United States. President Woodrow Wilson decided to enter the war to prevent the Entente defeat and work out a strategy to defeat Bolshevik Russia. Well before the war's end, Churchill was plotting an armed intervention to put the Tsar back on the throne. Barely had the conflict ended before a British Expeditionary Force was despatched to Russia to shore up the Tsarist generals, Denikin and Wrangel. The provisional government had suggested that they were perfectly happy to hand the Tsar and his family over to Britain, but the foreign secretary Lord Curzon was strongly opposed, fearing a class polarisation at home. Churchill and his associates hung the Tsar and his family out to dry. Neither the king nor his ministers were in a sentimental mood.

While Churchill had seriously underestimated the weaknesses of the Tsarist state, the Russian revolutionaries were more far-sighted. They understood that the Tsarist social formation harboured the most explosive accumulation of contradictions in Europe. Its feudal state apparatus had almost fallen apart in 1905,

---

1 For a detailed account of this phase, see Tariq Ali, *The Dilemmas of Lenin*, London, 2017.

but was saved temporarily by the Stolypin dictatorship.[2] But even this regime (much lauded in Russian universities today) failed to broaden the base of a formation that rested almost exclusively on the landed nobility, and whose ideological foundations were cemented in three basic principles: 'Autocracy, Orthodoxy, Nationality'. In other words, the Romanov dynasty, Russian Orthodox clericalism and Great Russian Chauvinism.

By 1914, however, more than half the population of the Tsarist state was non-Russian. A police state that institutionalised brutality through its colonies had created an intense hatred of the regime. In Azerbaijan, a reactionary elite of Muslim landlords kept the peasantry in serf-like conditions and were happy to collaborate with Moscow, including supplying soldiers to crush revolutionary Armenian organisations. In Guria, a statelet in Georgia, a promising revolutionary movement was put down by a Muslim general.

The emergence of Baku as an oil city radicalised the local population, but its influence on neighbouring regions was limited. In Chechnya and Dagestan (conquered in 1859), a radical banditry continued an intermittent struggle against the Russians. In the years leading up to the world war, the bandit leader Zelim Khan was regarded as a national hero, not unlike his contemporary Emiliano Zapata in Mexico. The Ingush, from the north east Caucasus, were employed by Russian landlords and industrialists as a defence against peasants and workers. Russia itself had long experienced unrest in all parts of the country, from peasant uprisings to serious opposition within sections of the officer corps linked to a liberal intelligentsia.[3]

---

2 Stolypin wanted to create a class of rich farmers (kulaks) separated from poor peasant labourers, to speed up the process of rural capitalism. He made some progress, but dividing the peasantry into rigid classes was not so easy without dismantling the privileges of the landed elites. On this the Tsarist state refused to budge.

3 Further details on these subjects can be found in my book *The Dilemmas of Lenin*. For a refreshing and stimulating account of the revolution, also published in the centenary year, China Miéville's *October*, London, 2017, is peerless.

The 1905 revolt was a serious indicator of what might lie ahead. In terms of political creativity, the spontaneous emergence of soviets – elected local parliaments in which workers, peasants and soldiers chose their own members – challenged the unrepresentative Duma, creating a situation of temporary dual power. The most violent areas of rural rebellion were Latvia and Georgia. Social and national oppressions had fused to produce a political explosion there that lasted longer than anything in the cities, where the army had to be sent to quell the insurrections.

And there was an additional factor. The revolutionary organisation that was attempting to weld all of these social forces together to challenge the most backward state in Europe was the most politically advanced in the world. Driven into exile, its leaders had assimilated the Marxist theory that was then the common sense of the major leaders of German Social Democracy. The archaism of the Tsarist state, with its long tradition of ramshackle 'administrative exile' (Pushkin under house arrest, Lenin in Siberia) and its incompetent spy networks, further undermined its own existence.

The First World War sealed the coffin of Russian absolutism. The Tsarist army had been the last solid bastion of the regime. With mass conscription of peasants made necessary by the war, the old reliability of a professional army was threatened. But no Russian Army – something else Churchill failed to grasp – would have been able to withstand the Imperial German Army. In 1914, Germany had the best-trained and best-equipped fighting force in Europe, as even France and Britain, their own armies swollen with colonial soldiers, were about to discover.

The under-discussed Eastern Front was a disaster from the beginning. The Russian advance into the Masurian Lakes was imperiously crushed at Tannenberg in the first weeks of the conflict. Over the next twelve months, the Germans pushed forward relentlessly, taking Poland and Byelorussia and inflicting huge losses. Brusilov's desperate offensives in 1916 resulted in some initial territorial gains, but these were rolled back by Ludendorff's carefully considered counter-offensive, in what was the worst single massacre of the war. Units of the Tsarist army fell apart. The casualty rates are illuminating. In three years of fighting, Russia lost more men than any of the other combatants had after four years: 2.7 million dead.

At the same time, there was turmoil in the Tsarist colonies in the East. The largest of these was Turkestan, whose regime Lenin compared to the French colonial operation in Algeria. The bulk of the native population was legally and topographically segregated from the colonisers. Rebellions were rare: one in 1898, another in 1916. The latter was savagely repressed, one of the last two defeats that Tsarist forces inflicted on the colonised. The other was in Kazakhstan and Kyrgyzstan. Here, in the decades before the war, the peasants had been driven off their fertile land in the northern black-earth belt by a million or so colonists. These included Cossacks and peasants whose presence created enormous tensions between the Tsarist empire and the displaced clans, culminating in a national rebellion in 1916. The reprisals wreaked upon the indigenous population were the final and worst atrocities of Tsarism. Hundreds of thousands of Kazakhs and Kyrgyz refugees fled to China, many returning to their homelands after the revolution.

The world war accelerated the Tsarist collapse, but many other factors were involved. Starvation stalked the Russian countryside. Absence of labour on the land resulted in the bad harvests of 1916. The weak but vicious Russian bourgeoisie, alarmed by the turn of events, united with an intemperate clique of nobles and denounced the Tsarist court for being 'pro-German'. Conspiracies were discussed openly in the parlours of the despairing nobility. Their solution was a military putsch to dethrone the Tsar. In this they were encouraged by equally desperate Allied diplomats in Petrograd. All the social contradictions of Tsarist Russia had now reached the point of rupture. The war, in Lenin's words, was the powerful 'stage-manager' of the last act. His own masterful slogan for the Bolsheviks was a precise response to the crisis: 'Land, Bread, Peace'.

The third year of the war witnessed an elemental explosion of the Petrograd masses. There was an acute bread shortage and a breakdown of supplies. Thirty thousand striking workers in the giant Putilov Mill demanded a 50 per cent wage rise. Strikers toured the city's factories and workshops pleading for solidarity. A general strike culminated on 25 February 1917 with a gigantic outpouring of workers and other large sections of the population. Led by women, they occupied the streets and squares of the city demanding 'Bread and Peace'. The Tsar was not in Petrograd at the time. He was in his tent, close but not too close to the frontline. He cabled the garrison commander: the demonstrations must be crushed. The orders were obeyed. A massacre ensued.

The next day, many soldiers expressed revulsion at what had happened, and 160,000 of them, a sizeable minority, sparked a regimental mutiny. By nightfall the Tsar's government had fled the city. Armed soldiers and workers were now masters of the boulevards. Who would occupy the political vacuum? A coterie of bourgeois politicians created a committee. The soldiers and workers, backed by the Bolsheviks and other left parties, revived the 1905 soviets. It was obvious who represented the majority. Three days later the Tsar abdicated. The February Revolution had toppled the centuries-old Romanov dynasty in eight days.

In April 1917, Lenin returned from his Swiss exile to Petrograd, prepared a set of theses for a Bolshevik gathering, and insisted that the country was ready for a second revolution that would end the war, distribute land to the peasants and feed the cities. He was opposed by senior leaders in his own party and criticised in the party newspaper, but persisted nonetheless. Within six months the Bolsheviks had won electoral victories in the key soviets and taken power.

In February 1917, Churchill had been preoccupied with his own career. After the disaster at Gallipoli he was in the political wilderness, concentrating all his political energies on getting a new Cabinet post. By April he was on full alert, fantasising about how only he could put the Tsar back on the throne. He saw, not incorrectly, that a triumph for Lenin's Bolsheviks threatened stability at home as well as in Europe and the United States. It would weaken the British Empire by encouraging native uprisings. Pleading endlessly with Lloyd George to take him back into the government, he confronted very real Conservative hostility to the prospect of his re-entry. Curzon warned Lloyd George: 'It will be an appointment immensely unpopular with many of your chief colleagues', and pointed out that while 'he is a potential danger in opposition, in the opinion of all of us, he will as a member of the Govt be an active danger in our midst'.

The chairman of the Conservative Party lodged a formal protest. In his view, and that of his party, bringing Churchill back would be 'an insult to the Army and Navy and an injury to the Country'. Lloyd George finally managed to get Churchill back as minister for munitions, where he cultivated an attachment to the use of chemical weapons, then at an early stage, but deployed over the next two years by the RAF against the Kurdish tribes resisting post-war British plans for the region.

For Churchill and the Entente powers the key issue now was to back a Russian regime capable of continuing the war. A German triumph on the Eastern Front was bound to lead to a Germany victory in the West too. Here was another moment when the British and French leaders should have proposed a ceasefire, given the stalemate on the Western front. National chauvinism, which had ignited popular fervour in August 1914, had lost its appeal. Soldiers were dying in droves, a generation destroyed. Small mutinies and desertions had begun in the armies.

But the Entente continued as before, and its supporters in Russia – conservatives and right-wing Mensheviks, reflecting the interests of the bourgeoisie – pushed to stay in the war. But they were opposed by many of their own supporters and outnumbered on this issue in the Petrograd soviet. The latter's Order No. 1, issued on 1 March 1917, instructed all army units in the garrison to keep their arms, elect deputies to the soviets and use their political rights to the full. That simple decree cut off any possibility of an orthodox transition to a bourgeois state. The soviet had declared their sovereignty over the means of violence on behalf of a future proletarian state.

In contrast, the Bolsheviks were virtually alone in demanding an immediate negotiated end to the war. And it was Bolshevik agitators inside the army, growing at a rapid rate, who accelerated the 'peace from below', encouraging the mass desertions that made the continuation of war impossible. Their stance on ending the war was one major reason why the Bolsheviks eclipsed other parties in the elections to the soviets in the cities.

Those electoral triumphs, particularly in Moscow and Petrograd, made it relatively simple for the October Revolution to succeed with hardly a shot fired. The Military Revolutionary Committee of the Petrograd Soviet, under Bolshevik leadership, made the formal decision to seize power. Trotsky announced that the provisional government had ceased to exist, while in a few words Lenin proclaimed the birth of a global socialist order, ending with 'Long live the victory of the world revolution.' It was simultaneously a declaration of intent and a call to action.

War and Revolution

Throughout Europe revolution was in the air. Soldiers and workers had seen through the pretensions of the warmongers. Casualties were mounting daily, and the agony of Verdun and the Somme in 1916 had led to a collapse of morale, especially in the French Army. A series of mutinies ensued. They were covered up at the time, but soldiers and officers on all sides knew what was happening (not unlike the rebellions of US GIs against their officers in Vietnam half a century later). At one stage, half the French Army was in open defiance of its high command, and replacement divisions had refused to be sent to the front.

Between the February and October revolutions, forty-nine French infantry divisions either mutinied or threatened insurrection. Russian military units stationed in France were meanwhile acting as couriers for the revolution in their own country, and pleading with French soldiers to do the same at home. Some officers were roughed up; a few were killed. Most fell into line. French soldiers were seen marching through their towns bleating like sheep to highlight their own sorry status.

The scene was memorialised decades later, to mark the sixtieth anniversary of the 'Great War', by the Austro-German poet Erich Fried, who paid the mutineers this tribute:

> For years the troops have gone
> Like lambs to the slaughter

> But these are bleating
> They are marching through the town
>
> They are marching
> And they are bleating like sheep
>
> By bleating they cease to be
> A herd of sheep.[4]

The February 1917 Revolution had created panic in Washington. The events in Petrograd made the US entry in the war inevitable, but it had been under serious consideration for some time. President Woodrow Wilson's pious homilies on 'liberty and justice and the principles of humanity' were always just for show. In a letter to a close friend in July of 1917, Wilson took off the mask: 'England and France have not the same views with regards to peace that we have by any means. When the war is over, we can force them to our way of thinking because by that time they will, among other things, be financially in our hands.'

The United States declared war in April 1917, and set up a special intelligence advisory committee to keep tabs on developments in Russia. One of its members was Allen Dulles, who would later, as the first boss of the CIA, effectively run the Cold War throughout the 1950s, together with his brother, John Foster Dulles.

Wilson was deeply concerned by the impact of the Russian Revolution at home. This was not an irrational fear. Although much of the American working class succumbed to the jingoism characteristic of the time, the traditions of working-class radicalism went deeper. Industrialisation in the United States had been particularly ruthless. Like other members of his class, Wilson would not have been insensible to the persistence of radical ideas in the decades that had followed. Well before the Russian Revolution, the class war at home had become a serious problem.

---

4 Erich Fried, 'French Soldiers Mutiny – 1917', in *100 Poems Without a Country*, trans. Stuart Hood, London, 1978.

In the United States, as in Britain, the resistance of the working-class-in-formation was seen as a threat to capitalism. White supremacy, before and after the US Civil War, had helped to keep workers divided. Despite this, there was an eruption of resistance.

Few capitalists would have disagreed with the assertion made by the International Workers of the World (IWW), nicknamed the Wobblies, that 'The working class and the employing class have nothing in common!' By 1912, when Woodrow Wilson won the presidency, the socialist newspaper *Appeal to Reason* had a paid circulation of about 700,000 and a pass-along readership many times that. Its pages are famed for their serialisation of Upton Sinclair's *The Jungle*, as well as for reports and class angles on national politics.

In the lead-up to the First World War, the paper opposed militarism, conscription and the war itself. Eugene Debs was an associate editor and a regular contributor. Founder of the American Railway Union – whose 1894 Pullman strike had shut down freight and passenger services in twenty-seven states until it was suppressed by 12,000 US army troops – Debs became a committed socialist while jailed during the strike. In 1905 he helped convene the IWW, and in 1912 ran against Wilson as the Socialist Party's candidate for president, winning around a million votes, roughly 6 per cent of the total in a four-man race.

Workers nevertheless enlisted in droves in 1917, and war profiteers had their hands outstretched. The *Appeal* changed its leadership, supported the war, and watched its circulation tumble. Not everyone wished to fall in line. On 27 June, three months after the United States entered the war, workers at the copper mines of Bisbee, Arizona, led by Wobblies, went on strike. Their demands were basic: improved safety measures, equal treatment of all mine workers, and the right to be paid a flat wage in US dollars rather than the debased company coupons that could be used only in the equally debased company store. More modest demands are difficult to imagine. The mine owners refused even to consider them, and accused their employees of being 'unpatriotic' and of sabotaging the war effort.

In July armed police and vigilantes arrested men in their homes and off the streets, and 'deported' some 1,200 Bisbee mine workers, dumping them in the New Mexico desert. Most were immigrants, many from southern Europe and Mexico. With rifles pointed at their heads, they were herded into cattle cars for the sixteen-hour journey. Parents, then as now, were separated from their children. The plan had been mooted and was carried out by the Cochise County Sheriff, Harry Wheeler, and by Walter Douglas, general manager of Phelps Dodge, the biggest mining company in the area, which also controlled many Bisbee establishments including the newspaper. The two had secretly deputised 2,200 men, including pro-company miners, in a Loyalty League.

It was a shot across the bow. The Wobblies were being warned to avoid Russian-style actions at home. And not just them. The Bisbee authorities established tribunals to determine the loyalty of others in the town, upon threat of deportation.

Every branch of the US state was instrumentalised in the drive against working-class militancy. The Supreme Court would rule that mass kidnapping across state lines did not qualify as a federal issue. The Court had already shown itself to be little more than a device to defend capitalist privileges. In 1915 it discarded laws that restricted the blacklisting of trade unions in Kansas. In 1918 it would throw out a federal child labour law that Wilson had supported. Five years later it overturned the minimum wage for women in Washington, DC. Back then, the Court was seen for what it was. Its chief justice, former US president and union-basher supreme William Howard Taft, openly weaponised the Court in order to foil, as he put it, 'socialist raids on property rights'.

The repression betrayed the government's unease. Congress passed the Espionage Act in 1917 and added the Sedition Act in 1918, which criminalised expressions of opposition to the war and sent about a thousand people to prison for what they said, including Debs. He had given a speech in Canton, Ohio, dealing with the nature of war: who decides it versus who dies in it. More than that, the speech was an indictment of the landlord, the plutocrat and their political servants: 'They tell us that we live in a great free republic; that our institutions are democratic; that we are a free and self-governing people. This is too much, even for a joke. But it is not a subject for levity; it is an exceedingly serious matter.'

He listed a bill of particulars. Wilson and his Justice Department, reading the text supplied by their agents in Canton and complicit reporters, must have also heard a warning:

> Socialism is a growing idea; an expanding philosophy. It is spreading over the entire face of the earth: It is as vain to resist it as it would be to arrest the sunrise on the morrow. It is coming, coming, coming all along the line. Can you not see it? If not, I advise you to consult an oculist. There is certainly something the matter with your vision. It is the mightiest movement in the history of mankind. What a privilege to serve it! . . . It has taught me the ecstasy in the handclasp of a comrade. It has enabled me to hold high communion with you, and made it possible for me to take my place side by side with you in the great struggle for the better day; to multiply myself over and over again, to thrill with a fresh-born manhood; to feel life truly worthwhile; to open new avenues of vision; to spread out glorious vistas; to know that I am kin to all that throbs; to be class-conscious, and to realize that, regardless of nationality, race, creed, color or sex, every man, every woman who toils, who renders useful service, every member of the working class without an exception, is my comrade, my brother and sister – and that to serve them and their cause is the highest duty of my life.
>
> . . . Yes, my comrades, my heart is attuned to yours. Aye, all our hearts now throb as one great heart responsive to the battle cry of the social revolution. Here, in this alert and inspiring assemblage our hearts are with the Bolsheviks of Russia.

Debs was arrested two weeks later and sentenced to ten years in prison. The Mexican revolutionary Flores Magón – exiled in the US, fascinated by the Russian Revolution and the prospect of a unity of workers of the world – was arrested after publishing a manifesto advocating the freedom of the 'human species'. He was sentenced to twenty-one years in Leavenworth Penitentiary, where he died. Bill Haywood and 100 other Wobblies were rounded up on Wilson's orders and tried in 1918 for labour activities and opposition to the war. Haywood was sentenced to twenty years but fled to the Soviet Union, where he became a labour adviser to Lenin until 1923.

In the post-First World War period, Woodrow Wilson was placed on a pedestal by many European politicians and historians as the author of the Fourteen Points, which liberated the small nations that had been part of the Hapsburg and Ottoman empires in Central Europe and the Middle East. The colonies of the European empires were left intact, with the exception of the German possessions in Africa. 'The world has been made safe for democracy', Wilson wrote in 1923:

> But democracy has not yet made the world safe against irrational revolution. That supreme task, which is nothing less than the salvation of civilization, now faces democracy, insistent, imperative. There is no escaping it, unless everything we have built up is presently to fall in ruin about us; and the United States, as the greatest of democracies, must undertake it.[5]

'Democracy', as Wilson's domestic programme demonstrated, was merely a word in lieu of 'counter-revolution'. Beginning in 1919, amid a post-war strike wave, thousands of men and women – anarchists, immigrants (especially Italians, Eastern Europeans and Jews), suspected 'Reds' by any other name – were arrested, imprisoned and deported in the Palmer Raids. A project of the attorney general and the Labor Department, the country's first Red Scare relied on investigations by a new Justice Department bureau, overseen by a young and ambitious J. Edgar Hoover. Fear of radicalism merged with a more free-floating nativism, casting immigrants as symbols of social peril. In what would become a cause célèbre on the left in the 1920s, two Italian workers with anarchist sympathies, Nicola Sacco and Bartolomeo Vanzetti, were falsely accused of murder, stitched up by a pliant court, and electrocuted. It sent a message: Step out of line and you could die. Wilson's invocations of the United States coming out 'upon those grand heights

---

5   Woodrow Wilson, 'The Road Away from Revolution', c. 8 April 1923, *The Papers of Woodrow Wilson*, vol. 68, Princeton, 1993, p. 323.

where there shines unobstructed the light of the justice of God'
sounded like the blarney they were.

In 2020, angry students at Princeton marched into the office of
university president Christopher Eisgruber and demanded that
Woodrow Wilson's name be removed from the buildings and
programmes that it adorned. Wilson had been president of
Princeton for eight years (1902–10) before ascending to national
office. The students succeeded in compelling Princeton to drop the
name, including from the Woodrow Wilson School of Public and
International Affairs. Their reasoning was linked not to foreign
policy but to another part of his record at home. A blog at the time
explained the basis of the students' anger:

> Easily the worst part of Wilson's record as president was his
> overseeing of the resegregation of multiple agencies of the federal
> government, which had been surprisingly integrated as a result
> of Reconstruction decades earlier. At an April 11, 1913, Cabinet
> meeting, Postmaster General Albert Burleson argued for segre-
> gating the Railway Mail Service. He took exception to the fact
> that workers shared glasses, towels, and washrooms. Wilson
> offered no objection to Burleson's plan for segregation, saying
> that he 'wished the matter adjusted in a way to make the least
> friction'.
>
> ... The Department of Treasury and Post Office Department
> both introduced screened-off workspaces, separate lunchrooms,
> and separate bathrooms. In a 1913 open letter to Wilson, W. E. B.
> DuBois – who had supported Wilson in the 1912 election before
> being disenchanted by his segregation policies – wrote of 'one
> colored clerk who could not actually be segregated on account of
> the nature of his work consequently had a cage built around him to
> separate him from his white companions of many years'. That's
> right: Black people who couldn't, logistically, be segregated were
> put in literal cages.[6]

---

6 'Woodrow Wilson was extremely racist even by the standards of
his time.' Dylan Matthews, blog, Vox.com.

Wilson was a white supremacist par excellence.[7] Racism was integral to his biography and political make-up. Born in the South and raised there before, during and after the Civil War, he took the Redemptionist view of Reconstruction, writing in an essay: 'Negro rule under unscrupulous adventurers had been finally put an end to in the South, and the natural, inevitable ascendancy of the whites, the responsible class, established.' In another text, written in 1881 but never published, he approved of the delegitimisation of black voters in the South, explaining to the perplexed that the reason was not because of their dark skin but because they had dark minds. Small wonder that Freud collaborated with William Bullitt to attempt a psychoanalytical biography of Wilson.

Small wonder too that Wilson, who supported the Reconstruction-era Ku Klux Klan, screened D. W. Griffith's much-lauded racist silent movie *Birth of a Nation* at the White House in 1915. Griffith, who conceived his hymn of praise to white supremacy as a tool of popular education, included three quotes from Wilson's earlier writings in the film's intertitles. The most incendiary of them is used to introduce the heroes of the drama: 'at last there had sprung a great Ku Klux Klan, a veritable empire of the South to protect the Southern country'.[8]

---

7   At the Paris Peace Conference in 1919 he sabotaged the Japanese delegation's attempt to add this token declaration of racial equality to the final treaty: 'The equality of nations being a basic principle of the League of Nations, the High Contracting Parties agree to accord as soon as possible to all alien nationals of states, members of the League, equal and just treatment in every respect making no distinction, either in law or in fact, on account of their race or nationality.' Wilson insisted that the vote on including this declaration – eleven out of seventeen members in favour, with the US, Britain, Australia and Belgium among the nays – was invalid because it wasn't unanimous.

8   Griffith chose not to use another part of Wilson's quote, speaking of the white men's need to 'rid themselves, by fair means or foul, of the intolerable burden of governments sustained by the votes of ignorant Negroes'; the film's visuals both make and sustain the point more wrenchingly than the words could.

This assessment of Reconstruction as a disastrous evil wrought by radical Republicans was not, however, peculiar to Wilson, the South or even Griffith's chief inspiration: Thomas Dixon Jr.'s grotesque 'historical' novel *The Clansmen*. It had become the formal history of the day, emanating from the so-called Dunning School of white academics, trained in the elite halls of Columbia University by William Archibald Dunning, a Northerner, and then, PhDs in hand, taking up residence in college history departments throughout the land. Griffith's film helped to revive the Klan, now as a largely middle-class national organisation using surveillance, threats, lynching and other violence against blacks as well as immigrants, Jews, Catholics and union radicals. Around the same time, Attorney General Palmer and his protégé Hoover were institutionalising their own version of what the young Wilson had once called (apropos the Klan) a 'secret club' to counter 'some of the ugliest hazards of a time of revolution'.

Germany, Pale Mother

In contrast to the United States, where the left was disorganised and the impact of the 1917 revolutions was thus limited, Europe was in revolt. Germany was electrified by the thunderbolt from Petrograd. Sailors mutinied at Kiel, soldiers refused to obey orders, and in 1918 the Kaiser was unceremoniously dumped. A radicalisation was in process. The political atmosphere in Berlin was volatile.

Three working-class parties competed for primacy on the left. The most important of these, the German Communist Party (KPD) – founded by the major leaders of the German left, Rosa Luxemburg, Karl Liebknecht and Leo Jogiches – had been in gestation for some time. Luxemburg had realised, well before Lenin, that there was a rotten streak in the German Social Democratic Party, which dominated the Socialist International. Her breach with Karl Kautsky had come as early as 1910–11, when the right-wing of the SPD had publicly defended Germany's imperial muscle-flexing with the despatch of the warship *Panther* to Agadir.

The Second International had appealed to all its parties to organise joint actions against the war danger. The SPD's Central

Committee refused. It trusted foreign ministry assertions that Germany did not intend war, and argued that if it took too strong a stand against colonialism this would damage its chances in the forthcoming elections. Luxemburg declared this 'a monstrous piece of treachery' and, as a result, a token action was organised against the adventurism in Morocco.

The elections of 1912 saw huge gains for the SPD. Winning 110 seats, it became the single largest party in the Reichstag. Kautsky declared this to be an event of 'world-historic significance', a view not shared in South West Africa. He was in celebratory mode: 'Although we have not won that overwhelming strength for which we hoped, still we have condemned the government and reaction to impotence.'

If that were the case why did the SPD leadership tone down its demands and abandon its independent propaganda in the election's second round in a miserable compromise coalition with the Liberal Progressives? Kautsky characterised the Liberals as the 'left-wing of the bourgeoisie based on the new middle class'. But, as many had predicted, the Liberals moved rapidly to the right, and the Kaiser had no reason to fear. The Reichstag approved an increase in armaments and the taxes to pay for them. This parliamentary cretinism paved the way for the SPD's fatal capitulation of 1914 and its aftermath: a deep division in the workers' movement that ultimately allowed the triumph of German fascism.

In 1918, however, the situation was volatile. In December, when the KPD emerged a month after Germany's capitulation, the Independents of the USDP, a left-wing breakaway from the old party, had already won over many radical members and intellectuals. In her address to the KPD's founding congress, Luxemburg laid out the foundation stones of a Socialist German Republic:

> The proletariat will use its political supremacy to gradually wrest all capital from the bourgeoisie: to centralise all instruments of production in the hands of the state, i.e., of the proletariat organised as the ruling class; and to increase the total of productive forces as rapidly as possible.
>
> Of course, in the beginning this can only be effected by means of despotic interference into property rights and into the conditions of

bourgeois production; by measures, therefore, which appear economically insufficient and untenable, but which, in the course of the movement, go beyond themselves, necessitate further inroads into the old social order, and are unavoidable as a means of revolutionising the whole mode of production.

The measures will, of course, be different in different countries.

Nevertheless, in the most advanced countries, the following will be generally applicable:

1) Abolition of landed property and application of all land rents to public purposes.
2) Heavy progressive taxes.
3) Abolition of the right of inheritance.
4) Confiscation of the property of all emigrants and rebels.
5) Centralisation of credit in the hands of the state by means of a national bank with state capital and an exclusive monopoly.
6) Centralisation of the means of communication and transport in the hands of the state.
7) Increase in the number of factories and instruments of production owned by the state; the bringing into cultivation of waste lands, and the improvement of the soil generally, in accordance with a social plan.
8) Equal obligation upon all to labor. Establishment of industrial armies, especially for agriculture.
9) Unification of agricultural and manufacturing industries; gradual abolition of the distinction between town and country.
10) Free education for all children in public schools. Abolition of children's factory labor in its present form. Unification of education with industrial production, etc., etc.

She went on to argue, at a Berlin public meeting called by the Independents, that parliamentary duelling with 'Junkers and bourgeois' on the merits or otherwise of socialism was a waste of time. 'Socialism does not mean getting together in a parliament and passing laws', she declared. 'Socialism means for us the overthrowing of the ruling classes with all the brutality [*loud laughter*] that the proletariat is capable of deploying in its struggle.'

Berlin itself appeared to be on the verge of a civil war. Christopher Clark provides a flavour of the city in December 1918: 'thronging with armed workers and units of radicalised soldiers – the most boisterous of these was the People's Naval Division, whose headquarters were the Royal Stables, an imposing neo-baroque building on the eastern side of Palace Square. There was talk on the extreme left of an armed uprising.'

Matters came to a head when the SPD/USPD/Liberal Progressive government ordered the sailors to leave the Royal Stables and they refused. The city's commander, Otto Wels, sent to enforce the order, was, according to some reports, spanked. The sailors and soldiers then surrounded the government building, occupied the telephone exchange and cut off the Chancellery from all contacts. However, SPD leader Friedrich Ebert used a secret line to request military intervention. The Royal Stables were bombarded with artillery shells for two hours, and the crowds surrounding the Chancellery were driven away.

As the news spread, anger grew. The USPD withdrew from the government. A huge crowd of socialists, communists and non-aligned workers surrounded the troops, argued with them and explained what was really going on. The soldiers listened, asked some questions, and then withdrew from the city. Berlin was now plunged into a pre-revolutionary crisis.

The right wing of the SPD, on Ebert's pleading, added Gustav Noske to the government's roster of senior ministers. This son of a weaver from Brandenburg, an industrial worker himself but besotted with militarist patriotism, now turned further to the right. He started by organising a Freikorps drawn from the dregs of post-war German society. These were the people embittered by defeat, whose ultra-nationalism served the needs of the SPD/military officers complex. Their hatred of the German left and the 'Jewish-Bolsheviks' in Moscow made them the perfect candidates for these militias.

The SPD leaders wanted to destroy the Berlin left. In the process of attempting to do so they fertilised the ground for fascism. 'Someone has to be the bloodhound,' boasted Noske, 'and I am not afraid of taking the responsibility.' On 15 January 1919, the Freikorps hunted and captured Rosa Luxemburg and Karl Liebknecht. Cavalry guards quartered in the Hotel Eden beat the two to death. Rosa's body was dumped in the canal. This was the founding moment of the bitter hatred felt by the KPD for the Social Democrats.

The anger burst beyond the confines of politics. George Grosz's savage cartoon of April 1919, published in the satirical journal *Die Pleite*, expressed much more than just pain on the left. A general unease took hold in the country among many not identified with the KPD or the USPD.

Brecht wrote two poems for Rosa Luxemburg, the first in 1919 before her body was found:

> So now Red Rosa has passed away.
> Where she lies none can say.
> She told the truth to the poor, that's why
> The rich decided she had to die.

The second, written some years later, with fascism on the threshold of power, served as her epitaph:

> Here lies, buried
> Rosa Luxemburg
> A jewess from Poland,
> A pioneer of the German working class
> Killed on the orders of
> The German oppressors. You, the oppressed ones,
> Bury your discord.

Failure of Churchill's Brainchild: Regime Change in Russia

The Berlin events of 1919 were a severe blow, but not of the sort that crushed political dissent. The punishment meted out to the defeated Germans at Versailles, followed by the economic crash of the late 1920s, accelerated the sharp polarisation in the country. Throughout the Weimar period (1918–33), the liberal ruling elite could not resolve the antagonism of interests. Neither the strength of the revolutionary forces nor the counter-revolutionary passions of conservatism and fascism could be subdued. The stage was being set for a new internal and external conflict. We shall return to Germany in the next chapter.

Meanwhile, as workers across the world found themselves both emboldened and imperilled in the winds of the Russian Revolution, the Entente powers had been deploying methods akin to those so vividly sketched by Grosz to defeat the revolution. Secretary of War Churchill was determined, as he put it, to 'strangle the Bolshevik baby in its crib'. Influential voices in Washington agreed.

What later became known as the Cold War began hot, in 1917, with the Allied intervention in the Russian civil war. On their own, the Tsarist remnants and their Black Hundred shock troops would have been defeated much earlier, saving many lives on both sides. Years later George F. Kennan, an early cold warrior, mellowed by age if not experience, described the political psychology of the West in relation to Russia in 1917:

> There is, let me assure you, nothing in nature more egocentrical than the embattled democracy. It soon becomes the victim of its own war propaganda. It then tends to attach to its own cause an absolute value which distorts its own vision ... *Its* enemy becomes the embodiment of all evil. *Its* own side ... the centre of all virtue. The contest comes to be viewed as having a final, apocalyptic quality. If *we* lose, all is lost; life will no longer be worth living; there will be nothing to be salvaged. If we win, then everything will be possible; all problems will become soluble; the one great source of evil ... *our* enemy will have been crushed; the forces of good will then sweep forward unimpeded; all worthy aspirations will be satisfied.[9]

---

9   George F. Kennan, *Russia and the West under Lenin and Stalin*, London, 1961. Nothing much has changed. If anything, the combined state/media projection of 'we are good, they are bad' has reached new heights in the wars of the twenty-first century. The 'war on terror' being the most recent example, one partially laid to rest by the 2021 defeat in Afghanistan (see Tariq Ali, *The Forty-Year War in Afghanistan: A Chronicle Foretold*, London, 2021).

Mounting an armed intervention against the Russian Revolution was the brainchild of Churchill, strongly supported by Wilson. For them, the Bolsheviks were the scourge of Western civilisation. Their very presence threatened the order instituted by capital and empire. Both leaders were ill-informed about Russian history, with its rich vein of rebellions for at least three centuries. They failed to recognise the organic nature of the revolution and, in the case of Churchill, glorified the Tsarist system with its dukes and princelings flanking the Tsar, leading his troops to disaster. As Churchill proclaimed: 'Of all the tyrannies, the Bolshevik tyranny is the worst ... the most destructive, the most degrading and ... far worse than German militarism.' Even his colleague Lloyd George was concerned that Churchill's Russian obsession was 'upsetting his balance'.

Once again, Churchill's hatred sprang less from his love of monarchy than from what he perceived as a danger to the British Empire. Likewise, US calculations had nothing to do with a love of democracy. Had the Anglo-US support for the White Russians in the civil war been successful, the new regime would likely have been composed of a deadly assortment of monarchists, liberals, conservatives and the fascists of the Black Hundred, experts in pogroms, whose members were the most vicious elements in the civil war, usually burning Jews after capturing a village or small town.

As it was, the revolution enjoyed support in the cities and important sections of the countryside. The Red Army created by Trotsky, the Commissar of War, developed into a mighty fighting force and saw off the threat to the revolution. It included many peasant-soldiers who had deserted the battlefields of the First World War, but who now fought to defend the regime that had ended their misery. In the next war, it was the continuation of this Red Army that, despite Stalin's brutal killing of its most gifted generals, would break the backbone of the Third Reich at Kursk and Stalingrad.

The revolution's troops faced the combined Entente armies, whose total soldiery numbered 100,000 men. The British contingent, totalling more than 15,000, included cannon fodder from the white dominions (ANZAC) and from colonial India, mainly Muslims and Sikhs. The French landed 10,000 soldiers in

Odessa. The United States sent a token force of 5,000. The Greeks despatched two divisions totalling 30,000 men; the Poles contributed 3,000, the Romanians 32,000. The Japanese sent 30,000 soldiers to occupy Siberia. Despite the numbers, what Churchill called 'our side' was soundly defeated.

Churchill's intervention proved to be a huge disaster on every level. Lloyd George and Wilson had initially decided against authorising a full-blooded military intervention to topple the Bolsheviks. They knew the risks such a course entailed. The mutinies in the Entente armies had given them much food for thought. The fear that their own soldiers might be reluctant to fight, together with growing working-class dissent at home, had seemed to settle the debate.

But Churchill persisted, eventually securing an agreement to utilise forces already assembled in Murmansk and Archangel. As Damien Wright has written, in the most detailed history of the Allied intervention, it 'was one of the most ill-conceived and poorly planned campaigns of the twentieth century. Overall it achieved little other than the loss of life and maiming of many hundreds of soldiers, sailors and airmen who had already given so much during four years of war on the Western front and in other theatres.' He goes on to explain:

> The many different White Russian and anti-Bolshevik factions remained divided, failed to agree on strategy and were often no match for the increasingly organised, efficient and motivated Red Army under the leadership of Leon Trotsky. In many cases units of the White Army defected en masse to the Bolsheviks, sometimes murdering their officers before doing so. On more than one occasion, White Russian troops mutinied and murdered their British officers before going over to the enemy. Corruption and inefficiency from the lowest and highest levels of leadership plagued the White Russian forces.[10]

---

10 Damien Wright, *Churchill's Secret War with Lenin: British and Commonwealth Military Intervention in the Russian Civil War, 1918–20*, Solihull, 2017.

By 1919, Churchill was getting desperate over the failure to defeat the revolutionary army. He was livid that the War Office had barred British troops from using poison gas. (The Red Army had not used it.) He fired off a letter to the Chief of Imperial Staff dated 25 January 1919:

> What is the reason for the injunction given at Archangel? Because an enemy who has perpetrated every conceivable barbarity is at present unable, through his ignorance, to manufacture poisoned gas, is that any reason why our troops should be prevented from taking full advantage of their weapons? The use of these gas shells having become universal during the great war, I consider that we are finally entitled to use them against anyone pending the general review of the laws of war which no doubt will follow the peace conference.[11]

'Every conceivable barbarity' clearly did not refer to the civil war as such, since Lenin and Trotsky wanted to win over as many White soldiers as possible. It was, instead, a reference to the Bolshevik decision to execute the Tsar and his family at the height of the civil war, in July of 1918. The Politburo that made this choice was concerned that the White forces might capture the Tsar and his family and use them as symbols during the war. Trotsky had initially favoured a trial, no doubt seeing himself in the role of principal prosecutor laying bare the historic crimes of the Romanovs on a world stage. It was the English, after all, who had been the first to try and execute their king, also during the course of a civil war. The French had followed suit in 1793 and guillotined both Louis XVI and Marie Antoinette. The Bolsheviks were following established precedent, but the exigencies of the civil war made a trial impossible. The Black Hundreds used this to some effect with their civil war slogan: 'The Jews have killed our Tsar.'

It is worth re-emphasising that after the February 1917 revolution and the abdication of the Tsar, the provisional government in Russia had suggested to the British that they could transport the

---

11 Churchill Archives, quoted in ibid., pp. 212–13.

Romanovs – Queen Victoria's grandson plus entourage – to the United Kingdom. Lord Curzon turned down the offer on the grounds that it would meet strong domestic opposition and strengthen the enemy within. Churchill could have waged a public campaign demanding a haven in England for the Tsar and his family. He could have consulted his ducal cousin about housing them at Blenheim Palace till more suitable accommodation was found. I doubt that this would have led to a Banbury Soviet and an armed insurrection in Oxfordshire. Yet Churchill abstained from this debate. Why?

One word can describe the British elite's refusal to grant refuge to the royal asylum-seekers: cowardice. The political leaders of Britain, including Churchill, abandoned the cousin of George V to his fate. Like many other families on both sides, the Romanovs became part of the collateral damage in the war between revolution and counter-revolution.

It soon became clear to many soldiers and not a few officers that Churchill's adventurism in Russia was turning out to be a disaster. The officer who famously went public with his criticism was a highly decorated South African lieutenant colonel, Jack Sherwood-Kelly VC, CMG, DSO, the commanding officer of the 2nd Battalion of the Hampshire Regiment. He was not a Bolshevik sympathiser by any stretch of the imagination, but was seen as 'a brave and independent thinker with strong moral principles'.[12]

Sherwood-Kelly's men had been trained in the use of poison-gas projectiles intended for an attack on Bolshevik blockhouses on the outskirts of the village of Alexandrova. Sherwood-Kelly wrote to his senior officer urging him to call off the assault: 'if the proposed operation is left to my discretion, I shall not carry it out. I am continuing to make all preparations in case you order me to carry out the raid.' The high command was aware that this was not the first time Sherwood-Kelly had objected to orders from above. There were reports that he was contemptuous of senior officers serving in North Russia and sharply critical of the conduct of the campaign, including the summary executions of White Russian soldiers who were preparing to change sides.

12   Ibid., p. 175.

Earlier, a censor had read and revealed the contents of a letter Sherwood-Kelly had written to a friend in England, in which he confided that the entire operation was a 'useless, aimless and ill-managed campaign', and that he 'could not bear any longer to see splendid soldiers, who had given years of devoted sacrifice in France, uselessly killed'. He was confronted with the letter by General Sir Henry Rawlinson, who informed him that it constituted suitable grounds for a court martial, but that Rawlinson was prepared to overlook the offence given Sherwood-Kelly's distinguished military record. He was, however, to be relieved of his command and sent back to England.

When he discovered that intrigues were continuing against him, the South African went public. On 6 September 1919, *The Daily Express* carried the following headline:

ARCHANGEL SCANDAL EXPOSED; DUPLICITY OF
CHURCHILL POLICY IN RUSSIA; THE PUBLIC
HUMBUGGED; FAMOUS VC APPEALS TO THE NATION

Sherwood-Kelly's open letter in the paper was devastating. Soldiers, he wrote, had been recruited under false pretences and told outright lies. They had assumed it was a defensive, low-level relief operation, designed to evacuate exhausted troops holed up in the Arctic. In other words, a genuine humanitarian intervention. That this was false rapidly became clear. In fact, he wrote, the soldiers were 'being used for offensive purposes on a large scale and far into the interior, in furtherance of some ambitious plan of campaign the nature of which we were not allowed to know'.

The result of all this was 'that the puppet Government set up by us in Archangel rested on no basis of public confidence and support, and would fall to pieces the moment the protection of British bayonets was withdrawn'. British lives were being lost 'in backing up this worthless enemy army [a reference to the White armies] and in keeping in power this worthless Government, and I became convinced that my duty to my country lay not in helping to forward a mistaken policy, but in exposing it to the British public'.

When British newspapers carrying Sherwood-Kelly's indictment reached North Russia they were widely circulated. As Petty Officer Telegraphist Reginald Jowett of *HMS Pegasus* wrote: 'Lt Colonel Sherwood Kelly's scathing indictment of the Government's policy, and general conditions in this area ... is causing a great deal of comment here, as we all know how true it is.' Jowett denounced the 'High Official' in the War Office as an 'armchair critic' who had no idea what conditions were like. 'All the men who have been up-river are unanimous in declaring that the conditions spoken of by Lt Col Kelly in his articles in the press are absolutely so.'[13]

Churchill, clearly the 'High Official' referenced, fulminated against Sherwood-Kelly and insisted he be tried. A court martial accordingly took place at Guildford, but a sympathetic court let him off with a severe reprimand. He resigned his commission two weeks later. When he died of malaria, aged fifty-one, in 1931, he was buried with full military honours.

Consider, by contrast, the revolution's approach to building support for and within the Red Army. It did so with often sharp but always frank debates on tactics and strategy in the leading bodies. Soviet citizens heard detailed public reports from the front. On one famous occasion, Trotsky was persuaded by the dramatist V. Meyerhold, then staging an epic play on the streets in Petrograd, to mount the stage and report directly to the huge audience on how the war was proceeding. The Commissar for War explained that it was not just a civil war, but that foreign armies of the imperialist powers were backing the Tsarist remnants and needlessly prolonging the conflict.

Churchill had no context for grasping this kind of struggle. At one critical point in the civil war, with Moscow and Petrograd both under attack from the White Guards and Kronstadt under temporary British occupation, Lenin had considered an evacuation from Petrograd. Trotsky and Stalin both opposed this strongly. The cradle of the revolution had to be defended and Lenin dropped the idea. Trotsky was despatched to take charge of the defence of the city. On the train he dictated a set of reflections on the civil war. He

13 Quoted in ibid., pp. 178–80.

mocked Churchill, who had boasted that the White Guards were close to victory and referred with contempt to the anti-revolutionary crusade undertaken by the fourteen Entente nations. More like 'fourteen geographic notions', Trotsky wrote; the Whites would have been far happier had they been sent 'fourteen Anglo-French divisions'. Churchill's rejoicings at imminent victory were premature, but Trotsky speculated on what might happen if counter-revolutionary forces could not be halted outside Petrograd:

> Having broken through this gigantic city, the White Guards would get lost in this labyrinth of stone, where every house will present them with an enigma, a threat or a deadly danger. From where should they expect a blow? From a window? From a loft? From a cellar? From behind a corner? From everywhere! We can surround some streets with barbed wire, leave other streets open and transform them into traps. All that is needed is that a few thousand people should be firmly resolved not to surrender ... Two or three days of such street fighting would transform the invaders into a frightened and terrified flock of cowards, surrendering in groups to even unarmed passers-by and women ...

As the tide began to turn, Petrograd was spared, but Trotsky's tactics would be deployed in the Second World War, and to great effect, during the battles for Stalingrad.

At another low point, Trotsky and Lenin considered what might have to be done if the key cities fell. Lenin remarked that in such an eventuality, the only serious option would be to shift to the countryside and mountains and wage a continuous guerrilla war. This became academic, as the White Guards began to lose support and the Red Army launched simultaneous counter-offensives on several fronts.[14] A British naval assault on Kronstadt was ultimately rebuffed.

---

14 A decade later in China, the defeats suffered by the communists in Shanghai in 1927 and Canton in 1930 left no other serious option for Mao Zedong and his comrades but to withdraw to the countryside – symbolised by the epic Long March – and create a politico-military red base in Yenan, the first major site of dual power in the country.

On 7 November 1919, the second anniversary of the revolution, Trotsky announced to the national executive of the soviets that the civil war had been won, that the White generals had fled, and that enlisted British prisoners of war had been released but officers were being brought to Moscow. George Lansbury, then a Labour MP and editor of the *Daily Herald*, had advised the Bolshevik leaders to free the soldiers, but to keep the officers hostage to force British recognition of the Soviet Union. Churchill had lost. His obsessions had led to more carnage. Another crime in the ledger.

There is an interesting footnote to this story. Not every member of the Churchill family was hostile to Bolshevism. The talented sculptor Clare Sheridan, Churchill's first cousin whom he adored and treated as a sister, shocked him one day by announcing at breakfast that she was desperate to go to Moscow, see for herself what was going on, and sculpt the heads of Lenin and Trotsky. Churchill worked himself into a rage, denouncing the two men and the Bolsheviks in general as criminals and monsters, etc.

Sheridan ignored him and established direct contact with a Soviet trade delegation then ensconced in London trying to end the British sanctions and embargo. The delegation was led by two veteran Bolsheviks, Lev Kamenev and Leonid Krassin. Kamenev, one of Lenin's oldest comrades and Trotsky's brother-in-law, agreed to see her. He was startled both by her beauty and her request, pointing out politely that Lenin and Trotsky were quite busy men, and it was unlikely that they would be able to see her. She persisted, meeting Kamenev on a number of social occasions, and, as the cliché goes, one thing led to another. Churchill's cousin bedded the Bolshevik leader. A weekend trip to the Isle of Wight sealed the bond.

Sly little Kamenev. Who would have guessed? Certainly not his close colleagues, or his wife. Clare Sheridan got her way. The Churchill connection must have amused both Lenin and Trotsky. Lenin sat for her but kept on working all the while. She recalls him as 'taciturn', though he described Churchill as 'our enemy who relies too much on the Court and the Army'. Trotsky invited her to accompany him on his train to the civil war front, but she declined.

She left Moscow late in 1920. On her return to England she was reported to have said: 'I was given comfortable quarters in a requisitioned house. Both Lenin and Trotsky are excellent sitters. I had eight hours with Lenin and twenty with Trotsky.' She was taken with the latter, and a flirtation ensued. She later wrote that Trotsky had asked her to inform her London friends that 'when Trotsky kisses he never bites'.[15]

She wrote in *The Times* that 'Trotsky talked pictures, art and literature. He had the head of a Mephisto. He had a wonderful personality and is full of fire. He has read the best English literature, and once said to me that if England had never done anything but produce Shakespeare she would have justified her existence.' Of Lenin she wrote: 'From the art point of view I think he is the most interesting man in the world. His eyes are most extraordinary. I modelled him in his room at the War Office while he was at work at his desk. His calmness in all circumstances is extraordinary. No matter how excited others get he always preserves his impassiveness.' The same could not be said for her cousin.

Sheridan's mother wrote to her on her return: 'I forgive you, darling, as I would even if you had committed a murder.' But for a long time Churchill never spoke to his cousin and she was temporarily exiled to the United States. On her part, she never forgave Stalin for 'murdering all my friends'. Churchill, in contrast, was not unduly upset by the extermination of 90 per cent of Lenin's Central Committee. This only made it easier to do business with Stalin when the next war erupted.

---

15 David Stafford, *Churchill and Secret Service*, London, 2013, p. 115.

6

Nine Days in May, 1926

Know thy enemy:
he does not care what colour you are
provided you work for him
and yet you do!
he does not care how much you earn
provided you earn more for him
and yet you do!
he does not care who lives in the room at the top
provided he owns the building
and yet you strive!
he will let you write against him
provided you do not act against him
and yet you write!
he sings the praises of humanity
but knows machines cost more than men.
Bargain with him, he laughs, and beats you at it;
challenge him, and he kills.
Sooner than lose the things he owns
he will destroy the world.
SMASH CAPITAL NOW!

Christopher Logue, poster poem, *Black Dwarf* (June 1968)

The interregnum between the two world wars presented a complex ensemble of inter-related possibilities. The political impact of the Russian Revolution on the West came at a time of ideological and economic crisis. Several European countries witnessed a growing polarisation between socialist revolution and fascist counter-revolution. Woodrow Wilson's cynical notion that an Allied victory in the First World War would 'make the world safe for democracy' ebbed away with remarkable rapidity.

In the common sense of the period, political democracy had failed miserably to provide any long-lasting solution to social and economic problems. By 1937, Richard Crossman, a social-democratic intellectual, confessed in his book *Plato Today* that 'we are uncertain what the democracy is for which we stand'.

The Bolsheviks were already reading the funeral rites for the British Empire. The threat was felt closer to home, however. In 1906, Lloyd George had warned his Liberal Party colleagues that, if 'we failed to remove the national degradation of slums and widespread poverty', Labour might sweep them aside. In his famous Limehouse speech the same year he described conditions in the mines. A short extract provides a flavour of the times, with the image of Prime Minister Asquith and Lloyd George knocking on the doors of mining magnates to plead for an extra ha'penny causing much merriment in the Tory press:

I was telling you I went down a coal-mine the other day. We sank into a pit half a mile deep. We then walked underneath the mountain, and we did about three-quarters of a mile with rock and shale above us. The earth seemed to be straining – around us and above us – to crush us in. You could see the pit props bent and twisted and sundered until you saw their fibres split in resisting the pressure. Sometimes they give way and there is mutilation and death. Often a spark ignites, the whole pit is deluged in fire, and the breath of life is scorched out of hundreds of breasts by the consuming flame.

In the very next colliery to the one I descended, just a few years ago three hundred miners lost their lives that way. And yet when the Prime Minster and I knock at the doors of these great landlords and say to them – 'Here, you know these poor fellows who have been digging up royalties at the risk of their lives, some of them are old, they have survived the perils of their trade, they are broken, they can earn no more. Won't you give them something towards keeping them out of the workhouse?' – they scowl at us and we say – 'Only a ha'penny, just a copper.' They say 'You thieves!' And they turn their dogs on to us and you can hear their bark every morning.

After the war, Prime Minister Lloyd George and other politicians promised a 'nation fit for heroes to live in'. But such promises were thin stuff. A year later a wave of strikes swept through the country, with Scotland in the lead. Red Glasgow became a symbol of 1919. Even during the war, socialists such as John Maclean, ferociously hostile to the war, had demanded a Scottish Workers' Republic. Jean McNichol, of Glaswegian stock herself, described what followed:

In April 1918 Maclean was again charged with sedition, on the basis of various phrases in his speeches (they included: 'tools should be downed', 'the revolution should be created', 'the Clyde district had helped win the Russian revolution'), and tried the next month, again in Edinburgh. His address to the jury, which Bell calls 'one of the most famous' speeches ever made in Scotland, lasted more than an hour and was a defence and a restatement of the views that had led to his arrest, alternately stirring and analytic. 'I am not here, then, as the accused; I am here as the accuser of capitalism dripping with blood from head to foot ... I have squared my conduct with my intellect, and if everyone had done so this war would not have taken place ... I have nothing to be ashamed of. Your class position is against my class position ... My appeal is to the working class ... They and they only can bring about the time when the whole world will be in one brotherhood, on a sound economic foundation ... That can only be obtained when the people of the world get the world, and retain the world.'

The jury found him guilty without even retiring to consider their verdict, and he was sentenced to five years' penal servitude. Lenin was among those who protested: 'Maclean is in prison because he acted openly as the representative of our government; we have

never seen this man, he is the beloved leader of the Scottish workers; he has never belonged to our party, but we joined with him.'[1]

Had this spirit and this intransigence spread after 1919, the
outcome of the 1926 General Strike might have been different. It
was not to be. Moreover, the state was prepared for action. On 31
January 1919, Churchill had ordered the deployment of the British
Army to Glasgow. They were stationed in George Square with
tanks and artillery at the ready. Force was used, and for many
Scottish families the memory remained strong, transmitted from
one generation to another.

Churchill, on his side, never had any problem squaring *his*
conduct with *his* intellect. In many ways, he symbolised the concordat that had been established between the landed nobility, agrarian
business and the bourgeoisie, both mercantile and industrial, from
the latter's emergence onwards. He moved with infinite ease from
one political party to another, from one cabinet position to the next.

In November 1924, Churchill was alarmed by the rise of Labour
to office (albeit as a minority government). British Intelligence did
its duty and engineered the fall of the government on the basis of
forgeries designed to out Ramsay MacDonald, the prime minister,
as a closet Bolshevik. Sensing a Liberal decline, Churchill became
a Tory once again, and found his way to the Treasury. His knowledge of finance and economics? Nil. One of his first acts was to
clash with his own civil servants, who thought his first budget was
irresponsible. The permanent secretary at the Treasury, Sir Warren
Fisher, confided to Neville Chamberlain that Churchill 'was a luna-
tic ... an irresponsible child, not a grown man'. Senior officials
were despondent: 'they never knew where they are or what hare
W.C. will start'.[2]

Churchill then argued with Chamberlain, now in command at
the ministry of health, on social reforms that the latter regarded as

---

1 Jean McNichol, 'The Atmosphere of the Clyde', *London Review
of Books*, 2 January 2020.

2 Neville Chamberlain, Diary entry, 1 November 1925, cited in
Clive Ponting, *Churchill*, London, 1994.

necessary to improve the everyday lives of working people. Chamberlain had suggested reforms related to the poor law, local authority rates, health insurance and the creation of local health authorities. He had envisaged twenty-three bills over three parliamentary sessions. Churchill opposed the measures, telling Lord Salisbury that 'the rich, whether idle or not, are already taxed in this country to the very highest point compatible with the accumulation of capital for further production'.

But this was just a warm up to his most significant act of fiscal lunacy: returning to the gold standard in 1925 on the basis of prewar parity resulted in the long economic crisis that followed. Churchill explained his conversion to ideas peddled by a bevy of top bankers – backed by Montague Norman, governor of the Bank of England – as being motivated by the need to prevent any drift of the British Empire: 'If we had not taken this action the whole of the rest of the British Empire would have taken it without us, and it would have come to a gold standard, not on the basis of pound sterling, but a gold standard of the dollar.' Primacy would exact a high price.

The leading liberal economist of the day, J. M. Keynes, dubbed Churchill 'The Wicked Chancellor'. In a series of articles refused by Geoffrey Dawson's *Times* but serialised in Lord Beaverbrook's *Evening Standard*, Keynes savaged the proposals for a return to gold. He was aware that Churchill 'had no instinctive judgement in financial matters' and that the bankers had pushed this through.

Keynes's articles were published soon after as a pamphlet titled 'The Economic Consequences of Mr Churchill', in which he lambasted the government, demonstrated the fallacies of its economic policies with forensic skill, and pointed out that 'improving the exchange by 10 per cent involves a reduction of 10 per cent in the sterling receipts of our export industries'. He denounced the injustice of what this entailed for workers – a 10 per cent reduction in wages – and posed the question as to how credit restrictions might also reduce wages, which he answered with particular respect to miners:

In no other way than by the deliberate intensification of unemployment. The object of credit restriction, in such a case, is to withdraw from employers the financial means to employ labour at the existing level of prices and wages. The policy can only attain its end by intensifying unemployment without limit, until the workers are ready to accept the necessary reduction of money wages under the pressure of hard facts ... Deflation does not reduce wages 'automatically'. It reduces them by causing unemployment ... Woe to those whose faith leads them to use it to aggravate a depression ... Like other victims of economic transition in past times, the miners are to be offered a choice between starvation and submission, the fruits of their submission to accrue to the benefit of other classes ... On grounds of social justice no case can be made out for reducing the wages of the miners. They are the victims of the economic juggernaut. They represent in the flesh the 'fundamental adjustments' engineered by the Treasury and the Bank of England.[3]

It was these 'fundamental adjustments' that created the basis for widespread labour unrest.

On 30 July 1925, the Miners' Federation leadership met with Prime Minister Stanley Baldwin, who had made it clear that a reduction in living standards was essential to revive industry by increasing profits. The next day, the *Daily Herald* reported a verbatim fragment of the conversation:

MINERS: But what you propose means a reduction of wages.
PRIME MINISTER: Yes. All workers in this country have got to face
   a reduction in wages.
MINERS: What do you mean?
PRIME MINISTER: I mean all the workers of this country have got to
   take reductions in wages to help put industry on its feet.

The trade unions had the best part of a year to discuss the proposal, prepare a proper response and mobilise public opinion. They failed. Not so the government. The Trades Union Congress, dominated by ultra-moderate forces, was reluctant to act for fear of

---

3 Robert Skidelsky, *John Maynard Keynes: The Economist as Saviour, 1920–1937*, London, 1992, pp. 203–4.

losing what it had already won over the years. In the interim the mine owners had threatened to reduce wages, but in order to avoid disturbances the government had provided a subsidy to enable the bosses to pay the miners at existing rates. During this period the government made serious preparations for a class war. The TUC, meanwhile, had greeted the subsidy as a victory and did nothing to organise for the battle that lay ahead. By the spring of 1926 the period of subsidies had come to an end.

A Royal Commission report, released in March, further stoked the fires. It ruled that the owners had a case, that wages should be reduced by 13.5 per cent and that government subsidies should end. However, it declared against extended hours, arguing that this would likely lead to two out of every hundred miners being killed within twenty years. It also opposed the blatant attempt to split the Miners' Federation.

Initially the TUC pushed the Federation to compromise and accept the Commission findings. But neither the miners nor their leadership were prepared to accept wage cuts. On 30 April they decided to act and issued the call for a strike.

That same day, the king, George V, signed a proclamation declaring that the miners' strike constituted a state of emergency. What was termed at the time as the King-in-Council had the power to take charge of the country in times of peace and war. It was, effectively, a dictatorship. The government announced that troops were moving into South Wales, Lancashire and Scotland. The navy was on standby. Mutiny, sedition or creating disaffection within the army, the police or the fire brigade would constitute an offence without benefit of trial. Civil commissioners – military officers, civil servants, notables – were appointed to districts throughout the country.

By May Day 1926, one million miners throughout the country were locked out. Their SOS to their fellow workers could not be ignored. A specially convened conference backed the miners by a huge majority (99.87 per cent), and the TUC General Council called for a general strike, though it carefully avoided using precisely those words so as not to create the wrong impression: 'co-ordinated industrial action' or 'a national strike' were the preferred terms. There were no revolutionary undertones what-soever.

But mass struggles have a certain logic, whatever their declared aim. The political consciousness of those taking part often tran-scends that of their leaders, and this was certainly the case with the miners and other sections of resistance on 3 May, when the action started one minute before midnight. Churchill feared the emer-gence of soviets, but the only revolutionary force embedded in the workers' movement was the Communist Party. Its national membership was only 5,000, and while its influence extended beyond that, it did not have sufficient weight to launch anything significant except on a local level.

'The General Strike', declared Prime Minister Baldwin on 6 May 1926, ratcheting up the rhetoric, 'is a challenge to Parliament and is the road to anarchy and ruin'. The TUC's response to this open declaration of war by the Conservative government was character-istic: 'The General Council does not challenge the Constitution ... The sole aim of the Council is to secure for the miners a decent standard of life. The Council is engaged in an industrial dispute.' This was no doubt true. And yet, timid as the TUC was, limited in its structure and aims, and with no capacity or intent for revolution-ary action, the government's response was rabid.

Two and a half million workers came out on strike. Printworkers at the *Daily Mail* refused to print the Establishment's daily lies, and the print operation was temporarily transferred to Paris. Churchill took charge, launching a government newspaper, the *British Gazette*, with newsprint commandeered from the tradi-tional Tory press, much to the irritation of the proprietors. This was one of the first examples of a newspaper expressly designed to create fake news for the purpose of engendering an atmosphere of fear. Churchill's ideological assault depicted the strike as a chal-lenge to the state by Bolshevik-inspired agitators. It was, he insisted, 'a deliberate, concerted, organised menace', whose aim was noth-ing less than the creation of 'a Soviet of Trades Unions' that would take over the 'economic and political life' of the country.

This was pure fantasy. Trotsky, responding from Moscow on 6 May, painted a somewhat different picture: 'We must look facts

straight in the face: the chief efforts of the leaders of the Labour
Party and of a considerable number of the official trade union
leaders will not be directed towards paralysing the bourgeois state
by means of the strike, but towards paralysing the General Strike
with the aid of the bourgeois state.' A prediction confirmed by the
TUC itself with its demand that '[a] strong warning must be issued
to all localities that any person found inciting the workers to attack
property or inciting the workers to riot must be dealt with immediately', and by the Labour newspaper the *Daily Herald* in an
editorial titled 'Trust Your Leaders'.

In addition to the daily propaganda sheet, Churchill helped mobilise blackleg labour via far-right organisations, including the League
of St George among others. In the main, however, it was the army and
navy that supplied the largest contingent of blacklegs and kept the
docks operating to secure food supplies. The universities were at that
time dominated by conservative students, many of whom answered
Churchill's call to keep the country moving, and boasted of their role
in defeating the strike, their first whiff of class war. Baldwin would
later claim that appointing Churchill editor of the *British Gazette* had
been one of his cleverer moves. It kept him too busy to provoke more
acts of violence. Churchill would boast in turn that it was the *Gazette*
that won the day for their side. Did he really believe that?

In fact, despite Labour Party/TUC pusillanimity, the country
was seriously divided. Only a minority of workers were ever on
strike. Beyond this, a million workers were unemployed. Yet only
tens of thousands of them volunteered to help the government.
Special constables were drafted like sheriff's deputies in the
American West. Otherwise, the mix opposing the strikers was
unsurprising: professionals of all sorts, ex-army officers, young
brutes from the Stock Exchange. A sizeable section of the middle
classes was hostile to trade unionism per se, and this was a chance
to punish the workers.

The politics of the TUC's own strike paper, the *British Worker*,
was revealing. In its very first edition it advised:

Do all you can to keep everybody smiling – the way to do this is to
keep smiling yourself. Do your best to discountenance any ideas of

violent or disorderly conduct. Do the thing that is nearest – that will occupy you and will steady your nerves. Do a little to interest and amuse the kiddies now that you have the chance. Do what you can to improve your health, a good walk every day will keep you fit. Do something. Hanging around and swapping rumours is bad in every way.

This view was challenged from below. A distinctive feature of the strike was the number of local bulletins and newssheets that emerged to counter Churchill's propaganda. Some had a daily circulation of around 10,000 copies, their effectiveness demonstrated by the unceasing attempts by authorities to suppress them. Most of these rank-and-file publications ignored the TUC's instructions to stick to the facts and not engage in comment or interpretation. In Newcastle, the *Workers' Chronicle* challenged the sanctity of private property, with one headline demanding 'Nationalisation of the Mines Without Compensation Under Workers' Control Through Pit Committees'.

In Monmouthshire, Wales, the miners' daily bulletin published an imaginary conversation between a striker and his young son:

'What is a blackleg, Dad?'
'A blackleg is a traitor, my boy. He is a man who knows not honour or shame.'
'Were there many blacklegs in the valley, Dad?'
'No, my boy. Only the stationmaster at Abersychan and two clerks at Crane Street Station.'

The TUC's advice to keep the strike passive provoked roars of laughter spiced with anger in many working-class communities. In his remarkable strike chronicle, *The General Strike May 1926*, Robin Page Arnot reported on daily events. His entry of 6 May (the third day of the strike) contains the following information:

Sir John Simon declared in the House of Commons that the strike was illegal. Interim injunction by Justice Ashbury against Tower Hill branch of Seamens Union. An appeal was made for special constables. Protest against strike from the Executive of the Institute of Journalists . . . [Shapurji] Saklatvala [a Communist MP] sentenced to two months imprisonment . . . numerous collisions between police and strikers in the streets: In Old Kent Road, London, crowd dispersed by police, several injured. In Glasgow, 66 arrests, several injured. In Edinburgh, 22 arrests.

East Fife in Scotland was a stronghold, having created a Defence Committee. Elsewhere, clashes with the police and blacklegs were increasing. Trams that were still running were overturned and burnt, while buses simply could not operate in Poplar and Bermondsey. In Edinburgh the football ground was used as a parking venue for impounded vehicles that were not validated by the unions. In Leeds a blackleg-operated bus was stopped by strikers carrying guns.

None of these actions reached national proportions. A minority was prepared to fight, but it was bereft of a political instrument. And its own leaders were preparing to capitulate in the most abject fashion. They did so nine days after the strike began. It was a shameless and unconditional surrender. George V, now beginning to understand the flexibility of Labourism, confided to his diary: 'Our old country can well be proud of itself, as during the last nine days there has been a strike in which 4 million people have been affected, not a shot has been fired and no one killed, it shows what a wonderful people we are.'

The Labour leaders and their intellectual advisers – MacDonald, Thomas, Clynes, Sydney and Beatrice Webb et al. – must have purred with delight at this royal appreciation of their own role.

What of Ernest Bevin, then head of the transport union? He had been one of the most radical members on the TUC's General Council, praising in strong language the conference delegates after they had agreed to strike: 'You have placed your all upon the altar of this great Movement, and having placed it there, even if every penny goes, history will ultimately write up that it was a magnificent generation that was prepared to do it rather than see the miners driven down like slaves.' After the surrender, a Versailles moment for the TUC leaders, Bevin did not waste too much time in deciding that class collaboration was a much better course than industrial action. Certainly for him. His career and standing in society blossomed. In time he would become Churchill's favourite Labour politician, loyal to the British State and its Empire for the rest of his life. An English Noske.

And what of the miners and their heroic leader A. J. Cook? They battled on till late that autumn. In a token act of *noblesse oblige*, the Prince of Wales (later Edward VIII, later still the Duke of Windsor) sent a donation of £10 accompanied by a note written by a flunkey on his behalf:

> H.R.H. necessarily cannot take sides in any dispute; but we all owe a debt to miners in the past, and everyone feels sympathy for their wives and children in their hour of distress. Besides, it would be an unsatisfactory end to any dispute that one side should have to give in on account of the sufferings of their dependents. H.R.H. is confident that with goodwill on both sides there will be a happy issue out of the present difficulties.

By then, however, embittered and angered at what they perceived as a betrayal by their fellow workers, the miners finally submitted rather than starve. Yet they would never forget those who had done them so much harm. Churchill became an object of hatred in Scotland, Wales and Northern England, as well as in large parts of London and a few other big cities, a hatred that was passed down from one generation to the next. The trade unions lost half a million members within weeks of the miners' defeat. When elected in 1929, the Labour government refused even to consider nationalisation of the mines. Ramsay MacDonald, the prime minister, said the timing was not quite right. With the crash of 1929 in the United States and the depression that hit Britain in 1931, the Labour leaders, genetically incapable of understanding – let alone combating – the capitalist crisis, simply decamped to form a coalition government with Tories and Liberals, leaving an isolated rump of party members in the House of Commons.

C. P. Scott, the editor of the *Manchester Guardian*, had long bewailed the division of 'progressive forces' in Britain. He feared that the formation of the Labour Party, the disputes among Liberals on Irish Home Rule, the First World War and the General Strike might lead to their displacement. An intimate of Gladstone, Lloyd George and Asquith, and regularly received at Downing Street, Scott appealed to both Labour and Liberals to come to terms. In November 1922 he wrote:

> It is impossible in any broad way to dissociate Liberalism from Labour. They have the same root in aspiration and purpose, the same resolve at all cost to place the welfare of the community above that of any class – Labour as representing by far the most numerous class may sometimes tend to forget this, but not for long ... At present they are forced into an unnatural antagonism by the limitations of an antiquated electoral system wholly unsuited to the needs of the day, but the moment that is reformed and proportional representation gives us a true mirror of the nation the truth will emerge ... They [Labour and Liberals] may never combine, but they should always understand, and in the main support each other.

He was aware that some in the Liberal Party were fooling around with the notion of making it an anti-socialist centre party. He was totally opposed to this route and warned: 'Liberalism, unless it is to be constructive, is a barren and impotent thing, and, reunion or no reunion, its destiny is the dust heap.' A hundred years later, Scott's views still resound in the pages of the newspaper he founded, as many in the parliamentary Labour Party, including its current leader, Keir Starmer, would like nothing better than a move to the centre. Two of his predecessors – Tony Blair and Gordon Brown – publicly expressed political affection for Mrs Thatcher. Tory leader and prime minister David Cameron never hid his admiration for Blair. Each begat the other. Given what 'progressive politics' means these days, Scott's model could now be easily extended to include a section of the Conservative Party as well.

It was Labourism that derailed the 1926 strike by insisting it remain a passive show of strength, instead of actively mobilising support for a miners' victory.

The British trade union movement after the defeat of Chartism was a defensive operation, its politics a combination of Liberalism and Methodism. The sickly political party it produced shared the same parentage. It was not without reason that Tom Nairn raged: 'What was written in the English sky, to correspond to the towering words of 1789, "Liberté, Egalité, Fraternité"? The shamanism of the British Constitution, an assorted repertoire of (largely fake) antiquities, the poisonous remains of the once revolutionary ideology of Puritanism, and the anti-revolutionary invective of Edmund Burke.'[4]

That Churchill was addicted to this medicine is hardly surprising. But the fact that most of the British Labour movement has been too is a disastrous shortcoming. Only a few Labour politicians (Tony Benn and Jeremy Corbyn among them) have been prepared to challenge the antiquated structures of monarchy, property and power. 'They work well' was the dominant view in all British political parties, so why bother with change.

---

4 Tom Nairn, 'The English Working Class', *New Left Review*, I/24, March–April 1964.

7

The Rise of Fascism

By ship, in cars, on foot, by plane or train
They came in haste to meet the simple salutation out of Spain
The word: Salud!
A short word for such a journey and ordeal
By plane or train, in cars, by ship, on foot!
But handed out with something made of steel
And with a friend's smile, it could seem a lot!
The word: Salud!
When from their trench mortars their grenades
Come whistling over us
This is the word with which his own class greets
For which he fights, their fight
On foreign soil and over foreign streets
And yet his own kind.

Bertolt Brecht, 'By Ship, In Cars,
on Foot, by Plane or Train' (1936–37)

In September 1919, as Churchill in his Whitehall den fumed over the Bolsheviks, the German Army, under revolutionary pressure, was forced to permit political debates among the rank and file, albeit with strict supervision. In a Bavarian unit, a thirty-year-old corporal, recuperating from war injuries (he had been gassed), observed the political scene in Germany. A communist uprising in Munich had been defeated only recently by the army. The corporal, too, had become obsessed with the Bolshevik victory in Russia.

A soldier in his unit had asked why Germany had lost the war and the company commander had thoughtfully assigned the promise-laden Corporal Hitler to compose a reply. Raul Hilberg, regarded universally as the greatest scholar of the Judeocide, takes up the story:

Hitler's answer, dated 16 September, 1919, is his first explicit writing about the Jews. In this lengthy memorandum, he stated that the Jews were exploiting nations, undermining their strength, and infecting them with racial tuberculosis. He went on to discuss anti-Semitism, making a distinction between an anti-Semitism of emotion, which could give rise only to temporary eruptions, or pogroms, without leading to a solution of the Jewish problem, and an anti-Semitism of reason, which would result in a series of legal measures aimed at the eventual elimination of the Jews . . . He referred to emotion (*Gefuhl*) as momentary. On the other hand, reason (*Vernunft*) is steady. He wanted this steadiness for the attainment of his goal, the total removal, disappearance, or elimination of the Jews, expressed in the German word *Entfernung*.

This critical core of Adolf Hitler's intellectual make-up was virtually ignored by his many sympathisers in the ruling circles of Britain and the United States. They were, to a surprising degree, emotional, casual anti-Semites. Hitler's political theology was understood much better in France, where an anti-Semitic intellectual tradition, strongly embedded in much of the conservative and Catholic right, pre-dated Hitler.

Churchill saw fascism as an extra-parliamentary current with its own armed bands that could defeat the communists. On this he remained consistent till 1937. His support for Mussolini was effusive, his hopes in Franco outlasted the war, and, for some years, he was impressed by Hitler and the sturdy, patriotic Hitler Youth. After the war was over, he supported using fascist remnants to defend Western colonial possessions in Asia and to keep Greece subjugated, in addition to polishing and reusing chunks of the defeated fascist states in Germany, Italy and France: police chiefs, military personnel, chiefs of intelligence, judges and magistrates were kept on active duty to help win the Cold War.

The question 'What is fascism?' first emerged from the flames of the first House of the People set on fire by the *Fasci di combattimento* (fascist bands) in Italy in 1919. In the action lay the answer. The Fasci were created by Benito Mussolini in Milan that year with a clear purpose: to oppose and destroy the socialists. It was a conflict that had begun in 1914 when pro-war groups had fought the Socialist Party's anti-war activists. Mussolini often boasted of the wounds he had collected during that conflict. His hardcore support came initially from the Arditti, the commando units who believed that, having saved the country, they should be allowed to run it. They were attracted to Mussolini's rhetoric of patriotism, his calls for social reforms and his hostility towards intellectuals.[1] But it was the combat against socialist revolutionaries that attracted support from capitalists and the state authorities.

Antonio Gramsci, the most far-sighted Marxist theoretician and political leader produced by the Italian left, explained the rural growth of the Fasci and their movement:

> The fact that their emergence coincided with the landowners' need to form a white guard against the growing power of the workers' organizations allowed the system of bands created and armed by the big landowners to adopt the same label of Fasci. With their subsequent development, these bands conferred upon that label their own characteristic feature as a white guard of capitalism against the class organs of the proletariat.

---

1 See Robert O. Paxton's *The Anatomy of Fascism*, London, 2004. This remains a succinct and extremely useful synthesis, despite the absence of any discussion on early Marxist theories of fascism produced at the time by Antonio Gramsci and Leon Trotsky. See also Dylan Riley's essay on Paxton's and Michael Mann's differing views on fascism in 'Enigmas of Fascism', *New Left Review*, 30, November–December 2004. Riley insists that 'interpretations of fascism are ... intimately bound up with alternative readings of the history of the twentieth century as a whole', a view with which I strongly concur.

Here was a new force prepared to defend capitalism and landlordism by illegal, violent and extraconstitutional methods. And to kill in doing so.

The debate on fascism continues to spawn books whose authors disagree over whether it was a revolutionary or a counter-revolutionary phenomenon. Rarely has the eruption of something new led to such a simultaneous theoretical and historical debate on its character, likely evolution and ultimate aims. The empirical evidence of fascism's rise in Italy and Germany suggested that it was the last response of a frightened bourgeoisie. Was it just that, or something more?

And what of the political hybrids it inspired in Austria, Spain, Japan, India, Hungary, Romania, etc.? It is ultra-fashionable in present times to decontextualise fascism – to ignore or to downplay how it came into existence and for what reasons. Why was it so popular with the elites? And why, in Germany, did a large bloc of the old ruling class, including the remnants of the Hohenzollern dynasty and other aristocrats, cling to the fascists as if their lives depended on it?

Despite the presentation of fascism these days by conservative and revisionist historians, the facts related to its rise remain stubborn: it was created to destroy and defeat the left, and would not have triumphed had the dominant classes refused their financial and political support. In a period of severe economic and political crisis, fascism specialised in making the poor fight against the poor.

What had so scared the dominant classes in Italy was the eruption of what became known as the *Biennio Rosso*, or 'Two Red Years', of 1919–20: a wave of militant strikes in the North, accompanied by factory occupations and the creation of workers' councils (incipient soviets); peasant eruptions in the countryside, including strikes, huge mass rallies, and clashes between peasant and fascist militias; the birth of a growing Marxist intelligentsia to replace anarcho-syndicalism; and, importantly, a general election in which the Socialist Party (PSI) emerged as the largest single party, which meant defeat for the ruling Liberal coalition.

The Socialist Party was a unified organisation. Moderate and revolutionary socialists argued endlessly over tactics, strategy and the Russian Revolution, but they did not splinter. They received the largest number of votes in most key areas: Emilia Romagna (60 per cent), Piedmont (49.7 per cent), Lombardy (45.9 per cent) and Tuscany (41.7 per cent). The Liberal lists won in Southern Italy. Elsewhere, the Christian-democratic Parti Popular Italia (PPI), founded in 1919 by a priest and backed by the Vatican to counter the Socialists, won 20 per cent of the vote and 100 seats in the Chamber of Deputies. It supported some social reforms, women's suffrage and proportional representation, but dissolved soon afterwards into warring pro-fascist and anti-fascist factions. Pope Pius XI, who took Peter's throne in 1922, signed a concordat with Mussolini and later helped Croatian fascist leaders escape justice after the Second World War. Many Catholic priests, in sharp contrast to the Vatican's collaboration, fought with the resistance and helped some Italian Jews escape their executioners.

The events of the *Bienno Rosso* included food riots in 1919, general strikes in Turin and Piedmont in April 1920, and a mutiny of soldiers in Ancona who refused to be transferred to Albania. It was obvious that semi-insurrectionary movements were emerging in both North and South. As the historian of Italian fascism Philip Morgan points out, the character of the movement in the South, where the Socialist Party was weak or non-existent, differed from that of the North: 'In the South it had a traditional shape: occupations of the *latifundia*. Spreading initially from Lazio in the spring to the autumn of 1919, coinciding with the demobilisation of Italy's peasant army, land occupations resumed in spring 1920 and were particularly intense in the autumn of 1920, affecting parts of Sardinia, Sicily, Calabria, Campania and Apulia.'[2]

In many cases the initiative was taken by demobilised soldiers, their ability to use weapons being as important as their political demands. Politically, it was the Catholic peasant leagues backed by the PPI who challenged the landowners. Unfortunately, both organisations were prone to accepting unnecessary compromises.

---

2 Philip Morgan, *Italian Fascism: 1915–1945*, London 2004, p. 39.

Two trade union confederations, one Catholic, the other Socialist, also emerged in this period. In 1920, Federterra, the agricultural trade union federation of the Socialists, had a million members. Its core membership consisted of landless labourers in Emilia and Apulia, but after the war the struggles between agricultural labourers and capitalist farmers were at their most intense in Lombardy, central Tuscany and Veneto. In most cases the Socialist-led peasants and labourers won the day. These victories created a new political consciousness among Italian workers, leading to a string of Socialist triumphs in local elections in the autumn of 1920.

While anti-Socialist coalitions won most cities, the increase in Socialist votes in the countryside swept aside the Liberal representatives of the landowners: 'In Siena province, 30 of 36 local councils went Socialist, as did 149 of 290 communes in Tuscany as a whole. In Emilia, the cradle of rural socialism, the PSI won control of a staggering 223 of 280 municipal councils, and in the province of Bologna alone, 54 out of 61.'[3]

The PSI had campaigned on a revolutionary programme, stating openly that its aim was to utilise the local town halls as institutions of power to challenge the bourgeois state on a national level. These municipal 'dictatorships of the proletariat' were far removed from parish-pump politics. They represented the victories of one class against another, and it was not totally surprising that a rich commercial farmer reported to his colleagues in the Bolognese agrarian association that there 'are occasions when I don't know whether I'm in Russia or in Italy'. He was worried, and rightly so. The combination of strikes and electoral triumphs based on mass mobilisations was a potent elixir, a warning that socialist revolution was on the way and could not be averted by using parliamentary methods.

This was the opinion of threatened middle-class professionals, the rural bourgeoisie and the capitalists. Their need for a tough counter-revolutionary organisation was met by the fascists. The Liberal leader, Giovanni Giolitti, refused to take fascism seriously.

---

3 Ibid., p. 43.

He believed Mussolini and his cohort could be tamed by power-sharing, and refused to discuss a parliamentary anti-fascist coalition with the Socialists – unless Mussolini was included! The reason for the Liberal intransigence on this issue was that many of the party's supporters preferred Mussolini to the Socialists. Observing the political chaos with glee, in 1922 the fascist leader announced his march on Rome. He was not fully confident that his legions could take and retain power, but he thought it worth a try. His ultimate success delighted conservatives throughout Europe.

Mussolini's mythomania portrayed the 'march on Rome' in fierce colours. The reality was somewhat different. The march itself was neither violent nor a decisive act. What actually took place was different from what was later presented. A coterie of courtiers and sycophants deliberately deceived the king, misinforming him that the army was refusing to defend Rome against the planned fascist march from Milan. A weak and pathetic figure, the king did not require too much prompting. He contacted Mussolini and offered him the prime ministership.

Mussolini immediately agreed. His Blackshirts arrived in Rome a full day after he had gratefully accepted the royal offer to form a new government. Fantasist that he was, he seriously considered ordering his train to a halt before it reached Rome and entering the city on a white horse. Instead, he came by sleeping car and went to the palace even as his black-shirted thugs were looting the houses of political enemies and force-feeding the editor of a liberal paper with castor oil, the 'fascist medicine'.

All the early fascist pledges made in the immediate aftermath of the First World War were unceremoniously dumped. Abolishing the monarchy? The king remained firmly ensconced on his throne. Land reform and expropriation of ecclesiastical property? An independent judiciary? Democratisation of local government? Empty promises, never to be realised. Fear and conformism gripped the country.

In 1927, five years after the fascists took Rome and Italy, Churchill went to meet with Il Duce. He was convinced early on that Mussolini and Italian fascism represented the only kind of extra-parliamentary force capable of defeating Bolshevism and its followers in Europe. The fascists could mobilise people in the streets, something that traditional conservative parties could not. 'If I had been an Italian,' he is quoted as saying during his trip, 'I am sure I should have been whole-heartedly with you from the start to finish in your triumphant struggle against the bestial appetites and passions of Leninism. But in England we have not yet had to face this danger in the same deadly form. We have our own way of doing things.'[4]

After one of his meetings with Mussolini, Churchill gushed to a crowd of waiting journalists:

I could not help being charmed, like so many other people have been, by his gentle and simple bearing and by his calm, detached poise in spite of so many burdens and dangers. Secondly, anyone could see that he thought of nothing but the lasting good, as he understood it, of the Italian people, and that no lesser interest was of the slightest consequence to him.

In an autobiography – published in several editions in Britain and the United States, with an admiring preface by the former US ambassador to Italy – Mussolini proudly quoted what Churchill had said about him. Churchill called Mussolini 'the Roman genius', 'the greatest lawgiver among living men', telling him 'your movement has rendered service to the whole world'. He lauded Italy 'with her ardent Fascisti, her renowned Chief, and stern sense of national duty'.

Small wonder then that the *New Leader* commented at the time: 'We always suspected that Mr Winston Churchill was a fascist at heart. Now he has openly avowed it.' Churchill's wife informed him that C. P. Scott at the *Manchester Guardian* was 'vexed over your partiality to "Pussolini"'. Churchill's praise had Pussolini purring.[5] Uncharacteristically, Churchill preferred to ignore Il Duce's imperial pretensions. Mussolini had made no secret of his

---

4 Martin Gilbert, *Winston S. Churchill. Volume V: Prophet of Truth, 1922–1939*, New York, 1976, p. 226.
5 Ibid.

desire to turn the Mediterranean into an Italian lake once again, if not to rival Britain and France.

Both conservative and liberal historians of Churchill are somewhat embarrassed by this extravagant praise and tend to side-step his more gory effusions. Roy Jenkins coyly refers to Churchill's Italian pilgrimage as part of a tourist trip that took in Vesuvius and ended with 'two encounters with Mussolini in Rome, after which he issued much too friendly statements'. Andrew Roberts executes a sleight of hand, quoting Churchill in 1923, when he was critical of the Italian dictator for destabilising the League of Nations, before opining: 'It would have been better for Churchill's reputation if he had stuck to this opinion ... but as time went on he began to see [Mussolini] as a bulwark against Communism, which he feared would spread westwards in post-war Europe.' Neither historian quotes Churchill directly, thus avoiding a discussion of his genuine enthusiasm for Italian fascism.

In 1926, a year before his trip to Rome, and now Chancellor of the Exchequer, Churchill expressed his admiration for Italian corporatism:

> Italy is a country which is prepared to face the realities of post-war reconstruction. It possesses a Government under the commanding leadership of Signor Mussolini which does not shrink from the logical consequences of economic facts and which has the courage to impose the financial remedies required to secure and to stabilise the national recovery.

Nor was he alone. Mussolini's fans included many English Conservatives, some of whom flocked to Rome for years after Il Duce's rise. One of them, Henry 'Chips' Channon, MP, confided to his diary on 6 July 1934:

> There is something classical in Mussolini's seaplane flying to Rome being struck by lightning. It would seem as if the Gods themselves were jealous of this dynamic man. Only once have I met him. It was in 1926 ... in Perugia. The whole town was en fete with garlands and bands and photographers and we were told that Il Duce was

arriving the next morning. At 4 am the next day the streets were crowded with singing, black-shirted boys. I got tickets for a lecture Mussolini was going to give at the University, and we duly arrived and found ourselves in a small room along with 40–50 other people, the cream of Perugian society. Suddenly the door opened . . . a little man, Napoleonic in stature, in a black coat, raised his right hand in a fascist salute and advanced down the room as the audience stood up . . . my Italian was never very good, nevertheless I understood every word he said. He held the audience spell-bound, and made cold chills run down my spine. It gave me more of a thrill than my interview with the Pope. When it was over we were led up, because we were English, and introduced to him and I shook his warm big hand . . . Now all our Roman friends meet him often, as during the past few years he has deigned to go out into Society.[6]

Another conservative diarist of the period, Harold Nicolson, wrote of the fascist allure at a time of personal frustration: 'Everything has gone wrong . . . I incurred enmities: the enmity of Lord Beaverbrook; the enmity of the BBC and the Atheneum Club; the enmity of several stuffies.' He had lost his job (a BBC contract for a series of talks on modern literature, terminated because he'd praised Joyce's *Ulysses*), failed in an election and was worried that 'my connection with Tom (Oswald) Mosley has done me harm'. But 'life is fun', and so he and Mosley tootled off to see Mussolini in Rome, with a later stopover in Berlin to check on the progress of Herr Hitler. It was January 1932. Mosley, a onetime Labour MP who would soon launch the British Union of Fascists, confessed his fantasies to Nicolson: 'Tom cannot keep his mind off shock troops, the arrest of MacDonald [Prime Minister] and J. H. Thomas [Secretary of State for the Colonies], their internment in the Isle of Wight and the roll of drums around Westminster. He is a romantic. That is his great failing.'

In Rome, Mosley was advised by Mussolini to adopt the title of fascist for his new party, but not to fool around with militarist

---

6 *'Chips': The Diaries of Sir Henry Channon*, London, 1967, pp. 37–8.

notions. Accordingly, he declared himself 'unimpressed' by the Italian dictator. Unlike Nicolson, Mosley was far more relaxed and encouraged by Hitler's continuing rise, and suggested to his friend that on their return to England they should seriously discuss the formation of a youth movement that 'would correspond to the S.S. or *Schutzstaffel* organisation of the Nazis'. Nicolson told Mosley he would be better off entering Parliament and confining his struggles to the House of Commons, which Mosley thought he could do 'with the backing of Winston and the Harmsworth press'.[7]

The Rise of Hitler

Hitler's rise to power had started with an attempt to mimic Mussolini. Munich was the setting for what became known as the Beer Hall Putsch of 1923. The fascists' plan was to kidnap the existing conservative state government in Bavaria and then to establish an alternative National Government in Munich and call on the army to back them. Since General Ludendorff had agreed to march with them, Hitler had assumed the army would follow suit. It was a serious misjudgement.

The Bavarian conservatives and the population at large remained loyal to their government, which ordered the police to preserve order. They did so, opening fire on the Nazi demonstrators. Fourteen Nazis and four policemen were killed, while Hitler and his colleagues were imprisoned. Ludendorff was arrested but released on his own surety. The German military high command refused to violate its own structures, and the Weimar Republic remained in place. The Beer Hall Putsch became the subject of mass ridicule, dismissed as a 'comic opera'.

The lesson learnt by Hitler in prison led him to forswear organising a putsch to seize power. For the time being he would remain, on the surface at least, a defender of constitutional niceties. By 1933 pursuit of that strategy had secured him ultimate power.

---

7 *The Harold Nicolson Diaries*, ed. Nigel Nicolson, London, 2004.

In both Italy and Germany, the reasons for the rise of fascism were the same, despite their variable social structures and levels of industrialisation, the different roles of the peasantry (significant in Italy), and their respective positions in the First World War, which Germany had lost while Italy ended up on the winning side. The impact of the war on employment, coupled with a growing social crisis, disrupted the routine functioning of parliamentary democracies. The historical function of fascism was twofold: to destroy the forces of the left that were disrupting the smooth operation of capitalism, and to restore the rates of profit.

Normally, parliamentary democracy is the most suitable system for elite rule because it permits a periodic reduction in social antagonisms through safety valves such as press freedoms, open academic discourse, local and provincial elections, etc. But this depends on a certain equilibrium of economic, social and political factors. When that equilibrium is disrupted by internal or exogenous forces – so the Austrian social-democratic economist Rudolf Hilferding argued – a form of fascism will appear attractive to certain layers of the population: an extreme form of bourgeois rule, a dictatorship of capital that takes over every aspect of social, economic, cultural and political life, even if this entails the political expropriation of sections of the bourgeoisie itself and the limiting of its off-duty pleasures. Max Horkheimer saw fascism 'as the most modern form of monopoly-capitalist society'. Richard Lowenthal added that it was also 'planned imperialism'. Both saw fascism as an expression of the deep crisis that afflicted actually existing capitalism, a dictatorship that, in order to defend the ruling class, took direct power away from the bourgeoisie.

Mussolini's ultra-nationalist ideology promised to make Italy great again by reconstructing a modern version of the Roman Empire. Anti-Semitism was not a necessary component of fascist rule, and early membership rolls of the Italian fascist party included the names of many Jewish businessmen. German fascism, due largely to Hitler's own obsessions, made anti-Semitism a core policy.

Freud, wrongly, thought this was the only concrete policy the fascists possessed, and, again wrongly, imagined that the infection would not reach plucky little Austria. In Europe and the United

States, most conservative and liberal politicians, and not a few on the left, minimised or ignored this aspect of fascism in their speeches and writings. Churchill, though not in office during the vital period of the 1930s, was of their number. Though he took a dislike to Hitler's imperial aspirations, he remained in a forgiving mood even as late as 1938. After Hitler criticised him for being a warmonger, Churchill's response was certainly not robust. Perhaps it was diplomatic. Here is his statement to the House of Commons on 6 November that year:

> I have always said that if Great Britain were defeated in war, I hoped we should find a Hitler to lead us back to our rightful position among the nations. I am sorry, however, that he has not been mellowed by the great success that has attended him. The whole world would rejoice to see the Hitler of peace and tolerance, and nothing would adorn his name in world history so much as acts of magnanimity and of mercy and of pity to the forlorn and friendless, to the weak and poor.
>
> Since he has been good enough to give me his advice, I venture to return the compliment. Herr Hitler also showed himself unduly sensitive about suggestions that there may be other opinions in Germany besides his own. It would be indeed astonishing if, among 80,000,000 of people so varying in origin, creed, interest, and condition, there should be only one pattern of thought. It would not be natural: it is incredible. That he has the power, and, alas! the will, to suppress all inconvenient opinions is no doubt true. It would be much wiser to relax a little, and not try to frighten people out of their wits for expressing honest doubt and divergences. He is mistaken in thinking that I do not see Germans of the Nazi regime when they come to this country. On the contrary, only this year I have seen, at their request, Herr Bohle, Herr Henlein, and the Gauleiter of Danzig, and they all know that.
>
> In common with most English men and women, I should like nothing better than to see a great, happy, peaceful Germany in the vanguard of Europe. Let this great man search his own heart and conscience before he accuses anyone of being a warmonger. The whole peoples of the British Empire and the French Republic

earnestly desire to dwell in peace side by side with the German nation. But they are also resolved to put themselves in a position to defend their rights and long- established civilizations. They do not mean to be in anybody's power. If Herr Hitler's eye falls upon these words, I trust he will accept them in the spirit of candour in which they are uttered.[8]

An essay Churchill wrote a year earlier had taken the same conciliatory line: Hitler 'was the child of the rage and grief of a mighty empire and race which had suffered overwhelming defeat in war'. The Führer sought revenge for that defeat, and 'in the fifteen years that have followed this resolve he has succeeded in restoring Germany to the most powerful position in Europe'. Germany was no longer prostrate at the feet of the victors. 'Whatever else may be thought of these exploits,' Churchill wrote, 'they are certainly the most remarkable in the whole history of the world.' Admiration and exaggeration apart, Churchill criticised the banning of the socialist and communist parties, the hatred for and persecution of the Jews, and the alarming assaults on Christianity in favour of the 'old gods of Nordic paganism'.[9] Did he really believe this or was it just for the record?

Trotsky's Warnings

In the Soviet Union, political conflicts and factional struggles within the Bolshevik Party had led to a victory for Stalin's faction at a time of setbacks abroad, in Europe and China. The defeated Trotsky was expelled, deprived of his nationality and sent into exile in Turkey. Kemal Ataturk despatched him to the isle of Prinkipo, where Byzantine Emperors had imprisoned their rivals.[10]

---

8   Quoted in Richard M. Langworth, 'Did Churchill Praise Hitler?', blog post, 25 June 2009, at richardlangworth.com.

9   Winston Churchill, 'Hitler and His Choice', in *Great Contemporaries*, London, 2012 [1937], pp. 251–7.

10   For further details, Isaac Deutscher's *The Prophet Outcast*, London, 2003 [1963], is indispensable.

Trotsky had been almost alone in warning, from 1931 onwards, of the dangers that lay ahead in Germany. A few years later, Bertolt Brecht, in his California exile, began work on what was to become one of the most savage attacks on the rise of Hitler and fascism. Brecht, together with Walter Benjamin, had read Trotsky's warnings, the following passage of which may have helped in the composition of *The Resistible Rise of Arturo Ui*, first performed a decade later:

At the start of his political career, Hitler stood out perhaps only because of his big temperament, a voice much louder than others, and a circumscribed mentality much more self-assured. He did not bring into the movement any ready-made programme, if one disregards the insulted soldier's thirst for vengeance. Hitler began with grievances and complaints about the Versailles terms, the high cost of living, the lack of respect for a meritorious non-commissioned officer, and the plots of bankers and journalists of the Mosaic persuasion. There were in the country plenty of ruined and drowning people with scars and fresh bruises. They all wanted to thump with their fists on the table. This Hitler could do better than others. True, he knew not how to cure the evil. But his harangues sounded now like commands and again like prayers addressed to inexorable fate. Doomed classes, like those fatally ill, never tire of making variations on their plaints or of listening to consolations. Hitler's speeches were all attuned to this pitch. Sentimental formlessness, absence of disciplined thought, ignorance along with gaudy erudition – all these minuses turned into pluses. They supplied him with the possibility of uniting all types of dissatisfaction around the beggar's sack of National Socialism, and of leading the mass in the direction in which it pushed him. In the mind of the agitator was preserved, from among his early personal improvisations, whatever had met with approbation. His political thoughts were the fruits of oratorical acoustics. That is how the selection of slogans went on. That is how the programme was consolidated. That is how the 'leader' took shape out of the raw material.[11]

---

11 Leon Trotsky, *The Struggle Against Fascism in Germany*, introduction by Ernest Mandel, New York, 1971.

As eloquently noted by his biographer:

> Trotsky's attempt to arouse the working class of Germany to the danger that threatened it was his greatest political deed in exile. Like no one else, and much earlier than anyone, he grasped the destructive delirium with which National Socialism was to burst upon the world. His commentaries on the German situation, written between 1930 and 1933, the years before Hitler's assumption of power, stand out as a cool, clinical analysis and forecast of this stupendous phenomenon of social psychopathology and of its consequences to the international labor movement, to the Soviet Union, and to the world.[12]

In discussing the rise and fall of fascism, one question tends to be either overlooked or underplayed. Was fascism inevitable or was it resistible? And if the latter, through which mechanisms? That a crucial sector of German capitalism favoured a period of order is an indisputable fact. Some may well have preferred a more rational form of irrationality, but others backed and funded Hitler's party. The fact that many owners of capitalist monopolies, as well as conservatives – parties and individuals – of many hues, favoured fascism embarrasses liberal historians today.

What of the German left? As discussed earlier, the two major parties, the social-democratic SPD and the communist KPD, were bitterly divided. The counter-revolutionary thrust begun by the right-wing SPD leaders Noske, Ebert and Scheideman in December 1918–January 1919, with the help of the Freikorps (ancestor of the future SA and SS), not only spilt the blood of Luxemburg, Liebknecht, Jogiches and Haase, it was also responsible for the assassination of thousands of workers by proto-fascist death squads between 1919 and 1921.

Was it possible to bridge that river of blood? Had the Comintern in Moscow reversed course, pushing the KPD to launch a serious unity offensive, calling on socialists and other parties to form a united front against fascism, the situation might have been

---

12 Deutscher, *The Prophet Outcast*, p. 103.

retrievable. The failure to analyse the specificity of fascism led to complete disaster in 1933. The far right in the SPD hated the KPD more than it did the Nazis. As for the KPD, it was on an ultra-left course, writing off the fascist threat as a temporary aberration. It referred to its opponents in the SPD as 'social-fascists', and one top KPD leader, Ernst Thälmann, infamously remarked, 'First Hitler, then our turn.'

The relationship of forces did *not*, however, initially favour fascism. In the May 1924 general elections, the SPD got 6 million votes, the KPD almost 4 million, the Centre Liberals 4 million and the Nazis 2 million. In December of that same year another election was called. The KPD lost a million votes to the SPD, whose total was now just under 8 million, the Centre was unchanged, and the Nazis dropped to 907,000. In the May 1928 elections, the pattern was more or less the same, with the Nazi vote down to 810,000. When the Depression hit Germany hard, there was a dramatic shift. In September 1930, the fascist vote increased seven-fold, to 6.5 million votes, with the SPD at 8.5 million and the Communists at 4.5 million, slightly more than the Centre at 4 million.

In his first essay-pamphlet after the 1930 election, Trotsky warned that the vacillating German bourgeoisie faced a choice: social democracy or fascism. In his view: 'Fascism in Germany has become a real danger, as an acute expression of the hopeless position of the bourgeois regime, the conservative role of the Social Democracy in this regime, and the accumulated powerlessness of the Communist Party to abolish it. Whoever denies this is either blind or a braggart.' The 'malarial character of the political curve', he argued, suggested that the tempo of the crisis would be speedy. A pre-revolutionary crisis and the strategic impotence of the revolutionary party could, in other words, lead to a horrible defeat. He appealed for an SPD–KPD pact to unite the working class against the Nazis, arguing that this would change the political dynamic overnight and become a pole of attraction for liberals as well as those who were despairingly falling prey to fascist demagogy.[13]

---

13   Trotsky, *The Struggle against Fascism in Germany*, pp. 9–31.

His appeal fell on deaf ears. The left's failure scarred working-class consciousness and members of both parties. Within two years Hitler was in power, with the support of the overwhelming bulk of the German elite. The KPD had run Thaelmann in the 1932 presidential elections. The SPD had refused even to put up its own candidate and insisted on voting for von Hindenburg as the lesser evil. He won, and in January of the following year appointed Hitler as Reich Chancellor.

During the Weimar period that preceded fascism, the German army, navy and air force had been quietly but consistently engaged in rearmament. Under the Nazis, after 1933, there was a sharp acceleration. A few tests were conducted, beginning with the occupation of the Rhineland in 1936, and their success meant that within a few years the Third Reich was ready for war. Visiting Bavaria in 1935, Churchill was impressed by the patriotic German youth singing nationalist songs as they marched through the streets.

If the virulence of inter-war nationalism in Germany was a response to the punishing conditions of the Versailles Treaty and the global economic crisis of the Great Depression, what of its British counterpart? British nationalism took the form of pride in and support for the British Empire on both a casual and an ideological level. The Empire was part of everyday life. It effortlessly dominated politics and culture. A large section of the labour movement was at one here with British capitalism.

Reducing this reality simply to the imperial loot that trickled down to the subaltern classes is an insufficient explanation. After all, imperial gains did not help the working class much in material terms. Reductions in wages, political repression of strikers and radicals, curbing of trade union rights, were, and remain, features of British capitalism. The 'harmony of interests' never existed at home or abroad. There was dissent, of course, as Priyamvada Gopal has strikingly demonstrated,[14] but it was dwarfed by mass identification with the Empire.

---

14 Priyamvada Gopal, *Insurgent Empire: Anticolonialism and the Making of British Dissent*, London, 2019.

For example, Ramsay MacDonald – leader of the Independent Labour Party, subsequently leader of the Labour Party and the first ever Labour prime minister – had opposed the First World War, but prior to that he had written a book that jolted many socialists. Its German-language edition of 1912 was edited and introduced by one of his main German equivalents, Eduard Bernstein.[15] MacDonald argued that while it was necessary to 'democratise' the empire, it was even more important to retain and maintain it.

Leaving no room for doubt, he explained that 'democratisation' did not mean self-determination in any shape or form for the 'inferior races', since it was abundantly clear they were incapable of governing themselves. He defended white rule in South Africa, justified racial segregation in the United States, and was totally indifferent to the civil rights of African Americans. As Labour prime minister, he practised what he preached and defended the empire as vigorously as Churchill.

Colonial rebellions against British imperialism found no favour with a large majority of the British Labour movement. MacDonald was fully supported by Labourist intellectuals assembled in the Fabian Society. Bernard Shaw wrote extensively defending the Empire. His principal contribution to Fabian theory on this subject was to proclaim the existence of 'higher and lesser civilisations'. Hardly original, this was a view shared by Churchill, Leopold of Belgium, their French and German equivalents, Woodrow Wilson and many others.

Hitler gave this belief in superior races a new twist in the 1930s by extending it for domestic use against Jews and later, in occupied territories, against the Slavs. They were *untermenschen* (sub-human). The triumph of the Nazis in 1933 marked a turning point in world politics. The largest state in Europe was now the bastion of counter-revolution against the Bolsheviks and revanchism against the imperialist powers that had humiliated it in 1919. Goebbels, the first effective spin-doctor of the twentieth century,

---

15 James Ramsay MacDonald, *Socialism and Government*, 2 vols, London, 1909; *Socialismus u. Regierung*, ed. Eduard Bernstein, Jena, 1912.

explained that the Versailles Treaty had resulted in the expulsion of 'Germany from the comity of powerful political countries', and that the principal function of the Nazis was 'to unite the people and once more lead it back to the comity of nations'. The same nonsense was repeated by Mussolini during Hitler's triumphal trip to Rome in 1938: all that the two countries wanted was 'justice, security and peace for all'.

In London, the Tory leader Stanley Baldwin was appealing for a different axis, also 'for peace and justice in the world', based on a deal between the two English-speaking powers. In a speech given at the Albert Hall in May 1935, just before becoming prime minister for the third time, he outlined his position:

> The combined powers of the navies, the potential man-power, the immediate economic power of a combined blockade, and a refusal to trade or lend money would be a sanction that no power on earth, however strong, dare face. It may be a hundred years before that desirable end may be attained; it may never come to pass. But sometimes we may have our dreams . . . I cannot but think, even if men cannot advocate it openly yet, that some day and some time those who follow us may see it and know that the peace of the world is guaranteed by those who speak our tongue.

The speeches of Hitler and Goebbels about 'peace' did have an impact, and there were conservative politicians in every European country who believed them, but Churchill wasn't convinced. Like others at home and in France, he hoped that the Germans would turn on the Soviet Union and destroy the Bolshevik menace before settling scores elsewhere.

Hitler and Mussolini soon provided evidence that the extermination of Bolshevism and Jewish Bolsheviks in particular was indeed their main strategic aim in Europe. The rehearsal for the larger conflict that was being prepared took place in Spain, when a military coup led by General Francisco Franco toppled an elected Republican government, a coalition of left and progressive parties. Churchill's position was clear from the start: 'I will not pretend that, if I had to choose between Communism and Nazi-ism, I would choose Communism.' First he embraced Mussolini, now Franco. Spanish history was far more complicated than implied by Churchill's stupid and reductionist comment. He was too blinded by his hostility to the left to see that Franco's victory would only strengthen fascism's stranglehold on Europe.

The Spanish Cockpit

As the respected Spanish historian Julián Casanova points out in his sober reassessment of the brief flowering and embattled fall of the democratic Republic, the civil war in Spain, triggered by a coup against a democratically elected government, was not a single war that might be defined simply as a contest between fascism and democracy.[16] It was that too, but there were many wars inside this one, some with long historical pedigrees: a war to settle deep social conflicts, precipitated by the complex chemistry of the first truly democratic regime in Spanish history; a war of class struggle; a war of religion, between obscurantism and modernisation; an ideological war around concepts of the nation and fatherland; a war between antagonistic political beliefs, waged in an international context characterised by the crisis of democracy and challenges from left and right, symbolised by communism and fascism.

The Popular Front in Spain had swept to victory in the 1936 election. Its official programme was innocuous, but it was clear to the dominant classes that the masses responsible for the victory wanted a social revolution that would transform Spain forever. In keeping with the continuities and discontinuities of Spanish history, a generals' conspiracy began to take shape, backed by the oligarchic bloc. Their objective was simple: a pre-emptive counter-revolution.

Revolts against the Popular Front government in army barracks in July 1936 provoked working-class uprisings in Madrid, Barcelona, Santander and virtually every other major city in Spain. These were accompanied by the creation of autonomous institutions: workers' councils and peasant collectives. Plainly, these were

---

16 Julián Casanova, *The Spanish Republic and the Civil War*, Cambridge, 2010.

not just defensive moves, but a declaration of intent backed by a muscular show of strength. The anarchist trade union confederation in Barcelona (CNT) and its socialist counterpart in Madrid and the North (UGT) exercised working-class sovereignty over factories, districts and brigades. The central government had no power in these zones. For a short period – nine months – there was genuine dual power in Spain, the only such example in the West. The *Economist* noted hopefully: 'We have the influence of Paris of 1848 and 1871 rather than the influence of Moscow in 1917', forgetting conveniently that the road from 1871 led to Moscow in 1917. It was the prelude to a popular revolution. Hence the military revolt.

Churchill could see that this was not a repeat of the 1926 General Strike in Britain, but a revolution backed by pro-Moscow socialists and communists and, in Catalunya, anti-Stalin communists and anarchists. Like most of Europe's conservatives and the two fascist dictators, Churchill backed the uniformed counter-revolution. In Moscow, Stalin was worried that no single party was in complete command to carry out Comintern orders. He was particularly concerned by Catalunya, where the anti-Stalinist POUM (and its strong backers in Soviet military intelligence), as well as the anarchists, refused to accept the line from Moscow. He authorised a virtual civil war within the left. Others, like Jan Berzin and his network of internationalist agents organised in the Fourth Department of the Red Army based in Western Europe, were desperate for a victory in Spain. They could see that it would be a blow against fascism and might even revive the demoralised working class in the Soviet Union.

The central government in Madrid, nervous and faltering as ever, agreed nonetheless to distribute arms to the workers and citizens opposed to the conspiracy. All the conditions for a revolutionary takeover were now present, but the workers' parties were divided. The military, under Franco's leadership, was not. The civil war commenced. As we shall see, Germany and Italy played a major role in sustaining Franco with arms, troops and training, most infamously with the Nazi bombing of the Basque town of Guernica. Britain and France preached and practised non-intervention. Léon

Blum, the Socialist prime minister at the head of a Popular Front government in France, was far too scared to help his comrades in Spain. International brigades from many countries were formed to fight on the side of the Republicans.

As Julián Casanova observes, Spain's fate was specific, but not so different from that of over half of the twenty-eight European parliamentary or quasi-parliamentary democracies of the interwar years that, by the beginning of 1939, had succumbed to dictatorial regimes. There was one big difference, however: the Spanish revolution was confronted by separatist tendencies in the Basque country and Catalunya, which accelerated during periods of dictatorship. The democratic task of national self-determination at home and decolonisation in Morocco would have helped to isolate and, possibly, defeat Franco, despite German and Italian support.

Franco's victory put paid to all such hopes, as an iron dictatorship began imprisoning, torturing and killing its civil war opponents, including university rectors and teachers. Book burnings were revived for the first time since the Inquisition had ordered the mass burning of Muslim libraries in Granada in the fifteenth century. The books being burnt now, apart from Marxist and socialist texts, included the works of Voltaire, Rousseau, Goethe, Flaubert, Balzac, Hugo, Dostoevsky, Fernando de Rojas, etc. Rooms in libraries where 'bad books' were confined became known as 'hells', and in a number of cases they were still in existence when Franco died in 1975.

Proportionately, the Basques and Catalans suffered the most, together with socialists and communists throughout the country. Spanish refugees flowed into France. Franco's dictatorship decisively shifted the relationship of forces in Europe. A confident and triumphant fascism now confronted bourgeois democratic France, imperial Britain and the Soviet Union.

The Nazi intervention on behalf of a pro-fascist clerical–military dictatorship in Spain was followed by the *Anschluss*, as Hitler's forces marched into Austria in 1938. Austrian social democrats had strongly favoured a union with Germany in 1919, but the proposal was brusquely rejected by the Entente as premature. Hitler's return to his native country was popular there, and a strain of fascism, on some levels more virulent than the German variety, took root in Austrian soil.[17]

The march into the Rhineland, the intervention in Spain, the Anschluss: three test runs had been successful. Hitler was now poised for a war to take Europe. Both appeasers inside the British Conservative Party and, a little later, Franklin Roosevelt in the White House believed that resistance to the Nazi war machine could not possibly succeed. They wanted a pre-war deal, a 'separate peace' with Hitler, failing to see that it would not be worth the paper on which it was written. All attempts by the Soviet Union to create an alliance with France and Britain were rebuffed.

Counterfactual history is never satisfying, but there are few who doubt that, had Britain done a deal with the Third Reich, the United States would not have intervened militarily in Europe, unless it appeared that the Soviet Union, on its own, might defeat the Nazis.

There was much that Churchill simply failed to understand in this period. Enamoured of Mussolini, impressed by Hitler's organisation, an advocate of Franco's triumph in Spain, he failed to see the steel curtain festooned with swastikas that was threatening Europe, and that Hitler's ascent meant a revival and consolidation of German imperialism. When he finally grasped the gravity of the threat too many opportunities to deal with it had been lost.

Churchill's position on Spain was a case in point. Writing in the *Evening Standard* on 10 August 1936, he was insistent on British and French non-intervention:

> Meanwhile it is of the utmost consequence that France and Britain should act together in observing the strictest neutrality themselves and endeavouring to induce it in others. Even if Russian money is thrown in on one side, or Italian and German encouragement is given to the other, the safety of France and England requires absolute neutrality and non-intervention by them.

---

17   It is difficult to understand the savage depictions of the country in the novels of Elfriede Jelinek outside this context.

Given the scale of the German and Italian intervention, compared to which the International Brigades were puny, the non-interventionists effectively handed over the country to Franco. Churchill's support for the General on every level was never in doubt. As Paul Preston recounts in his highly acclaimed work on the Spanish Civil War, most of the atrocities were carried out by Franco's forces. To these Churchill and others turned a blind eye:

> Winston Churchill's reaction to the situation in Republican Spain was representative of the perception of events in upper-class and official circles. When the new Spanish Ambassador Pablo de Azcarate arrived in London in early September 1936, he was introduced by his friend Lord David Cecil to Churchill. Although Azcarate arrived with a reputation as a highly respected functionary of the League of Nations, a red-faced Churchill angrily rejected his outstretched hand and stalked off muttering, 'Blood, blood . . .'[18]

Two months later, on 2 October 1936, Churchill penned another column for the *Evening Standard*. This time he targeted the execution of hostages in Madrid by the Republican side. Civil wars are never pretty. It depends which side you're on. The Madrid executions were heavily criticised within the Republican camp and *El Socialista* published a strong editorial the day after Churchill's column titled 'Moral Obligations in War': 'The life of an adversary who surrenders is unassailable; no combatant can dispose of that life. But that is not how the rebels behave. No matter. It is how we should behave.' Churchill admitted that Franco's gangs regularly 'shoot a proportion of their prisoners taken in arms', but insisted this was not comparable to what he called the 'tortures and fiendish outrages in the lowest pit of human degradation' committed by Republicans. Therefore, he concluded, 'It would be a mistake alike in truth and wisdom for British public opinion to rate both sides at the same level.' In other words, Franco was better than the Republicans. Blinded by

18 Paul Preston, *The Spanish Holocaust: Inquisition and Extermination in Twentieth-Century Spain*, London, 2012, p. 295.

class and imperial prejudices, Churchill fully backed European fascism against its enemies on the left.

He never changed his mind on Franco. As far as he was concerned, the Spanish dictator was an all-weather friend, unlike Stalin and the Red Army who could only be temporary allies. On Germany, before most other Tory leaders, he realised that Hitler could not be appeased. Rearmament was the key. Once he had achieved that, he was satisfied. He organised a fightback against Germany and was lucky when Hitler spared the British Expeditionary Force in France. British propagandists were quick to transform a defeat into a victory. But within the army most soldiers and officers were only too aware how close they had been to disaster.

8

Japan's Bid for Mastery in Asia

Here war is simple like a monument:
A telephone is speaking to a man;
Flags on a map assert that troops were sent;
A boy brings milk in bowls. There is a plan

For living men in terror of their lives,
Who thirst at nine who were to thirst at noon,
And can be lost and are, and miss their wives,
And, unlike an idea, can die too soon.

But ideas can be true although men die,
And we can watch a thousand faces
Made active by one lie:

And maps can really point to places
Where life is evil now:
Nanking; Dachau.

W. H. Auden, Sonnet XVI from *In Time of War* (1939)

The opening of Japanese hostilities against China in July 1937 launched the Second World War and made a future clash with the United States and Britain virtually inevitable. By December that same year Japanese forces had captured some of the most important ports and cities, including Shanghai and Nanjing. A million Chinese citizens were now under occupation.

Western leaders failed to perceive the real significance of this conflict. They saw it as a minor episode, a relatively harmless extension of Japan's continuing occupation of Manchuria since September 1931. The conquest of Manchuria had clearly violated the charter of the League of Nations, but Churchill was strongly opposed to any retaliatory action. He saw Japan as a bulwark of order in the Far East that might deter Soviet expansionism in the region and prevent the breakup of China. On 17 February 1933 he spoke to the far-right Anti-Socialist and Anti-Communist Union, a gathering of kooks and extremists: 'I do not think that the League of Nations would be well-advised to have a quarrel with Japan ... I hope we shall try in England to understand a little the position of Japan, an ancient state, with the highest sense of national honour and patriotism.'[1]

A few weeks later he emphasised this view further, comparing the Japanese occupation of Manchuria to British rule in India: 'It is in the interests of the whole world that law and order should be established in Northern China.' International law could be flouted with impunity so long as there was no threat to British economic interests. Appeasement? Without any doubt.

Churchill had never taken the Japanese threat seriously. In the late 1920s he declared there was not the 'slightest chance' of war with Japan in his lifetime. He only saw Japan as a threat when it was already too late. Prior to that, Britain had viewed the Japanese as a strategic partner that might be helpful in negotiating the shifting balance of power in Asia. From 1902 till 1922, the two island monarchies were staunch allies. Japan had fought with the Entente in the First World War. When the time came to renew Britain's treaty with Japan, the Foreign Office was nervous. Churchill argued that not to renew it could well be regarded as a hostile act.

The dilemma was supposedly resolved at the Washington Conference in 1922, when the United States, Britain and Japan signed a multilateral agreement to cooperate in order 'to promote arms control and international stability in Asia'. The Japanese leaders took this as a green light to prepare for something they had

---

1   Quoted in Clive Ponting, *Churchill*, London, 1994, pp. 359–60.

long desired: the occupation and punishment of China and the removal of the British Empire in Asia.

Churchill had refused to believe, partially for racial reasons, that Singapore was under any threat from Japan. Five years after the Japanese, with Churchill's verbal support, began the conquest of China, his beloved Singapore fell with the humiliating surrender of the British Army.

During the interwar years, Japan was still an underestimated global player. Treated by Western imperial powers with a mixture of condescension, racism and outright contempt, Japanese politicians fell into a parallel trap. They overestimated themselves. From their point of view, the naval battle in which they defeated Tsarist Russia in 1905 was the greatest such battle in modern history. It's not every day that the entire fleet put out to sea by a major Western imperial power is destroyed in the course of an afternoon. The capable strategist behind this triumph was Marshal Admiral Tōgō Heihachirō, who had trained as a naval cadet in Britain for seven years (1871–78). He hero-worshipped Nelson and was thrilled when the Anglo press later described him as 'the Nelson of the East'.

He was less pleased by other aspects of everyday life in Britain. He belonged to a respected samurai family, was an ardent Japanese nationalist, and did not appreciate his fellow cadets at Dartmouth addressing him as 'Johnny Chinaman'. After the 1905 triumph he became a revered figure, second only to the emperor. After his death, the attack on Pearl Harbor was modelled on his tactics against Russia.

Tōgō's victory was part of a larger plan. Japan wanted to be a dominant power in Asia. Observing the British occupation of India and the US dominance of South America via military interventions, Japanese military and court thinkers asked: if them, why not us? But how had Japan risen so rapidly? In the case of Germany, also a latecomer to the imperial world, its rise could be directly observed and the kaiser and the king of England were first cousins. In contrast, Japan was invisible for reasons of geography and race.

On the eve of the First World War, East Asia had become the fulcrum of an inter-imperial struggle. Till their military defeat, the Chinese Qing dynasty had been regarded as the dominant politico-military-cultural force in the region. No longer. While the West never colonised China directly, by 1914 they owned most of the country's economy. Aware who their future rivals would be, the Japanese nonetheless fought alongside the Entente powers against the German-led alliance. As Europe recovered from the disaster, there was a shift of global interest eastwards, with both the United States and Japan inspecting the prizes before the final match.

In Korea in the late nineteenth century, the Japanese pro-consul had instituted a set of bourgeois reforms with the signed approval of the king and prime minister. As historians have stressed, these were by no means insignificant:

> 208 separate laws were from the end of 1894 endorsed by the king: class distinctions, slavery, the exam system, even the clothes Koreans wore, even the long pipes that symbolised yangban status, were abolished ... new and stable coinage circulated, new tax laws unified the extraction system ... the practice of punishing whole families for the transgression of individual criminals came to an end. No more would the high officials ride in sedan chairs, hustled along by several groaning wretches ... for Koreans who had groaned under the yoke of an aristocracy that, as it neared total collapse, seemed only to exact more privilege for itself, the reforms were a welcome antidote.[2]

Japan now formally incorporated Korea as a colony on the European model, and added Sakhalin island and the Russian concessions in Manchuria to their list of imperial properties in the region.

The US president Theodore Roosevelt wondered whether Japan's 1905 victory over Russia 'may possibly mean a struggle between them and us in the future'. Meanwhile in Russia itself, revolutionaries and not a few bourgeois liberals rejoiced at the defeat of their own autocracy. Lenin spelt out his views in some detail. Japan was a modern bourgeois state, more progressive than the Russian autocracy:

---

2 Bruce Cumings, *Korea's Place in the Sun: A Modern History*, New York, 2005, pp. 120–1.

Progressive, advanced Asia has struck an irreparable blow against reactionary and backward Europe ... The criticism of the autocracy formulated by all advanced Russians, by the Russian Social-Democracy, by the Russian proletariat, is now confirmed by the criticism of Japanese arms ...

The war of an advanced country with a backward country has once again played a great revolutionary role, as has happened many times in history. And the class-conscious proletariat, resolute enemy of war, which is the inevitable result of all class rule, cannot conceal from itself this revolutionary work that has been accomplished by the Japanese bourgeoisie in its victory over the autocracy. The proletariat is hostile to every bourgeoisie ... but this hostility does not relieve it of the necessity of distinguishing between the representatives of a bourgeoisie that is playing a progressive role or a reactionary role in history.[3]

Japanese successes in colonisation and occupation ended all doubts in London. A new island-empire had been born. Britain moved rapidly to conclude an alliance with Japan. Other powers upgraded their legations in Tokyo to full embassies. Tensions between Japan and its Entente allies first emerged before, during and after the First World War, but they were mainly expressions of nervousness at the sight of a non-white imperial power behaving as an equal.

By the late 1930s, however, Japan's chessboard moves in the region had begun to seriously concern the West. Writing in 1938, Churchill insisted that Japanese insolence on the global stage needed to be kept under strict watch, especially in China:

Several unpleasant things have happened. British policemen in the International Settlement of Shanghai have been punched and manhandled by Japanese soldiers in a manner which shows a deep-seated hatred towards white people. Japanese apologies for sinking the American gunboat *Panay* and killing considerable numbers of

---

3 V. I. Lenin, 'The Fall of Port Arthur', *Vperyod*, No. 2, 14 January 1905.

American citizens have not carried conviction either to the Government or to the people of the United States. A Japanese Admiral, by name Suetsugu, of whom the world had not previously heard, has declared himself in favour of driving the white race out of the Far East, and immediately after this declaration this Admiral has acquired a controlling position in making Japanese plans.[4]

The world had not yet heard too many Japanese names. Nor had Churchill. The last sentence quoted was false. Nobumasa Suetsugu, together with more senior admirals – Kato, Ogasawara and, especially, Tōgō – had since 1922 formed the core of a naval lobby that was extremely unhappy with the post–First World War order dominated by the Western victors. They opposed disarmament and insisted that Japan desperately needed to upgrade with a fleet of submarines and a naval air force.

Churchill's pique regarding race was amusing in the circumstances. So much anger at being treated in the same way by the Japanese as the Western powers had treated – and continue to treat – Asians, Africans and indigenous tribes in the Americas. He even complained that the Chinese were receiving better treatment than the 'non-yellow races, and in particular and unhappily, the British and Americans'.

This was patently untrue, but what angered Churchill most was the existence of a sovereign, independent and imperialist Japan. Hence the characteristic, patronising Churchillian whinge:

All this is too bad, because it was the British and Americans who cordially fostered and aided for many years the modernisation of Japan. No nations in the civilized world have watched with so much practical sympathy the great advances that Japan has made in the

---

4 Winston Churchill, *Step by Step: Political Writings, 1936–1939*, London, 2015 [1939], p. 145. One might add that the Japanese apology, however perfunctory, was at least offered. In contrast, Churchill's admirer Margaret Thatcher refused to apologise for the gratuitous sinking of the Argentine light cruiser, the *General Belgrano*, in 1982, during the Malvinas/Falklands war. The vessel had been moving away from the warzone.

last fifty years. Certainly no other governments have done so much to befriend Japan or have yielded themselves more readily to the hope that Western science and knowledge would be in this case a unifying force between Japan and her world companions.[5]

Emperor Hirohito or a minion might easily have retorted that, since Western science and knowledge was not a unifying force in the West, why should it be so with Japan? The reason Hirohito was preparing to enter into an alliance with the Axis powers was not because ultra-nationalist secret societies now controlled his army and navy, but because Germany and Italy had no colonies in East or South Asia. Britain was the most powerful colonial power in the region, and the United States was a dominant player. The Pacific was not yet an American sea, but was en route to becoming so.

In 1924, a Japanese officer, Lieutenant Colonel Hashimoto Kingoro, had proposed in his book *Addresses to Young Men* what needed to be done to move Japan forward. I doubt whether Churchill knew of this text but, as a fellow islander, he would surely have sympathised with the argument stated with such force and without civilisational adornments:

> There are only three ways left to Japan to escape from the pressures of surplus population . . . emigration, advance into world markets and expansion of territory. The first door, emigration, has been barred to us by the anti-Japanese immigration policies of other countries. The second door is being pushed shut by tariff barriers and the abrogation of commercial treaties. What should Japan do when two of the three doors have been closed against her?

Other Japanese militarists asked why their country should be satisfied with 142,270 square miles to feed 60 million people while British colonies like Australia and Canada had more than 3 million square miles to feed 6.5 million mouths each. There was a deadly imperialist logic in Japan's decision to take China and destroy British properties in Asia in order to push back their major rival in

---

5   Ibid.

the Pacific, the United States. They had not decided on the exact order for the latter part of their plan. Which is why the Second World War began with the Japanese invasion of China proper on 7 July 1937 (and ended in Japan on 6 August 1945 when the bomb dropped on Hiroshima). From Asia it spread to Europe, before returning home with Japan's reckless, if not totally irrational, attack on Pearl Harbor on 7 December 1941.

The invasion of China was not simply a matter of an island-kingdom challenging a decaying continental empire on its own. The imperial leaders in Tokyo assumed that they could take China while their Axis allies, primarily Germany, conquered Europe and planted the swastika on the Kremlin. Hitler and Hirohito had even planned a victory summit in Vladivostok.

Had all this gone according to plan, the United States would have been in a weak position and an isolationist current might have swept through the country, forcing Washington to sign a peace treaty. Hirohito, his warlords and the imperial bureaucracy had decided that the conquest of China was desirable, achievable and economically necessary. If the British had taken and pillaged India, why should Japan stay out of China? In terms of imperialist immoralities there was no reason why, in their drive to become a global power, they should behave any differently from their rivals.

They knew full well that China had never been eaten whole throughout its 3,000 years of recorded history. The Chinese state was the oldest and most continuous in the world. On previous occasions the Celestial Kingdom had suffered blows in the North. The Great Wall had been penetrated. But peace treaties, the birth of the Yuan Empire and regular intermarriages between the Mongol princesses and the Han nobility had produced a hybrid elite and helped enlarge the size of the imperial gene pool. All this had helped resolve, temporarily, some of its problems.[6]

Chinese civilisation had dominated the region. Its religions, its

---

6 Mark Elvin's *The Pattern of the Chinese Past*, Stanford, 1973, remains the finest social and economic history of China in English. The ideas in it grew from the stimuli Elvin received at the Department of Economic History at Glasgow University from early 1968 onwards.

rites and rituals, its principal language, its calligraphy, its literature, had influenced Japanese culture as well. Much more so than
the ultra-nationalists liked to acknowledge. All that, now, lay in
the past. The Japanese conquest would be a complete oedipal take-
over: economic, political and military.

Like so many major conflicts (the assassination in Sarajevo
unleashing a European civil war in 1914 comes to mind), this one
emerged from an unplanned encounter: a clash in July 1937 between
Japanese and Chinese soldiers on the Marco Polo Bridge, some
thirty kilometres south of Beijing. Tokyo ordered the conflict to be
rapidly resolved by local officers on the spot, but exchanges of fire
and some loss of life carried on for three days. Officers on the ground
on both sides secured an armistice, ensuring a three-week respite.

In Tokyo, however, it was decided not to let an opportunity like
this go to waste. Hirohito cut short his vacation and returned to
the capital. The hawks insisted that the Chinese nationalist government was seriously misbehaving, and that its refusal to accept the
legal independence of the conquered territory, Manchukuo, and
subsequent violations in the demilitarised zone separating it from
Northern China, had only increased tensions.

There was only one permanent solution: to treat the recent incident as a serious provocation and mount an immediate counter-
attack 'to defend Japanese lives and property'. The hawks had few
doubts regarding the Japanese military's ability to rapidly inflict a
crushing defeat on the Chinese and establish suzerainty over the
whole country. This view was strongly supported by the Japanese
Army in Manchukuo and by the South Manchurian Railway
Company, in which Hirohito's extended family were deeply invested.

More senior and less rabid officers in the General Staff advised
caution. Generals Ishiwara and Torashiro had been concerned by
another clash, this one between Japanese troops and Soviet Red
Army units on Kanchazu Island in the Amur River. Two Soviet
gunboats had been destroyed. The generals warned of a possible
Soviet counter-offensive and opposed the despatch of more troops
to Northern China. The emperor temporarily backed this view,
expressing dissatisfaction with those in his entourage who were
backing the expansionists.

However, after further discussions, Prime Minister Konoe and his Cabinet performed a volte-face and voted unanimously in favour of sending more troops to Northern China. One of Konoe's principal advisers on China was the journalist and scholar Ozaki Hotsumi, who had been recruited to work for Soviet military intelligence by Richard Sorge, now well settled in Tokyo. The decision to send troops to China was indirectly influenced by both these men as well, reducing the military pressure on the Soviet Union.

The Republic of China

The 1911 upheaval in China led to the overthrow of the decaying, rotten-ripe Qing Dynasty, the declaration of a republic, and the elevation of a prominent nationalist democrat, Dr Sun Yat-sen, who had long fought on both a literary and a military level against the Qing. He denounced the seventeenth-century Manchu takeover of China as a huge national tragedy, and himself converted to Christianity as a way to break with the dead past of his own country. The nation's politics had radicalised during Sun Yat-sen's years of exile in Japan, leading to the disintegration of the Chinese state and of the Qing dynasty it had sustained for over three centuries.

It was not easy to dismantle the old state, however. Everything was in a complete mess. At its head, the monarchy had fatally wounded itself with its total incapacity to move forward, making it increasingly dependent on the British Empire. In truth, the Opium Wars, Elgin's barbaric decision to torch the Summer Palace, the Taiping rebellion, the Muslim rebellion and the creation of a fiercely anti-Qing, anti-Manchu Islamic Sultanate in Yunnan had made the Qing dynasty disposable.

Sun Yat-sen spent most of his time in party-building. To him must go the enormous credit of having founded the first serious political party in modern China. The Guomindang (GMD) started life as a staunchly republican, nationalist offering. During its early years it was an umbrella for all those who wanted to move the country forward. It received an enormous impetus from the May

Fourth movement launched by Beijing students in 1919, a great democratic cultural revolution that blamed the country's rotting culture for all the sins that were then on display.[7] The argument may have lacked sophistication, but its importance as a stimulus to further radical intervention should not be underestimated. From this mighty politico-cultural movement that erupted two years after the Russian Revolution there emerged a shoal of intellectuals – Lu Xun and Chen Duxiu among the most prominent – whose essays and debates in both written and spoken form enlightened an entire generation.

This process also laid the basis for the formation of the Chinese Communist Party (CCP) in 1921. In Moscow, the Comintern leaders, excited by the turn of events in China and intent on creating a united front against the imperialist powers, engaged in an attempt to unite all anti-imperialist and anti-warlord forces. They had some success. Having been denied support by the West, Sun Yat-sen turned to the Soviet Union and agreed to work with the CCP. The First United Front was formed in 1924, and both parties worked together to form the National Revolutionary Army (NRA). Their aim was to rout the warlords who had created their own armed principalities in different parts of the country, end the chaos, and unify the country. The Whampoa Military Academy was created, with Soviet advisers brought in to help train the cadres of the new army. Many of the communist and nationalist military leaders were students of the academy, which gave lectures on strategy and tactics, one of which concentrated on the recently concluded civil war in the Soviet Union.

Sun Yat-sen's death from cancer in March 1925 marked a turning point, something that Moscow failed to appreciate. Growing tensions between the right-wing of the GMD – led by Sun Yat-sen's brother-in-law, Chiang Kai-shek – and the CCP were ignored. The left-wing faction of the GMD (which included Sun Yat-sen's widow, Soong Ching-ling) was not as powerful. The Chinese

---

7   See Rebecca E. Karl, *China's Revolutions in the Modern World: A Brief Interpretive History*, London, 2020, which contains a stimulating chapter on the May Fourth movement.

communists, very much under Moscow's influence, complied with a suicidal Comintern instruction that, despite all the difficulties, they should remain allied to the GMD. The horrendous costs of following this instruction paved the way for Mao Zedong's hegemonic grip on the party and a change of strategy.

It was by now obvious to most Chinese leaders that the United Front was no longer viable. Ferocious GMD repression of CCP organisations took place in April 1927 in Shanghai and, three years later, Guangzhou. A Comintern observer witnessed the disarming and dismantling of the peasant organisation, carried out by landlords with GMD backing, but did nothing. Mao Zedong, who since 1924 had been assigned by his party to work full-time at the Peasant Movement Training Institute, also observed the disaster, and was angered by the inactivity of the Comintern. He left the Institute and moved on to work with the peasant movement in Hunan in defiance of Stalin's instructions.[8] His text, 'An Investigation of the Peasant Movement in Hunan', soon became a classic of the Chinese revolutionary movement, analysing the class divisions within the peasantry and refusing to treat the bulk of the rural population (a huge majority of the country) as an undifferentiated mass.

There were communist successes, however. In Shanghai the CCP defeated the warlord army controlling the city, leading in 1927 to the birth of the Shanghai Commune, a beacon for other Chinese cities. Then the inevitable happened. After only six weeks Chiang Kai-shek turned on the communists and GMD militias attacked the Commune on 12 April. The ensuing bloodbath was memorialised in André Malraux's powerful 1933 novel, *Man's Fate*. One of the main communist leaders, Zhou Enlai (the first post-revolution prime minister of China), was portrayed sympathetically as Kyo Gisors. The novel was the first literary recognition in Europe that Asia was playing an important role in world politics. Malraux depicted the highs and lows of the struggle, the suffering, the crushed hopes and the final defeat. What was striking was the enormous respect Malraux exhibited for the Chinese Communist

8 Ibid., pp. 72–4.

Party, its activists and the workers who flocked to participate in and defend the Commune.[9]

The Chinese civil war, inaugurated by the Shanghai massacre and the simultaneous executions of at least 10,000 communists in several other cities, lasted for a decade. The GMD, now on the payroll of rural landlords and urban capitalists, was on the ascendant. Fierce debates inside the CCP after the April 12 incident slowly led to a change in outlook. The communists had lost the cities, and a strong fascist grouping in the GMD – the Blueshirts, specialised in targeted killings and massacres – had gained the upper hand. The decimation of the Changsha Soviet by the GMD in 1934-5 forced a decision.

Where possible the CCP went underground. The Long March to Yanan was the outcome of a huge defeat, but Mao Zedong had won the argument. Reality triumphed over 'theory' or 'bookism', as Mao referred to various left-wing dogmas at the time. Meanwhile, the GMD was recognised as the official government by the West and the Soviet Union. The Red base established in Yanan was ignored. In Moscow, Stalin had concluded that the CCP could never win.

The idea that the post-Sun Yat-sen GMD represented a democratic alternative to the CCP is belied by the facts. While most mainstream assessments today, Rebecca Karl informs us, 'positively evaluate the GMD's efforts at modernising state and society, a small number of scholars has broken with this formalism to emphasise the

---

9 The novel attracted a cluster of serious filmmakers. Eisenstein came close to filming a version at the time. In the 1980s, Bernardo Bertolucci wanted to adapt it, but the Chinese government expressed a preference for the second project on his list, which became the Hollywood spectacular *The Last Emperor*, not his best work by any means. Michael Cimino was also attracted by its epic character, but he died while making notes on the project. Malraux himself, in his Gaullist reincarnation, was slightly embarrassed by the novel, insisting that it was a depiction of 'lived experience' rather than an expression of support for the Chinese Revolution. Given that he didn't spend that long in Shanghai, this remark puzzled some of his former friends.

fascist ideological bases of GMD practices'.[10] The conservatives and the Blueshirts were determined to wipe their own slate clean of anything that smacked of socialism. Sun Yat-sen's heirs, with Chiang Kai-shek in the lead, would concentrate on a 'conservative revolution', in other words on the institutionalisation of an authoritarian state based on a defence of existing class privileges. Sun Yat-sen's widow refused to accept this view and was far more sympathetic to the Chinese communists.

What might or might not have happened in China had Hirohito refused to authorise the transformation of the country into a Japanese occupation zone is still debated in academic circles. What is indisputable is that Japan's war on China altered the political landscape. Chiang Kai-shek famously stated that the Japanese occupation was a disease that could be cured, whereas the CCP was a 'cancer that had to be rooted out'. By adopting this approach, the GMD lost China. Its incapacity to defend its people led eventually to mass desertions from the GMD to the communist armies. Some saw the beginnings of this in the GMD's early failure to resist the Japanese attack on Nanjing, ordered by Hirohito and designed to inflict a defeat of such magnitude that China would no longer resist.

The Nanjing Massacre

On the morning of 13 December 1937, barely a month after they had taken Shanghai, Japanese tanks entered Nanjing and General Matsui's army took the city. There was no resistance. The GMD government had decided to retreat. The rich and well-off had followed in their wake. The poor were left to their fate. What followed was six weeks of pure horror. Without doubt this was one of the worst crimes of the Second World War, and yet one will find scarcely a reference to it in the 1,065 pages of Churchill's *Memoirs of the Second World War*, published in 1959, or in the French historian Henri Michel's 947-page classic account, *La Seconde Guerre Mondiale*, published in 1975. American war

---

10 Karl, *China's Revolutions*, p. 75.

historians are marginally better. In one case a single mention, in another case a paragraph.

What explains the amnesia? Not simply Eurocentrism, but the Cold War and the post-war drive to integrate Japan at all levels: moral, political, economic, military and monarchical. To acknowledge what happened at Nanjing would have led to questions being asked as to why the Allies had preserved Hirohito and his throne. The stubborn refusal of the Japanese government to admit to the scale of the crime is also linked to Hirohito. To this day, Sino-Japanese relations remain enveloped by the dark shadows of this atrocity.

The most informative account in English appeared in 1997: *The Rape of Nanking* by Iris Chang. As a young girl, Chang had first heard stories about Nanjing from her parents, both academics who left China for Taiwan after the Revolution. The facts are now not disputed by most historians, other than the nationalist variety in Japan. Chang writes of what happened after the city fell in December 1937:

Japanese soldiers began an orgy of cruelty seldom if ever matched in world history. Tens of thousands of young men were rounded up and herded to the outer areas of the city, where they were mowed down by machine guns, used for bayonet practice, or soaked with gasoline and burned alive . . . Years later experts at the International Military Tribunal of the Far East (IMTFE) estimated that more than 260,000 non-combatants died at the hands of Japanese soldiers at Nanjing in late 1937 and early 1938, though some experts have placed the figure at well over 350,000.[11]

11 Iris Chang, *The Rape of Nanking*, New York, 1997, p. 4. Chang uncovered so much about the massacre that it affected her own mental health. Promoting her book in numerous locations, and recounting the horrors, was an extremely painful experience, almost as if she was living through it herself. She became suicidal and finally took her own life on 9 November 2004. She was thirty-six years old. In one of three suicide notes, she wrote: 'I can never shake my belief that I was being recruited, and later persecuted, by forces more powerful than I could have imagined. Whether it was the CIA or some other organisation I will never know. As long as I am alive these forces will never stop hounding me.'

Chang's descriptions of the mass rapes carried out by Japanese soldiers are unbearable. She does not exaggerate. Over the six weeks after the occupation, at least 1,000 women of all ages were mass-raped every single day. Those who helped save lives were in the European quarter. Ironically, the head of the German Association in Nanjing, John Rabe, was also the leader of the expatriate Nazi Party. Chang describes him as the 'Nazi Schindler' who allowed as many local people to take refuge as was possible. His diaries record his shock and outrage. He complained politely to the Japanese authorities who, even more politely, ignored him. He finally reported directly to Hitler:

> They would continue by raping the women and girls and killing anything and anyone that offered any resistance, attempted to run away from them or simply happened to be in the wrong place at the wrong time. There were girls under the age of 8 and women over the age of 70 who were raped and then, in the most brutal way possible, knocked down and beat up. We found corpses of women on beer glasses and others who had been lanced by bamboo shoots. I saw the victims with my own eyes – I talked to some of them right before their deaths and had their bodies brought to the morgue at the Kulo hospital so that I could be personally convinced that all of these reports had touched on the truth.[12]

Having been a historical footnote for so long, Nanjing now appears to be the centre of a state-created historical memory of the occupation years. It helps to create a post-Mao national unity in China by relegating the civil war and the 1949 revolution that emerged from it to the national museum.[13]

12 Quoted in ibid., p. 119.
13 The upgrading of the Nanjing massacre has also led to the recovery of a lost novel, *Nanjing*, completed in 1939, the result of two months intensive labour by the poet and literary critic Ah Long (*Nanjing xueji*, Beijing, 1987, untranslated). See Michael Berry, 'The Lost Novel of the Nanjing Massacre', in David Der-wei Wang (ed.), *A New Literary History of China*, Harvard, 2017. For an account of Hu Feng and his victimisation by Maoist bigots, there is a moving account by his widow, Mei Zhi, *F: Hu Feng's Prison Years*, trans. Gregor Benton, London, 2013.

Iris Chang's account, dismissed by some as exaggerated, received strong confirmation from Herbert Bix, who quotes from standing orders to military units that specified the killing of all prisoners, civilian and military, and the burning of houses. There were no specific orders to 'rape' Nanjing, but after the city fell the Japanese soldiers went 'on an unprecedented and unplanned rampage of arson, pillage, murder and rape. The resulting slaughter continued in the city and its six adjacent rural villages for three months.'[14]

Hirohito's Crimes

The assault on Nanjing was led by Hirohito's fifty-year-old uncle, Prince Asaka, who was the senior-most officer at the height of the massacres and rapes. There is no basis whatsoever for whitewashing the emperor. He presided over meetings at the imperial headquarters throughout the war. All major operations required his assent. It was Hirohito who had insisted on the rapid conquest of China using 'shock and awe' methods. The continuing attempt to defend him, with far-right thugs still trying to disable or kill his critics, ignores the central role he played in the attempt to build the Japanese Empire.

Short of stature, given to nervous twitches, shrill-voiced, near-sighted, tense, and never at ease in his body, Hirohito was not exactly the cloaked replica of a traditional samurai. Worshipped as a divinity by the ignorant, even they might have recoiled at the thought of him leading them to war in military uniform, which never suited him as it had done the kaiser, the tsar or the king-emperor. But he was more intelligent than all of them. He was also

---

14   Herbert Bix, *Hirohito and the Making of Modern Japan*, New York, 2000, p. 333. Two decades after it was published, Bix's portrayal of Hirohito remains unmatched. It is strongly recommended to Churchill fans, since it was the Japanese emperor's decision to destroy the British and French Empires in Asia. After the fall of Singapore that Churchill had predicted would never happen, the writing on the wall was inscribed in Japanese characters.

strong-willed and, more than anything else, he wanted to reign and rule.

Unlike his grandfather, the Meiji emperor, who had indulged his prodigious appetites on every level, Hirohito put self-discipline above sexual or culinary pleasures. His life was frugal and strictly regulated. His education was dominated by militarism. The most capable admirals and generals would arrive at the palace to give him lectures on American theories of sea power and the use of infantry. That was what he enjoyed most, but it did not exempt him from the more tedious stuff, such as economics or constitutional and international law (which he needed to learn in order to understand what aspects could later be violated). Experts on Western history, diplomacy and political philosophy, race and imperialism completed his education.

He was thrilled when he was nineteen years of age to be given command of company-sized units of the Imperial Guard. A trench was dug inside the palace compound enabling him to practise using a machine-gun. After his succession to the throne seven years later, he was rarely out of uniform. The bizarre enthronement ceremonies organised by the palace elite carried on for a year, climaxing in the secret ritual of his deification – an 'awe-inspiring mystery' as the ultra-loyal press and newly established national radio had it – consummating his symbolic marriage to his progenitor, the sun goddess Amaterasu Omikami, while lying in the foetal position, wrapped in a quilt, on the sacred *shinza* bed.

In power, as Bix demonstrates, Hirohito was the more than willing 'active agent' of his and the ruling elites' interests, 'neither an arch-conspirator nor a dictator but a leading participant' in the major political and military events of his reign: 'Like a silent spider positioned at the centre of a wide, multisided web, Hirohito spread his filaments into every organ of state and the army and navy, absorbing – and remembering – information provided by others.'[15] For the court elite, 'constitutional monarchy' was simply a protective cover that enabled the emperor to rule while remaining unaccountable.

---

15 Ibid., p. 179.

Bix portrays Hirohito as a devious, clever politician, and skilfully charts every shift and turn. We see how, from 1926 onwards, Hirohito and his close advisers began a succession of anti-democratic initiatives to strengthen the *kokutai* – the emperor-based polity – and impose an aggressive, militarist-chauvinist nationalism from above, characterised by mass arrests, forced recantations and executions.

A coercive conformism was imposed on the press and intellectual life as well. The target of these divine measures were communists, workers and peasant activists. Hirohito's prerogative of *tosuiken* – the autonomy of supreme command – was never surrendered to anyone. Slightly nervous about Western condemnations of the invasion of Manchuria, he was gleeful and triumphalist at the Kwantung Army's success. His refusal to criticise the criminal depredations of his young officers in China encouraged them to even worse excesses, in the name of 'divine Japan'. After the Nanjing rapes and killing, a mass toast to the emperor was proposed by soldiers and officers, while General Matsui rode on horseback, followed by his infantry, through empty streets in Nanjing. A thoughtful Prince Asaka had ordered that everyone living in the vicinity of the victory march be slaughtered just as a precaution.

As the conflict developed into a full-scale war, Hirohito was involved in decision-making on a daily basis, authorising, inter alia, the use of poison gas, and 'signing off' on the campaigns against guerrilla bases that became known as the *sanko*, or the three 'alls': kill all, burn all, loot all. Bix argues with conviction that Hirohito was a 'real war leader' who 'carefully examined and sanctioned the policies, strategies and orders for waging wars of aggression'.

Occupation and Civil War in China

In China, the incapacity of the GMD to defend either Shanghai or Nanjing, preferring to flee rather than fight, left a deep mark on Chinese national consciousness. If the 'nationalist' party and government had failed so dismally, was there any possibility of salvation? The 1937 Japanese invasion had forced the GMD and the CCP to agree a United Front once again and cast their differences aside till the Japanese were forced out of the country.

Konoe's attempts to win over Chiang Kai-shek by insisting that the Japanese were only in China to drive out the Western powers and wipe out the communists could not and did not succeed, though some Blueshirts in the GMD did begin a period of open collaboration with Tokyo. Even if Chiang had been tempted, he knew full well that open collaboration would only strengthen the CCP.

The GMD and CCP fought separately against the Japanese, but as the US generals Hurley and Marshall noted and reported back to the White House, the communist armies were better led, more reliable, politically motivated and had a rapport with the people. The GMD forces were lazy, corrupt to the core and often unreliable. The CCP leadership were adepts at understanding and using the grand narrative supplied by their country's history. The historian Gregor Benton, whose classic work on the Chinese Red Army's tactics from 1934 to 1938 is the most detailed study of this period, is insistent that the Red Army survived 'because it took [the ancient military philosopher] Sunzi's precepts to heart while its opponents in Chiang Kai-shek's military academies ignored them'.[16] As a result, while Chiang's forces had overwhelming superiority in numbers, their tortoise-like advances and lengthy stationary periods added to the predictability of their moves.

The CCP's military strategy, though underplayed by many official historians, was as crucial as the Long March in preserving the remnants of defeated party-army units that would two years later act in unison under a single military-political high command,

---

16 Gregor Benton, *Mountain Fires: The Red Army's Three-Year War in South China, 1934–1938*, Berkeley, 1992, p. 19. The dramatic story of the Chinese Communists in southern and central China, long hidden in the shadow of the Long March, has been brilliantly reconstructed in this 700-page history, using oral interviews, legends, letters, documents and local archives to show how they survived terrible isolation and the repressive GMD counter-revolution. It's a story confined to a region, but it enriches the 'grand narrative'.

confronting the Japanese and taking full advantage of the truce agreed with the GMD.

In Tokyo in 1941, the emperor was about to make a final decision that would determine his own country's future and that of China. There was a sharp difference of opinion within the Japanese political and military elites as to whether it was time to launch a war against the United States. The military was pushing for a time limit on diplomacy. The US sanctions against Japan had irritated even those who did not want to extend the war, but Prime Minister Konoe, constitutionally the only adviser permitted to Hirohito, opposed any new war. The militarists, however, were stubborn.

Drawing on the scholarship of a new generation of Japanese historians, as well as palace documents and the memoirs and diaries of aides and chamberlains, Herbert Bix details the emperor's intimate involvement in the planning of Pearl Harbor. From the beginning of November 1941, Hirohito engaged in intense discussions with his high command, cross-questioning chiefs of staff over minute details in their daily briefings, and fussing obsessively over the exact wording of the war rescript. On 8 December (Tokyo time) he received the first reports of the attack at 2.30 a.m., and from then on was in constant meetings. His naval aide Jo Eiichiro noted in his diary: 'Throughout the day the emperor wore his naval uniform and seemed to be in a splendid mood.'

One of the documents uncovered by Bix was a verbatim report of the crucial imperial conference on 5 September, where the views of the 550 BCE Chinese military philosopher Sunzi were once again brought into play:

ADMIRAL NAGANO: If Your Majesty will grant me permission, I
    would like to make a statement.
EMPEROR: Go ahead.
NAGANO: There is no 100 per cent probability of victory for the
    troops stationed there ... Sunzi says that in war between states of
    similar strength, it is very difficult to calculate victory. Assume,
    however, there is a sick person and we leave him alone; he will defi-
    nitely die. But if the doctor's diagnosis offers a seventy per cent

chance of survival, provided the patient is operated on, then don't you think one must try surgery? And if, after the surgery, the patient dies, one must say that was meant to be. This indeed is the situation we face today.

EMPEROR: All right, I understand. [He answered in a better mood.]

KONOE: Shall I make changes in tomorrow's agenda? How would you like me to go about it?

EMPEROR: There is no need to change anything.

Reminded by his prime minister that it was not too late to reverse the decision or to delay it, Hirohito refused. The next day, as the Imperial Conference continued, the main item on the agenda was the finalisation of the exact date for the strike. The documentation prepared for the emperor by General Sugiyama made it very clear that the United States could not be overpowered militarily, and therefore it was difficult to predict when the war would end. It would be a protracted struggle. The first step would be to smash the British Empire in South and South-East Asia, thus taking Britain effectively out of the war. This would 'produce a great transformation in American public opinion', meaning that 'a favourable conclusion to the war is not necessarily beyond hope'.

Sugiyama and the high command had agreed on a plan whose success depended on taking over British, French and Dutch colonies in South and East Asia for both strategic and economic reasons. Simultaneously, 'we shall work with Germany and Italy to break up the unity of the United States and Britain'. This would put Japan in an impregnable position, since it 'would see us link up Europe and Asia, guiding the situation to our advantage'. Success here and 'we might see a hope of coming out of the war at least even with the United States'.[17]

On the third day of the conference, Hirohito expressed a real concern that the Soviet Union might attack from the north, and insisted that a three-pronged war would be extremely difficult to sustain. His generals reassured him on this question. Winter was

17 Bix, *Hirohito*, pp. 410–13.

not far away and, leaving all other considerations aside, the Red Army was not crazy enough to despatch its divisions in deep snow.

Meanwhile, diplomatic exchanges with the United States were continuing. Prince Konoe had indicated to Washington that he was prepared to meet President Roosevelt on a ship in neutral waters, for an urgent summit to resolve all major issues. Hirohito agreed to an early October time limit for the negotiations. He quoted to his chiefs of staff a famous *tanka*, written by the Meiji emperor expressing concern on the eve of the 1905 Russo-Japanese war: 'Across the four seas all are brothers. / In such a world why do the waves rage, the winds roar?'

On hearing this, the chiefs of staff feigned humility and promised to give peace a chance. Hirohito still gave them permission to mobilise for the offensive in the south, but wanted reassurance. He asked the chief of the general staff: 'But if the Konoe–Roosevelt talks go well, you'll stop, won't you?' The response: 'Indeed, your majesty, we will.' Few believed that the United States would agree to the talks. They didn't. The principal proponent and strategist of the new war, Admiral Yamamoto, visited Konoe a few days later and tried to calm him down: 'I don't know about the army, but as you try and adjust diplomatic relations [with the United States] you don't have to worry about the navy. The coming war will be protracted and dirty, and I don't intend to sit idle on the flagship neglecting my duty.'

Both men still assumed that a summit with Roosevelt was possible, and Konoe asked what he should do if they were in the middle of the talks and the attack was launched. Yamamoto advised deception: 'If the talks at sea break down, don't assume a defiant attitude. Depart leaving everything vague. And the fleet will take action while you are *en route* home.'

Konoe, convinced that the die was cast, resigned four days later. Whereas earlier he had strongly favoured the Germans and defended the Axis powers, now he became convinced that Germany would lose and that a Japanese victory was improbable. He genuinely wanted a deal with Roosevelt to safeguard Japan's future interests. But he had lost the confidence of Hirohito, not to mention the pro-Axis leaders of the armed forces.

The war minister, Hideki Tojo, was desperate for Konoe to get out and let the rest of them complete the job. Konoe's departing advice to the emperor was that Prince Higashikuni be appointed his successor. Hirohito refused and appointed Tojo instead, a clear signal, if any was needed, that he wanted a warrior to run the war. He was close to Tojo throughout the war, bad-mouthing Konoe for lacking 'firm beliefs and courage'.[18]

At further meetings in November, the emperor became totally convinced of the need to fight the United States and intervened on every level, including supervising and checking the details of the war rescript that would be distributed when they launched the attack. A scholar of Chinese classics at the court had drafted the document. Its essence was clear: 'For its existence and self-defence', the Kingdom of Japan was preparing to obliterate Anglo-American imperialism in Asia.

On Sunday/Monday (in Japan) 8 December 1941, Hirohito gave the signal for the attack on Pearl Harbor. Tojo's 'War of Great East Asia' had begun. Five and a half months prior, on 22 June 1941, Hitler's armies and air force had launched Operation Barbarossa, the invasion of the Soviet Union. These two events would, within a few years, lead to the crushing defeat and humiliation of the Axis powers, but not before Japanese barbers had exposed the bald patches of the European empires.

The fall of Singapore in February 1942 – to a Japanese army half the size of Britain's 'impregnable fortress' – was the most devastating blow inflicted on the British Empire in the Asian war. A year prior, British code-breakers had intercepted Hitler's message to the Japanese foreign minister, Yousuke Matsuoka. The German leader insisted that the Japanese assault Singapore and take Malaya. He was convinced that this would be a body blow from which Britain would not be able to recover. Churchill complacently believed that Singapore could not be taken. The British

---

18   After the war, Prince Konoe, who had tried to stop the attack on Pearl Harbor and favoured a withdrawal from China, was arrested as a possible war criminal. The emperor remained untouched, courtesy of General MacArthur and the United States.

naval base was strong and well prepared. The forests in the hinter-land were impenetrable. How could the 'little Japs' cross them? He declared that Singapore was the 'Gibraltar of the Far East', a slightly absurd analogy, given that it was only Franco's neutrality vis-à-vis the British and the Americans that had prevented the fall of Gibraltar. In the event, the naval dockyards were captured by the Japanese. How could Churchill have imagined that a naval base with hardly any warships (most of them were in the Middle East) could defend itself. And before long the 'little Japs' had swept through the forests as well. On 15 February 1942 the British Army surrendered and 90,000 men were taken prisoner. Churchill blamed the local commanders, but the underestimation of Japan was his own responsibility. This defeat marked the beginning of the end for the British Empire, regardless of Japan's ultimate fate.

9

The War in Europe: From Munich to Stalingrad

The golden fruits
Of Stalingrad's toil:
Peace, contentment, highest honor.
And behind every window
Rustles news
About our joyous future.

Anna Akhmatova, 'The Victory' (May 1944)

A long night slowly enveloped Europe after the fascist triumphs in Italy, Germany and Spain. All that democratic Europe's ruling classes could see, however, was false dawns. Self-deception was widespread. In an entry on 6 July 1938, the conservative diarist Harold Nicolson noted:

> Chamberlain (who has the mind and manner of a clothes brush) aims only at assuring temporary peace at the price of ultimate defeat … We have lost our will-power, since our will-power is divided. People of the governing classes think only of their own fortunes, which means hatred of the Reds. This creates a perfectly artificial but at present most effective secret bond between ourselves and Hitler. Our class interests, on both sides, cut across our national interests. I go to bed in gloom.

What must have depressed him was that, a few months earlier, Churchill himself had refused to reject the idea of doing a deal with

Hitler. At the Conservative Party Conference at Scarborough in October 1937, he went out of his way to declare his full support for the foreign policy of the Chamberlain government. There had been differences in the past on rearmament, but these had been amicably resolved, so, Churchill advised, 'let us indeed support the foreign policy of our Government, which commands the trust, comprehension and the comradeship of peace-loving and law-respecting nations in all parts of the world'. The following week he informed his readers in the *Evening Standard*: 'War is NOT imminent'.

Leaving aside the politicians, nobody auditing British industry would have guessed that hostilities with the Germans were only a few years away. Close trade ties and foreign exchange negotiations remained in full flow. During one of his table talks in 1938, after the invasion of Czechoslovakia, Hitler was reported to have said that 'in a direct conversation conducted in German with a decent and straightforward Englishman, he would have no great difficulty in finding a satisfactory settlement for existing issues'.[1] The German ambassador in London, Herbert Dirksen, made not-so-discreet-inquiries and suggested a list of people who might be suitable for a meeting with Hitler, a list that included R. A. B. Butler. Not much came of this particular initiative, but economic appeasement continued regardless till the summer of 1939.[2]

A combination of ignorance – the failure to understand the nature of fascism – and a ferocious class hostility to the Soviet Union typified the mindset of many conservatives and not a few leaders and supporters of the Labour movement. In the case of the latter there was an additional factor: the tormented collective memory of the First World War. That horrendous experience had affected most working-class families. The maimed and the traumatised were still alive in numerous households.

The horror of that war lay at the roots of British pacifism,

---

1 *Documents and Materials Relating to the Eve of the Second World War, Vol. II, Dirksen Papers*, Moscow, 1948, p. 178.

2 Martin Gilbert and Richard Gott, *The Appeasers*, London, 1963, Chapter 14, contains detailed accounts of the economic collaboration that continued till just before the European war commenced.

typified by the Peace Pledge Union and a hostility to rearmament, let alone a new war. Tory and Labour politicians were aware of this fact. Chamberlain's appeasement of the fascist dictator was not seen as such by many, till the *Anschluss* and the occupation of Czechoslovakia began to concentrate minds. Popular support for the prime minister's attempt to negotiate with Hitler began to decline only after the summer of 1939. He was perceived as someone trying to stop a new war, and Hitler's constant invocations of 'peace' continued to deceive some. Within the Conservative Party, Chamberlain remained hugely popular even after his resignation and replacement by Churchill in 1940.

But it had become clear that German rearmament was proceeding apace. Hitler, like his admirers in Japan, was also in search of an imperial backyard. German political theorists sympathetic to the new nationalism made no bones about saying as much in public. The Monroe Doctrine became a universal model: if South America was the strongly patrolled and economically dominated backyard of the United States and its corporations – an arrangement designed to keep its European rivals at bay and decided unilaterally by President Monroe in 1823 – why should the Germans not take Europe, or the Japanese abstain from imperial activity in China and South-East Asia? To each power its own backyard.

After the Munich agreement between Germany and Britain in 1938, which agreed yet more concessions to Hitler (including Czechoslovakia), divisions continued in the British Parliament. The difference between the appeasers and Churchill lay in what Nicolson had already noted. Chamberlain, Halifax and the businessmen supporting them thought that the class interests of those who ruled Britain, and of those on whose behalf they did so, would be best served by doing a deal with the German upstart. Churchill realised a short time before the others that Britain had to keep up with the Germans on the rearmament front, if not as preparation for war, then at the very least to maintain the pressure in negotiations.

By 1939 he had realised that what was really at stake was the British Empire and British sovereignty. For that reason, he wanted to offer a carrot, but with the stick clearly visible. The Germans had let it be known that they wanted their old colonies back, and the British were not opposed to this if it was part of a larger settlement. Both sides preferred that the Soviet Union be defeated first, something that was in the perceived interests of both the fascist dictatorships and the capitalist democracies, i.e. France and Britain.

That was not to be. The Germans correctly understood that a premature attack on the Bolshevik fortress, before a proper hinterland had been acquired, could backfire. In 1936 Soviet military strength was overwhelming compared to that of Germany. Contrary to popular legend, at no point did the Wehrmacht possess military superiority over the Red Army on the frontier. On the contrary, the Soviet superiority was staggering: seven to one in tanks, with 24,600 in readiness against 3,500 Panzers; four to one in planes.

In the Soviet war games carried out in 1936, Marshal Tukhachevsky was placed in command of the 'German party'. John Erickson, the foremost historian of the Red Army, describes how Tukhachevsky's strategy and tactics predicted with astonishing accuracy the lines of the actual German attack in June 1941. Tukhachevsky demonstrated how the Red Army could easily be outflanked with a 'surprise blow' in the first-wave attack. Erickson describes what happened next:

> At this point, Marshal of the Soviet Union Yegorov, Chief of the General Staff, intervened. As director of the war-game, he proposed a different notion, based on the preliminary mobilisation of the 'Red Party' . . . Tukhachevskii's proposals . . . 'met powerful opposition were rejected in their entirety' . . . Stripped of any strategic acuity, the war-game represented nothing but a frontal, meeting engagement in the form of the frontier battles of 1914 – of indecisive outcome. Tukhachevskii was 'deeply disillusioned'.[3]

Tukhachevsky refused to be silenced. In early 1937, he gave his last lecture at the General Staff Academy, determined to correct what he regarded as serious flaws in the thinking of Yegorov and other top commanders, as well as rebuke General Isserson for his over-optimism in which the 'peal of victory' drowned all else:

---

3   John Erickson, *The Road to Stalingrad*, London, 1975, p. 3.

Operations will be inestimably more intensive and severe than in the First World War. Then, frontier battles in France lasted for two to three days. Now, such an offensive operation in the initial period can last for weeks. As for the Blitzkrieg which is so propagandised by the Germans, this is directed towards an enemy who doesn't want to and won't fight it out. If the Germans meet an opponent who stands up and fights and takes the offensive himself, that would give a different aspect to things. The struggle would be bitter and protracted; by its very nature it would induce great fluctuations in the front on this or that side and in great depth. In the final resort, all would depend on who had the greater moral fibre and who at the close of the operations disposed of operational reserves in depth.[4]

Six months later, in June 1937, Stalin and his underlings decided to purge the top ranks of the Red Army. Tukhachevsky together with Generals Uborevich, Yakir, Primakov, Putna and Edleman were accused of 'treason' and executed. The following year, Marshal Yegorov, who had argued with Tukhachevsky in the war games, disappeared, reported dead. Marshal Blyukher, commander of the Soviet forces in the Far East, was executed in November 1938. General Vatzetis, a senior commanding officer during the civil war, was arrested in the interval between his lecture and the questions at the Frunze Military Academy.

'The decimations', writes Erickson, 'snaked back into past enmities; Tukhachevsky himself had incurred the hatred of Stalin in 1920.' A combination of blunders, vanity and jealousy on the part of Stalin and Marshal Voroshilov had led to a serious setback in the Russo-Polish war of 1919–21. In his reports to Lenin and Trotsky, the Marshal had been diplomatic in his use of language. It was well-known that most of the Red Army high command regarded Stalin's crony Voroshilov with total contempt. The 'incompetent, mediocre, bungler' now got his revenge.

---

4 Quoted in ibid., p. 5. Three years later the high command of the French Army didn't want to, and didn't, fight the Germans, thus enhancing the myth of German invincibility.

It is difficult to estimate which helped Hitler more: the continuous British appeasement after 1933 or Stalin's decision to have the most gifted Red Army leaders shot in 1937–8. What is virtually indisputable is that the old Soviet high command would have surprised the Germans, seen them off much earlier, shortened the war and saved millions of lives.

In Germany itself, the Third Reich was fully aware that there remained strong pockets of communist and social-democratic support within the working class and throughout the country. A defeat or a series of military setbacks in the Soviet Union might puncture German nationalism. Much safer, they thought, to take Western Europe first, utilise its resources to build German strength, and save the big beast for later. What about the 'world-island' in Northern Europe? The Germans would have preferred a Quisling monarchy, with the Duke of Windsor restored to the throne and the British Empire neutralised from its centre by Germany and destroyed on its periphery by Japan.

Hitler's decision to create a European union from above, by force, was unacceptable to London and Paris. Britain had assembled a counter-revolutionary bloc to resist Napoleon's attempt to take Europe, and 1815 had settled the debate. Could it repeat that triumph again with hardly an ally left in Europe? Chamberlain, the French prime minister Daladier and their supporters had gone too far in appeasing the Germans. They had to be stopped, Churchill argued, before the situation became completely untenable. This position was, roughly, the same as that adopted by the Labour Party, which provided Churchill with support in Parliament. Unlike Churchill, the Labour leader Clement Attlee and his party had supported the Republican side in the Spanish Civil War, and Attlee himself had dusted down and donned his old First World War army uniform to pay a visit to the International Brigades fighting on the battlefront. After the war Attlee turned back anti-fascist Spanish refugees.

Failure of Appeasement, and the Hitler–Stalin Pact

Things had been going incredibly well for Berlin, so much so that they were surprised by the decision of the British and French

governments to make Poland the *casus belli*. It was this that necessitated a rushed and temporary alliance with Stalin, giving the
Russians sovereignty over half of Poland as a bribe, while the
Germans sorted out Europe. Stalin, as we shall see, took the pact
much more seriously than did his German counterpart. Senior
Soviet generals, intelligence agents and diplomats were extremely
sceptical, justifying it only as offering some badly needed breath-
ing-space to fully prepare the USSR for war.

Churchill's role in the year leading up to September 1939 and
during the war years has been written about at such length and in
such detail that it barely needs summarising. He was the only serious ruling-class politician who understood by late 1938 that a failure to resist the Third Reich would lead to disaster, first for the
British Empire and then for Europe. This was not yet the view of
the Conservative Party, or of Geoffrey Dawson, the editor at *The
Times*. Lord Rothermere (a fascist sympathiser) ensured that his
newspaper, the *Daily Mail*, propagated the same appeasement
views in more extreme fashion. The excitement on the government
benches in the House of Commons, when news finally came that
the Führer had agreed to a 'peace' summit with Chamberlain and
invited him to Munich, is best described by a participant:

My eyes stole up to Mrs Fitzroy's gallery and I saw Mrs Chamberlain
listening intently. A lovely figure sitting by her made me a gesture of
recognition and half-waved; it was the Duchess of Kent. Behind her
was a dark, black figure, and I looked again and recognised Queen
Mary, who never before in my recollection has been to the House of
Commons . . .

[Chamberlain's] great speech continued for an hour . . . magnifi-
cently the Prime Minister led up to his peroration, but before he got
to it, I suddenly saw the FO officials in the box signaling frantically
to me; I could not get to them as it meant climbing over 20 PPS's, so
Dunglass [the future Sir Alec Douglas-Home] fetched a bit of paper
from them which he handed to Sir John Simon [foreign secretary]
who glanced at it . . . and excitedly tugged at the PM's coat;
Chamberlain turned from the box on which he was leaning, and
there was a second's consultation. 'Shall I tell them?' I heard him

whisper. 'Yes', Simon, Sam Hoare and David Margesson all nodded . . .

The PM . . . told how he had telegraphed both Hitler and Mussolini this morning; he had sought Mussolini's eleventh-hour help and intervention, and how the *Duce* had not let him down, but acted promptly. How foolish the anti-Italians now looked, and Anthony Eden's face – I watched it – twitched, and he seemed discomfited . . . and then the PM played his trump ace and read the message . . .

'That is not all. I have something further to say to the House', and he told how Hitler had invited him to Munich tomorrow morning, that Mussolini had accepted the same invitation . . . every heart throbbed and there was born in many, in me, at least, a gratitude, an admiration for the PM which will be eternal. I felt sick with enthusiasm, longed to clutch him – he continued for a word or two and then the House rose and in a scene of riotous delight, cheered, bellowed their approval . . . Peace must now be saved and with it the world.[5]

Churchill had long argued that fascism was fine, more or less, as long as it used its strength and popular support to combat Bolshevism on every front at home and abroad. He had, as described in a previous chapter, supported Franco and, by extension, the Italian and German intervention in the Spanish Civil War to ensure victory. Was there ever a doubt in his mind? Did he really think it might end in Spain? Did nobody point out to

---

5 *'Chips': The Diaries of Sir Henry Channon*, London, 1967, pp. 170–1. To get an idea of what many in the British ruling class, both the royals and the princes of industry, actually thought of Churchill and Hitler, I cannot recommend too strongly Sir Henry Channon's Diaries, an indispensable social history of the upper classes of that period. I have quoted from them earlier, though a few choice entries were deleted by an early editor, Robert Rhodes James. One of them is a crucial note on the day Churchill became prime minister. The censored sentences describe a sad gathering of appeasers at the club. After a reflective silence, 'Rab [Butler] remarked: "We now have a half-breed as a Prime Minister."' The reference was to Churchill's white American mother. It would take the war and the Cold War before the pure-blooded realised that they were all now political half-breeds.

him that the Germans and Italians were using Spain as a test run for a wider war? If so, there is no evidence of it in his writings of the period, only the expression of a pious hope that Spain itself might unite under the victors of the war: Franco and the Catholic Church. The Popular Front government in France offered moral support to the Republic but opted for non-intervention.

Britain and France had sacrificed Czechoslovakia: the Munich Agreement was signed in September 1938 and violated by Hitler in March 1939. The Czech government surrendered. Five months later, on 1 September, the Germans marched into Poland, which boasted the fourth largest army in Europe. The symbolic resistance was courageous – cavalry against tanks – but ineffective. Polish nationalism crumbled. The German high command, genuinely surprised by the speed with which they had swallowed three countries whole, began to take the Corporal more seriously. When he informed them that the next target was France, they did not flinch. When he further pointed out that he would be in effective charge of the operation, they nodded their approval. Since it was France, there were a few old scores to be settled.

Would the Maginot Line hold? The French were not over-confident and their military leadership was politically divided. In a letter to his wife, de Gaulle had described Munich as a 'capitulation that will give us a short respite, like the aged Madame du Barry on the revolutionary scaffold begging, *"Encore un petit moment, M. le bourreau"*.'[6] France's military strategy was essentially defensive, and they could do nothing after Poland fell except wait for the German attack. Here too, de Gaulle was prescient. Writing to his close friend and political ally, Paul Renaud, a month after war had been declared, he argued that Germany would demoralise France psychologically by making them wait, knowing full well how depressing inertia can be for an army. 'In my humble opinion', he suggested, 'there is nothing more urgent and necessary than to galvanise the

---

6 Julian Jackson, *A Certain Idea of France: The Life of Charles de Gaulle*, London, 2018, Chapter 5.

French people instead of comforting them with absurd illusions of defensive security.'[7]

I doubt whether by 'galvanising the people' he meant arming them and training them to resist, but that was what was needed, and it would have been extremely useful during the Vichy years when France was a German protectorate. The Resistance did emerge, but later. The British had despatched a strong Expeditionary Force to help shore up French defences in 1939. It was too early then to visualise or predict the speed with which a total catastrophe might occur and envelop the country.

Wehrmacht commanders had delayed the invasion of France (to Hitler's great irritation) by insisting that Norway had to be occupied first. Its 15,000 miles of coastline rendered it vulnerable. The British Navy had already imposed a blockade, cutting off North Sea access to the Scandinavian peninsula. This threatened the flow of Swedish iron and ore supplies that were essential for German munition industries and the rearmament programme. Two phone calls from Berlin, and Denmark was occupied in the course of a weekend. Sweden's Socialist government rapidly affirmed its neutrality. The Norwegians fought back vigorously but were overwhelmed. A British submarine transported the king, his family and courtiers to London.[8]

In 1940, as the Panzer divisions assembled on the borders of France and Belgium, disorganisation in the French military was complete and irremediable. But this was not just a technical or strategic deficiency. France was politically divided. The 1936 Popular Front government under Léon Blum had been attacked for being the French version of the 'Bolshevik–Jewish conspiracy'. Many on the conservative right, hostile to Jews and communists alike, were mildly or strongly sympathetic to fascism. This included a majority of French military leaders. It was their refusal to inspire and lead their forces that led to an early French capitulation.

---

7 Ibid.

8 The Norwegian resistance fought back much more effectively against the German war machine than did several of its European counterparts.

Few could imagine that Britain would survive the fall of France, and nobody believed that with the whole of Europe under the iron heel of Germany, the Americans would intervene. In that critical year, the choice for most people on the right (in Europe as a whole) was not Hitler or Churchill, but rather Hitler or Stalin, and (like Churchill on Spain) they had no doubt on this score. It is this that helps explains the lack of a unified will to resist. The French communists had paralysed themselves by remaining silent as the German armies poured in. This stemmed from a blind loyalty to Moscow, where the Nazi–Soviet Non-Aggression Pact had been in force since 23 August 1939.

Hitler, who took over direct command of the French operation, was himself surprised by the speed with which the Maginot Line collapsed. After all, the Allies had 144 divisions, three more than the Germans, and a huge advantage in terms of artillery and tanks. They had fewer fighter planes, but overall they could have resisted. It was the moral and political collapse of the French high command, rather then technology, that led to the defeat.

The course of events was straightforward. On 10 May 1940, the Belgian and Dutch ambassadors in Berlin were summoned to the foreign ministry, where Ribbentrop informed them that their countries would soon be occupied and they should bid farewell to their sovereignties. The Dutch prevaricated. Four days later the Luftwaffe bombed Rotterdam, killing 800 civilians. The next morning, the Dutch surrendered. Their Queen fled to London. Belgium was taken a fortnight later, and then came the fall of France. Hitler and his generals received the French surrender in the same train compartment in which the Germans had surrendered in 1918. The Führer pranced and hopped around for the benefit of the German press. Revenge for the humiliating Treaty of Versailles was now complete. The rapid victory in France did more to enhance Hitler's reputation than any other single event of the war. He was, Goebbels announced, 'in utter bliss after his grandiose triumphs'. For the next few years, the generals would rarely question his military decisions. But the political and military leaders of the Third Reich would look back with regret at their strategic error in not finishing off the British when the opportunity was there.

The French people had awaited the invasion with a mixture of indifference and fear, eerily recalling the mood that had existed in 1814, a year before Waterloo, as recorded by Henri Houssaye in his book, *1814*:

> The invasion terrified the population, but France cast down did not have a tremor of revolt. The metaphysical idea of the violated homeland which had in '92 [1792] ... such a powerful action on a nation young and rejuvenated by liberty, that idea did not did not arouse a people aged by war, weary of sacrifices and avid of rest. The brutal and material fact of foreign occupation with its adjunct of evils, requisitions, pillage and assaults, murder and incendiarism were needed to awaken the anger and hatred.

The 'metaphysical idea' was Saint-Just's remark, 'The fatherland is the centre of honour.' Too much blood had flowed down the Seine for that to be effective in 1940. Many hardcore French nationalists were included in the Vichy government. De Gaulle's followers were a small minority.

For Churchill and his generals, the big question after the fall of France was how best to get British troops out and back home as soon as possible. Here the Germans were helpful. The advance made by General Heinz Guderian – the leading German strategist on tank warfare and a proponent of *blitzkrieg* – had been relentless, until to his great annoyance he was ordered by Hitler to stop. It was this fateful decision by the Führer that enabled Britain to rescue as many troops as they could by any means necessary.

The romantic image of little boats ferrying soldiers from one shore to another was useful propaganda, but it was the Royal Navy that brought most of them back. Stranded in France himself, as the Germans swiftly reached Boulogne and Calais, Harold Nicolson's nerves were on edge. He had managed to obtain a suicide pill in case he was captured. His diary entry for 1 June 1940 is terse but reflects the mood:

> We have now evacuated 220,000 men [in fact 370,000, a figure that included 110,000 French soldiers], which is amazing when I recall

how we feared we should lose 80%. But there are few grounds for enthusiasm really, except moral grounds. We have lost all our equipment. The French have lost 80% of their forces and feel that we deserted them. It will constitute a real problem to recreate good relations between the forces ... the French with their tendency to attribute blame to others will be certain to say we thought only of rescuing the BEF and let them down.[9]

Few historians doubt that, had the German advance not been unilaterally halted, a German occupation of the United Kingdom, Churchill or no Churchill, would have become a reality. There would have been no alternative in that case but to berth the Royal Navy in US ports as Roosevelt had suggested – an offer that a fuming Churchill had turned down.[10]

What lay behind Hitler's reasoning? Historians remain divided. The argument that the German Army was tired and over-stretched is unconvincing. No German general accepted this version, though Rundstedt was in cautious mode, perhaps recalling an old Prussian maxim: 'Man kann sich totsiegen!' ('You can triumph yourself to death!'). More likely, realising Hitler's reluctance, he simply told him what he wanted to hear.

The decision came from Hitler alone. It's difficult to believe that it was made purely on military grounds. The Führer had already annoyed his military leaders by interfering in operations already in motion. With German troops thirteen kilometres away from Dunkirk, he ordered them to stop. The German chief of staff, General Halder, expressed his anger in his diary: 'The tanks and

---

9 *The Harold Nicolson Diaries*, ed. Nigel Nicolson, London, 2004, p. 249. The French did attribute blame and they were correct in this case, since Churchill had promised Reynaud that 'equal sacrifices' would be made. Fifty thousand French soldiers guarded the perimeter at Dunkirk, while the British escaped. Strafing by the Luftwaffe was half-hearted, in accordance with Hitler's instructions.

10 In *Dunkirk, The Men they Left Behind* (London, 2008), the military historian, Sean Longden describes in moving detail the fate of the 40,000 British soldiers that Churchill left behind and who were forgotten till the end of the war.

military units are standing still, as if nailed to the spot between Bethune and Saint-Omer, after command from the highest level, and are not allowed to attack ... As things stand it will take weeks to clear out this pocket. It greatly damages our prestige and our further ambitions.' Whatever the reasons, Hitler's decision was political.

General Guderian was livid. As the leading war strategist he had amended Manstein's plan, attacked France on two fronts, and enabled a victory within six weeks. If the decision had been a military one, then Hitler would have been speaking with Halder and Guderian rather than Rundstedt, generally regarded within the German high command as a yes man. It was later claimed that Rundstedt had demanded a pause so that the infantry could catch up with the Panzers. This view is not fully convincing. It was a *post factum* explanation for Hitler's own mistake. The generals commanding the operation did not think they needed to wait for anyone to complete what was now little more than a mopping up operation.

Hitler's own explanation a few days later, when the magnitude of his error became obvious, may well have been concocted, but it contains more than a grain of truth. He informed his colleagues that the decision to halt the advance had indeed been political. Its aim had been to sign a peace treaty with Britain: 'The Army is the backbone of England and the Empire. If we destroy the invasion corps, the Empire would fall apart. Since we are neither willing nor able to take on its inheritance, we have to give the Empire a chance. My generals failed to understand this.'[11]

The only problem with this explanation is that, even if this was the motive, Hitler could have dictated his terms to a new government in Britain after Guderian had mopped up the British Expeditionary Force. Undoubtedly, the peace treaty envisaged would have been on the model he was about to propose to the French military leaders Weygand and Petain in France. Whatever else, most German military historians agree that this huge mistake cost Germany the war. Hitler's not-so-trusted old friend and

---

11   Volker Ullrich, *Hitler: Downfall 1939–45*, London, 2020, pp. 103–4.

deputy, the neurotic Rudolf Hess, flew over on a secret mission to Britain in 1941 to suggest a peace deal. When informed of this, Churchill snorted and returned to finish watching the Marx Brothers' antics on screen. His choice was correct.

Recently released documents make it clear that Britain had nothing to do with this trip. The initiative had come from Hess alone, a delusional figure in the Nazi hierarchy, whose action enraged Hitler. British intelligence was certainly aware of the letter sent on Hess's behalf to the Duke of Hamilton, suggesting a rendez-vous. He was not impeded as he flew over the Scottish coast, near the Duke's estate, but was picked up immediately after parachut-ing, interrogated at length and locked up. He claimed he had made the trip without informing anyone, a one-man peace mission. This turned out to be true.

On being told of the failed operation, an angry Hitler demanded an immediate investigation as to how Hess had been allowed near an airport, despite strict instructions to the contrary. He was well aware of the neurosis that afflicted Hess, who had developed a phobia: Germany could not and must not fight a war on two fronts, since that would lead to disaster. He considered peace with Britain to be essential as the Reich turned its attentions eastward with Operation Barbarossa. Having failed to persuade his own leader, he thought he'd try his luck with Churchill. In Berlin, Hitler ordered Goebbels to release an official press statement referring to the letter Hess had left behind for his leader. This letter, Goebbels said, revealed 'in its confused nature the unfortunate signs of a mental breakdown, giving rise to fears that Hess has become the victim of delusions'.

Operation Barbarossa

The Continent, with some exceptions in Eastern Europe, was now under German sovereignty. Britain would be dealt with later. Stalin had dismissed reports of an impending German invasion, even though they came from Soviet spies strategically placed in the German military and diplomatic apparatuses, as well as from US intelligence and Churchill. One of the top Soviet agents was

Richard Sorge, embedded in the German embassy in Tokyo. His reports were impeccable.

Sorge had quickly penetrated the German community of journalists and businessmen in Tokyo, and became a close friend of General Eugen Ott, appointed Germany's ambassador to Japan in 1938, and of his wife, Helma, who fell in love with Sorge. (Ott knew Sorge was sleeping with his wife, but seems to have tolerated it in the belief that women found Sorge irresistible.) It was in the ambassador's safe in the embassy that Sorge first discovered some details of Hitler's plans for Operation Barbarossa.

Sorge sent the information to Filipp Golikov, the military intelligence chief in Moscow, where Stalin had wiped out most of his opponents in the Bolshevik Party, including almost every member of the 1917 Central Committee. Golikov, a timeserver and a mediocrity by any standard, was in a state of permanent fright. Lieutenant Colonel Erwin Scholl, who was also stationed at the Tokyo embassy, returned from Berlin in May 1941. The news he brought back was sensational, and Ott wasted no time in sharing it with Sorge. On 31 May, Sorge cabled Golikov:

> Berlin informed Ott that the German attack will commence in the latter part of June. Ott 95 per cent certain that war will commence . . . Because of the existence of a powerful Red Army, Germany has no possibility to widen the sphere of war in Africa and has to maintain a large army in Eastern Europe. In order to eliminate all the dangers from the USSR side, Germany has to drive off the Red Army as soon as possible.[12]

Ott had provided the barest of outlines, but Scholl provided Sorge with the information in full: 170–180 mechanised divisions were already close to the Soviet border, and the assault itself would encompass the entire front. The German general staff had few doubts that the Red Army would collapse, and that the Wehrmacht would take Moscow, Leningrad and Kiev. They would then take

---

12 Owen Matthews, *An Impeccable Spy: Richard Sorge, Stalin's Master Agent*, London, 2019.

control of the Trans-Siberian railway and establish direct contact with the Japanese forces in Manchuria.

Stalin, still basking in the so-called triumph of the Nazi–Soviet Pact, refused to believe any of it. 'You can send your "source" . . . to his fucking mother,' he told Golikov. On the message itself he scribbled: 'Suspicious. To be listed with telegrams intended as provocations.'

Unlike the Germans, who saw the Non-Aggression Pact as necessary but temporary, Stalin had illusions that it might be lasting. Owen Matthews quotes from a 1966 interview with Marshal Zhukov, conducted by Lev Bezymensky, a Soviet historian and war veteran. In January 1941, Zhukov and others had warned Stalin of ominous German troop movements. Stalin wrote to Hitler, asking politely whether these reports were true. Hitler replied that they were, but he swore 'on my honour as a head of state that my troops are deployed . . . for other purposes. The territories of Western and Central Germany are subject to heavy English bombing and are easily observed from the air by the English. Therefore I found it necessary to move large contingents of troops to the east where they can secretly reorganise and rearm.' Stalin believed him.

Marshall Zhukov told an interviewer some decades after the war that by early June 1941 it was obvious to most of the high command that the Germans were preparing to invade. He had showed Stalin 'staff maps with the locations of enemy troops entered on them':

> A few days passed and Stalin called for me . . . he opened a case on his desk and took out several sheets of paper. 'Read', said Stalin . . . it was a letter from Stalin to Hitler in which he briefly outlined his concern over the German deployments . . . Stalin then said 'Here is the answer' . . . I cannot exactly reproduce Hitler's words. But this I do remember precisely: I read the 14 June issue of *Pravda* and in it, to my amazement, I discovered the same words I had read in Hitler's letter to Stalin.

It was Molotov who broke the news of the invasion to Soviet citizens. For a fortnight, Stalin made no public appearance. When he finally addressed the nation, his speech was leaden at the start, but improved as it went on, even if its ideology and language were reminiscent of 1812 rather than 1917. He pledged fierce resistance and a scorched-earth policy.

In the updated 2001 edition of *The Soviet High Command*, John Erickson makes clear that the Red Army's response was not a foregone conclusion:

> The system lived perpetually on a narrow knife-edge. How frighteningly narrow was brought home to me in a singular exchange with Chief Marshal of Artillery N. N. Voronov . . . Knowing he was present at the very centre of events during the early hours of Sunday, 22 June, I asked him for his interpretation. His final remark was quite astonishing. He said that at about 7.30 a.m. the high command had received encouraging news: the Red Army was fighting back. The worst nightmare had already been overcome. Red Army soldiers had gone to war, 'the system' had responded and would respond.[13]

On 22 June 1941, the German Army marched bravely to its graveyard. For the next four years, two of the most powerful armies in the world would be locked in combat from the Baltic to the Black Sea. Within a few weeks the Panzer divisions were occupying territory the same size as Germany. Morale was high. It was still summer. Stalin had released many imprisoned generals and senior officers who had been arrested but not felled in 1937–8. They went straight from prison to the front.

The Soviet Union bled profusely. The fate of the globe was hanging in the balance across the vast spaces of the USSR. Anxieties and hopes were attuned to the noises emanating from distant battlefields. Hope, fear and despair were now linked to the fighting that was turning the snow red on the frozen rivers of Russia. Might the losses suffered on the Vistula, the Spree, the Danube and the Seine be reversed on the Neva, the Volga, the Don and the Azov Sea? Nobody was yet sure. The Polish Marxist historian Isaac

---

13 John Erickson, *The Soviet High Command: A Military–Political History, 1918–41*, London, 2001, p. xx.

Deutscher, writing from his London exile in 1941, saw the war being transformed into a battle between revolution and counter-revolution:

Since 22 June 1941 the Russian Revolution has once again begun to forge unbreakable links with the European labour movement. These links are proving stronger than all the opportunistic manoeuvres of Soviet diplomacy in recent years. It was not the Russian Revolution that in September 1939 shared the torn body of Poland with German fascism. In those unhappy September days Russia had not shown her true revolutionary face – no revolution in history has yet taken on the shape of a jackal scrounging the battlefield. The face which was then turned towards the despairing worker and peasant was the totalitarian mask imposed by the post-revolutionary bureaucracy. Now history is stripping off that mask and revealing the Revolution's true countenance: bleeding but dignified, suffering but fighting on. Cruelly, but justly, history is putting an end to all cynical masquerades.

What is left of those congratulatory telegrams in which the Kremlin spoke high-sounding words about 'the Russo-German friendship cemented by blood spilled in common'? How many other castles, built not so much in the air as on the wrongs done to nations, were to be 'cemented' by the wretched Kremlin architects? On the very eve of 22 June, Moscow was still trying to salvage its friendship with the arch-executioner of Europe by recognizing his occupation of Yugoslavia, Greece, and Norway. The shadow of total war was already darkening the German-Soviet boundary when communiques and denials, laboriously produced in the offices of the Narkomindel, tried to prove to an incredulous world that the giant concentration of German troops presented no danger to the Soviet Union, and that nothing had yet clouded the friendship between Berlin and Moscow. Ostriches hatched in eagle's nests were timorously burying their heads in diplomatic sands refusing to admit that a storm was imminent. But an approaching storm does not usually wait for the ostriches to trot out to confront it.[14]

14 Isaac Deutscher, '22 June 1941', *New Left Review*, I/124, November–December 1980.

1942: The Decisive Year

The First World War led to the collapse of three large empires and four royal dynasties: the Hapsburgs, Ottomans, Romanovs and Hohenzollerns. The remnants of their empires had been picked up by the British and French in the Middle East, new nation-states had been agreed by Woodrow Wilson in Europe, and the Russian Revolution had spread to many of the contiguous Tsarist colonies, which were willingly or unwillingly integrated into the Soviet Union.

In the Middle East, the British had created a mosaic of new states, modelled on what was happening in Europe. A 'line in the sand' created Iraq. British troops had occupied Kurdish cities – Mosul, Kirkuk and Suleimaniya. Syria was split apart. Contemporary Lebanon still remains in large measure the artificial creation of French colonialism it was at the outset – a coastal band of Greater Syria sliced off from its hinterland by Paris to form a regional client dominated by a Maronite minority that had long been France's catspaw in the eastern Mediterranean. Saudi Arabia was a British product, leased to Ibn Saud and family, with the literalist dogmas of the Wahhabis thrown in as the agreed ideological condiment.[15]

All this was under threat in 1942, as the German Army under Field Marshal Rommel moved closer and closer to British colonies. Churchill, as ever when imperial possessions were threatened, was extremely concerned. What he did not fully grasp, though he was not completely unaware of the possibility, was that even an Allied victory would not save the blood-drenched Empire. By now, beyond the stresses caused by the ongoing conflicts in Europe and in the East, it was a financially, politically and morally bankrupt enterprise. Nationalists in the Middle East – especially in Baghdad,

---

15 This sect regarded the rest of Islam as its enemy. It was quite relaxed about Western imperialism, with which it has happily collaborated for over a century. The Gulf statelets were at that time tiny fishing villages, for the most part, and all the British Empire needed to do was to pick a trusted family of servitors.

Cairo, Alexandria and Damascus – made no secret of the fact that they were hoping for a German victory.

The decomposition of the British Empire was not due to Japanese military advances alone. In the first months of 1942, Japan had taken Malaya, Singapore, Java, the Philippines and Burma. Hirohito and Tojo's armies had conquered these colonies with less than 200,000 men. In Singapore alone, as described earlier, the British Imperial Army had lost 140,000 soldiers, most of them as prisoners of war. The subjected peoples had chosen not to fight for the British, and Malaya had witnessed large-scale mutinies in the army. A mass uprising in Kedah had threatened the Sultan, who had been kidnapped by his own son, Tunku Abdul Rehman, who offered to collaborate with the Japanese and broadcast an appeal to the population not to resist the invaders.

Earlier, in 1940, Japan had occupied Indochina, with the collaboration of Vichy France. The latter continued to administer the colony, saving the Japanese a lot of problems. If any single example were needed to demonstrate the affinities of Axis fascism and European imperialism, it was provided by this experience of dual imperialism in Indochina from 1940 to 1945. It was also the only example outside China of an armed resistance by communists and some nationalist groups to Japan (more precisely, to the dual imperialism). Elsewhere, organised nationalists preferred to take the Japanese at face value or, at any rate, use them against long-established European empires: Ahmed Sukarno against the Dutch in Java; Subhas Chandra Bose and, indirectly, Gandhi against the British in India.

In North Africa, Rommel's panzer divisions had reached El-Alamein. A huge crowd gathered in Alexandria to chant 'Forward, Rommel, forward'. The Egyptian masses wanted a British defeat. The adage often used by imperial powers to justify uneasy alliances – 'the enemy of my enemy is my friend' – could also be deployed by its unwilling subjects.

The fall of Tobruk had exposed fissures in the British military high command. Twenty-five thousand British soldiers had been taken prisoner. Churchill mourned the loss and partially understood the cause. He later wrote:

This is one of the heaviest blows I can recall during the war. Not only were its military effects grievous, but it had affected the reputation of the British armies. At Singapore eighty-five thousand men had surrendered to inferior numbers of Japanese. Now in Tobruk a garrison of twenty-five thousand [actually 33,000] seasoned soldiers had laid down their arms to perhaps one-half of their number.[16]

In a personal letter to Churchill, the blundering General Claude Auchinleck apologised abjectly, if somewhat incoherently, and accepted full responsibility (as form dictated) for the disaster. He was duly sacked and sent eastwards. Sycophantic Indian officers would nurse the Auk's wounded ego and aid his recovery. But, in truth, the problem went much deeper than the mistakes of a single person.

The scale of the military debacles in Singapore and Tobruk angered many soldiers and citizens. At home, Churchill and his government were confronted with strong political opposition and a serious energy crisis. The military failures led to confrontation in the House of Commons, where the unofficial leader of the opposition, the Welsh Labour MP Aneurin Bevan, challenged both the conduct of the war and the outmoded class structures of the officer corps in the British Army. He taunted Churchill: 'Had Rommel been British, he would never have risen above the rank of sergeant.' Bevan pointed out the sad state of affairs where the 'staff colleges of the army have no textbook on the co-ordination of air and land forces'. He highlighted the presence in Britain of five or six Czech, Polish and French generals who were not being used in the war. Why? It might be hurtful 'to our pride', but they would do a better job than the 'inefficient' generals currently in charge. Gifted Englishmen were available as well. Bevan shone the torch on one such person, a veteran of the Spanish Civil War who had fought with some success against the side Churchill had supported:

There is a man in the British Army – and this shows how we are using our trained men – who flung 150,000 men across the Ebro in Spain, Michael Dunbar. He is at present a sergeant in an armoured

16 Winston Churchill, *The Hinge of Fate*, New York, 1950, pp. 343–4.

brigade in this country. He was Chief of Staff in Spain; he won the battle of the Ebro, and he is a sergeant in the British Army. The fact of the matter is that the British Army is ridden by class prejudice. You have got to change it and you will have to change it. If the House of Commons has not the guts to make the Government change it, events will . . . you have to purge the army at the top. It will have to be a drastic purge, because the spirit of the British Army has to be regained.[17]

The Member for Ebbw Vale had stirred a hornet's nest, but even those serving officers who stood up to reply were forced to admit the truth of some of the points he had made. Bevan could and should have reminded Parliament of an army it had once created, a new model army, whose captains and soldiers, clad in russet jackets, had transformed the shape of the country. The old ruling families they had defeated had regained their positions after the restoration of the monarchy and the House of Lords. The King's Army had been carefully reconstructed. Over the years, hereditary privileges and wealth had led to the purchase of commissions. The stink of privilege had even survived the trenches of the Great War. Bevan spoke for the voiceless, for the hundreds and thousands of soldiers who had to face this largely talentless hierarchy of saluting parrots every single day.

As for the energy crisis, it had arisen because war production was almost exclusively based on coal. Weekly average coal production had fallen by three-quarters of a million tons from 1939, and a further shortfall was predicted for 1943. The conditions in which the miners worked were appalling. And with good reason they did not trust politicians. Above all, they loathed Churchill. In other words, even in 1942, class hatred trumped national patriotism. A 1944 inspection by visiting technical experts from the United States confirmed that:

the centre of the [production] problem is the bad feeling and antago-nism which pervade the industry and which manifests itself in low

17   Aneurin Bevan in House of Commons Debate, 2 July 1942.

morale, non-co-operation and indifference. In almost every district we visited, miners' leaders and mine owners complained of men leaving the mines early, failure to clear the faces and voluntary absenteeism.[18]

Churchill, Attlee and Bevin (the so-called worker's leader in the Cabinet) decided with Cabinet backing to keep the report under covers. They informed Parliament it was a 'secret' document. This was a blatant lie. The reason given to the Cabinet was that the publication might promote 'anti-Americanism' in the country, if it were interpreted as an undesired American interference. This excuse is barely credible. The anti-Americanism that existed at this time was mainly confined to members of the ruling classes and sections of the Foreign Office. The only possible reason for suppressing the report must have been a fear that it might provoke a strike or, at any rate, increase class awareness. The government hurriedly set up their own Committee on the Coal Mining Industry. Its conclusions would not be too different, but were more moderately expressed.

Stalingrad

Meanwhile the most critical battle of the entire European war was about to begin on the banks of the Volga, outside Stalingrad (now Volgograd). Hitler had ordered the Sixth Army and the Fourth Panzer division to take the city whatever the cost. For extra support they had Romanian and Hungarian troops guarding the rear.

The city, then called Tsaritsyn, had seen tough battles during the civil war. In June 1919, Churchill had authorised a tank intervention by the British Expeditionary Force to aid General Denikin's White Army. Major Euan Cameron Bruce was awarded the DSO for his courage and audacity in the battle that led to the city being taken back from the Bolsheviks. The Whites were lucky. The Red military commander was the aforementioned Voroshilov, Stalin's crony, then the head of the Military Committee in the city. Serious

---

18   Quoted in Correlli Barnett, *The Audit of War: The Illusion and Reality of Britain as a Great Nation*, London, 1986, pp. 64–5.

misjudgements by Voroshilov, regarded by many of his contemporaries as a dunce, had led to the defeat. The White victory was temporary. Reinforcements from Moscow arrived and by January 1920 the city was taken back by the Red Army. Denikin's army came close to destruction and fled towards the Crimea, never to recover. In 1942, however, the enemy was stronger and more determined, its officer corps and soldiery poisoned with anti-Semitic and anti-Slav ideologies.

The Führer had wanted the war to be over by December 1941 at the latest, with Moscow captured and Leningrad starved to death, followed by the ceremonial destruction of the cities. Leningrad had to go, declared Hitler: 'This is the city where Bolshevism started, and in this city, Bolshevism will be utterly destroyed. This is the nemesis of history – harsh perhaps, but just.' Many on the European right would have agreed with him and joined in the celebrations. But the *blitzkrieg* failed. Unlike the French, the Red Army fought back.

Arming the people in Moscow and Leningrad helped to prevent the fall of the two key cities of the Revolution, and in Stalingrad and Kursk the Red Army broke the backbone of the Third Reich. Though the role of the Soviet air force should not be underestimated. Soviet bombers slowed down the advance of the Wehrmacht to Moscow.

In Stalingrad the battle lasted for over five months, and the tactics that had to be deployed were those that had been almost perfected by Trotsky and Tukhachevsky in the civil war two decades prior, as explained in detail by John Erickson in his three indispensable books on the Red Army. Stalingrad is not the only major battle of the war to have been commemorated in many books and several movies. They vary in quality. There is one written masterpiece: Vasily Grossman's novel *Life and Fate*.

Grossman was the war correspondent for the Red Army newspaper in Stalingrad throughout the battle, before moving on to Kursk. In his novel the city becomes an emblem for a country at war. There is chaos, blind obedience and a cohort of intellectually challenged officers and commissars. The citizens and the rank-and-file soldiery are the collective hero. Their courage can never be questioned. But in this they are not completely alone. There are also the officers and men who live in 'House No 6/1', for whom the author reveals a real sympathy, contradicting his own Tolstoyan philosophic ramblings elsewhere in the novel. The inhabitants of 6/1 fight because they possess independent minds and a fiercely critical spirit. Most are former members of the left opposition destroyed by Stalin. This is Grossman's homage to the prescient voices of the twenties and thirties. The Revolution speaks through them and others like them throughout the country. They tell us that without the freedom to discuss, criticise, think, write and suggest alternatives, there can be no socialism. During an interrogation by the Divisional Commissar, the least political inmate of 6/1 reveals:

> I can't make head or tail of what's going on in there ... they all seem terrified of this Grekov, but he just pretends to be one of the lads. They all go to sleep in a heap on the floor, Grekov included, and they call him Vanya. Forgive me for saying so, but it's more like some kind of Paris Commune than a military unit.

Even as the siege of Leningrad continued (it was to last 900 days), Hitler was attempting to reduce Stalingrad to rubble. After months of savage fighting, with German losses increasing every day and supply lines broken, Field Marshal Von Paulus refused to sacrifice any more German soldiers.

The Battle of Stalingrad had begun in summer on 23 August 1942. It ended in the depths of winter on 2 February 1943. The total casualties were estimated at 2 million, making it the fiercest battle of the Second World War. Hitler was enraged by the surrender. A field marshal, twenty-two generals and a quarter of a million soldiers, mainly German but also Italians, Spaniards, Hungarians and Romanians, were now Soviet prisoners of war. Moscow and Stalingrad were liberated. Leningrad would follow.

The German far right and the fascists had blamed the German Jews for their defeat in the First World War. There was nobody else to blame now. The master race had suffered a body blow at the hands of the *Untermensch* (including women soldiers and officers) and Jewish resistance groups in other parts of the country. When he first heard of the surrender, Hitler remarked to Goebbels that Paulus 'could have freed himself from all sorrow and ascended into eternity and national immortality, but he prefers to go to Moscow'. He did, and after the war he preferred to live in East Germany, only too aware of how many former Nazis had been integrated by the West into virtually every single structure of the Bundesrepublik.

Hitler never recovered from Stalingrad. According to Goering, it aged him fifteen years and he suffered a nervous breakdown, not showing himself in public for weeks. The German security service reported the public reactions to his first appearance on a newsreel after the Stalingrad defeat. He looked 'exhausted', 'tense' and 'aged'. But he was was still determined to carry on.

In an attempt to avenge the defeat at Stalingrad, the German high command agreed on Operation Citadel, a battle to defeat the Red Army on the Soviet salient around Kursk in western Russia. This time the Soviet forces were fully prepared on every level and morale was high. The German offensive was halted before it could seriously penetrate the Red Army defences. German losses were huge, and after three days Hitler called off the battle. It was the largest tank battle of the war. The Red Army had triumphed. Grossman's equivalent in another medium was Dmitri Shostakovich, whose Leningrad Symphony and astonishing string quartets were a homage to those who had held out in the grimmest of circumstances.

There would be no more German offensives in the Soviet Union, only defensive battles, followed by retreats. Even as Hitler was digesting the latest disasters from the Eastern Front, he was informed that a combined American-British advance had led to the occupation of western Sicily. The Italians, as expected, had retreated, and there was little doubt that the two Allied powers would soon be heading upwards to the mainland.

10

The Indian Cauldron

> Life: *enough of this poetry*
> *We need hard, harsh prose;*
> *Silence the poetry-softened noises;*
> *Strike with the stern hammer of prose today!*
> *No need for the tenderness of verse;*
> *Poetry: I give you leave of absence;*
> *In the realm of hunger, the world is prosaic*
> *The full moon is scalded bread.*

Sukanta Bhattacharya, 'Hey Mahajibon' (O, Great Life) (1944)

During the interwar period India was in a state of continuous turmoil. The reforms of 1919 – which had promised increased political participation of Indians in government but denied them power – were regarded by most Indians as ill-intentioned and offering very little. In Parliament in 1917, Edwin Montagu, the secretary of state for India, had declared 'the gradual development of self-governing institutions, with a view to the progressive realization of responsible government in India as an integral part of the British Empire'. The result was a build up of pressure from below.

The British Empire clearly faced a choice: it could grant India dominion status or it could rule largely through repression. The failure to grant the first necessitated the second.

The Pashtuns, Punjabis, Bengalis and Malabari (now Keralans) saw the rise of mass movements and terrorism on the pre-revolutionary Russian model. Peaceful marches were violently broken up by the police. The 1919 massacre in Jallianwala Bagh in Amritsar is the best known, but there were others. The Moplah peasant uprising in Malabar in 1924 was deliberately misinterpreted by Raj ideologues. The Chittagong Armoury Raid in April 1930 was an audacious attempt to seize police and auxiliaries' weapons and launch an armed uprising in Bengal. The raiders were revolutionaries of various sorts, united by the belief that only an armed struggle inspired by the Easter Rising of 1916 (they called themselves the IRA: Indian Republican Army) could rid them of the British. The plan was to take government and military officials hostage in the European Club where they hung out after work, seize the bank, release political prisoners, destroy the telegraph offices and telephone exchanges and cut off all railway communications.

They partially succeeded, but could not capture the British officers and civil servants. It was Good Friday. The European Club was empty. Despite this, the main leader of the uprising, Surya Sen, assembled their forces outside the police armoury, where he took the salute as IRA members (numbering under a hundred) paraded past him. They hoisted the Indian flag and declared a Provisional Revolutionary Government. The British swiftly took back control and guerrilla warfare ensued. The IRA was outnumbered. A traitor gave away Sen's hiding place. He was captured, tortured and, together with another comrade, hanged. Other prisoners were packed off to the Andaman Islands.

In Lahore, the capital of the Punjab, a twenty-two-year-old, Bhagat Singh, who hailed from a staunch anti-imperialist family, decided with a handful of supporters to carry out two missions in 1930. The aim of the first was to assassinate the British police officer who had badly beaten up the nationalist leader, Lala Lajpat Rai, at a demonstration in Lahore. But they shot the wrong police officer. The second was to throw a few bombs into the Central Legislative Assembly in Delhi when it was empty. Bhagat Singh declared they did so because they wanted the noise of the blast to wake up India.

In prison he became a communist and wrote that terrorist tactics were not useful, but he refused to plead for mercy. Gandhi half-heartedly spoke on his behalf to Lord Irwin, the liberal Viceroy, but was rebuffed. Bhagat Singh and two comrades, Sukhdev

Thapar and Shivaram Rajguru (all members of the tiny Hindustan Republican Socialist Party), were hanged in Lahore Jail in 1931.[1]

There were similar events on a lesser scale elsewhere, and peasant uprisings too, the largest of which, in modern Kerala, shook the landlords and their British protectors. The peasants were mainly poor Muslims. They were defeated and the leaders of the revolt despatched to the Andamans for fifteen years. In 1935, the British realised the seriousness of the situation and passed a second Government of India Act through the House of Commons.

Churchill was vehemently opposed to the new law but was out of office. The Act provided for a controlled provincial autonomy, with the governors in each province holding reserve powers to dismiss 'irresponsible' governments. The tiny franchise was somewhat enlarged, and in 1937 the dominant Congress Party virtually swept the board in provincial elections, with the crucial exceptions of the Punjab and Bengal where secular-conservative, landlord-run parties obtained majorities.

Within two years of these elections Britain was at war. The Congress leaders, astounded that they had not been consulted before India was dragged into the war, instructed all their provincial governments to resign in protest and refused to offer support for the war. All this confirmed Churchill's prejudices. He simply refused to grasp Indian realities.

The volume of protests and resistance from the end of the First World War till the late thirties had been rising with each passing year. Gandhi himself, in his South African phase, was a staunch Empire-loyalist. His view that 'the British Empire existed for the benefit of the world' neatly coincided with that of Churchill, and the Indian lawyer was not in the least embarrassed at acting as a recruiting sergeant during the First World War. He moderated these views when he returned to India and reinvented himself as a political deity. He was happy to mobilise the masses, but on a 'moral level'. He would leave statecraft to the politicians, mainly Nehru and Patel.

---

1   In yet another example of narrow-minded fanaticism, Pakistan's Islamic extremist parties have, till now, vetoed any monument in their memory to mark the spot.

Though when they needed his imprimatur during crisis times (Partition and the Indian occupation of Kashmir), he always obliged.

Gandhi's decision to make the Congress a mass party by appealing to the vast countryside had increased its size and political weight. In an overwhelmingly Hindu country, Gandhi had used religious symbols to mobilise the peasantry. This began to alienate Muslims, and since the Brahmins dominated the Congress leadership, the 'untouchables' knew their grievances would never get a hearing. Despite this, Gandhi, Patel and Nehru built a formidable political machine that covered the whole of India. The 1937 elections demonstrated as much, and it's worth pointing out that in the north-western frontier province bordering Afghanistan, the predominantly Muslim Pashtuns had voted for the Congress Party as well.

The decision to take India into the Second World War without consulting its only elected representatives was yet another avoidable error on London's part. The British underestimated the change in mood among the masses and some of their leaders. Had they consulted Gandhi and Nehru, offering them a fig-leaf to support the war, things might have panned out differently. The Congress leaders felt they had been treated shabbily and, after internal discussions that lasted a few months (revealing a strong anti-war faction led by the Bengali leader, Subhas Chandra Bose), they opted to quit office.

The British Viceroy immediately began to woo the Muslim League, and vice versa. The League's leader gave full-throated backing to the war as did the conservative pro-British elected governments in Punjab and Bengal.

When, on 22 December 1939, the Congress Party announced its decision to resign and did so a week later, Jinnah declared that henceforth 22 December should be celebrated as a 'day of deliverance' from Congress rule. Ambedkar, the 'Untouchables' leader, provided strong backing, saying he 'felt ashamed to have allowed [Jinnah] to steal a march over me and rob me of the language and the sentiment which I, more than Mr Jinnah, was entitled to use.' Surprisingly, Gandhi also sent his congratulations to Jinnah for 'lifting the Muslim League out of the communal rut and giving it a national character'. Little did he know where this would lead.

Emboldened by the emergence of an anti-Congress minority, the Viceroy, Lord Linlithgow expressed some optimism:

> In spite of the political crisis, India has not wavered in denunciation of the enemy in Europe, and has not failed to render all help needed in the prosecution of the war. The men required as recruits for the Army are forthcoming: assistance in money from the Princes and others continues to be offered: a great extension of India's effort in the field of supply is proceeding apace.[2]

With this in mind, Linlithgow was confident he could survive the storm. When the Congress ministers resigned en masse, the Viceroy ordered the arrest of its leaders and activists. They were released in December 1941 as the British attempted to reach some accommodation. Gandhi was carefully studying the development of the war in Europe as well as Japanese moves closer to the region, and wondering whether the British might be able to hold out. He was not yet sure. The local impact of Operation Barbarossa was the release of imprisoned Communist Party leaders and militants, who now came out openly in support for the war. Gandhi continued to wait. It was the humiliation inflicted on the British in Singapore in February 1942 that led to a change of course. The Congress leaders began to think about calling for a Quit India movement and, in this fashion, declared their own (partial if not complete) independence from the British. Gandhi had engineered Bose's isolation within the Congress, but he was very critical of Nehru's anti-Japanese militancy. Nehru had suggested that Congress should organise armed militias to fight against the Japanese were they to take India. Gandhi reprimanded him strongly. He should not forget that Japan was at war with Britain, not India.

In contrast to Gandhi's handwringing and delays, the Bengali Congress leader, Subhas Chandra Bose, always deeply hostile to the notion of offering any support to the British war, went on the offensive. Of the entire Congress high command, he was the most

---

2 Quoted in Srinath Raghavan, *India's War: The Making of Modern South Asia, 1939–1945*, London, 2016, p. 25.

radical nationalist. He began to work out a master plan that owed more to the organisers of the Chittagong Armoury Raid than to Gandhi. Bose did not believe that peaceful methods could prevail. They were fine at certain times, but the situation was now critical. Britain had insulted India by taking its young men away once again to fight in inter-imperialist wars. Bose wanted to create an Indian National Army and began to explore all possibilities.

In 1942 Churchill agreed that Sir Stafford Cripps, the left-wing, former ambassador to Moscow, be sent to India to meet with Nehru, Gandhi and other leaders and plead with them to help Britain. If they agreed, he could offer a verbal pledge of independence after the war. However, before Cripps could depart, bad news came from South-East Asia: Singapore had fallen. Churchill blamed the men in the field. The British Army had not fought back effectively: 'We had so many men in Singapore – so many men – they should have done better.' As stressed above, it was a huge blow.

Cripps arrived in India, but few were willing to listen to his message. Jinnah's Muslim League and the Communist Party were backing the war, but so speedy was the Japanese advance that Gandhi genuinely believed they might soon be negotiating Indian independence with Hirohito and Tojo rather than Churchill and Attlee. When Cripps insisted he was offering Congress a 'blank cheque' they could cash after the war, Gandhi famously riposted: 'What is the point of a blank cheque from a failing bank?'

After Cripps returned empty-handed, Churchill pinned his hopes for a stable Indian army largely on Jinnah and Sikandar Hyat Khan, the leader of the Unionist Party and elected Premier of the Punjab, a province crucial to the war effort in terms of manpower and for being the granary of India. When, after Cripps's return, Churchill said 'I hate Indians. They are a beastly people with a beastly religion', he was expressing a long-held view, but in this instance was referring to the Hindus who had badly let him down.

Bose, now detached from the Congress Party, had already spent time in Berlin a year earlier. He had asked senior Nazi civil servants to facilitate the release all Indian prisoners of war held by the Germans to him. He would then create an Indian National Army (INA) and take it to India to open a new front against the British.

'How do you propose to transport them?' he was asked. Bose replied that he was intending to do so via the Soviet Union. At this point, the Germans, deeply immersed in planning Operation Barbarossa, told Bose that would be impossible. June 1941 was not far away.

Bose's single meeting with Hitler didn't go too well. He had read *Mein Kampf* and found that the Führer's insulting remarks regarding Indians were not that different to Churchill's. He argued with Hitler but was told that the Japanese might be a better bet and that he should get to Tokyo as soon as possible. Bose accepted the advice. The Japanese were far more receptive. After the fall of Singapore, Bose had his INA. It was a unified, secular force that fought against British army units in Burma.

Hatred for Bose intensified on the pro-British side, but the INA initiative increased his popularity in India as a whole. If the Japanese took Kolkata and Delhi, Bose would become the de facto leader of an Indian government. Gandhi and Nehru were only too aware of this possibility. Churchill's hatred for India and Indians grew each day as the bad news came in. Leo Amery, his old friend and secretary of state for India in the war cabinet, wrote: 'On the subject of India, Winston is not quite sane ... I don't see much difference between his outlook and Hitler's.' Amery had suggested a far-reaching deal with India which granted virtual dominion status before the war, but the Chamberlain government was not ready to agree to this. Churchill never would be ready to 'preside over the liquidation of His Majesty's Empire'.

In August 1942, the Congress leaders felt they could no longer remain inactive. The spectre of Bose and the fear of a Japanese occupation made the usually ultra-cautious Gandhi somewhat reckless. At the All India Congress Committee he launched the Quit India Movement, demanding that the British get out immediately. Huge crowds gathered; acts of mass civil disobedience were carried out. Thousands of Congress activists and all its leaders were locked up. Bose felt strongly that the Quit India Movement would not succeed unless Nehru and Gandhi armed the masses to fight back. This they would never do. It went against the grain of the strategy they had adopted for many decades. Bose was secure and confident in his own strategy, despite his over-dependence on the Japanese.

The Bengal Famine

In the middle of a world war, with political battles raging in different parts of the subcontinent, a new disaster occurred. This time in Bengal.

Bengal was the first region occupied by the British. From the late eighteenth century its land was ruthlessly used to grow opium, in what the historian Mike Davis has described as 'the biggest drug transaction in world history'. The gigantic drug profits accrued by the East India Company from the 1820s onwards paid for the direct costs and permanent overheads (the army in particular) involved in expanding the Empire to the rest of India.

Here was imperialism in action. Kolkata, designated as the imperial capital, was developed, and a sprinkling of natives were educated in English. In the rest of the province all that happened was the destruction of local handicrafts, the creation of a landed oligarchy and the modernisation of poverty. The opium grown in Bengal was transported from Kolkata to Canton. The Chinese market for the drug was expanded by the two Opium Wars (1839–1842 and 1856–1860) fought by the British to the detriment of China. They laid the ground for a huge growth in trade. 'This extraordinarily one-sided trade', writes Davis, had by 1868 led to a situation where British India 'supplied 36 per cent of China's imports but bought less than 1 percent of its exports'. The sale of Bengal opium was a key link in 'the chain of commerce with which Britain had surrounded the world'.[3]

How did this global chain work? A. J. H. Latham described it in his classic account, *The International Economy and the Undeveloped World, 1865–1914*:

> The United Kingdom paid the United States for cotton by bills upon the Bank of England. The Americans took some of those bills to Canton and swapped them for tea. The Chinese exchanged the bills for Indian opium. Some of the bills were remitted to England as profit; others were taken to India to buy additional commodities, as

3 Mike Davis, *Late Victorian Holocausts*, London, 2001, p. 300.

well as to furnish the money remittance of private fortunes in India and the funds for carrying on the Indian government at home.[4]

Jute was not as profitable as opium, but then its trade did not require gunboats, though commodity sales were greatly helped by war: the Crimean War and US Civil War saw a huge rise in demand and profits. First shipped from Bengal in 1795 by the East India Company, four decades later pure jute yarn was being made and sold in Dundee. A report published by the Indian Industrial Commission (1916–18) – by 1918 consisting of ten members, only four of whom were Indians, and one of these was the Parsi magnate Sir Dorabji Jamsetji Tata – stated that 'the annual average value of the jute trade to Bengal has been computed at 10,000,000 pounds', and went on to point out that 'the association of the Calcutta jute industry with the east coast of Scotland has throughout remained intimate'.

No need to guess who the dominant partner was. The majority of European staff working in senior and junior managerial capacities at the jute mills in Bengal were Scottish. By 1918, cheap migrant labour from other parts of India made up 80 per cent of the workforce. Locals were not trusted by recruiting agents. All the workers lived in abject conditions. A tiny proportion of the profits from opium and jute could have created a system in which health clinics, schools, sanitation and tolerable housing units were built throughout the province, as they were in the white dominions. This was the Bengal created by a ruthless Empire.

The institutionalised poverty that characterised British rule in India and led to countless deaths is often underplayed or ignored by 'culturalist' historians. The treatment of Bengal was particularly vicious, decades before the wartime famine. An official report written by Dr Bentley, director of the Public Health Department in Bengal for the year 1927/8 was unsparing in its details. A million and a half Bengalis were dying every year from malnutrition, curable diseases, and lack of health facilities. These included 750,000 children under fifteen years of age. It was a 'dietary on which even rats could not live for more than about five weeks':

---

4   Quoted in ibid.

Their vitality is now so undermined by inadequate diet that they cannot stand the infection of foul diseases. Last year 120,000 people died from cholera, 350,000 from malaria, 350,000 from tuberculosis ... On an average 55,000 newborn infants die every year of tetanus.

That is why many British administrators viewed famines as little more than added extras.

Nothing much had changed twenty-five years later. 'Over five million people in Bengal starved or died in epidemics because of the man-made famine in 1943.' This inscription appears on screen over the last shot of Satyajit Ray's searing film *Distant Thunder*, a masterwork in its own right. The scale of the Bengal famine, which lasted almost two years from late 1942 to 1944, was not known to many people in India at the time. The nationalist leaders were in prison, while the Muslim League and the Communist Party were immersed in the war. There was an additional factor: some narratives of the famine underplay 'the enrichment of Indian industrialists' – Gandhi's great friend and benefactor G. D. Birla among them – who enthusiastically supported stripping the countryside of rice in order to feed their factory workers engaged in wartime production. Their pursuit of profit played a role in the mass starvation, yet this aspect has been largely absent from most historiography of the famine – in part, one author suggests, by over-emphasising the explanatory power of 'culture' and underestimating or even ignoring political economy.[5]

That between 3.5 and 5 million people died only became known after independence, and the first serious scholarship on the famine only began to be published decades later. But the British knew. Linlithgow's successor as Viceroy in 1943 was Archibald Wavell, who received regular reports from Bengal and was taken aback by the scale of the catastrophe. Though 'official' statements by Leo Amery and his civil servants downplayed the casualties, they were challenged immediately by Bengali politicians and cultural figures.

Satyajit Ray, the finest filmmaker the subcontinent has ever

---

5   See Janam Mukherjee, *Hungry Bengal: War, Famine and the End of Empire*, London, 2015.

produced, was convinced that the 5 million figure was, in all likelihood, an understatement. During the late 1970s and 1980s, I visited Kolkata regularly. We had informal conversations, one of which I recorded till he was discussing other film directors and told me to switch off. I kept notes, nonetheless. We talked mainly about the state of world literature and cinema, which was how the subject of the famine came up.

Distant Thunder, based on a novel by Bibhuti Bhushan, was Ray's take on the famine, filmed in colour. We discussed the politics of the 1975 movie, his most radical and for that reason subjected to criticism by Pauline Kael in the *New Yorker* and, for a different reason, by Jonathan Rosenbaum in *Sight and Sound*, among others. Ray was enraged by both reviews. Rosenbaum was 'ignorant, couldn't tell Indian women apart ... it appears he wanted an epic'. As for Kael, 'she can't understand that certain subjects require different faces and different camera movements'. Kael had found some of these shots 'jarring' and, while she liked the film, she was taken aback by its 'politics'. She suggested that Ray was trying to expatiate his own guilt.

It was this that angered him most. Why should he feel any guilt at all? Just for not having experienced the famine first-hand because he lived in the city? He had been in his early twenties when it happened, but 'we all knew about it, if not the exact numbers. Kolkata was full of refugees, begging on the streets. It was a heart-rending sight. We knew that thousands of people were dying in the villages and we knew why. Churchill was intensely disliked in Bengal.'

Of all the charges laid against Churchill in relation to India, one of the most damning is the accusation that he was responsible for the Bengal famine. Indian historians are not united on this issue. Some think that Churchill's verbal attacks on and utter loathing for Gandhi are even worse crimes. But rude words are usually ineffective. It is true that Churchill denounced the Indian leader as a 'malignant subversive fanatic' and 'a seditious Middle Temple lawyer, now posing as a fakir of a type well known in the East, striding half-naked up the steps of the Viceregal palace'. The governor of Bombay, Lord Willingdon, described Gandhi 'as a Bolshevik and for that reason dangerous'.

But had Gandhi been a subversive, Bolshevik fanatic, the British would have faced many more problems in the 1920s. Some got very worked up when Churchill suggested that Gandhi's 1932 'fast unto death' was fake, and alleged that glucose was being dissolved in the water he drank. The correspondence between Churchill and Linlithgow on this issue reads like satire today.

Most Indians at the time would have seen the invective as a badge of honour. To be insulted by the enemy was part of the struggle. The only reason for taking offense would be that since Gandhi was, in fact, fighting for a peaceful, orderly and gradual transfer of power, the abuse was unfair. For some Gandhi was a deity, and they were pained by the harsh words. In any case, insulting him was a joke compared to the mass starvation that swept Bengal in 1943, when crucial food supplies were diverted to the war effort, malnutrition was widespread, and millions of people starved to death.

The response to this is to compare India's share of world GDP to that of Europe. In 1700, India's share was 22.6 per cent, while Europe's was 23.3 per cent. In 1820, seventy-seven years after the British East India Company had taken Bengal, before expanding rapidly to the rest of the subcontinent, India's GDP share had fallen to 15.7 per cent while Europe's had risen to 26.6 per cent. In 1890, two decades after the year-long Great Uprising was defeated, India's share had tumbled to 11 per cent and Europe was now on 40.3. Five years after independence and seven years after the end of the war, India was on 3.8 per cent and Europe on 29.7. Prior to the British colonisation, as many modern historians have pointed out, Indian peasants and agricultural labourers were not the 'half-naked beggars' that some later became during British rule. Eighteenth-century figures indicate that the poorest agricultural labourers in Chennai/ Madras earned more in real terms than their counterparts on English farms. By 1990, the income of the average British household was twenty-one times higher than its Indian counterpart. The reason? Industrial–capitalist imperialism. The huge burden placed on the shoulders of India was imposed by Britain.

It is common practice these days to ascribe the responsibility for famines to the decisions made by individuals. Liberal, anti-communist historians blame Mao personally for the disastrous famine that followed the Great Leap Forward, and Stalin for the impact of the coercive, ill-conceived industrialisation in the Ukraine. According to this logic, Churchill's name should certainly be added to the list of those responsible for the millions of deaths in Bengal. A population of 60 million was reduced by 5 million in just under three years.

Churchill's callousness is not in doubt: Malthusian remarks such as 'Indians breed like rabbits' (similar statements are often made about Irish Catholics) were criminally negligent. What was also criminal, once it had become clear what was going on in Bengal, was the refusal to declare a state of emergency in the province, immediately reverse the policies that starved the people of food, and send in rice and flour from other parts of the country. This was a crime for which Churchill certainly, but also the entire wartime coalition including Attlee and Bevin, were responsible. They never protested or suggested counter-measures to deal with the crisis. Churchill thought the figures were being exaggerated by mendacious Indians, when the truth was that the British were trying desperately to stop the flow of information from spreading throughout India or reaching Britain.

Churchill made no direct reference to this horror in his history of the war. Perhaps a subconscious guilt led to his oblique and false statement: 'No great portion of the world population was so effectively protected from the horrors and pitfalls of the world war as were the peoples of Hindustan . . . They were carried through the struggle on the shoulders of our small island.'

Viceroy Wavell was a bit more sensitive, pointing out to the British government that the famine 'was one of the greatest disasters that had befallen any people under British rule'. He was concerned that it would hugely damage Britain's reputation. Here he was wrong. Official and tame historians made sure that the episode was wholly, or in large part, whitewashed.

How else to explain the absence of the famine from the entire volume of the *Oxford History of The Twentieth Century*. It gets a few lines (very few) in Max Hastings's 600-page opus *Finest Years*, on Churchill's war. Boris Johnson thought it best to leave the subject unmentioned in this Churchill biography, despite the fact of his having an Indian mother-in-law. Not a single historian writing on

Attlee, deputy prime minister in the war cabinet, mentions the famine or the discussions of it among ministers. For what was a man-made disaster, the refusal by so many historians to touch on the subject borders on the grotesque. Had Hitler taken Europe and done a deal with the United States, the Judeocide would undoubtedly have been treated the same way, and not just in Europe.

Three important books that have broken the wall of silence are Mike Davis's pathbreaking study *Late Victorian Holocausts: El Niño Famines and the Making of the Third World* and works exclusively on the famine by two North America–based Bengali scholars, Janam Mukherjee and Madhusree Mukerjee. There are also innumerable articles, such that the picture we now have is virtually complete. What exactly happened?

Bengal at the time was a province of 60 million people, roughly half Hindu, half Muslim, 90 per cent of whom inhabited 90,000 villages. Its 20,000 miles of waterways wound their way through dense forests, making over half the villages inaccessible except by boat. Hunger stalked these villages even in times of normality. Livestock dependency (as in Ireland) was low, and the population survived on rice and fish. The word of the British administrator was law.

The province had always been prone to cyclones, and its eastern part, now Bangladesh, remains under constant threat on this front. A number of cyclones hit the coast in 1942, but it was the tsunami in November of that year that flooded the region around the Ganges Delta. The low elevation in Bengal meant that the tsunami rolled far inland, destroying farmland and rice fields. Salt water poisoned ripe crops. The wave also carried the fungal disease known as 'rice blast', which struck the paddy fields. This reduced the average rice crop in coastal and surrounding areas by a third. The effects of this disaster were made worse by the fact there had already been a drought. To add to the punishment, the Damodar River burst its banks, flooding the Burdan district of Bengal, devastating villages, drowning even more rice fields and causing an outbreak of cholera.

Scarcity led to price rises and hoarding, and starvation was widespread. But the worst killers at this early stage were the epidemics, with malaria taking more lives than cholera. There was no free national health system in Britain, so it would have been utopian to expect the same ruling elite to create one in India. The hospitals that existed were of reasonable quality, but were located only in the big cities and reserved mainly for the use of whites and the native rich.

With Japan's lightning conquest of British-ruled Burma in the spring of 1942, the restless mega-colony found itself at the forefront of an inter-imperialist war, waged within the larger configurations of the Second World War. Alas, it was the poorest Bengalis who were now facing a slow annihilation. Had the Japanese taken Kolkata, as many nationalists (and not simply supporters of Bose) had hoped, the jubilation would have been short-lived. The famine would have proceeded unchecked.

Despite all the disasters, the 1943 harvest was only 5 per cent less than the average of previous years. It was not the lack of food that killed millions. It was simply that the food was made inaccessible on orders from the highest levels of the imperial bureaucracy in Delhi, who were carrying out instructions from London. The feeding of armies and those engaged in daily production for the military were given priority. A further factor was the Bengali government's advice that people should stock up on grain after the Japanese advance, which further decreased supplies. There were also US and Chinese troops in northeast Bengal and Assam, creating a further drain on food.

The only Indian politician who offered more than sympathy was Subhas Chandra Bose. The news had reached him in Japanese-occupied Burma, where his INA was fighting the British. His offer to the Indian government to send Burmese rice to the starving Bengali villages did not even merit a reply, even though he had suggested it would be transported in civilian trucks.

Churchill had no doubt whatsoever where the food should be sent. His chief adviser on food distribution in Britain was a close friend, the scientist Fred Lindemann ('The Prof'), a German by extraction. He was not universally popular. His arrogance and closeness to Churchill angered many in Whitehall, who felt that their meticulously researched facts and statistics were being misused, twisted and unnecessarily abbreviated by 'the Prof' to cater to Churchill's prejudices and instincts.

The sobriquet attached to Lindemann was either 'Baron Berlin' or worse. When he worked at 'S-Branch' (a group of academic economists tasked with analysing data), a few daring colleagues used to hiss 'SS' as he passed by. He clearly needed an English name. Churchill obliged. The Prof became Lord Cherwell. Nothing else changed. In an interview with *Harper's Magazine* after her book *Churchill's Secret War* was published, Madhusree Mukerjee explained how well-matched Churchill and Cherwell were:

> Judging by a lecture that Cherwell gave in the 1930s, he regarded colonial subjects as 'helots', or slaves, whose only reason for existence was the service of racial superiors. In drafts of this talk, he outlined how science could help entrench the hegemony of the higher races. By means of hormones, drugs, mind control, and surgery, one could remove from slaves the ability to suffer or to feel ambition – yielding humans with 'the mental make-up of the worker bee'. Such a lobotomized race would have no thought of rebellion or votes, so that one would end up with a perfectly peaceable and permanent society, 'led by supermen and served by helots'.
>
> In November 1943, Cherwell urged Churchill to hold firm against demands for famine relief. Else, he warned, 'so long as the war lasts [India's] high birth rate may impose a heavy strain on this country which does not view with Asiatic detachment the pressure of a growing population on limited supplies of food'. That is, he blamed the famine on the irresponsible fecundity of natives – and ignored the devastation of the Indian economy by the war effort. He also elided the fact that the War Cabinet was preventing India from using its ample sterling balance or even its own ships to import sufficient wheat.[6]

In response to rising prices in Bengal, families sold anything that was of any value: radios, bicycles and even the metal roofs of their huts. They would trade household items such as pots and pans for even a tiny amount of rice. They sold what little land they possessed. A quarter of a million families lost all their land during the famine. Increased prices also led people to turn to the cursed money lenders, leeches who did not forbear from charging high interest rates.

---

6   Scott Horton, 'Churchill's Dark Side: Six Questions for Madhusree Mukerjee', *Harper's Magazine*, 4 November 2010.

Less is known about the foraging that took place during the famine, as it was subsumed under the larger story of the Second World War and the area was closed to journalists for much of the time. We do know there were incidents of cannibalism and that some Brahmin women preferred death to going in search of food, let alone accepting it from 'lower caste' people or Muslims. It is difficult to feel sympathy for them. There were internal refugees, too, with the poor making long marches from the countryside to the city. Three-quarters of a million reached Kolkata and the suburban villages surrounding it. Some of the more enterprising peasants raided food depots. They had nothing to lose.

In the week ending 9 October 1943, just under 2,000 deaths were recorded in Calcutta alone, with 1,600 the week before. In contrast, Amery reported that from 15 August to 16 October 1943, roughly 8,000 people had died in Calcutta from malnutrition. The journalist K. Santhanam, a former member of the Legislative Assembly, believed 100,000 people were dying in Bengal each week.

The chief press adviser to the Bengal government did everything in his power to stop word of the famine from reaching Britain. The government itself ceased reporting daily deaths by starvation. Every possible effort was made to underplay the scale of the famine. The war had put everything else, including human lives, on hold.

Fearing the Japanese Army might soon be sweeping into eastern India, the war cabinet in London imposed a scorched-earth policy, known as 'Denial', which involved stripping Bengal's coastal districts of 'surplus' rice supplies and seizing local transport in order to prevent it falling into the hands of the invading forces. Wartime mobilisation brought an 'authoritarian resolve' to the predatory dynamics of colonial rule, Janam Mukherjee argues: the British Governor of Bengal, Sir John Herbert, sidelined the elected provincial government under Fazlul Huq – a genial anti-communalist populist, whose somewhat misjudged slogan in the 1937 elections had been 'Lentils and Rice!' – and appointed an English official, L. G. Pinnell, to implement Denial at top speed.

Pinnell approached a well-known supporter of Jinnah's Muslim League, the rice merchant, M. A. Ispahani, offering his company 2 million rupees to carry out the operation. The predictable 'hue and cry' from the other parties prompted Pinnell to appoint four more Denial agents on a party-communalist basis for 'balance' – leading, Mukherjee writes, to even more chaos and corruption. In April 1942 Pinnell called for a levy of 123,000 tons of 'surplus' rice; stocks were seized by force where farmers resisted, while compensation payments drove up prices across the board.

In May, Pinnell turned his attention to boats: 43,000 vessels were destroyed or confiscated over the next few months, crippling the 'essential riverine transport infrastructure' upon which millions of the poorest Bengalis depended; boat owners were compensated, but not those who leased them for their livelihoods; potters and fishermen were left destitute. At the same time, as Mukherjee points out, rice was still being exported from Bengal: 45,000 tons in January 1942 rising to 66,000 tons in April.

It was at this point that the refugees from Burma arrived. The Japanese victory there led to some 600,000 Indian workers fleeing the country, at least 80,000 dying on the 600-mile march to the Bengal border. While the British Imperial government did its best to look after Europeans fleeing the Japanese advance, the Indians were left to fend for themselves. The survivors increased the demand for rice in Bengal at precisely the time when Denial was stripping stocks bare.

Adding to the indigent were thousands of peasant families evicted wholesale by the British authorities for the purposes of military expediency: 36,000 people from Diamond Harbour, 70,000 from Noakhali and so on. Many of these deportees were left particularly vulnerable and would be among the first to perish with the onset of mass starvation.

Responding to the widespread anti-Denial protests, a Congress resolution of 10 July 1942 called for full compensation for any loss of landed property or boats, which it said should not be surrendered until compensation was settled. From London, the war cabinet declared that the Congress 'Denial resolution' – moderate enough – amounted to treason. Amery urged Linlithgow to adopt harsher measures with regard to Gandhi and the Congress leadership, rather than 'merely punish the wretched villager who refuses to hand over his boat or his bullock cart'.

Meanwhile, 'the poor were on the move by the millions, trudging through the monsoon rains, now half-naked, falling by the wayside and dying, or straggling into urban areas to beg for food'. What passed for a health system was 'in shambles: under-organized, understaffed and lacking in basic supplies'. Bengal's official surgeon-general would describe the famished as 'mere skin and bone, dehydrated, with dry furred tongues, sores on lips, staring eyes'.[7]

Viceroy Linlithgow, whose attitude towards the mass starvation had been to ignore it as far as possible, was replaced in October 1943 by Wavell, whose imperial *cursus* included the suppression of the Arab Revolt in Palestine, and humiliating defeat in Malaya, Singapore and Burma. Prior to that he had served in Kenya, Cyprus and Somaliland. This was the itinerary of many officers in the imperial legions. Churchill had found him a disappointing military commander (i.e. Wavell had disagreed with him), and sent him off to New Delhi to get him out of the way. Churchill regarded him as 'a good average colonel' who would have made 'a good chairman of a Tory association'. This was a bit unfair.

Wavell was far too well read and cultured to be just that, and in fact, after touring Calcutta incognito with his wife, he instructed the military to help with relief, committing a full division to the effort. On Wavell's orders, the destitute refugees were gradually transferred to army camps from November 1943 onwards and meagre rations were allocated. However, the compulsory round-ups in Kolkata, in an attempt to clear the city of begging skeletons, led to the separation of families and related social disasters. Husbands abandoned their wives, children were sold or left to die. Widows in joint family homes were discarded like unwanted rubbish. Mass prostitution flourished as isolated women and children were kidnapped and sold into brothels. By the end of 1943, well over 3 million Bengalis had died.

Wavell acknowledged the famine and tried to do something about it, despite being regularly thwarted by London. He remained unpopular with his masters. Churchill asked in a mocking telegram why, if food was so scarce, had Gandhi not died yet?

'Wavell's star rose high at an early stage of the war', his friend

---

7   Mukherjee, *Hungry Bengal*, pp. 121, 129.

Basil Liddell Hart later wrote. 'The glow was the more brilliant because of the darkness of the sky.' Churchill regarded him as too cautious, while Wavell thought Churchill's understanding of military tactics hadn't developed much since the Boer War. Churchill wanted his warlords to be more like himself, bullying, insensitive and adventurous. Wavell was a bookish introvert. If there had ever been a proper Commission of Enquiry into the famine, he would have provided valuable evidence to counteract the inhumanity displayed by Churchill and Attlee in the war cabinet.

As the skies of Bengal darkened with the smoke of burnt bodies, Wavell did his best to convince London of the necessity for large-scale imports of food grains, enlisting the support of the commander-in-chief of the Indian Army, Claude Auchinleck, and of the chiefs of staff in London. Wavell continued to request food through February and March 1944, going so far as to threaten his resignation. He exhausted every avenue, including the newly founded United Nations Relief and Rehabilitation Authority (UNRRA), without success. To Churchill's outrage, Wavell approached Roosevelt directly, asking for US ships to bring grain to a battered subcontinent beset by famine and hunger. Roosevelt, together with Congress and the US media, remained indifferent. They did not wish to offend Churchill. Australia and Canada both offered aid, but there was no available shipping.

In March 1944 the British government offered 400,000 tons of wheat in exchange for 150,000 tons of rice. In June, Wavell managed to extract 200,000 tons from the war cabinet, but this was still too little in his eyes. Churchill then requested US aid himself in mid 1944, but shipping had been committed to the European conflict.

The war cabinet was unmoved, with Churchill observing that the starvation of the 'anyhow under-fed Bengalis' was less serious than that of the 'sturdy Greeks'. According to Amery, writing in his journal, 'Winston so dislikes India and all to do with it that he can see nothing but waste of shipping space.'

Wavell's intervention appeared to have stabilised the situation in Calcutta by the end of the year, but mass starvation continued in the countryside. As winter drew on, the predicament of the rural poor was worsened by chronic cloth shortages, so that many died not only homeless and starving but literally naked. For propaganda purposes, however, the famine was supposedly now under control. The war cabinet still resisted Wavell's requests for food imports. The first half of 1944 saw an increase in the death rates, as epidemics took hold on a weakened population; deaths from malaria would peak that November. Another 2 million people died of hunger, disease and exposure during 1944.

In Calcutta, 'the urban poor lived on the absolute margins of life and death', in stark contrast with the increased profits that Indian industrialists were making. In December 1944 the new governor of Bengal, the Australian politician Richard Casey, recorded his horror at the living conditions he encountered on a tour of Calcutta's slums: 'Human beings cannot let other human beings exist under these conditions.'[8]

The situation remained serious in 1945, when the failure of the monsoon rains brought fears of another famine. In January 1946, Wavell warned Frederick Pethick-Lawrence, the Attlee government's Secretary of State for India, that the food situation was once again critical. Pethick-Lawrence acknowledged that 'India's need is unquestionable', but made it clear that there would be no increase of food imports. Instead, he recommended that the food ration in the cities be cut to make existing supplies go further. In these conditions, with independence now on the horizon, the attempts by rival Indian politicians to blame the catastrophe on their opponents – especially the unelected Muslim League government, which had presided over the worst of the famine – fell on fertile ground.[9]

Communal divisions, however, were still not all-encompassing. There were unified mass protests in November 1945 and February 1946 against the trials of Indian National Army soldiers taken prisoner in Burma by the returning British troops: Muslim League, Congress and Communist flags were tied together in a gesture of political unity – 'testimony to a sense of solidarity with which the population of Calcutta understood their highly uncertain collective fate'.[10]

---

8 Ibid., p. 194.
9 Ibid. See also John Newsinger's review of Mukherjee's book in *New Left Review*, 96, November–December 2015.
10 Mukherjee, *Hungry Bengal*, p. 202.

In that same fateful year, 1946, the naval ratings in Bombay and Karachi went on strike and seized battleships of the Royal Indian Navy. In its entire history, the British Empire had never faced a mutiny on this scale in its armed forces. A huge general strike erupted in Bombay in solidarity with the sailors. The strike committee was completely non-communal, its leaders – Hindus, Muslims and Sikhs – making it clear they would only 'surrender to a Free India, not the British'. The radical poet and songwriter Sahir Ludhianvi expressed the anger of many in his poem dedicated to the sailors who rebelled:

> O, Leaders of our Nation
> Lift your heads,
> Look into our eyes,
> Whose blood is this,
> Who died?
>
> You showed us the direction
> You painted our destiny
> You blew on the embers
> Now you shrink from the flames;
> You appealed for waves
> And now seek shelter from the storm.
>
> We understand all;
> Hope now lies in compromise
> Colonial pledges always wise
> Oppression was just a fairy tale!
> The foreign promises let us hail!
> Yes, accept their protestations of love
> The people rise from below, you take fright above.
> The old legacy will not die.
> O leaders of the nation,
> Whose blood is this?
> Who died?[11]

---

11 My translation.

Nevertheless, political leaders continued to channel the anxieties and frustrations of the masses into a more sectarian mould. Congress and Muslim League leaders pleaded with the sailors to give up, promising protection. The naval ratings believed them. Free India made sure that not a single 'mutineer' was taken back into the navy. Pakistan, surprisingly, was far more generous in taking them back after Independence.[12]

On 16 May 1946, the Attlee government's Cabinet Mission to India published its proposal for a united, independent India with wide-ranging regional autonomy, intended to preclude the formation of a separate Muslim state of Pakistan. The Congress leadership at first agreed to the proposal, but soon began to back away on the grounds that the Muslim League would be over-represented. On 10 July, Nehru rejected the plan unequivocally. The Muslim League called a 'direct-action day' four weeks later to agitate for the creation of Pakistan.

In *Hungry Bengal*, Janam Mukherjee insists that starvation provided an essential underpinning for the horrific outbreak of communal/ethnic violence in Calcutta in August 1946. The *hartal*, or general strike, called by the Muslim League on 16 August, divided the city along lines already hardened by the dehumanising effects of the famine. Groups of Muslims on their way to a rally at the Maidan, Calcutta's central park, attacked shops that had not closed, while armed Hindus tried to block their route. The upshot was 'five days of largely unrestrained murder, looting, arson, mutilation, torture and dislocation' that left much of the city in ruins. At least 5,000 were killed, although the real figure is almost certainly higher. On 28 August it was reported that there were 189,015 people displaced by the violence being sheltered in relief camps, but as Mukherjee points out, the total figure of the displaced was much higher: many fled the city altogether – 110,000 by train and unknown numbers on foot – while thousands more took shelter with friends and relatives. Mukherjee

---

12 B. C. Dutt, *The Mutiny of the Innocents*, Bombay, 1971. Dutt, one of the naval ratings involved, had written one of the first pamphlets inciting the revolt, calling on the sailors to 'recognise the enemy' and 'love India'.

estimates that some 10 per cent of the city's population were displaced by the violence. At least the new governor of Bengal, Sir Frederick Burrows, was able to take comfort in the fact that the riots were 'communal and not – repeat not – in any way anti-British'.[13] What could be more perfect?

The Bengali social reformer Ram Mohan Roy had said many decades earlier that 'what Bengal thinks today, India thinks tomorrow'. He was referring to the rich culture and radical political consciousness of the Bengali people. The 1946 riots prefigured the partition of the subcontinent. They took place at a time of renewed starvation, as a society already brutalised by years of hunger finally began to unravel. While the occasion was the Muslim League *hartal*, the cause was 'very specific and identifiable tensions' in the city. It was a 'localized battle for the control of city blocks, alleyways, and neighbourhoods'.[14]

Wavell's introduction of rationing in 1944 had meant that who 'belonged' in the city and who did not became a life-and-death question: not belonging meant repatriation to the un-rationed countryside. In August 1946, as Mukherjee puts it, 'that decision was taken into unofficial hands'. Sporadic violence continued even after the city had been occupied by 45,000 troops and the rioting had officially come to an end, with people still being driven from their homes and sometimes murdered.

Mukherjee's account makes absolutely clear that, in order to protect the Raj from a Japanese threat that never materialised, the British state sacrificed the lives of some 5 million people. The war cabinet maintained an attitude of callous indifference. In Churchill's case, the indifference was strongly tinged with racism. The Bengal famine was no natural disaster but 'the direct product of colonial and wartime ideologies and calculations that knowingly exposed the poor of Bengal to annihilation through deprivation'; 'a grievous crime was committed in broad daylight', one that is still unacknowledged.[15]

---

13 Mukherjee, *Hungry Bengal*, pp. 220, 235.
14 Ibid., p. 215.
15 Ibid., pp. 252, 260.

The British were far from alone in perpetrating this crime, as we have seen. Indian elites and political leaders, largely unmoved by the suffering in the countryside, were both accessories and beneficiaries. Here, Mukherjee highlights a crucial silence in Indian historiography. These classes still rule India – and Pakistan – today. Mukherjee describes travelling the Bengali countryside while doing his research: 'Hunger seemed still everywhere – haunting the shadows, moaning in dingy corners, written on the faces of young children on street corners, gnawing at the spines of middle-aged sweepers, and silently ravaging the collective consciousness of society at large.'[16] As he observes more generally:

> The profound and pervasive links between war, famine and riot are tortured and complex, but they are also manifest. They are, moreover, far from uncommon. Wherever there is civil war, ethnic violence, communal riots, or any other type of horizontal violence – particularly in the global South – look for the hunger that preceded it, and it is more often than not very easily found.

~

During his first trip to India in 1898, Churchill had read Macaulay's essays and admired them greatly – till he came across the historian's strictures on the founder of the Churchill dynasty. Macaulay then became a 'rogue'. Churchill did not record his views on Macaulay's essay targeting Warren Hastings, the second Governor-General appointed by the East India Company. Stationed in India, Churchill must have read it. Did he underline the concluding paragraph and recall it in later years? Probably not. He should have. Macaulay concluded his essay thus: 'Those who look on his character without favour or malevolence will pronounce that, in the two great elements of all social virtue, in respect for the rights of others, and in sympathy for the sufferings of others, he was deficient. His principles were somewhat lax.'

---

16 Ibid., p. 258.

Macaulay's essay had been provoked by Edmund Burke's savage impeachment address in the House of Lords in 1788, indicting Hastings for 'high crimes and misdemeanours' on behalf of the House of Commons. That Hastings was a rogue is beyond doubt. He wanted to make money, and in those early days of British rule in Bengal and neighbouring regions he looted at will. The fact that he stole from the rich to make himself richer shocked polite society.

The following extract from Burke's speech indicates what he might have thought of Churchill presiding over a famine that cost 5 million lives.[17]

My lords, I do not mean now to go farther than just to remind your lordships of this – that Mr. Hastings' government was one whole system of oppression, of robbery of individuals, of spoliation of the public, and of supersession of the whole system of the English government, in order to vest in the worst of the natives all the power that could possibly exist in any government; in order to defeat the ends which all governments ought, in common, to have in view. In the name of the Commons of England, I charge all this villainy upon Warren Hastings, in this last moment of my application to you.

My lords, what is it that we want here, to a great act of national justice? Do we want a cause, my lords? You have the cause of oppressed princes, of undone women of the first rank, of desolated provinces and of wasted kingdoms.

Do you want a criminal, my lords? When was there so much iniquity ever laid to the charge of any one? No, my lords, you must not look to punish any other such delinquent from India. Warren Hastings has not left substance enough in India to nourish such another delinquent.

My lords, is it a prosecutor you want? You have before you the Commons of Great Britain as prosecutors; and I believe, my lords,

---

17 Burke was adopted as a counter-revolutionary conservative after the French Revolution, which he attacked. His texts were used for similar purposes against the Russian Revolution. But as this impeachment speech reveals, there were other sides to him. For a stimulating essay, see Francis Mulhern, 'Burke's Way', *New Left Review*, 102, November–December 2016.

that the sun, in his beneficent progress round the world, does not behold a more glorious sight than that of men, separated from a remote people by the material bounds and barriers of nature, united by the bond of a social and moral community – all the Commons of England resenting, as their own, the indignities and cruelties that we offered to all the people of India.

Do we want a tribunal? My lords, no example of antiquity, nothing in the modern world, nothing in the range of human imagination, can supply us with a tribunal like this. We commit safely the interests of India and humanity into your hands. Therefore, it is with confidence that, ordered by the Commons,

I impeach Warren Hastings, Esquire, of high crimes and misdemeanours.

I impeach him in the name of the Commons of Great Britain in Parliament assembled, whose parliamentary trust he has betrayed.

I impeach him in the name of all the Commons of Great Britain, whose national character he has dishonoured.

I impeach him in the name of the people of India, whose laws, rights and liberties he has subverted; whose properties he has destroyed; whose country he has laid waste and desolate.

I impeach him in the name and by virtue of those eternal laws of justice which he has violated.

I impeach him in the name of human nature itself, which he has cruelly outraged, injured and oppressed, in both sexes, in every age, rank, situation, and condition of life.

My lords, at this awful close, in the name of the Commons and surrounded by them, I attest the retiring, I attest the advancing generations, between which, as a link in the great chain of eternal order, we stand. We call this nation, we call the world to witness, that the Commons have shrunk from no labour; that we have been guilty of no prevarication; that we have made no compromise with crime; that we have not feared any odium whatsoever, in the long warfare which we have carried on with the crimes, with the vices, with the exorbitant wealth, with the enormous and overpowering influence of Eastern corruption.

My lords, it has pleased Providence to place us in such a state that we appear every moment to be upon the verge of some great mutations. There is one thing, and one thing only, which defies all mutation: that which existed before the world, and will survive the fabric of the world itself – I mean justice; that justice which, emanating from the Divinity, has a place in the breast of every one of us, given us for our guide with regard to ourselves and with regard to others, and which will stand, after this globe is burned to ashes, our advocate or our accuser, before the great Judge, when He comes to call upon us for the tenor of a well-spent life.

My lords, the Commons will share in every fate with your lordships; there is nothing sinister which can happen to you, in which we shall not all be involved; and, if it should so happen that we shall be subjected to some of those frightful changes which we have seen – if it should happen that your lordships, stripped of all the decorous distinctions of human society, should, by hands at once base and cruel, be led to those scaffolds and machines of murder upon which great kings and glorious queens have shed their blood, amidst the prelates, amidst the nobles, amidst the magistrates, who supported their thrones – may you in those moments feel that consolation which I am persuaded they felt in the critical moments of their dreadful agony!

My lords, if you must fall, may you so fall! but, if you stand – and stand I trust you will – together with the fortune of this ancient monarchy, together with the ancient laws and liberties of this great and illustrious kingdom, may you stand as unimpeached in honour as in power; may you stand, not as a substitute for virtue, but as an ornament of virtue, as a security for virtue; may you stand long, and long stand the terror of tyrants; may you stand the refuge of afflicted nations; may you stand a sacred temple, for the perpetual residence of an inviolable justice!

Considering the House of Lords 'a sacred temple' to combat tyranny was a far-fetched notion even then, and Burke's shameless flattery did not work. Hastings was acquitted. The process had lasted almost two years and had bankrupted him. His reputation never fully recovered. Nobody ever suggested impeaching Churchill, or Attlee, his co-partner in colonial war crimes.

11

Resistance and Repression

The partisan
Knows she'll be killed.
In the red glare of her rage
She sees no difference
Between dying and being killed.
She's too young and healthy to fear death
Or feel regret . . .

Nazim Hikmet, *Human Landscapes* (1941–5)

What of occupied Europe? The resistance movements against fascism were uneven. Churchill kept a close watch, for they would play an important role in shaping the post-war order. A distinction must be made between the actually existing Resistance – a minority in most cases, but one that fought politically and military against the fascists, mainly under communist leadership – and conservative patriots that included, especially in France, a handful of monarchists.

This courageous minority was in sharp contrast to the silent or imagined Resistance, in a broader sense of the word, that was adopted by many towards the tail end of the war, in most cases after the defeat of fascism. It encompassed a sizeable segment of the population that had never participated in any oppositional activity, that had ridiculed its existence, that attempted in later years to obscure its memory and history, but that also used the myth of the Resistance shamelessly in the aftermath of the war to legitimise the new political order that was installed in the wake of the Allied victories in Italy, France, Belgium and Luxembourg.

In Germany itself, effective and consistent anti-fascist resistance was virtually confined to the underground Communist Party of Germany (KPD). There were, of course, small groups of students, extremely courageous and determined, who denounced the regime in public and sacrificed their lives. Despite KPD efforts, armed struggle was impossible, as was any effective, as opposed to purely symbolic, public defiance. KPD members, supporters and voters had numbered in the millions, most of them factory workers. Soon after Hitler was installed as chancellor in January 1933, the KPD was banned, its offices sealed, its leaders hunted down, its militants tortured, imprisoned and killed.

The KPD leaders had insisted that Hitler would not last long, and for a while communists and fascists fought it out on the streets. This ended very rapidly. As the KPD began to understand the scale of the defeat and its implications, they reorganised and resisted as best they could. One form the resistance took in fascist Germany was to act as the ears and eyes of both Moscow and London. The Russians were greatly helped by KPD sympathisers who had infiltrated the upper echelons of the state machine and regularly supplied information to the 'Red Orchestra', the most effective spy network in occupied Europe.

There were others who, through accident of birth, were situated in helpful class locations. Take the three daughters of General Kurt von Hammerstein, who, as chief of the army from 1930 to 1934, was the most senior officer of the Reichswehr. He served Hitler for a year before retiring, but was asked to return in 1939. Hammerstein was a conservative, but unlike many of his fellow officers, he was hostile to the Nazis and not simply contemptuous in class terms. His daughters had gone to school and university in Berlin, coming of age during the febrile years of the Weimar Republic. In 1933, the oldest, Marie Luise (Butzi), was twenty-five, her sister, Helge, a year younger, while Maria Therese was twenty-two. All three were KPD sympathisers. Helga had left school at sixteen and joined the KPD a year later; her younger sister followed in her tracks. They were fond of their parents, but, as Helge explained later:

I read the Marxist classics, including Engels, also Ludwig Feuerbach, *The German Ideology* and even *Das Kapital*, and suddenly thought I understood the world, that I had found a key to understanding a mixed-up world. I had the feeling that with historical materialism I had firm ground under my feet, and was, for the first time, as happy again as I had been at fourteen when the world began to open up to me. For a while, I saw my parents and their friends principally as representatives of their class, and, although I was still living with them, I stopped taking part in their life.[1]

It was Butzi and Helge who first cast eyes on notes their father had made during an exhausting session with Hitler in late 1933. The new chancellor had informed Hammerstein that the primary task of Germany was to attack and destroy the Soviet Union. After reading the detailed notes, they waited for the right moment, typed them up, and within a week they were on the desk of General Berzin at the Fourth Department of the Red Army.

Stalin preferred not to believe this information. Leo Roth, a close comrade in the KPD and a lover of Helge, had taken huge risks to get the notes out. He soon had to flee Germany, but was arrested and shot on Stalin's orders. Pure paranoia on the Soviet dictator's part. Later, Maria Therese helped to transport Jews out of the country and soon left herself, along with her husband, to live in Japan. Butzi, whose life was recently dramatised in the German soap opera *Babylon Berlin*, moved to East Berlin in 1949 where she practised as a lawyer, dealing mainly with Jewish clients.

Another example, now famous, is that of Sophie Scholl, the twenty-one-year-old college student who distributed anti-Nazi leaflets in Munich in 1943, and went to the scaffold uttering the words: 'What does my death matter, if by our action thousands of people will be awakened and stirred to action?' Her nobility echoes that of another prisoner at another time in another Munich, where a workers' uprising had been throttled on 3 May 1919. Eugen Leviné, the leader of the short-lived Bavarian Workers' Republic,

---

1 Hans Magnus Enzensberger, *The Silences of Hammerstein*, Kolkata, 2009, Kindle loc. 693–7.

defiantly confronted the court that was about to sentence him to death with the following words: 'We Communists are all dead men on leave. Of this I am fully aware. I do not know if you will extend my leave or whether I shall have to join Karl Liebknecht and Rosa Luxemburg. In any case I await your verdict with composure and inner serenity.'

In 2000, the eminent West German historian Hans Mommsen produced what has been hailed as the definitive account of resistance under the Third Reich. He expressed some irritation with media exaggerations of the role played by the resistance and also with 'both the CDU/CSU and, more cautiously, the SPD, who have been seeking to present the resistance as their political legacy'. Mommsen stressed that the fascist dictatorship 'had its roots in German society as a whole', and was critical of the positions taken by the SPD and Free Labour Unions who, 'as late as 30 January 1933 adopted a stance "with both feet on the ground of legality"'. In this fashion 'they failed to see that this "legality" had long ago become a tool in Hitler's hand, even though Benito Mussolini had already demonstrated how, without a breach of the prevailing constitution, it was possible to take the road to dictatorship'.

The SPD's failure to combat the far right in 1919 boded ill for what was to come. In 1932 – at the time of the so-called Papen putsch when the social-democratic government of Prussia was eliminated – Carl Severing, the minister of the interior, made the infamous statement, *Ich weiche vor dem Gewalt* ('I yield before violence'). After a lieutenant and two soldiers had entered his office he swiftly abrogated all the authority he had accumulated over the last fourteen years in just five minutes. This did not augur well either for the SPD or for Germany.

Since this was where legality led, the only real resistance was elsewhere. Mommsen emphasised that the 'resistance cannot be measured by the criteria of its outward success', and was critical of those in the newly unified Germany who refused to accept the reality of wartime communist resistance:

> It is unjust to dismiss communist resistance on the grounds that they were fighting for a 'totalitarianism' analogous to Nazism. They

were fighting the Nazi evil, and sacrificing themselves for their cause, with just as much courage as other German resistance movements. We should regard the various forms and directions taken by the resistance in their totality as a mirror of existing political alternatives to National Socialism in German society.[2]

What requires some explanation is why there were no mutinies within the rank and file of the German Army, even after the series of defeats that began with Stalingrad in 1943. The Eastern Front should have been an obvious site for rebellion. German soldiers had been extremely well indoctrinated in the master-race mythology. The brutalities of the Wehrmacht in the Soviet Union were on a par with those of the SS and were directed against the Jews but also the Slavs. The killing of Soviet prisoners of war, the mass rapes and the barbarianism of the invaders have been well documented. Vasily Grossman's despatches from the war zones made no attempt to sanitise what he saw. He described how the Germans treated Soviet peasants and others as if they were animals.

Soldiers who thought and behaved like this could neither mutiny nor surrender or desert to the enemy. It was the top layers of the mainly aristocratic and conservative officer corps that wanted to get rid of Hitler. He was tolerated when he took Czechoslovakia, Poland and France, but Stalingrad and Kursk? They knew they could not win the war, and, since that was the case, in order to save Germany a separately negotiated peace with the United States and Britain was the only solution.

By 1944 it was too late. Neither Roosevelt nor Churchill would have considered a separate deal, as was made clear in response to the feelers put out by the Germans. As early as 1941 and again in 1943, the head of the Abwehr, Admiral Wilhelm Canaris, was busy attempting to arrange a separate peace between Germany and Britain. He and Sir Stewart Menzies, 'C' of MI6, shared a deep hostility towards communism, and no doubt hoped it wasn't too late to unite fascism and democracy against the Soviet Union.

---

2   Hans Mommsen, *Germans Against Hitler: The Stauffenberg Plot and Resistance Under the Third Reich*, London, 2005, pp. 24–5.

Circumstantial evidence suggests that the two had a head-to-head meeting on safe territory: Franco's Spain. However, their efforts were sabotaged by Kim Philby, the Soviet intelligence operative embedded in British intelligence. Philby is said to have paralysed the paperwork. Whatever Menzies' intentions, there is no evidence that either Churchill and his war cabinet or the British military high command were in favour of capitulation.

The German high command was sometimes prone to wishful thinking. They talked a lot without doing anything. In 1943, for instance, senior officers mooted doing the business when Hitler visited the Eastern Front to lunch with his generals. It was discussed quite seriously, with Field Marshal Gunther von Kluge being warned in advance so that he could keep out of the line of fire. He objected to the details, arguing that 'It was not seemly to shoot a man at lunch', and pointed out that there might be casualties among 'senior officers [including himself] who would have to be there and who could not be spared if the front was to be held'. He was passively sympathetic to Stauffenberg's effort in 1944, but shot himself after it failed. Better that, he thought, than to be renditioned by the Gestapo.

The desperation to find 'good Germans' who stood up to Hitler led sometimes to absurdities. The collapse and disorientation of the Marxisant left in the 1990s provided revisionist historians with many opportunities to 're-evaluate' the Nazi past. It was claimed, for instance, that German physicists could have produced the atomic bomb but chose not to do so. Heisenberg, in particular, has been portrayed as a German patriot, supposedly out of sympathy with the Nazi regime, and the German physicists generally as being reluctant to build the bomb since the very idea was abhorrent or, as some said, impractical. This was not the view expressed by Joseph Haberer in his exemplary study of scientists under the Nazis, *Politics and the Community of Science*. Having consulted the original transcripts, he summarised the initial reactions of the interned physicists to the news of Hiroshima thus:

All the interned scientists, with the exception of von Laue and possibly Hahn, reacted in the following pattern: first, despondency and questions about how and where did we fail? How did the Americans do it? Expressions of personal failure and self-castigation followed: if they had worked harder, had tried to convince the Government to give full support, they probably would have beaten the Americans. A search for scapegoats followed these first two reactions. This included recriminations by some younger scientists to the effect that older colleagues, especially Heisenberg, had blundered and were to blame for the failure. Scientific leaders (such as Heisenberg and Weiszäcker) blamed the German Government for short-sightedness and for failing to support 'real' science.

Vichy on the Seine

Churchill remained extremely sceptical of the notion that there was a serious 'internal resistance' to Hitler. Newsreel images of the genuine mass celebrations that greeted early Nazi victories were too fresh in his mind to harbour any illusions. After the victories of the Red Army in 1943 and 1944, a separate peace negotiated by Britain and the United States with Canaris and Goering would have been seen for what it was: a betrayal and a capitulation. Apart from anything else it would have made a civil war in France and Italy inevitable.

The rapid fall of France in June 1940 was a huge blow to Churchill and the British political and military elites. They were now committed to a war against the Third Reich and engaged in a process of re-composition, one crucial aspect of which was the creation of a National Government. Labour MPs were needed to buttress Churchill against Conservative hatreds and indifference. During his early days as prime minister, the applause when he entered the House of Commons or delivered a speech was largely confined to the Labour benches, as many diarists noted at the time.

France's abject political surrender (the government that negotiated the 'peace' included two members of the Socialist Party), the capitulation of its army and the indifference of a large part of the country to the German occupation posed several questions for the British. The French Communist Party, trapped by the Stalin–Hitler pact, was paralysed. Questions arose in London. The most important of these was whether there would be a spontaneous Resistance and, if so, who might organise and lead it from within and without. And, if it had to be created from scratch in a country where traditional republican-conservatism was seriously divided, what might be the best mechanism?

Hitler had set up a collaborationist French government that continued to run the country, but with economic and political sovereignty effectively resting in Berlin. As far as the Germans were concerned, the priority was not the political composition of that government – though the removal of Jews and communists was a prerequisite – but rather its ability to stabilise the country, avoid a civil war and keep trade (loot) moving. This was virtually what they got with the regime in Vichy.

At the very beginning, it was not the Third Reich that asked Pétain to target the Jews and put them in holding camps. That was a French initiative, as historians have now proved without any doubt. The myth of a united France waiting patiently for the General to arrive on a khaki tank, a France with just a handful of traitors, was destroyed some decades ago by several foreign historians, with Robert Paxton torpedoing the work of most French historians.

The wartime resistance in France was a complicated and murky business. A melange of lies and cover-ups made all the more so later by the myths that grew up around it, stories that most French citizens knew were manufactured but that were considered necessary to save the 'honour' of France. There were two dominant versions of the Resistance story. The Resistance was essentially set up both from within and without. The external resistance was formed by the British SOE, aided and abetted by General de Gaulle's oddball outfit of patriotic nationalists, ultra-right monarchists and well-meaning uniformed hangers-on. The internal resistance comprised indigenous versions of the latter as well as communists (after June 1941) and leftist sympathisers based mainly in the factories and underground cells.

The Gaullists insisted that de Gaulle personified France. And the General himself began the post-war period with the blatant lie that France had been 'liberated by herself, by her own people with the help of the armies of France, with the support and aid of the whole of France, of fighting France, of the only France, of the true France, of the eternal France'. Apart from ignoring the role of Britain and the United States, this completely underplayed the support given to Hitler by the men and women of Vichy. And what of Vichy? Dismissed with an imperious wave of the hand: They were a tiny aberration – *'quelques malheureux traîtres'* – a few unfortunate traitors. Most of France knew perfectly well that this hallucinatory notion was complete nonsense.

Asked when the Resistance had begun, de Gaulle was characteristically modest. It had begun with *his* decision to go into exile, *his* declaration from London on 18 June 1940, *his* BBC broadcast to France exhorting the nation to join him in the fight that lay ahead. De Gaulle's flight to London and his appeal should not be underestimated, but their significance relates essentially to the post-war phase. An alternative to Vichy had been created with its headquarters in London.

An alternative version was given by the French Communist Party (PCF). The party glossed over the awkward period when the Stalin–Hitler Pact had paralysed the majority of communists throughout Europe. Its claim that it had been strongly opposed to the Nazis from the start of the occupation was exploded in 1977 by *Le Monde*. The newspaper asserted that in 1940 the Comintern had instructed its French section to get permission from the occupying authorities to publish its paper, *L'Humanité*, legally. The claim shocked many PCF members and was vigorously denounced and denied by the party's leaders. They gave up when decisive evidence emerged (probably courtesy of French intelligence archives) that revealed the allegation to be true. *Le Monde* included examples of articles for possible future publication in a legal edition of the paper. One of these referred to Georges Mandel, a former minister of the interior, as 'the Jew Mandel'.

While the official PCF line was to attack Vichy unequivocally, it simultaneously called for 'fraternisation' with German soldiers. There were acts of individual heroism, of course. The immensely gifted young French novelist Paul Nizan broke with the PCF, enlisted to fight the advancing Germans, and died at Dunkirk. Like the few other communist dissidents who broke ranks, he was vilified. Nizan was memorialised in a very moving essay by his school friend and comrade, Jean-Paul Sartre, as a model for political commitment:

> Nizan was a killjoy. His was a call to arms and hatred. Class against class. With a patient, mortal enemy, no quarter can be given: it is kill or be killed, there is no middle way. And no time for sleep. All his life, with his graceful insolence and his eyes lowered to his fingernails, he had repeated: 'Don't believe in Father Christmas.'[3]

The PCF justifiably stressed its own role – '*le parti des 75,000 fusillés*' – at the peak of the resistance and praised the working class for both its passive and active opposition to Vichy and the Germans. This was certainly true of a large minority. Unlike de Gaulle, the communists denounced all those who had collaborated as 'bourgeois class enemies'. Their alternative to Gaullism was not based in London, but on the battlefields of the Soviet Union, and there is little doubt that after Stalingrad and Kursk PCF membership grew rapidly, as did the resistance of all varieties.

Despite all this and despite the heroic acts of the French Resistance, the most awkward truth that neither Gaullist nor communist confronted was that a majority of the Resistance was non-French in ethnic terms. The underground included Spanish refugees from Franco's blood-letting, anti-fascist Italians, Armenians, Arabs, Jews and others who, in total, outnumbered the natives.

This truth was brought home by Marcel Ophüls' *Le Chagrin et la pitié* ('The Sorrow and the Pity') a four-hour documentary made in 1969 that challenged both versions of the Resistance. It provided enough evidence from French and German newsreels to make the Gaullist versions seem absurd. Their patriotic nationalism had not been the moving force in the Resistance, and the overwhelming majority of the French people had not favoured it.

---

3 Nizan's great novel, *The Conspiracy*, written in 1938, was published by Verso in 2011 with a Foreword by Sartre.

The 1968 political and cultural upheavals in France (as well as Germany, Italy and Japan) had made such films possible. The state broadcaster ORTF refused to show the film and it started life in independent cinemas in 1971, almost three years after completion. To this day, most French people have not seen it.

In contrast, the film's clear-sightedness was challenged by the morally ambiguous works of the novelist Patrick Modiano who also co-scripted Louis Malle's weak effort, *Lucien Lacombe*, criticised by the critic Serge Dany for lacking any social and political context. It was not a surprise that Modiano won the admiration of many collaborationists or that the literary prize he received (in May 1968!) was presented to him by a former close adviser of Pierre Laval. The evocation of the occupation period as a puzzle that is impossible to solve is now even more in vogue in countries like Italy, Greece and the former Yugoslavia. The desire to veil the communist resistance and bury it in the sea motivated many, especially political turncoats whose illusions about Stalin had been betrayed.

How did Churchill view de Gaulle and his entourage, now settled in London and behaving as if they were the French government? The two men were similar in some ways. The first a politician whose favourite pastime was playing soldiers and whose interference in military affairs often annoyed those at the receiving end. The other was born and bred a soldier, whose decision to intervene in politics immediately after the war (and later to topple the Fourth Republic) was not as popular as he liked to believe.

The fact remains that France was not freed from the Vichy government and its German overseer by the French Resistance, but by the United States and Britain after D-Day. The ten Allied divisions that landed in Normandy on 6 June 1944 were accompanied by 177 French commandos, needed more as translators and guides than anything else. Churchill understood de Gaulle's weaknesses, but he also knew that support for the PCF was growing by the day (it would become the largest single political party in France after 1945). An alternative was necessary, and de Gaulle's self-belief and identification of himself as the embodiment of the patriotic French state made him the most suitable bourgeois choice to run post-war France.

Churchill loved the idea of restoring monarchies wherever he could. It was impossible to do so in France, but having observed de Gaulle from close quarters, he knew that *le General* was the next best thing. As I have pointed out more than once, Churchill gave enormous priority to Europe's colonial empires and their post-war stability had to be maintained even if the ultimate price to be paid was the organisation of a smooth transition of the empires from Europe to the United States. It was for this reason that Roosevelt and Churchill seriously considered foisting two tame French colonialists cooling their heels in North Africa – Admiral Darlan and General Giraud, who they had managed to wrench away from Vichy – on the French people.

The Gaullists, backed on this by the PCF, were able to thwart Washington's plan. Darlan was conveniently assassinated. Roosevelt was compelled to come to terms, on an unstable basis, with the Gaullist–PCF forces. De Gaulle was in total disagreement with any notion, however abstract, of handing over French colonies to the United States, though that was what eventually happened in Indochina, if not in Africa. De Gaulle insisted that he was the sole guardian of French sovereignty together with his officers and soldiers, even though only a handful of the French troops brought to Britain after Dunkirk agreed to serve under him. In fact, the Gaullist Resistance organisation was outnumbered by the PCF and independent anti-fascist groups. Many non-communist, fellow-travelling intellectuals mingled easily with the PCF wing of the resistance, living their daily lives through the communist friends they had chosen. After the war, some felt they had lost their way and either abandoned politics or moved over to the General. De Gaulle was nonetheless insistent in 1944 that he was the saviour of 'French honour' at a critical point in the nation's history, and he would go on to make all the key decisions on civilian administration and the temporary structures that needed to be put into place.

It was his stubbornness in identifying French sovereignty as embodied in his person and his Resistance organisation that annoyed both Roosevelt and Churchill. Stalin openly asked whether a nation that had collaborated so fully with the Germans should be assigned a share of Germany and a seat on the United Nations Security Council. This was the reason for his clashes and arguments with Roosevelt and Churchill. De Gaulle demanded that he be in charge of drafting an agreement on civil matters. Churchill pointed out that this could not be done without Roosevelt's approval, and that one of his key representatives had to be present. When de Gaulle refused to accept this, and threatened to boycott what the Allies were up to, Churchill was provoked into a fury: 'each time we have to choose between Europe and the open sea, we shall always choose the open sea. Each time I have to choose between you and Roosevelt, I shall always choose Roosevelt.' This was the essence of British foreign policy from then on.

It was this same experience that led de Gaulle to formulate his own thoughts on the post-war order: Neither Washington nor Moscow but France and French sovereignty. That is why he later pulled France out of NATO. The defence of French imperial interests was a central Gaullist precept. Those who have elevated de Gaulle to the status of a giraffe-god are, in their vast majority, opponents of these very precepts today. Praise of de Gaulle, Atlanticism, and acceptance of the German economic *Anschluss* are the hallmarks of contemporary France. When Chirac refused to back the Iraq war in 2003, his socialist opposite number Françoise Hollande, as revealed by Wikileaks, rushed to the US embassy to explain to the ambassador that this would not have happened had he been president.

This, therefore, is the legacy of 1944. De Gaulle, Churchill and Roosevelt agreed that most of the Vichy underlings – technicians in every field, including in the courts, the prisons, the army and the police – should remain part of the 'Liberation'. De Gaulle, sentenced to death in absentia by Pétain, had Pétain tried and sentenced to death, though this was commuted to life imprisonment (he spent the rest of his life on a benighted prison-island, a French speciality).

In 1992 President Mitterrand, who had worked for Vichy in the early years of the war, visited Pétain's tomb. Whether he did so as a sign of forgiveness or to revive the comradeship of his youth is a question of interpretation.

The Civil War in Italy

It is a great pity that the French Resistance never found a historian with the capacities of Claudio Pavone, whose huge book on the Italian Resistance continues to dominate the historiography on this subject in that country, despite the gradual rehabilitation of Mussolini by Berlusconi, Meloni and Salvini.[4]

Italy was different from the other countries in Europe – it had given birth to fascism. Mussolini had ruled the country for over a decade before Hitler's triumph in 1933, which reversed the relationship of forces. The Italian dictator hated playing second fiddle, failing to realise that it was the only space available. Tantrums, like the invasion of Greece without informing Hitler, backfired sensationally. The Greek Army chased the Italians out of the country, forcing the Germans to occupy Greece and delay the launch of Operation Barbarossa. Italy's setbacks in the war and the German disasters on the Eastern Front began to create fissures in Italian society. It was no secret that the Americans were planning a landing somewhere in the south. Would it be Sardinia or Sicily?

From 1943 onwards, the king and senior military figures, including Marshall Bagdolio, began to discuss the dumping of Mussolini and offering a peace treaty to the Allies, a Vichy in reverse. At the same time there was dissension from below. On 5 March, the workers at the Rasetti factory in Turin went on strike. Two days later they were joined by workers at nine other factories. By the end of the month virtually the entire city was at a standstill. Gramsci's political birthplace had come to life again. Four months later, even as the strikes were crossing city boundaries and affecting many other northern towns, the Allies landed at Sicily.

---

4   As a left-wing minority used to chant: 'Berlusconi, Meloni, Salvini non sono Mussolini, eppure tutti quanti ne sono innamorati' (Berlusconi, Meloni, Salvini are not the same as Mussolini, but yes, they love him nonetheless).

The king, Vittorio Emanuele III, realised that the only way he could survive was by rapidly dissociating himself from Mussolini. On 24 July, soon after Rome was bombed for the first time, the Fascist Grand Council met and adopted a motion that was critical of Mussolini. The next day, Il Duce went to call on the king, but was asked for his resignation and arrested by armed soldiers.

During the forty-five days that followed, popular demonstrations broke out all over the country to celebrate the end of fascism. The Duke of Addis Ababa (as Badoglio was mocked by many British officers) ordered a brutal response, while the king fled south to safety. The Germans invaded Italy to counter the collapse of fascism. Things came to a head on 3 September, when the Italian Army eventually dissolved, surrendering to Berlin. Over half a million soldiers were taken prisoner by their former ally and transported to Germany. Meanwhile, a secret armistice between Italy and the Allies was signed.

The Italian Resistance emerged out of this chaos. Hitler ordered the German Army in Italy to organise Mussolini's escape and create an alternative government. The instruction was carried out by SS officer Otto Skorzeny and Mussolini was placed at the head of the German puppet Republic of Salò in the north.

To complete the picture there was the growing strength of the Italian communists. In January 1943, the Italian Communist Party (PCI) had consisted, at most, of a few thousand members. Many of them had been exiled internally or had fled voluntarily, first to Spain where they fought with the Republican Army, later to France. Hundreds had been imprisoned. Their most gifted and independent-minded leader, Antonio Gramsci, had died in a fascist prison. The chief prosecutor in his case had demanded a sentence 'to stop his brain from working for twenty years'. His second-in-command, Palmiro Togliatti, was in Moscow.

By the end of 1943 the PCI had quadrupled its membership. Within a few years, the party had won the support of millions. How and why? Its role in the Resistance was the decisive factor. For a decade from the mid-1940s, the PCI and the PCF were the hegemonic parties of the left in Western Europe. In Greece and Yugoslavia, communist-led Resistance movements had been extremely effective and were on the verge of taking power. This was the peak of communist influence in Western Europe, and was used by Churchill and, more importantly, the United States to justify the Cold War in the Continent.

Claudio Pavone starts his magisterial history of the Resistance by quoting two important young left-wing intellectuals, Vittoria Foa and Italo Calvino. Foa, released from prison in August 1943, left his copy of Vico for his cellmate Bruno Corbi, with a dedication. They were Vico's words but expressed Foa's sentiments: 'by various and diverse ways, which seemed like hazards and were in fact opportunities'. Foa himself would later write: 'During the Resistance and, for a brief moment, at the Liberation, all had seemed possible to us.'

Three years later, Calvino focused on another section of the political panorama. On 15 September 1946, in a text titled 'Homer the Anti-militarist', written for the Turin edition of the PCI paper *L'Unita*, he posed an interesting question:

> What in fact is *The Odyssey*? It is the myth of the return home, born during the long years of 'naja' [military service] of the soldiers who have gone off to fight in distant places, of their anxiety about how they will manage to get home, when the war is over, of the fear that assails them in their dreams of never managing to make it home, of the strange obstacles that appear on the journey. *The Odyssey* is the story of the eighth of September [referring to the end of the Second World War], of all the eighth of Septembers in History: the need to return home by hook or by crook, through lands fraught with enemies.

The September 1943 armistice with the Allies also marked the beginning of large-scale Italian partisan resistance against the Nazi occupation, reaching over 100,000 members by April 1945, of which 35,000 were killed. The defeat of Mussolini and the fascist state he embodied was carried out largely by the Anglo-American armies with the Resistance forces as a crucial auxiliary. It had been agreed at Yalta that Italy and France – fascist and proto-fascist in their make-up – would be the patrimony of the West, i.e. the United

States. That those who sang *Marechal, nous voila*, did so with the *Marseillaise* inscribed on their hearts. Carmen Callil, in *Bad Faith*, her revealing biography of Louis Darquier, Vichy's 'Commissioner for Jewish Affairs', suggested that 'while there was compliance, resignation, fear, despair, self-interest, betrayal and shame, a strong sense of sullen, hungry fury growls through these years of the new French Fatherland'.

In Italy the anti-fascist movements had been larger from the very beginning, and in 1945, radical liberal politicians in the mould of Carlo Rosselli and Piero Gobetti insisted that pre-Mussolini Italy had never been democratic and, hence, a new democratic tradition had to be created afresh. They argued that a 'progressive democracy' was needed to root out fascism and the conditions that had created it and brought it to power. Some of this was embedded in the new constitution. Gobetti's wife Ada later explained what they had meant:

> In a confusing way I sensed . . . that another struggle was beginning; longer, more difficult, more tiring, even if less bloody. It was no longer the question of fighting against cruelty and violence, but . . . of not allowing that little flame of solidarity and fraternal humanism, which we had seen born, to die in the calm atmosphere of an apparent return to normal life.

The new Italian prime minister, Ferruccio Parri, startled the National Assembly by reiterating Rosselli's view: 'I do not believe that the Governments we had before Fascism were democratic.' Responses were not slow in coming. Pope Pius XII hurriedly sanctified private property, while Alcide De Gasperi, the most intelligent leader ever of the Christian Democrats, spelt out his political programme thus: 'anti-Fascism is a contingent political phenomenon, which will at a certain moment be overturned by other political ideals more in keeping with the feelings of Italian public life, for the good and progress of the nation'.

Did those other political ideals include fascism? De Gasperi would have replied in the negative at the time, but others like him later began a rehabilitation process, including Renzo De Felice with an eight-volume biography of Mussolini. Their arguments were depressingly unoriginal: fascism had not been a response to the threat of a workers' revolution, and Italian fascism was different to its German counterpart. The prettifying of Italian fascism by Berlusconi, Melone and Salvini is a continuing process in the country today.

From the point of view of Truman and Churchill, De Gasperi was a model anti-communist. Intelligent, politically astute and a skilful tactician, he outmanoeuvred his PCI rival Palmiro Togliatti with great ease. What the PCI needed was a Gramsci. Instead, what they got was a Comintern apparatchik and a cadre of Stalinist politicians who ran the outfit. Togliatti was neither a serious theoretician nor a clever politician. During the civil war in Spain he had revealed his true character as a cynical and cold-blooded operator who did as he was instructed. On his return to Rome from Moscow in 1944 he made it clear that there was no revolution in sight and ordered the Resistance to disarm itself.

It is true that there was no objective basis for a socialist revolution, despite the waves of workers' strikes. Any such attempt, had it been made, would probably have been drowned in blood by a combined operation: the Allies would have united with the right and far-right parties to crush the PCI, similar to what they were doing in Greece at exactly the same time.

Whether the Resistance should have stored its weapons for future use rather than meekly hand them over was a related, but separate, tactical issue. Where the PCI went hopelessly wrong was in doing a political deal with De Gasperi that handed over all their trump cards. In one of his essays on Italy, Perry Anderson sketched out how the failure of the PCI led them to exclude themselves from national politics:

When the war came to an end, Italy was ... not treated like Germany, as a defeated power, but as a chastened 'co-belligerent'. Once the Allied troops were gone, a coalition government, comprising the left-liberal Partito d'Azione, Socialists, Communists and Christian Democrats was faced with the legacy of Fascism, and the monarchy that had collaborated with it. The Christian Democrats, aware that their potential voters remained loyal to the monarchy, and recognising that their natural supports in the state apparatus had been the routine instruments of Fascism, were resolved to prevent anything comparable to German de-Nazification. But they were in a minority in the cabinet, where the secular left held more posts.

At this juncture the PCI, instead of putting the DC [Christian Democrats] on the defensive by pressing for an uncompromising purge of the state – cleaning out all senior collaborationist officials in the bureaucracy, judiciary, army and police – invited it to head the government, and lifted scarcely a finger to dismantle the traditional apparatus of Mussolini's rule. So far from isolating Christian Democracy, Togliatti manoeuvred to put its leader, De Gasperi, at the head of the government, and then joined with the DC – to the indignation of the Socialists – in confirming the Lateran Pacts that Mussolini had sealed with the Vatican. The prefects, judges and policemen who had served the Duce were left virtually untouched. As late as 1960, 62 out of 64 prefects had been minions of Fascism, and all 135 of the country's police chiefs. As for judges and officers, the unreconstructed courts acquitted the torturers of the regime and convicted the partisans who had fought against them, retrospectively declaring combatants of the Fascist Republic of Salò legitimate belligerents, and those of the Resistance illegitimate – the latter hence liable to summary execution after 1943, without penal sanctions for the former after 1945. These enormities were a direct consequence of the actions of the PCI. It was Togliatti himself who, as minister of justice, promulgated in June 1946 the amnesty that enabled them. A year later, the party was rewarded with an unceremonious ejection from the government by De Gasperi, who no longer had need of it.[5]

With historical revisionism still in full flow, the equation of the Soviet Union with the Third Reich remains useful for current needs in Poland, Hungary, Croatia and the Ukraine. The Italian cinema

---

5 Perry Anderson, 'The Invertebrate Left', *London Review of Books*, 12 March 2009.

offers an interesting contrast. Compare Bertolucci's epic *1900* with the Taviani brothers' *Notte di San Lorenzo*. The former film is a cleverly choreographed depiction of the rise of the working-class movement in northern Italy and the birth of Italian communism, portrayed with great sympathy. Made as a popular film with Hollywood stars playing key roles, it served its purpose. *Notte di San Lorenzo* depicts fascists and the Resistance fighting blindly with each other in a corn field. What is there to choose between them? The Tavianis register the changes in political temperature well, even though the film is pure rubbish.

For Churchill and Truman to defend the old-new structures of the Italian state on the grounds that the rage and cunning of the Soviet Union should never be underestimated was to deliberately misunderstand that country's policy. Churchill had recounted to his physician, Lord Moran, how once, after supper in Stalin's apartment in the Kremlin in 1942, the Soviet leader had turned to him and asked why he feared Russia. The Soviet Union had no intention of trying to conquer the world. Churchill muttered unconvincingly that he recalled a similar conversation with Ribbentrop. In fact, the deal made before Yalta – that Italy was part of the US domain and that the British could do what they wanted in Greece – was never challenged by Moscow and the two communist parties in those countries stayed in line. As Eric Hobsbawm once pointed out: 'one might even argue that the excesses of anti-communism were inversely correlated to the degree of the communist threat. In Germany and the USA, the two democracies which limited or abolished the legality of communist parties, the political appeal of the local parties was negligible.'[6]

6   Eric Hobsbawm, 'History and Illusion', *New Left Review*, I/220, November–December 1996.

12

The Origins of the Cold War:
Yugoslavia, Greece, Spain

Tighten your leather belts, workmen of Flanders!
The old man of Downing Street breakfasts early today with
*   the 300 men who betray you.*
Bake your seed grain, peasants of the Campagna!
There will be no land. Neapolitan stevedores
On the walls of houses you will be daubing:
'Bring back the Stinker!' Today in the full light of noon
The old man of Downing Street was in Rome.

Keep your sons at home, mothers of Athens!
Or light candles for them: tonight
The old man of Downing Street is bringing back your King.

Get up from your beds, Labour peers!
Come and brush the old man of Downing Street's bloody coat!

Bertolt Brecht, 'The Old Man of Downing Street' (1944)

In Western Europe the Resistance took different forms, determined by the Allies and the American and British armies. In Yugoslavia and Greece no outsider armies were required to defeat the Germans. As the Allied leaders began to contemplate total victory, the future shape of Europe would assume became a crucial issue. Churchill would play an important role again, but by now he was only too aware that US industry and Soviet manpower and industry had won the war. The British Empire was bankrupt. Key decisions would henceforth be made or agreed by Roosevelt and Stalin. It was necessary to pretend otherwise for public consumption, but for how long?

Churchill thought long and hard on how to prevent the largely communist Greek Resistance from becoming too dominant. Likewise with Yugoslavia. Bringing back the monarchy in both countries was his favoured choice.

The citizens of the United States and his Majesty's subjects in the United Kingdom had watched from afar as the Red Army had fought and won key battles. Admiration, not nervousness, was the dominant feeling among many citizens not sympathetic to the Axis powers. In October 1944, Stalin and Churchill met in Moscow at the 'Tolstoy Conference'. Here, on a famous piece of paper, Churchill and Eden obtained their temporary friend's agreement on the British plans for Greece, but Stalin wanted Romania and Bulgaria in return. That too was agreed.

Pleased that he had got his way, Churchill was in a good mood. Fortified by a glass or two, he said to Stalin: 'It's a pity God didn't seek our opinion when he built the world.' The Georgian's response: 'That was God's first mistake.' Did the two scoundrels laugh and open another bottle? Quite likely. Whatever the case, the Greek people had been betrayed, resulting in a civil war that followed the end of the Second World War and later a vicious military dictatorship, courtesy of NATO.

At Yalta in 1945, Stalin agreed to a division of 'spheres' in Europe and pledged no interference in Italy or France, where the two communist parties had been transformed into mass parties thanks to the Resistance they had led and the stunning military triumphs of the Red Army. The full meaning of the Yalta agreement has often been obscured, with Western ideologues regularly describing it as a necessary concession to Stalin. This is misleading. Yalta was always a double-edged sword. Not only did it license the Soviet control of Eastern Europe, it also approved a strong and hegemonic US presence in Western Europe, a presence essential to the establishment of NATO and a hegemony reinforced by what appear to be permanent US military bases in

Germany, Italy and Britain, further strengthened by the growth of nuclear weapons systems and their implantation in Western Europe.

Stalin agreed that Franco's Spain, Salazar's Portugal, Greece and Turkey should be a Western preserve and that Germany would be under a four-power occupation. He reluctantly agreed to France being one of these powers, since the Vichy regime had to all effects and purposes been part of the Axis network. It was also agreed that France would be a member of the United Nations Security Council. An unnecessary concession, some thought, but Churchill was determined to have at least two decaying European empires seated at the top table. It did not succeed in its real aim, which was the integration of Gaullist France in Anglo-American projects for the future. That came later.

As far as Greece and Yugoslavia were concerned, the piece of paper suggested Greece be part of the Western sphere and Yugoslavia a zone shared 50–50 by the US/Britain and the Soviet Union. It was a badly conceived plan. But not the only one. At Yalta, Roosevelt and Churchill also discussed the conditions under which the Soviet Union might enter the war against Japan. All three leaders agreed that, in return for Soviet participation in the Pacific theatre, Russia would be granted a sphere of influence in Manchuria after Japan's surrender. This would include a chunk of Sakhalin, a lease at Port Arthur, a share in the operation of the Manchurian railroads, and the Kuril Islands. They were clearly not following developments in China too closely. The way events turned out in Yugoslavia and Greece suggested that decisions made at the top table are not always accepted by people below. The Balkan experience was a striking reminder of this reality.

Yugoslavia: Partisans versus Fascists

At 2.30 a.m. on 6 April 1941, the Yugoslav ambassador had signed a friendship pact with Moscow, both sides hoping it might deter a German invasion, given that the Stalin–Hitler Pact was still in operation. No such luck. A few hours later the Luftwaffe took off from Bulgarian airfields, violated Yugoslav air space and subjected Belgrade to continuous and heavy bombing. Simultaneously, the Wehrmacht crossed the Austrian–Slovenian border at Maribor and moved to take Zagreb. By 8 April the Second German Army had reached Belgrade. On 10 April, Italian, Hungarian and Bulgarian forces invaded the country and dismembered it as Hitler had planned.

That same day, the 'Independent State of Croatia' was proclaimed under the leadership of the Ustashe, whose *Poglavnik* (Führer) Ante Pavelić had been brought back from Italy where till now he and his band of Catholic fascists had been sheltered by Mussolini and provided spiritual succour by the Vatican. Pavelić expanded his control to Bosnia-Herzegovina, giving Mussolini a big thank-you present in the shape of central Dalmatia. The Italians also occupied southern Slovenia including Ljubljana. They took Montenegro as well, before falling on a large chunk of Kosovo and attaching it to Albania, which was already under their control. The Hungarians were awarded the Vojvodina, and the Bulgarians were given their own lollipop in the shape of Macedonia.

The Yugoslav Army had proven useless. Its generals capitulated to the Germans on 17 April, with tens of thousands of soldiers flee-ing desperately in all directions. The Germans took 344,000, mainly Serb, prisoners; another 300,000 managed to get away. King Peter II and his government fled to London via stopovers in Athens and Palestine. Within eleven days the Axis had taken another country without meeting any resistance.

The Communist Party of Yugoslavia (CPY) was surprised by the total collapse of the army, which had been brought up on patriotic Serb traditions of fighting hard against the Ottoman Empire in the nineteenth century and the Hapsburgs during the First World War. Three years later, the CPY leader Milovan Djilas confessed to Dmitri Manuilsky, a leading Comintern apparatchik: 'We made the mistake of thinking the majority of officers, together with the General Staff, would resist the Germans. It did not happen. Most of them surrendered . . . There was no serious resistance; it was a triumphal march.'

Why was the CPY not prepared in 1941? The party had a tragic history. It had been subjected to massive repression under the monarchical dictatorships since 1918, and been banned in 1921.

Later, in Moscow, Stalin's purges had wiped out some of the best cadres of the party. Tito survived because he kept his head down and had a powerful protector in Georgi Dmitrov, the Bulgarian communist and long-time Comintern leader.

Here we had a classic example of a party subordinated to Moscow, and semi-paralysed by the Stalin–Hitler Pact that prevented it from even conducting sabotage against the occupiers. Tito, an ethnic Croat, refused to accept the fragmentation of Yugoslavia, denounced the fascist Croatian state created by the Third Reich, and pledged to re-unite his country. On 8 May 1941, Moscow recognised the Axis dismemberment of Yugoslavia. They expelled the ambassador after informing him that there was no longer any juridical basis for the existence of a Yugoslav mission in Moscow.

Four days previously the CPY leaders had convened a delegate conference in Zagreb where the leadership had strongly denounced the German breakup of the country and Tito had insisted that they start preparations for an armed struggle against all the occupying powers. He broke with Stalinist orthodoxy and stated that the fight against the fascists was simultaneously a struggle for power against the local bourgeoisie and its allies. He informed his comrades that he was speaking of a socialist revolution.

Unlike Stalin, the Yugoslav leader knew that the Germans would not delay too long before invading the Soviet Union. A military committee was set up, whose aim was to create clandestine, unified Yugoslav armed groups in every occupied region. The underground leadership felt it would be safer in Belgrade than Zagreb, where a section of the population was intoxicated by the lure of independence and where Pavelić was already pre-empting the Germans by persecuting, torturing and imprisoning Roma, Jews and Serbs. As far as these groups were concerned, three alternatives faced them: one-third to be exterminated, one-third deported and the rest forced to convert to Roman Catholicism.

Even the Germans were slightly horrified by the treatment of the Serbs. Subsequently at Nuremberg this exterminism was judged to be genocide. Serbs put the number killed at 750,000; the German figures are 350,000. Pavelić was prepared to safeguard the Bosniaks as long as they accepted they had been born Croatians and, in some cases, where Muslim gangs agreed to kill Serbs. Many did so to survive. Others enlisted as German auxiliaries.

The two Resistance movements in the Balkans that impressed the Allies were both led by the communist parties of Greece and Yugoslavia respectively. In the latter case, a majority of SOE observers in the field, or special envoys like Fitzroy MacLean sent to assess Tito, were impressed by the Croat communists and appalled by the alternative. The Croat nationalists – the Ustashe – were led by men who were straightforward fascists and collaborated openly and happily with Hitler, providing armed militias to combat Tito's multi-ethnic guerrilla army. In Serbia the Chetniks did not collaborate openly, but their hostility to Tito was on a par with that of the Ustashe. No sane British presence in Yugoslavia could have advised anything else but supplying Tito's forces with arms and supplies. Churchill's son Randolph had been parachuted into the country and he, too, was impressed by the communist-led resistance. The only dissenting voice was that of the novelist Evelyn Waugh, who took an early dislike to Tito, an irrational prejudice rather than a philosophical assessment, a trait for which he was already known.

The Resistance that was fighting defensive battles on the peaks and in the chasms of Montenegro combined a tough discipline and dogmatism. The Wehrmacht they were fighting against displayed the same levels of brutality against southern Slavs as it did in the Soviet Union. Their Ustashe allies, keen to display their total embrace of fascist values, were even worse. Tito, the undisputed leader of the Yugoslav Resistance, and his comrades on the leadership hailed from all nationalities. Tito, a Croat; Kardelj, a Slovene; Djilas, a Montenegrin; Ranković a Serb. The major political thrust of the Resistance stressed the unity of the embryonic Yugoslav state being created in the mountains. The Kosovars, then and postwar, were never fully integrated.

Yugoslavia, China and Vietnam were the three states where the effective resistance, led by the communist parties, resulted in revolutions. The party-armies were also institutions of a dual power. The spirit of the Yugoslav resistance was recalled decades later by the SOE radical, Basil Davidson, as he observed, with sadness, the break-up of Tito's Yugoslavia:

> In September 1943 I was with the Partisan Third Corps when it took the Croat-held town of Tuzla in northern Bosnia by storm. After days of fighting the enemy lost several hundred killed and as many wounded; there were also, according to my notes, rather more than two thousand Croat prisoners. These prisoners of war were conscripts of the 'Croat Independent State' promoted by Hitler. After that tough battle these prisoners lost their weapons and their footwear, boots being rarer in the Partisan Army than weapons.
>
> But they did not lose their lives or their liberty: they were quickly set free and sent home with the advice, cheerfully enough conveyed, that they waste no time in getting themselves rearmed and captured again. After that grim war Tuzla managed to grow into a flourishing town, and repeated calls for peace and reconciliation which have come from there during these last few years have seemed to me to recall and revive the Partisan experience of *bratstvo i jedinstvo*: the 'brotherhood and unity' for which the Partisan brigades had fought.

Why did the British back Tito? It was a strategic decision necessitated by the defection of the Serbian Chetnik commanders to the Axis in 1942. At that time only the Chetniks could have effectively sabotaged enemy communications. Instead, they began to help the Germans. Churchill reacted angrily. He first reduced the supply of weapons to them and then, after all appeals and inducements had failed, decided to cut off all further supplies in 1943.

This left Tito's partisans as the only available force in the country. Two years earlier, on 15 April 1941, the CPY had, after heated debates in the leadership, come out in support of an armed uprising against enemies within and without to transform Yugoslavia. They condemned the Nazi occupiers and those collaborating with them, the monarchic government's betrayal, and the deliberate fostering of chauvinism linked to ethnic hatred, arguing instead for a 'real independence of the Yugoslav peoples' on the basis of which 'a new, fraternal community will be built'.

Tito had moved the party's underground headquarters to Belgrade. Here, disguising himself as a Czech businessman working for Skoda, he found accommodation four doors away from General Schroder, the German commandant in Belgrade. The atmosphere in occupied Belgrade was graphically described by Djilas:

> Patrols during the night, darkness and continuous shots from all over the city. The Jews with yellow ribbons, with fear and anger, hunger and death, somber faces of citizens, and young Germans, gay and arrogant, with prostitutes and cameras. Flights of airplanes toward Greece and Romania. First local newspapers at the service of the occupiers.

German complacency reached a peak. They boasted openly to the local bourgeoisie in Zagreb and Belgrade that they were on their way to the Soviet Union. In April and May 1941, Tito sent urgent messages to the Comintern ('Grandpa' in code), via the Soviet military *attaché* in Belgrade, warning that the Nazi storm was about to hit the USSR. *Nach Moskau* was being painted on German tanks, and German generals were openly saying at dinner parties that they would enter the Soviet Union 'like a knife through butter'. On 31 May, Tito sent 'Grandpa' a message that made it clear the CPY was preparing to launch a general uprising on the day the German troops invaded Russia. Stalin, besotted with the Germans, refused to believe this information.

The week after the invasion, Tito sent an urgent message: 'We are preparing an armed revolt against the occupiers, since our people are ready to fight. Tell us, what do you think? We are short of arms. Can we get some quickly?' Back came the reply from a senior Comintern leader, Georgi Dimitrov, instructing Tito, on behalf of Stalin (ever-loyal to his deal with Churchill), not to confuse liberating the country from fascism with the socialist revolution. Tito, who had worked for a short time at the Putilov factory in Petrograd, and had heard Lenin speak, was puzzled. He later confided to the Yugoslav historian Vladimir Dedijer that it took him some to understand what was at stake:

If we would do as Moscow wanted, we could never develop our insurrection. In our condition, this directive would signify the liquidation of the uprising even before it started. On 6 April, the old regime, with the king at its head, abandoned the Yugoslav people to the mercy of the conquerors, and what was left of the state's apparatus passed in the service of the occupiers. This demonstrated its fragility, abandoning the Yugoslav tradition of fighting for national independence, confirmed in 150 years by thirty-nine revolts and ten wars against foreign forces. In Yugoslavia, a popular revolt against the occupiers was unimaginable if it would not assure the people that they would be given a chance, after the war, to have a new truly patriotic government with an administration that was firm enough not to allow Yugoslavia, in spite of her natural riches, to resist colonization by the great powers, to hold fast against ethnic oppression, and to see that the majority of the people would not live in misery.

Tito survived his visits to Moscow largely because Dimitrov backed him as the person to be trusted in Yugoslavia. He kept an ultra-low profile, avoiding unnecessary contacts, keeping aloof from petty intrigues. He once saw Stalin, hiding behind a pillar watching the proceedings of the Comintern. Nothing more. He never met him nor asked for a meeting. The real battles came later, when independent Yugoslavia and its leaders made it clear that they were not prepared to play the role of Stalin's pawn.

Half-hearted efforts by Stalin and Churchill to get Tito to accept the return of King Peter as the titular head were politely rejected. Churchill did not create a fuss. Yugoslavia had no strategic value as far as the British Empire was concerned. Tito's triumph lay in the fact that the Communist Party he headed and the Resistance it had created was multi-ethnic in character, uniting workers and peasants, students and intellectuals, against fascism. It was the only force capable of doing so. Chetnik, Ustashe and some Bosniak detachments collaborated openly and willingly with the Third Reich.

Tito disregarded Stalin's instructions and went all out for a socialist revolution. Popular support and a surge in self-confidence followed this decision. When Stalin threatened punishment, Tito's response was to warn the Soviet leader that any attempt to topple the Yugoslav government would be met with resistance. The Yugoslav population would be armed. For this 'crime' Tito was hounded out of the international communist movement. He wore the stigma as a badge of honour. Only after Stalin's death was normality restored.

Triumph and Tragedy in Greece

What was acceptable for Yugoslavia was strictly forbidden in Greece. The principal reason was Greek's strategic location in the Mediterranean. Its sea-lanes were vital routes for the British Empire. Piraeus and Crete were regarded as essential ports. The establishment of a communist state after a popular resistance was anathema to Churchill. A senior Foreign Office mandarin, Eyre Crowe, had set down the parameters of imperial policy in 1907, and these still guided politician and bureaucrat alike:

> The general character of England's foreign policy is determined by immutable conditions of her geographical situation on the ocean flank of Europe as an island state with vast areas of colonies and dependencies whose existence and survival as an independent community are inseparably bound up with the possession of preponderant sea power.

Though articulated decades earlier, this was still accepted by the Admiralty and the political class when it came to developing strategy and tactics from 1942 onwards. Combined with his own naval fetish, Crowe's words explained Churchill's obsession with Greece and his ruthless determination to gain control there, however high the cost in both hardware and human lives. It was to offer one of the clearest views of imperialist banditry in action.

A number of SOE agents in the country were aware that what had allowed the British to come in after the German withdrawal was the political weakness of the Resistance. One SOE officer, C. M. Woodhouse, was clear: 'I have no doubt at all that ELAS [the National Popular Liberation Army] could have taken Athens. That would have made a British landing extremely difficult.' The British intervention in Greece was designed first to block and then to crush the Resistance, with the aid of a semi-fascist right that had sustained the monarchical Metaxas dictatorship from 1936 to 1940, and often using security battalions that had helped police the Nazi occupation. This was a crime of the highest magnitude. The most successful anti-Nazi Resistance in Europe was snuffed out by Churchill and the British Army in one of the bloodiest moments of the war.

The civil war unleashed by London cost the lives of at least 600,000 Greeks out of a population of 7 million. Severed heads and bodies of executed partisan leaders were casually displayed in public squares. The British embassy in Athens justified this grotesque policy by excusing the exhibition of severed heads as 'a regular custom in this country which cannot be judged by western European standards'. By today's standards and usages, the British Army and its Greek auxiliaries were guilty of serious war crimes, some bordering on genocide.

The Greek Civil War came about because, with Stalin's approval, Churchill had been granted Greece as Britain's 'sphere of influence'. The problem was that most Greeks, barring the collaborators, were not in favour of this solution. The communist-led Resistance had played a major role in harassing and pushing back the German Army, and few serious observers at the time doubted that Greece belonged to the left. Churchill decided to crush this possibility.

British forces were sent to occupy the country, and in the post-war period they armed and backed the Greek right, including many who had helped the Germans. The Greek communist leaders in Athens could have followed Tito's example and disregarded Moscow's instructions, which in this case were that they should work with the British and allow their troops to disembark in Athens in 1944. Churchill was not interested in any notion of a National Government that included the Resistance. Orders were given to disarm and disable ELAS, the main Resistance force. Even as D-Day was being celebrated in London, British troops were engaged in a brutal and bloody war against the Greek Resistance. A war that lasted two years and more.

Churchill played a central part in the rape of Greece, and is still regarded by older generations in that country as a tyrant and a butcher. The fact that his leading accomplices in this crime included his wartime Labour lieutenants, Clement Attlee and Ernest Bevin (who continued the policy after 1945), does not excuse his role in the slightest.

In a heated debate at the Labour Party Conference in December 1944, Bevin had defended Churchill to the hilt. In a confused, mendacious and ill-informed speech, he had not been able to reply to Labour MPs and delegates who were shocked by what their country was doing to Greece. Aneurin Bevan, given five minutes to speak, was loudly applauded when he informed the conference that: 'Only three bodies of public opinion in the world have gone on record in his [Churchill's] support, namely fascist Spain, fascist Portugal and the majority of the Tories in the House of Commons.' The trade union wielders of the block vote were not impressed. They backed the fore-lock-tugger Bevin. The Labour Party Conference thus added another body (its own) in support of Churchill's terror in Greece.

The British atrocities in Greece embarrassed more than a few in the SOE, British intelligence and the army at the time. There were too many people around who, though ashamed and angry at what was being done, kept silent. Churchill was particularly enraged by the hostility of *The Times*, and fulminated against the paper in the House of Commons. He knew the editor, Robert Barrington-Ward, well, but was unable to convince him to change his line. A few Labour MPs challenged the government in a sharp debate in the Commons in December 1944, forcing Churchill and his heir, Anthony Eden, onto the defensive, but to no avail.

Though the British disgrace would soon be covered up, sanitised and forgotten in Britain, or amalgamated with the Cold War trope of 'freedom versus communism', the Greeks did not forget.

The story had begun in the summer and autumn of 1942 with the emergence of the National Popular Liberation Army (ELAS), the military wing of the National Liberation Front (EAM). In terms of its military effectiveness, spread of support and creation of popular, elected village assemblies with women getting their first chance to vote and participate in decision-making, the Greek Resistance was ahead of its Yugoslav counterpart. There was one huge difference, however: the Greeks did not have a Tito. That is, a political leader capable of taking decisions in the Greek interest, regardless of Moscow's needs and wishes.

Despite this, the two organisations had an excellent record of resistance against the occupying German forces. Within a year they had millions of members and supporters. EAM was operating effectively as a provisional Greek government. This was shown when, in 1943, General Speidel, the supreme commander of the German forces in the country, issued a civil mobilization order specifying that 'every male inhabitant of Greece aged between sixteen and forty-five must carry out work' when required to do so. EAM called for a general mobilisation against the order. This type of resistance was unheard of in any other occupied country.

The Axis high command were, appropriately as it later turned out, lodged in the Hotel Grande Bretagne (as later were the British high command). They had machine-gun nests on the roof and armed soldiers cordoning off some areas, but the crowd was so huge that those watching events from the hotel balconies were not able to locate their soldiers. The crowd started singing the Greek national anthem, repeating the last two lines ad infinitum, 'Hail Liberty', 'Hail Liberty' . . .

The detailed description of this event in Dominique Eudes's classic account of the Greek Resistance is astonishing. When the German troops first opened fire they did so in the air. The crowd decided to move on to the ministry of labour, where they had been asked to present themselves. The building was guarded by two companies of the Carabinieri. 'They aimed their rifles at the advancing crowd,' writes Eudes, 'and machine-guns commenced their irregular barking, scything down the front ranks like wheat. A few puny pistol shots answered as the machine-guns cut into the mass of people; the demonstrators were going berserk, gripped by a blind, irresistible determination, exalted by the mad ancient war-cry of Greece: *Aera! Aera:* wind, tempest, delirium.'[1]

The insurrection, for that is what it had become, continued, and 200,000 Athenians confronted the fascist occupiers. EAM called for strikes in the public sector, which duly occurred. Ministries were captured by the masses and set on fire, as filing cabinets were

---

1 Dominique Eudes, *The Kapetanios: Partisans and Civil War in Greece, 1943–1949*, London, 1973, p. 36.

emptied and records burnt. The telephone exchange workers came out on strike, disrupting communications. The Gestapo arrested the strike leaders, beating and torturing them. They were left in a cellar to be dealt with the next day, but managed to escape. Eudes takes up the story:

> The past fortnight's demonstrations had cost them dear, but the Athenians prepared to march on the machine guns once again. Groups formed in every part of the town. The streams converged into a sea of humanity; German and Italian patrols were widely dispersed in emergency patrols and the fighting started early in the morning. When the first procession came into sight of the academy, machine guns opened fire without warning. German soldiers dropped grenades from the roofs into the packed flesh of the crowd, wreaking terrible carnage. But the Athenian sea was flowing into the centre of the city from all directions: innumerable, anonymous, trampling the first cordons under foot . . . a quarter of the population of Athens. 200,000 people marching empty-handed through a hail of bullets.

As they reached the ministry of labour they realised that there were ten times as many soldiers and police as there had been on the last occasion:

> The first wave of demonstrators hesitated, eddied – a moment of uncertainty: the wave that piles itself up for a slow moment before breaking on the shore. *Aera! Aera!* The Athenians charged, insane but irresistible, transported towards their objective with a battle-crazy momentum that could not be touched by mere blood, by a scattering of deaths. Grenades and machine-guns were useless. The demonstrators reached the defenders within seconds and the soldiers were overrun, trampled, snatched up and torn to pieces by the multitude. Flames rose once again from the Ministry buildings. The bloodshed continued in the district until every file and every office had been reduced to ashes.[2]

---

2 Ibid., pp. 37–8.

Damaskinos, the Archbishop Primate of Greece, called on the German chargé d'affaires, Herr Altenburg. 'If the "civil mobilisation" [order] is not cancelled by 7 March, the church bells will ring the alarm as a sign of supreme emergency. Doubtless the Reich will make its own assessment of the consequences.' Altenburg wanted a compromise. Damaskinos stood firm. Altenburg rang Berlin, appeared relieved, and informed the Archbishop: 'The civil mobilization has been dropped.' Shaken by the Red Army's victory at Stalingrad, the German high command wanted troops to shore up the Eastern Front. Three days previously, referring to the Greek people, Hitler had muttered: 'We must have done with these lice!' The lice had won a huge victory, proclaimed on every wall in huge red letters by EAM's newspaper – broadsheets plastered on walls all over the country. The Resistance won more and more popular support.

The British, meanwhile, were engaged in non-stop manoeuvring to marginalise EAM and ELAS. They had created their own resistance group, the National Republican Greek League (EDES), under the command of a chancer, Napoleon Zervas, a colourful and charming rogue, who had always hedged his bets. Two EDES officers close to him were working with the German occupation as well. In October 1943 there were armed clashes between ELAS and EDES in which the pathetic qualities of the latter were on full display. London blamed ELAS and asked SOE to cease all supplies to them. The latter protested publicly, accusing EDES of collaborating with the Germans. A month later at a meeting of the war cabinet, with Labour in full agreement, it was decided to destroy the power of the communist-led Greek Resistance. Roosevelt was duly informed and raised no objections.

In Greece itself, from 1943 to 1944, ELAS refused to surrender to the British on any level. They carried on administering villages in the mountains and zealously guarded their support bases in Athens and smaller cities. A stalemate had been reached. But Churchill was not squeamish on these matters. He decided on a test of strength. The Greeks had fought Mussolini in 1940, continued the struggle against the Italians and Germans in 1941, and in the following two years targeted three fascist armies belonging to the Germans, Italians and Bulgarians. In October 1944 the Greek Resistance chased the Wehrmacht out of Greece. Two months later, the British Army under General Scobie's command launched a war against ELAS. A thirty-three-day battle shook Athens and Piraeus. ELAS was compelled to retreat and many partisans fled to the mountain villages, in zones that been liberated some years prior to the German defeat.

Churchill was triumphant. His instructions to General Scobie had been clear. Athens was to be treated as a 'colonial city':

> You are responsible for maintaining order in Athens and for neutral-izing or destroying all EAM-ELAS bands approaching the city. You may make any regulations you like for the strict control of the streets or for the rounding up of any number of truculent persons ... It would be well of course if your command were reinforced by the authority of some Greek Government ... Do not, however, hesitate to act as if you were in a conquered city where a local rebellion is in progress ... We have to hold and dominate Athens. It would be a great thing for you to succeed in this without bloodshed if possible, but also with bloodshed if necessary.

First welcomed, the British were now hated and despised. General Scobie, 'the sneer of cold command' permanently etched on his face, became a special target for ribald satire. Children in Athens mocked Scobie in the streets, singing songs that often linked his atrocities to his private parts. The lines changed regularly as the songs were constantly updated. A December 1945 version of the song featured in Theo Angelopoulos's masterly epic on Greek history, *The Travelling Players*:

> There's a knot in Scobie's willy,
> so to let off steam he gives the order
> to find a little boy in Kolonaki
> There's a knot in Scobie's willy,
> and if these knots come undone
> what will that mean for British policy, General Scobie?
> More knots will come, you can try a thousand tricks,

pile up weapons to bring back the king, but you won't succeed.
The people won't accept fascism from this royal lineage.
They will defeat this British policy.
There's a knot in Scobie's willy . . .[3]

In 1986, Channel 4 Television broadcast a three-part documentary series, *The Hidden War*, a project fully backed by the C4 supremo Jeremy Isaacs, and produced by the feminist documentarist Jane Gabriel. The Greek consultant was Professor Gella Skouras, who organised the crucial interviews with former partisans returning from exile. It was a bravura display of oral history. Detailed interviews with both SOE agents and Greek partisans, punctuated by archive footage that most viewers had not seen before, created a huge impact. The film's exposure of deep British involvement in handing power to the most retrograde right-wing elements in Greek society angered those whose role it laid bare.

Sections of the 'great and the good' had been stung in public, and letters on gilded stationary poured in. Having handed over Greece to the far-right in this 'cradle of democracy', they had been rewarded on their return home with knighthoods and peerages, and many were given prominent posts in political, academic and civil service establishments. Several had written or collaborated with other authors to produce Chatham House versions of history. The official spook version was Bickham Sweet-Escott's effort, published by Chatham House in 1954. Sir Geoffrey Chandler published *The Divided Land* in 1959. Sweet-Escott's brother-in-law, Eddie Myers, published *Greek Entanglement* in 1955. Even Sweet-Escott was compelled to admit that, under the British, 'resistance became very nearly a crime and collaboration very nearly a virtue'. A British soldier interviewed for the documentary, Chris Barker, expressed the confusion in the ranks: 'I thought we'd come to liberate the Greeks, but within what seemed to be a short space of time, we were actually killing them. And, more to the point, British chaps were dying in a cause that I couldn't quite understand.' This was the source of the 'outrage'.

---

3   Translated by Stathis Kouvelakis and David Fernbach.

Nicholas Henderson (ex-Foreign Office) demanded and obtained a meeting with Isaacs to register his own complaint first-hand. Noel (Lord) Annan, who had drafted the Broadcasting Act that created Channel 4, went slightly berserk, as revealed by his letter to Jane Gabriel. The guru of the 'great and the good' cast aside the mask:

> You are either very naïve or an unashamed fellow-traveller – which is it? Your series on the return of the Greek Communists was the most scandalously biassed [*sic*] programme I have seen for sometime . . . I suspect that you will answer by saying that all you were doing was to depict the tragedy of those Greeks who were forced into exile for thirty years . . . implicitly you portrayed the British officers and officials as either fools or Nazi collaborators. Greek politics are very difficult for those who don't know Greece to understand.[4]

Just in case he's been misunderstood, Annan insists that he holds no brief for American policies or the 'detestable colonels who imprisoned some of my Greek friends when they came to power'. In that case, the question could be posed, why did he hand over Greece to the Americans in the first place. A collapsing British Empire that rained terror on Greece after the German defeat was not obliged to do so. Annan was angered because the 'British officers who risked their lives in the war were so traduced'. The programmes were critical of what the British officers did in Greece, not 'in the war'. That they were obeying Churchill and Scobie's orders is obvious, but as the Nuremberg tribunal was to pronounce a year later, 'obeying orders' was not an excuse that should be accepted by any judicial tribunal in the future.

An informal agreement was reached: Channel 4 shamefully promised that the 'offending series' would never be shown again.

In the documentary, C. M. Woodhouse probably said more than

---

4 Geoffrey Chandler wrote to her: 'You are at best naive, or at worst dishonest.' When Gus MacDonald (later a Blairite adornment in the House of Lords) read out Chandler's letter on the C4 programme *Right to Reply*, the knight-spook withdrew his remarks and 'apologised unreservedly'.

was necessary and later regretted having done so: 'Our aim was to divide ELAS units into small groups led by British liaison officers answerable to GHQ in Cairo.' The reason for this was obvious. If the British allowed things to proceed as they were, ELAS's large-scale guerrilla army would form the core of the post-war Greek Army and bring Greece under left-wing control. 'Our aims were irreconcilable . . .'

On this all sides could agree. It was simply that Churchill was determined to inflict a defeat that would serve as an example both to the Greeks and to any others who might have similar ideas. His line of thinking was characteristic: there could be no peace without a British victory in Greece. It was pure banditry.

ELAS saw the British intervention as an attempt to take over the country in league with the king and right-wing groups who had supported Metaxas, the Greek version of Franco and Salazar. Woodhouse confirmed this in his own fashion: 'The Foreign Office wanted a situation where there was no resistance at all. A Foreign Office official actually said "the best sabotage would be no sabotage at all".'

The tragedy of the Greek Civil War was that it could have been won by the Greek left. Its position in the country was hegemonic. But within the Resistance, the *Kapetanios* based in the mountains were not politically strong enough to challenge the official leaders of Greek communism. The guerrilla leader Aris Velouchiotis was an extremely gifted military commander, but he was not a Tito. If analogies have to be made, he was much closer in temperament and values to a leader from a different time: the Mexican revolutionary, Emiliano Zapata. He, too, was killed in circumstances that have still not fully come to light.

Throughout 1942 and 1943, the Greek Resistance, led by communists, had fought against the occupying German Army via a combination of mass mobilisations and guerrilla actions. Two general strikes in Athens and Piraeus in April and September 1942 had compelled the Germans to increase wages and salaries, set up soup-kitchens for working people, and to state in public that no food would be exported from Greece. There was also a passive resistance against Greek 'slave labour' being despatched to

Germany. When questioned, every Greek potentially destined for German factories became deaf, dumb or illiterate. Greeks were transported by force, but their number was far less proportionally than that of all other conquered countries.

On the military front, the Resistance provided valuable support to the Allies. Brigadier Eddy was sent by GHQ in Cairo as a liaison officer with ELAS. The first action ELAS carried out after his arrival was to blow up the Gorgopotamos bridge, a vital conduit for transporting German supplies to Rommel's forces in Africa. Both Generals Montgomery and Maitland-Wilson expressed their gratitude in public. Even Churchill allowed a message in his name thanking the Resistance for 'the great help you are giving to the Allied cause'. The message was sent in September 1943. Two months earlier, the Greek government-in-exile, stationed in Cairo and consisting of monarchists and conservatives, had been told by the British that the destruction of EAM/ELAS was a political and strategic necessity.

Churchill had given the green light to bring back the king. Roosevelt was equivocal but agreed. The stage was set for the British Army to occupy Athens and unleash a vicious repression. The criminal nature of this enterprise was no secret; it was effectively the first action taken in what later became known as the Cold War. That is what explains the sensitivities of Lord Annan and others forty years later. Churchill and the British politico-military establishment had too much blood on their hands.

It would take some effort to make the Soviet Union the enemy again, but it had to be done, and McCarthyism in the US and a milder version in Britain (under a Labour government) proved effective. By this time the agreement at Yalta between Roosevelt, Stalin and Churchill had kicked in. The partitioning of Europe took place.

Greece was the transition point for the Cold War. Here the Second World War morphed into a war against communism and revolution, as it would soon do in China, Vietnam and Korea. After the German defeat, integrating fascists into the new armies fighting for 'freedom and democracy' became Western policy. It was to serve the needs of the new cold and hot wars that Churchill (flanked by US President Harry Truman) announced 'An Iron Curtain has descended on us' in his famous speech at Fulton, Missouri on 5 March 1946, which became the ideological pillar of the Truman Doctrine. After his electoral defeat in 1945, Churchill took on the role of a world statesman, the crutches happily supplied by Truman and his successor. But the 'special relationship' was always a one-sided affair, with ruffled feathers occasionally soothed by Washington to make the transfer of imperial power as amicable as possible.

In Greece and Yugoslavia, as we have seen, communist-led Resistance movements had been extremely effective and were on the verge of taking power. The Greek Civil War was still in progress. If the iron curtain had descended anywhere it was in Greece, and the person who had pressed the button to lower it was Churchill. Seven months previously, Truman had pressed another button. This one was nuclear and had obliterated two civilian targets: the Japanese cities of Hiroshima and Nagasaki. Western and Russian intelligence services knew perfectly well that the Japanese were preparing to surrender. The main reason to try out the nuclear weapons was as a shot across Russian bows: We've got it, you haven't.

The butchery in Greece was thus the real announcement of the Cold War. Stalin's takeover of Eastern Europe had already been agreed. The Soviet Union, with 20 million dead and a wrecked infrastructure, was not planning to invade anyone. Stalin had kept his side of the Faustian pact and let Churchill take Greece. Those Greeks who cursed both of them had the right idea. One of the most celebrated Greek partisans, Manolis Glezos – who had scaled the Acropolis during the German occupation and torn down the swastika flag – was in Moscow a year or so after Khrushchev's denunciation of Stalin had shaken the world. Glezos later described his meeting with Khrushchev in an interview with two journalists, Ed Vulliamy and Helena Smith. In a lengthy essay for the *Guardian* they wrote:

> Glezos wanted to know why the Red Army, having marched through Bulgaria and Romania, stopped at the Greek border. Perhaps the Russian leader could explain.
> 'He looked at me and said, "Why?"'
> 'I said: "Because Stalin didn't behave like a communist. He

divided up the world with others and gave Greece to the English."
Then I told him what I really thought, that Stalin had been the cause
of our downfall, the root of all evil. All we had wanted was a state
where the people ruled, just like our [then] government in the
mountains, where you can still see the words "all powers spring
from the people and are carried out by the people" inscribed into
the hills. What they wanted, and created, was ruled by the party.'

Khrushchev, says Glezos, did not openly concur. 'He sat and
listened. But then after our meeting he invited me to dinner, which
was also attended by Leonid Brezhnev [who succeeded Khrushchev
in 1964], and he listened for another four and a half hours. I have
always taken that for tacit agreement.'[5]

Vulliamy and Smith, to their credit, also provided a rare pen-portrait
of the British civil servant in charge of police operations in Greece.
This was Sir Charles Wickham, whose track record included the
founding of the RUC in Ireland. His mentality was not dissimilar to
that of Adolf Eichmann. These were men who carried out instructions from above using the most efficient methods possible:

Sir Charles Wickham had been assigned by Churchill to oversee the
new Greek security forces – in effect, to recruit the collaborators.
Anthropologist Neni Panourgia describes Wickham as 'one of the
persons who traversed the empire establishing the infrastructure
needed for its survival', and credits him with the establishment of
one of the most vicious camps in which prisoners were tortured and
murdered, at Giaros.

From Yorkshire, Wickham was a military man who served in the
Boer War, during which concentration camps in the modern sense
were invented by the British. He then fought in Russia, as part of the
Allied Expeditionary Force sent in 1918 to aid White Russian Czarist
forces in opposition to the Bolshevik revolution. After Greece, he
moved on in 1948 to Palestine. But his qualification for Greece was
this: Sir Charles was the first Inspector General of the Royal Ulster

5   Ed Vulliamy and Helena Smith, 'Athens 1944: Britain's Dirty
Secret', *Guardian*, 30 November 2014.

324

Constabulary, from 1922 to 1945 ... The head of MI5 reported in 1940 that 'in the personality and experience of Sir Charles Wickham, the fighting services have at their elbow a most valuable friend and counsellor'. When the intelligence services needed to integrate the Greek Security Battalions – the Third Reich's 'Special Constabulary' – into a new police force, they had found their man.

A few years after the stunning victories of the Red Army against the Third Reich, three Tory prime ministers – Churchill, Eden and Macmillan – excused the blood-letting in Greece, describing it as a necessary war against 'communist bandits'.

But it was not just the Tories who were happy to see Greece suffer. The day after Churchill lost the 1945 election, the British ambassador in Athens received a message from Ernest Bevin, the new Labour foreign secretary: 'There will be no change of policy.'[6] Bevin was a born Empire-loyalist and made no bones about the fact. He stated more than once how much he loved the British Empire. Within twenty-fours of Labour taking office, all the hopes of the Greek left were betrayed.

Greece was left denuded of an effective opposition to the right-wing governments imposed or fully supported by NATO. Left-wing MPs were harassed or killed, as in the case of the popular Greek deputy, Grigoris Lambrakis, brought into the public eye with Z, the striking debut film by Costa-Gavras that stunned younger audiences. To Churchill's crimes was added the daily repression that became part of everyday life for many Greeks.

The atrocities committed by Greek fascists and the army after the Second World War laid the basis for the NATO-supported military coup in 1967, designed to prevent the election of any Greek government that offered the mildest challenge to the existing

---

6 John Saville, *The Politics of Continuity: British Foreign Policy and the Labour Government 1945–46*, London, 1973. For those who think that Tony Blair was an aberration, this book provides a powerful corrective. The haze of sepia-tinted nostalgia that surrounds the Attlee government, largely because of the NHS and mine nationalisations, should be pierced in order to get a better view of its reactionary foreign policy.

political and ideological structures of the Churchill–Scobie state. The result was a vicious regime that reopened island prisons, engaged in large-scale torture, imprisoned the great Greek composer Mikis Theodorakis and numerous others, and forced many students and intellectuals to flee the country.

In 2020, a Greek court judged that the far-right 'Golden Dawn' party, the lineal descendants of Greek fascism, were criminal gangsters who had committed numerous murders. They were deprived of their parliamentary privileges in Greece and many of its core leaders and some members are confined to prison. The EU Parliament remains their last remaining base of operations. It is a great pity that the court was not asked to provide a retrospective verdict on those who made these developments possible, supposedly in the name of 'democracy and freedom' in 1944.

Churchill and Franco

Hitler and Mussolini had sustained Franco at the very start of his bloody career in 1936, when he launched a military coup to topple an elected government. In this endeavour he was backed internally by the far right and the Catholic Church, both in Spain and elsewhere on the Continent. French and British non-intervention was also helpful in buttressing the fascist backing from elsewhere. However, without strong Italian and German support, it's unlikely that Franco would have won. In his epochal history of the conflict, Hugh Thomas emphasised this point. The Italians alone despatched 75,000 soldiers and volunteers to aid Franco. The flow of weapons from Italy to Spain, begun in 1936, continued till 1939. These included '350 Fiat CR 32 fighters and ... 100 Savoia 79s ... 1,672 tons of bombs, 9 million rounds of ammunition, 10,000 machine-guns, 240,000 rifles ... Ninety-one Italian warships and submarines took part in the civil war.'[7]

In April 1937, to speed up proceedings, Hitler sent in the Luftwaffe under the command of Von Richthofen to bomb

---

7 Hugh Thomas, *The Civil War in Spain*, London, 2012, pp. 937–40.

Guernica, the first aerial raid on defenceless civilians in Europe, a war atrocity that shocked many at the time.

Churchill carried on supporting Franco both during and after the Second World War, almost single-handedly keeping him in power during the early post-war years. As in the case of Greece, here too Churchill's actions were governed by what he regarded as British interests, his preference for fascism against 'international Jews and communists', and his refusal to accept advice to the contrary from within the establishment. He was aware that the mood in Britain was sympathetic to the Spanish Republic. In October 1936, for example, thousands of workers in London ignored the injunctions of the Labour Party and threats from the state and marched against a British Union of Fascists rally in Cable Street in the east of the city. It was this kind of anti-fascist activity that led to a spurt in the size of the left-liberal and Marxist intelligentsia prior to 1939. Churchill mocked them and hated the pacifists among them, but he would need them in the run-up to the war.[8]

Two important Conservative leaders were not in favour of keeping Franco in charge of Spain. Anthony Eden expressed his views mildly, but Sir Samuel Hoare (later Lord Templewood), a one-time 'appeaser', was punished for his sins by being sent as Special Ambassador to Franco's Spain between 1940 and 1945. Churchill, on his sixth day as prime minister, had hesitated, but was convinced by a mean-spirited Halifax that this would be the best place for Hoare.

Factional rivalries in the Foreign Office, expressed loftily in written disagreements, emerged slightly differently in post-retirement diaries and memoirs. Alexander Cadogan, a senior mandarin at the Foreign Office, was a prime example. He knew that sending Hoare to Madrid was the easiest way to get rid of a very senior Conservative politician. Hoare went quietly. On Hoare's appointment Cadogan commented: 'Dirty little dog has got the wind up and wants to get out of this country.' Comment Two: 'They all agreed to send him out . . . as long as I see the last of Sam, I don't care what happens.' Speaking with Halifax a month later: 'I said

---

8   See Francis Mulhern, *The Moment of Scrutiny*, London, 1979, Chapter 2, 'The Claims of Politics'.

there was one bright spot – there were lots of Germans and Italians in Madrid and therefore a good chance of S.H. being murdered.' In that same period he couldn't resist another jibe: 'He'll be the Quisling of England when Germany conquers us and I am dead.' On the day the Spanish government formally accepted Hoare as ambassador, Cadogan expressed a sigh of relief: 'Thank heaven. Good riddance to v. bad rubbish.'

On his return to London in 1945, the 'English Quisling' produced a quick book, *Ambassador on Special Mission*, informing the Foreign Office that 'my object is to make the complete case against Franco as soon as possible'. No dice, old boy, was the response from Churchill and chums. The response from Labour's foreign secretary, Ernest Bevin, was not dissimilar. Unlike Churchill, the one-time appeaser Hoare had developed a real loathing for Franco and the Falangists.

An important influence on Hoare was the British writer Gerald Brennan, willingly stranded in Andalusia, and extremely knowledgeable about the country at large. He was well aware of what was taking place in the Basque country (where torture and prison were experienced by at least 50 per cent of families), and Catalunya, too, was drowning in repression, including a ban on the use of the Catalan language. Brennan was a mine of information, some of which appeared in Hoare's useful political memoir.

On one occasion, when 'neutral' Spain mobilised Falangist student supporters to give a warm send-off to the Blue Division on its way to fight together with its Axis benefactors against the Soviet Union, the demonstration ended in front of Falangist headquarters, where it was addressed by Franco's newly appointed hard-line interior minister, Ramón Serrano Suñer. Anti-British sentiment was rife in fascist Spain, and some of the students were sent off on a stoning diversion. They pelted the British embassy with government-provided stones neatly stored in bags. Hoare summoned Serrano Suñer on the telephone. It was a heated exchange. Serrano Suñer provoked the Special Ambassador by inquiring whether the embassy needed more policemen for protection, to which Hoare famously responded: 'Don't send more police, just send fewer students.'

On 12 June 1945, in a despatch from the Madrid embassy,

Counsellor R. J. Bowker reported that while officially the attitude of Great Britain and the United States was one of 'cold reserve', 'General Franco knows that neither power is going to use force to turn him out. Meanwhile commercial exchanges with both Powers proceed on a substantial scale and there are good prospects of building up post-war economic relations of benefit to all three parties.'

Bowker reported that Franco's cockiness was explained by his firm belief that the Western Allies would soon be at war with the Soviet Union, and could not afford to antagonise Spain. Within the country the right-wing opposition, i.e. the monarchists, were splintered into factions, the other parties subjected to fierce police repression, and the exile community even more divided. These realities formed the basis for Franco's self-confidence.

Western fears of a powerful Soviet Union turning westwards were baseless. The economic, social and structural damage suffered by the USSR was of such magnitude that neither Stalin nor the Red Army Marshals could think seriously about another round of wars, let alone one which involved the United States. It is true that Stalin worried endlessly about a second round of revenge the Germans might plan once they had recovered. He proposed a neutral, unified Germany on the Austrian model but this was rejected by the Allies. The only feasible solution that remained for Moscow was a permanent division of the country that chimed in with behind-the-scenes Allied thinking.

Franco was the illegitimate offspring of these Cold War priorities. Stalin should have insisted that the dictator be removed, a new constitution drawn up and elections held, as in Italy. Had the Soviet leader made this one of the key demands at Yalta or before, Franco would have lost and ended up somewhere in South America. Spain would have been spared another thirty years of the terror and torment.

Throughout the war Churchill and Roosevelt had no doubt whatsoever that the Soviet Union was the enemy of the future. This had been US policy from Woodrow Wilson onwards. Churchill had hoped that Hitler would do the job for the West, but history turned out otherwise. The Soviet role in winning the war had made it genuinely popular in the Western world. It took a bit of time to transform this image, but the West, under US leadership, persevered. Churchill was only too happy to be wheeled on stage whenever required.

Elsewhere, the military and political forces of the United States and Britain worked with former fascists in Germany, Italy, France, Korea and Japan to integrate and promote parties they could join, armies they could enlist in, and a variety of bombs they could develop to safeguard capitalist democracy. There was no need for any of this in Spain. Franco, like the more astute of the Japanese generals, had already forecast such a development.

Contemporary critics of what happened in Eastern Europe after Stalinisation tend to ignore the mess on their own side: the maintenance of the dictatorships in Spain and Portugal, the creation of one in Greece, the retention of fascists in state institutions, including the army, air force and police in Italy and Japan, and to a lesser extent in Germany. Since most of them are Euro-Atlanticists, the South and Far East of Asia remain mysterious regions. Many of the far-right, semi-fascist groups active today descend, directly or indirectly, from the fascists and collaborators of yesteryear.

Franco and the Portuguese dictator Salazar could have been brought down at the tail end of the war with economic sanctions and military threats. Spain was heavily dependent on oil, and the West had kept it supplied throughout the war. The United States had a tougher approach than Whitehall. Dean Acheson complained that 'the British thwarted all our efforts to use to the utmost our considerable powers to limit Franco's help to Germany'. Foggy Bottom bluntly informed Downing Street there was no basis for negotiations with fascist Spain. As Acheson later described: 'Franco's purposes were hostile, his officials' statements mendacious and their statistics falsified. With no confidence in the facts, there could be no confidence in the bargain.'

On US insistence, supplies were cut off for two years. Acheson continues:

As stocks sank to the point of exhaustion, cries of anguish would begin in Madrid, be taken up by the US Ambassador to Spain, Carlton J. H. Hayes, and by London, echoed by our Petroleum Adviser ... and be derided by most of the American government and press. When it reached a crescendo after two months ... a tanker or two would be released amid a chorus of vituperation.[9]

Circumstances (i.e. Churchill) did not permit more stringent action. Later on in his wartime recollections, Acheson recalls his irritation at 'the apparent sincerity with which, until almost the end of the war, the neutrals and British alike voiced fear of German occupation to justify trade with the enemy'.

Churchill had long made it clear that, in a choice between Franco and the elected leaders of the Republic, he would prefer the uniformed dictator. During the war he authorised the use of 10 million dollars to bribe Franco's generals if they promised to hold their leader back from going over completely to the Axis powers. The operation was handed over to the British naval attaché, Captain Alan Hillgarth, whose real job was head of intelligence and counter-intelligence in the Iberian peninsula.

The plan was to prevent Franco from becoming a 'belligerent' for at least six months. On the surface it appears to have worked, but it was Hitler's refusal to alienate Pétain and Vichy by acceding to Franco's colonial greed that marked a turning point. Had the war gone well for the Third Reich, the Spanish dictator would have caved in and done as he was told, but his instinct for self-preservation came into play after the Soviet victories at Stalingrad and Kursk. On Churchill's advice, Franco pulled out the 20,000-strong Blue Division in 1943, though thousands of Spaniards had already died and hundreds were POWs in the Soviet Union. Several thousand refused to return and understandably, given their politics, joined the Waffen SS.

Roosevelt was squeamish about having Franco in the Western camp. To push through some cosmetic changes, Churchill softened his position slightly and suggested that he might accept a pro-Western government as long as the monarchy was restored and a Bourbon was put back on the throne. Democracy had very little to

---

9 Dean Acheson, *Present at the Creation: My Years in the State Department*, New York, 1969, pp. 53, 54, 55.

do with any of this. Franco, without too much difficulty, outmanoeuvred the old man in Downing Street. There would be no
monarch while Franco was in power from 1939 to 1975; King
Juan Carlos would be his successor. Churchill hid his displeasure.
Denial of membership in NATO was considered a rap on the
knuckles. Franco was unbothered. A pliant king and a far-right
government was Churchill's preferred solution in most
circumstances.

Though he suggested in the *Daily Telegraph* on 30 December
1938 that, 'as a good English patriot', his support for Franco had
waned after Germany and Italy intervened in the civil war, two
years later he said something very different to the Duke of Alba,
Franco's ambassador in London. Over a lunch (fixed by Cadogan),
Churchill informed the Duke that: 'We desire the best and most
friendly relations with you and if they should change you can be
sure that it will not be our fault. We are determined, and I have
intervened personally in this matter, to help so far as we are able in
the provisioning of Spain.'

In his memoirs of the Second World War, another version is
offered: 'In this quarrel, I was neutral. Naturally I was not in
favour of the Communists. How could I be? ... if I had been a
Spaniard they would have murdered me and my family and
friends'. Why should this have been so? Because, he writes, the
Spanish government 'was in the hands of the most extreme revolutionaries'. This was not the case, and was definitely not so at the
start of the conflict.[10]

Dealing with Churchill on Spain, wrote Dean Acheson, the US
secretary of state, was tiresome, but 'the role played by Mr
Churchill . . . was my first experience of what was to recur often in
the next decade – that is of a relatively weak ally, by determined,

---

10 See Richard Wigg, *Churchill and Spain: The Survival of the
Franco Regime, 1940–1945*, Sussex, 2008. This is a meticulously
researched account. Wigg was a foreign correspondent of the old school,
writing for *The Times* for twenty-seven years in Latin America and
Spain. Reprinting Foreign Office/MI6 handouts was never his
stock-in-trade.

sometimes reckless, decisions, changing and even preventing action by a much stronger one charged with ultimate responsibility'. General de Gaulle was to demonstrate this; so was Syngman Rhee in Korea.

After the death of Franco, the Moncloa Pacts that marked the 'democratic rupture' were implemented by the Spanish state in 1976. Political parties and trade unions were legalised – an undoubted blow as far as some sectors of the Spanish bourgeoisie were concerned, since they preferred a dictatorship. Over four decades Spanish capitalism had developed, and in the last fifteen years of the Franco regime prospered, thanks to a 'state of exception'. During that period it was the repression of the working class that had fuelled the 'economic miracle', producing Japanese-style growth rates. The years 1964–71 saw remarkable growth. Thanks to Franco, Spanish industrialists lost only between twenty and twenty-five minutes of work per annum per worker due to strikes. The state had, for forty years, sent armed police into the factories to brutalise and arrest strikers; it banned working-class opposition and imprisoned all dissenters. To legitimise its economic power under a new political hegemony, Spanish capitalism needed to have free trade unions with which to dialogue. But they clung on to other privileges from the past, some of which hardly form part of a developed bourgeois democracy.

On their own, the Moncloa Pacts did little to address the national question. Catalans were offered nothing on the political front, while Basques continued to be tortured under the Spanish Socialist Workers' Party government. The more intelligent Francoists ended up in the Popular Party (PP). In 2018, the openly fascist VOX party – long gestating inside the PP and now enraged by Catalunya's demand for a referendum on self-determination – came out into the open and was surprised by its own success, joining the list of Lazarus-like parties in other parts of Europe. Catalan activists and politicians are still in prison at the time of writing. The echoes of the past have got louder.

13

The East Is Dead, the East Is Red: Japan, China, Korea, Vietnam

can we forget that flash?
suddenly 30,000 in the streets disappeared
in the crushed depths of darkness
the shrieks of 50,000 died out

TŌGE Sankichi, 'August 6' (1951)

The Second World War officially ended where it had begun: in Asia. What had started with what seemed at the time to be a minor clash of arms between Japan and China, on the Marco Polo Bridge outside Beijing, came to an unimaginable end with Truman's decision to test the newly created atomic bomb on Hiroshima and Nagasaki. The handover of European and Japanese colonies in Asia to the United States was part of a global process. Unlike Europe, where the Yalta agreement (with the Yugoslav exception) was enforced by both sides, in Asia resistance turned into new wars of liberation.

The conflict in Asia did not end as it had in Europe. Japan was defeated, but new enemies had been sighted. These 'enemies' had fought the Japanese Empire in China, Korea and Vietnam, where the Second World War had shifted gears and slipped into anti-colonial mode. The French, unable to bring themselves to fight the Third Reich, had no problems in killing the Vietnamese. The men of Vichy, backed by de Gaulle, were wreaking havoc in Vietnam and Algeria. The panic that had set in after the 1917 Russian

Revolution, slightly masked during the world war, gripped the West again, especially after the 1949 communist victory in China.

The domino theory (or permanent counter-revolution) became US State Department orthodoxy and dissent was silenced by McCarthyism. At its crudest, the argument went like this: if we let go of these countries, international and regional communism will be emboldened to 'challenge freedom and democracy'. Where? In South Asia, the Greater Middle East, the Mediterranean.

To prevent such a calamity, more wars had to be fought. The weakened European colonial powers were already on the retreat. The United States took charge and began to construct its own empire, the existence of which was categorically denied. In private, the imperial bureaucracy had no illusions about 'freedom and democracy'. They knew perfectly well who supported them. In February 1948 the Policy Planning Staff at the State Department wrote a straightforward assessment that spelt out what the national interest required: effectively a collection of puppet states grouped together in regional alliances and security pacts with the United States and Great Britain in particular.

> We have about 50% of the world's wealth but only 6.3% of its population ... Our real task in the coming period is to devise a pattern of relationships which will permit us to maintain this position of disparity without positive detriment to our national security ... We should cease to talk about vague and unreal objectives such as human rights, the raising of living standards, and democratisation ... We should concentrate our policy on seeing to it that key areas remain in hands which we can control or rely on.

At one of the Yalta sessions in February 1945, Roosevelt had attempted to resolve the 'colonial problem' in Asia. He suggested to Stalin that Hong Kong be returned to GMD China and Korea should become a trusteeship, with Britain firmly excluded Indochina would be granted independence and not handed back to France. Stalin became nervous, since he had done a deal with Churchill on Eastern Europe and the Far East at the 'Tolstoy Conference' in Moscow the previous year. Churchill threw a tantrum: 'I will not have one scrap of the British territory flung into that area . . . I will have no suggestion that the British Empire is to be put into the dock and examined by everybody to see if it is up to their standard . . . I will not consent to forty or fifty nations thrusting interfering fingers into the life's existence of the British Empire.'

Roosevelt calmly responded that he was referring to 'enemy possessions'. This Churchill grumpily accepted, but these 'possessions' were post-1918 League of Nations Mandates. It was agreed that the UN (about to be formed) could interfere in and examine British-controlled territories, though this was never implemented. Churchill backed the French 100 per cent and insisted that they should not let Vietnam become independent. Ho Chi Minh had already declared the country independent in 1945 and huge mass mobilisations had welcomed the event. It was not to be. The French resumed the colonial war, backed by the British, and after 1954 the United States took over and carried on until 1975.

The rest of Asia should have seen the nuclear targeting of Japanese cities as a portent of what was to come, even if not via nuclear weapons. The literal destruction of every building in North Korea (1950–53) was fully supported by Churchill and Attlee. By any definition, the destruction of Japanese cities was a war crime. The combined casualties were almost a quarter of a million people, overwhelmingly civilians. The effects on the survivors were traumatic. Civilian casualties caused by incendiary and nuclear bombing were horrific. Civilian deaths in Tokyo were 97,031; in Hiroshima 140,000; in Nagasaki 70,000; in 63 other cities 86,336.[1]

The Germans apologised for what had been done by the Third Reich; the French covered up the crimes of Vichy; Churchill never regretted the horrors inflicted by Bomber Command on German cities in raids that began in mid-1942. The most conservative

---

1   John W. Dower, *War Without Mercy: Race and Power in the Pacific War*, New York, 1988, p. 298. There was no Japanese equivalent of Kurt Vonnegut's antiwar novel *Slaughterhouse-Five*, conceived when he was a prisoner in Dresden during the terror bombing of that city. At least 25,000 civilians perished in the ensuing firestorms.

estimates suggest that 410,000 civilians, 70,000 prisoners of war and slave labourers from countries under German occupation were killed during the course of the war. In Dresden, 25,000 were killed in two hours. Fifty per cent of the built-up area in all of Germany's major cities and towns was destroyed. The punishment of civilians on this scale far outstripped the German bombing of British cities.

Presidents of the United States have continually defended, some more loudly than others, what was inflicted on Japan in 1945. Churchill, who rarely held back from explaining his own position on important events, concurred. Here we discover him in full flow on the importance of nuking Japan:

> British consent in principle to the use of the weapon had been given on July 4, before the test had taken place. The final decision now lay in the main with President Truman, who had the weapon; but I never doubted what it would be, nor have I ever doubted since that he was right. The historic fact remains, and must be judged in the after-time, that the decision whether or not to use the atomic bomb to compel the surrender of Japan was never even an issue. There was unanimous, automatic, unquestioned agreement around our table; nor did I ever hear the slightest suggestion that we should do otherwise.[2]

In fact, John Galbraith, who opposed using the bombs, argued (like a few others) that a Japanese surrender was imminent. Churchill rejected this. Always keen on punitive measures, regardless of locale, he conjured visions of a lengthy, crazed Japanese resistance that might cost a million more US lives and half as many British losses. It was pure rubbish, the froth of imperial fantasy.

The Tory MP Chips Channon was far more circumspect, noting in his diary entry of 5 August 1945: 'The world has been electrified, thrilled and horrified by the atomic bomb; one has been dropped in Japan today. It devastated a whole town and killed a quarter of a million people. It could mean the end of civilization.' Not for Churchill. With Japan on its knees, its people dying from

---

2 Winston Churchill, *Triumph and Tragedy*, London, 1953, Chapter 19.

radiation diseases, all was well, and one day they would realise it had all been done for their sake anyway:

> Now all this nightmare picture had vanished. In its place was the vision – fair and bright indeed it seemed – of the end of the whole war in one or two violent shocks. I thought immediately myself of how the Japanese people, whose courage I had always admired, might find in the apparition of this almost supernatural weapon an excuse which would save their honour and release them from being killed to the last fighting man.

When Churchill visited the United States in January 1953 to attend a farewell dinner for Truman, he should not have been too surprised to discover that Dean Acheson had prepared an after-dinner 'mock trial' in his honour at the White House. Churchill was in the dock for war crimes, accused of complicity in the use of nuclear weapons. The outgoing President Truman avoided being handcuffed to the British leader, since he was needed as the Presiding Judge. The event was later described by the president's daughter in her memoirs. Were they simply making light of an appalling war crime, or was this an attempt at some form of collective therapy? Was Acheson's conscience still in recovery mode? Whatever the reason, the episode is not without interest. Margaret Truman's description, as conveyed here by Richard M. Langworth, has Churchill's words in italics:

> 'During our last weeks in the White House, Prime Minister Churchill arrived for a visit. My father gave him a small stag dinner to which he invited Secretary of Defense, Robert Lovett, Averell Harriman, General Omar Bradley and Secretary of State Dean Acheson. Everyone was in an ebullient mood, especially Dad. Without warning, Mr. Churchill turned to him and said . . .'

> *Mr. President, I hope you have your answer ready for that hour when you and I stand before St. Peter and he says, 'I understand you two are responsible for putting off those atomic bombs. What have you got to say for yourselves?'*

Robert Lovett asked: 'Are you sure, Prime Minister, that you are going to be in the same place as the President for that interrogation?'

Lovett, my vast respect for the Creator of this universe and countless others gives me assurance that He would not condemn a man without a hearing.

Lovett: 'True, but your hearing would not be likely to start in the Supreme Court, or, necessarily, in the same court as the President's. It could be in another court far away.'

I don't doubt that, but, wherever it is, it will be in accordance with the principles of English Common Law.

Dean Acheson, who liked to tweak Churchill about Britain's diminished stature, then spoke up: 'Is it altogether consistent with your respect for the Creator of this and other universes to limit His imagination and judicial procedure to the accomplishment of a minute island, in a tiny world, in one of the smaller of the universes?'

Well, there will be a trial by a jury of my peers, that's certain.

Acheson: 'Oyez! Oyez! In the matter of the immigration of Winston Spencer Churchill, Mr. Bailiff, will you empanel a jury?'

Each guest accepted an historic role, wrote Margaret Truman. 'General Bradley decided he was Alexander the Great. Others played Julius Caesar, Socrates and Aristotle. The Prime Minister declined to permit Voltaire on his jury – he was an atheist – or Cromwell, because he did not believe in the rule of law. Then Mr. Acheson summoned George Washington. That was too much for Mr. Churchill. He saw that things were being stacked against him:'

I waive a jury, but not habeas corpus. You'll not put me in any black hole.

'They ignored him and completed the selection of the jury. Dad was appointed judge. The case was tried. The Prime Minister was acquitted.[3]

During this visit Mr. Churchill confessed to Dad that he had taken a dim view of him as President when he had succeeded Franklin Roosevelt. "I misjudged you badly", the Prime Minister said. "Since that time, you, more than any other man, have saved Western civilization."[4]

A revealing tale. The Chief War Criminal was the Presiding Judge, the principal accused was acquitted, Western civilisation was in safe hands again, and all was well in the world.

The fact that Stalin, Churchill and Attlee all approved of the nuclear strikes does not absolve the United States. They built the bomb, they tested it, Oppenheimer found a suitable quote from the Hindu scriptures to express a few misgivings, the pilots obeyed orders and observed the mushroom cloud formation. Was the awed indifference displayed by Western citizens at the time just one more example of the deep hold that imperialist ideology exercises with its embedded racist and civilisational death wish.

Several weeks before the bombing, secret Japanese documents were captured by US forces, including one sent by the Japanese Supreme Command in Tokyo to some of its most loyal and fanatical generals in the field based in Java. They were informed that Japan was about to surrender, but there was no need to panic. The surrender should be viewed as a truce that might last five or six years, after which war would be resumed on a still vaster scale, this time between the United States and Soviet Russia. In this Third World War, Tokyo predicted, the services of Japan would be needed by the Americans because Western Europe, if only from fear of Russia, would be reluctant to join in. The battleground, therefore,

---

3   Had Sitting Bull, Harriet Tubman and Edmund Burke been members of the jury, it might have returned a split verdict.

4   Richard M. Langworth, 'Churchill on Trial: Washington, 1953', at richardlangworth.com, quoting Margaret Truman, 'After the Presidency', *Life*, 1 December 1972, pp. 69–70.

would be largely in the eastern part of the Soviet Union and in Manchuria. Japan would play a leading part. It didn't turn out exactly like that, but in stressing common hostility to the Soviet Union and the necessity of a US–Japan alliance, the Supreme Command was not completely wrong either.

What these and other intelligence documents revealed was that the Japanese were preparing to surrender. Had this been allowed to happen, who knows, perhaps the emperor might have committed hara-kiri. The use of nuclear weapons had little to do with Japan supposedly refusing to surrender or 'saving American lives'. It was a crude, but effective, demonstration of power by the United States, a warning mainly to the Russians, but also to the Europeans. Rarely has a new global empire announced its arrival on the world stage in such a destructive fashion.

Hatred for the Japanese reached such a pitch in the United States that the wartime internment of Japanese-American citizens, even though many were fighting in the US Army against those of similar ethnic origins, was accepted by most US citizens.[5] Had the US decided on a similar measure against Muslim Americans after 9/11, I doubt there would have been too many protests. At one point the comparison of 9/11 with Pearl Harbor was being touted by so many pundits that many Muslim-Americans became fearful. The eternal junior ally Britain institutionalised spying on Muslims in schools and universities and at home in order to stress that the wars in the Middle East were a Muslim problem and had little to do with US/EU foreign policy. The fact that censorship and surveillance are now state policy in Britain, backed by all three parties in Parliament, says a lot that is not often said in public.

A refusal to accept any responsibility for war and destruction has usually been the hallmark of imperialist states. And, as John W. Dower reveals in his sober and careful study of race in the Pacific War, attitudes to the Japanese as a people had always been hedged

---

5   The first serious cultural critique came in 1955, with John Sturges liberal movie, *Bad Day at Black Rock*, which highlighted anti-Japanese racism and xenophobia in the country. Spencer Tracy played the good American and Robert Ryan his ugly counterpart.

with qualifications of one sort or another. The weaponised psycho-babble deployed against the Japanese was part of a project to dehumanise and mystify them. What you cannot understand has to be inferior. A lot of this type of material became common usage in US and Western propaganda during the Second World War.

Other criticisms levelled against the Japanese were that they were genetically conformist and permanently 'child-like'. Compton Pakenham, a British officer who had mixed in elite circles in Tokyo, wrote long essays for *Newsweek* in 1945 designed to reassure readers that nuking the Japanese variant of the yellow peril was not such a big deal. Their psychology was warped, their sinister cynicism was repellent, they were like no other nation in the world. Ellis Zacharias, the US Navy's top intelligence authority on Japan, helped out with some reflections of his own, bordering on the comical. The Japanese were a 'strange, inscrutable and peculiar phenomenon'. Well before Pearl Harbor, as Dowyer recounts, Barbara Tuchman had contributed a 'clinical note' on the Japanese to *Foreign Affairs* in 1936, which included this choice paragraph: 'So completely divorced is the Japanese mental process from the Occidental, so devoid of what Westerners call logic, that the Japanese are able to make statements, knowing they present a false picture, yet sincerely believing them. How this is accomplished it is impossible for a foreigner to understand, much less to explain.'[6]

The degree of conformity on this issue is striking, especially given that one of the charges against the Japanese people was that of excessive conformism. Childishness and immaturity, emotional backwardness, and a permanent inferiority complex were regarded as immutable aspects of the Japanese character. Gregory Bateson and Margaret Mead, distinguished anthropologists though they were, also promoted such views. In a 1942 book on Bali, the couple wrote that 'the Japanese, lacking respect for their own culture, perceive their inevitable inferiority and feel insulted when they meet this self-respect in others'.

These sentiments were taken up by others who gave it a new twist. The American journalist Edgar Snow felt that subconsciously

---

6 Dower, *War Without Mercy*, pp. 96, 97.

'the individual Japanese is aware of his unfortunate intellectual and physical inferiority to the individual Korean and Chinese, the two peoples subject to his god-Emperor. He is forever seeking compensation.' Hence the humiliations and brutalities Japan inflicted on its colonial subjects.[7]

Staunch defenders of China against the Japanese occupation and atrocities, such as Pearl Buck and Lin Yutang, were so shocked by the scale and crudeness of anti-Japanese racism in the United States and Britain that they predicted a war between the white and non-white worlds within a generation. What they did not foresee was how right-wing and liberal Japanese politicians, guided by their divine emperor and with their country permanently occupied by US troops, would work hard to defeat the Japanese left, create an effective one-party state, learn to love baseball and Hollywood movies, and become 'normal' just like the citizens of the West. It was as simple as that. The atomic bombs had supposedly wiped the slate clean. All the old cancers had disappeared. All that was needed was strict control. The US base in Okinawa was the last resort if Japanese leaders did not do as they were bid by the White House, a situation that prevails to this day.

China and Korea

After the conquest of Japan, the attention of the US leaders shifted to the region as a whole, where the stage was set for national uprisings in Vietnam and Korea (colonial possessions of France and Japan respectively). In both countries the local communists had led a resistance to the Japanese. More worryingly for the United States and its allies, a civil war in China was about to resume and, here too, the Chinese Communist Party was gaining momentum. The stars were predicting a revolution.

US and Allied atrocities in the Korean war (1950–3) included executions of POWs, the use of germ warfare, and the destruction of the entire infrastructure of North Korea. How did this come about?

---

7   Quoted in ibid., pp. 131–3.

Korea had been a Japanese protectorate and subsequently a full-blown colony of the Japanese Empire. Japan's defeat in 1945 had created a situation unexpected by Churchill and Truman. In virtually all the Japanese colonial possessions in the region, the subsequent nationalist resistance was led by communists. In China, the Guomindang (GMD) had been bruised so badly by its ambiguous attitude to the Japanese that large-scale desertions to Mao Zedong's armies had made the civil war a bit one-sided. The Chinese Revolution therefore became an inevitability.

Though the elite sectors in Chinese society had collaborated with the Japanese, as had the French with the Germans, the degree of collaboration varied from region to region. There was no real equivalent to the Vichy government. As in France, there has been a marked reluctance in both China and Taiwan to discuss the subject of collaboration.

To take just one example. The Shanghai film industry produced over 200 films under the Japanese occupation. One would have expected Mao's last wife and comrade, Jiang Qing, herself a product of the Shanghai cinema industry, to have set up a commission to evaluate these films. How many were pro-Japanese propaganda and how many were 'pure entertainment'? Given their popularity throughout the country, one assumes that most were in the latter category. Xiao Hong's comic masterpiece written during the war, *Ma Bo'le's Second Life*, opens with the line: 'Ma Bo'le was a coward even before the war.' The book portrays a cross-section of Chinese society during the occupation, but despite two movies based on the author's life, the novel itself has not been filmed.

More generally, Mitsui, Mitsubishi and other Japanese companies and banks dominated the market with the help of their Chinese counterparts. The latter went over to the GMD and funded it ferociously during the four-year civil war to little effect. The Chinese communists had gradually built a mass organisation throughout the country. They had turned guerrilla warfare into an art, as the Japanese and the GMD knew only too well. As the Pacific War ended, the Truman administration kept Japanese troops under US control, sent 50,000 US marines and $4 billion to keep Chiang Kai-shek afloat, and transported half-a-million GMD soldiers in

US planes to Manchuria to prevent a communist take-over. None of this worked. Truman baulked at the thought of direct intervention and Britain was no longer capable. China, after all, was not Greece, and too close, geographically, to Singapore, a disaster seared in Churchill's memory.

Chiang, as mentioned earlier, had said that the Japanese were a disease that could be cured, but the Chinese communists were a cancer that had to be rooted out. In fact, the cancer of corruption was now asphyxiating his own party. Desertions were weakening his armed forces, and in city after city the communist armies were being welcomed as liberators. Several OSS veterans who knew China had warned Truman that this would be the likely course of events. Now he knew.

Churchill, Roosevelt and Truman had supported Chiang Kai-shek and his GMD as the only legitimate solution for China. Weaponry from the US and Britain flowed down the Burma Road to arm GMD forces. He was taken along to several international meetings, and his China had been promised a seat on the Security Council in the forthcoming United Nations. Chiang was seen by Churchill as a Chinese version of de Gaulle.

But perceptions on the ground in China were different. Many non-communists had developed a strong aversion to the collaborationist wing of the GMD, to its main leader and to its large-scale corruption. The Chinese Communist Party and its armies were seen as the most effective force in resisting the Japanese occupation. The GMD's failures, despite massive Western support on every level, paved the way for the victory of the communists.

Chiang retreated to Taiwan, a former colony of Japan. Here he provided a glimpse of what might have happened to the mainland had he won: a regime of terror, theft of land, crushing of the indigenous people. This was the 'democratic alternative' to Mao Zedong. For a while, Taiwan was the official China for much of the Western world. Nixon's trip to the PRC in 1972 was to change all that.

Had Korea been left alone by the United States, there is little doubt a communist revolution would have been in the offing. As Bruce Cumings has argued in two books and several essays over the years, the strongest political force in the country after the

Japanese collapse was the Korean Communist Party. Apart from all other factors, at least 100,000 Koreans had fought with the Chinese Red Armies against the Japanese in China. A number of these had earlier joined the Long March under Mao's command to the Yenan outpost. American policy-makers understood that the native Korean forces (those groups that had loyally served the Japanese for many years) were not strong enough to stave off the revolution, usually described in the Western parlance of that period 'as Soviet expansionism'.

Stalin now committed another huge blunder. With the Red Army almost within walking distance of Pusan, he agreed to Truman's request to allow US troops to occupy the southern part of the peninsula. Why? The US had insisted they and they alone should occupy Japan. All the Soviet Union needed to do was to permit Korean communists to set up a government that would have mass support, unlike some of the Allied creations in eastern Europe. It was the 'Soviet expansionists' who permitted the United States to expand into Korea, creating the setting for the subsequent three-year war. Stalin had misread Hitler, Churchill and Truman in turn, with disastrous results.

The pro-Japanese elements in Korea were hurriedly corralled into a new Korean Army. The result was mayhem and ultimately a divided peninsula.

Bruce Cumings's carefully researched history of the Korean War recounts many horrific incidents of kidnappings and rapes carried out by the Republic of Korea (ROK) forces and US troops alike. Like the Japanese before them, the US soldiers targeted Korean women as use-objects. Neither country has paid compensation to the women who were brutalised non-stop during the wars. One of the worst atrocities alleged by the North Koreans occurred in the southwestern town of Sinchon:

> hundreds of women and children were kept for some days in a shed without food or water, as Americans and Koreans sought information on their absconded male relatives; when they cried for water, sewage from latrines was dumped on them. Later they were doused with gasoline and roasted alive. In November 1987, together with a Thames Television crew, I visited the charnel house and the tombs,

examined original photos and newspaper stories, and spent the day with a survivor; we came away convinced that a terrible atrocity had taken place although the evidence on its authorship was difficult to document.[8]

The Kim family took charge of the North, while far-right forces backed by the US took the South, with military fascists ruling the country directly on two separate occasions. South Korea is still occupied by the US, while North Korea is now a nuclear state. The dreaded weapon guarantees its sovereignty, as became clear during Kim Jong-un's heated intellectual exchanges with Donald Trump in 2018.

Vietnam

The US were stalemated in Korea, but in Vietnam they were beaten by a Communist Party that fought with courage and determination. Rarely have two Western imperial powers been defeated in succession by the same generation of leaders. The French had been confident that they would crush the Vietnamese resistance. They had referred contemptuously to General Vo Nguyen Giap as a 'bush general'. They imagined that because they had white skins and had won some battles, they were invincible. Mao Zedong once remarked with characteristic realism that: 'In real life we cannot ask for "ever victorious" generals.' Giap agreed with this wholeheartedly, but he knew that the morale and fighting spirit in his National Liberation Army had reached a peak by 1954. He would

---

8 Bruce Cumings, *The Korean War: A History*, New York, 2010, pp. 194–9. In 1950, at the Conservative Party Conference, Churchill had warned the Soviet Union not to forget that the atomic bomb existed to protect Korean democracy. The killings and executions were defended by ROK President Syngman Rhee and the US ambassador. They were part of an exterminist plan, a politicide intended to destroy Korean communism and its domestic allies. Cumings stresses that one reason many North Koreans are reluctant to unify with the South at some stage is because memories of the atrocities are deeply embedded in their collective consciousness passed on from one generation to another.

later explain that the support enjoyed by the Vietnamese Communist Party was linked to the role it had played in 1945:

> The general insurrection of August 1945 was an uprising of the entire people. Our entire people, united in a broad national front, with their armed and semi-armed forces, unanimously rose up everywhere, in the countryside and the cities, and conquered political power at a favourable political conjuncture, when the Japanese imperialists had lost the war, their Army was in a process of disintegration, and their lackeys were demoralised and powerless ... the practice of the August 1945 general insurrection had a highly creative content. In a former colonial and semi-feudal country like ours, the revolution of national liberation does not necessarily take the form of a protracted struggle or that of an armed uprising in the cities, but it is quite possible for it to combine, in a creative manner, these two forms of struggle.[9]

In the 1946 elections that followed Vietnam's Declaration of Independence the preceding year, the communist Viet Minh had done extremely well. Ho Chi Minh, the leader of the Vietnamese Communist Party had received the highest vote, with General Giap a close second. In negotiations with the French at Fontainebleau, it was the military leader who took a slightly tougher stance:

> They [the French] are making preparations to land their forces in Indochina. In a word, and according to latest intelligence, France is preparing herself to reconquer our country ... The Vietnamese people will fight for independence, liberty and equality of status. If our negotiations are unsuccessful, we shall resort to arms.

And that is what happened. The French Army, reluctant to fight the Germans in the recent war, showed no objections whatsoever to fighting a colonial war. They got their comeuppance at Dien Bien Phu: a humiliating defeat with the senior French officer

---

9 Vo Nguyen Giap, *The Military Art of Peoples War*, Monthly Review Press, 1970, pp. 167–8.

committing suicide rather than surrender. It was the end of France's ambitions in Asia. However, the Americans were less inclined to let the victory stand. Eisenhower refused to permit nationwide elections as per the Geneva Accords of 1954, because, as he famously stated, 'in any free election the Communists would win 80 per cent of the seats'.

Instead, they decided to replace the French by setting up a series of puppet regimes. When that didn't work, they entered the arena themselves in 1960, suffered their first military setback at Ap Bac in 1961, and continued to send in more and more troops over the next decade and a half. It was the Vietnamese people and their country that paid a heavy price. The resistance was heroic, the cost high: half a million US soldiers killed 2 million Vietnamese and wrecked the ecology of the country. Chemical weapons were utilised throughout the war. Countless numbers were raped, tortured, put in concentration-camp-style 'strategic hamlets' and brutalised. A US Marine officer immortalised himself by uttering the following words after his troops had burnt a whole village together with most of its population: 'The only way to save Ben Tre was to destroy it.' This was the cruel, unrelenting logic of imperialist wars.

The refusal of the Vietnamese to be defeated triggered the largest protest movement in the history of the United States, which infected the army as well. In April 1975 the tanks of the National Liberation Front entered Saigon. US personnel and a few hangers-on fled in helicopters. It was the first time the United States had ever been defeated in such fashion. Kabul in August 2021 was similar, but a different model.

The rebellion that shook Europe in the 1960s created the space to question and criticise how the Second World War and its aftermath had been presented. The fact that urban terrorist organisations emerged in three Axis countries – Germany, Italy and Japan – was the clearest sign that sizeable segments of the new generation were repelled by the failure to settle accounts with fascism.

14

Castles in the Sand:
Re-mapping the Arab East

... and if you could forget the screams
say the ears
then you could stop courting danger
then you could sail far away like a fig in a ship's belly

that has been plucked and is free of its tree
then you could be free like a grain of sand in the wind
free at last
of the native land you have lost

The world goes on turning
One must forget what has been
Don't be dumb
says the wind
blowing across from those who drove you away.

Erich Fried, 'Invitation to Forget' (1978)

Historical facts don't always speak for themselves. They are often forgotten or lost in interpretation. Especially in this century. In the case of the Arab East, for example, it is essential to see the past as the key to the present. The re-mapping of the region is still in progress: the Middle East has become the focus for a sustained military intervention by the United States and its allies. To understand why, we must return to the early decades of Churchill's imperial career.

The Ottoman Empire's decision to ally with the German Reich in the First World War led to the loss of all its colonial possessions after the defeat in 1918. Even before the war formally ended, Britain and France had decided to divide the spoils. Preparatory intrigues had begun as early as September 1914, a month into the war, with Kitchener (then Secretary of State for War) despatching a mendacious handwritten letter to the Sharif Hussein of Mecca and his son Abdullah. They were the leaders of the Hashemite clan, descended from the Prophet Muhammad's tribe, who were the Ottoman-appointed Guardians of the Holy Cities. Kitchener's missive contained an offer:

> Till now we have defended and befriended Islam in the person of the Turks. Henceforth it shall be that of the noble Arab. It may be that an Arab of true race will assume the Khilafat [Caliphate] at Mecca or Medina, and so good may come by the help of God out of all the evil, which is now occurring. It could be well if your Highness could convey to your followers and devotees who are found throughout the world and in every country the good tidings of the freedom of the Arabs and the rising of the sun in Arabia.[1]

Kitchener did not live to savour the British triumph. His old sparring partner took his place and presided over the new additions to the British Empire and the creation of new states and frontiers, thus providing an impetus to the proto-nationalist movements that already existed in the big cities of the departing Ottomans. Kitchener's aim, which Churchill carried through, was to find and shore-up the allies they would need in these lands. India provided a useful model: pick and choose from the existing elites.

The Hashemites and the Al-Sauds were prioritised in the Peninsula. A bunch of unsavoury individuals, bandwagon careerists and well-known crooks – addicted to collaboration with

---

1 Quoted in Elizabeth Monroe, *Britain's Moment in the Middle East, 1914–1956*, London, 1963, p. 27.

whoever might be the occupying power – were given key posts (as has been seen again recently in Afghanistan, Iraq, Libya and the Yemen). Empires are always in search of trustworthy collaborators, but there is no such thing as a collaborator loyal to one power. Those who don't flee the fall of 'their' empire are always in search of its possible replacements.[2]

There were 100,000 British and Indian troops in Mesopotamia under Churchill's charge when he was secretary of state for war. Egypt had been semi-autonomous during the Ottoman period, but Churchill now wanted a rapid transfer of even its truncated sovereignty to the British Empire. Egyptian nationalists protested strongly. There were public demonstrations in Cairo. In 1920, Alfred Milner, the colonial secretary and a staunch imperialist, suggested that the Ottoman arrangement with Egypt was not a bad idea: the British should simply step into Ottoman robes and footwear and carry on as before.

T. E. Lawrence had done something similar to good effect by uniting some of the peninsular tribes against the Ottomans. Churchill fumed at the very thought. Two years later, in an address to his constituents, he denounced all nationalist movements, especially in Egypt and India, arguing that 'the millions of people hitherto sheltered by superior science and a superior law [were showing] a desire to shatter the structure by which they live and to return blindly and heedlessly to primordial chaos'.[3] He was still smarting at the way he'd been sidelined by Curzon and General Allenby (high commissioner in the region) in 1921, when they did a deal with Egypt.[4]

---

2   The most recent example of this was the behaviour of the Afghan puppet president Ashraf Ghani in August 2021. The Taliban had agreed he could stay for a few months to ease the transition. Instead he fled with truckloads of dollars to the Gulf. As the US had no alternative, the Taliban flag fluttered over the presidential palace before the agreed date.

3   Speech in Dundee, 11 November 1922, quoted in Clive Ponting, *Churchill*, London, 1994, p. 250.

4   The period has been movingly evoked in Naguib Mafouz's *Cairo Trilogy*.

Egyptian nationalists were seeking a meaningful independence, but after negotiations Britain got everything it wanted: total military control of the Suez Canal area, of defence, protection of foreign interests, with Sudan named as the country Britain would 'protect' and, if there was any doubt in any mind, Egyptian foreign policy would be locked in to that of the UK. Churchill had no reason to whinge at all, but he did. The very idea of negotiating with the Egyptians to obtain consent from a subjected elite was anathema to him. Once again he went into tantrum mode, telling anyone prepared to listen that he would 'fight to the end'. Four days later he accepted the Cabinet decision and voted for the Allenby Plan.

Churchill's main worry was that the Egyptian model would encourage Indian nationalists to demand the same, and that this would be a threat to the Empire. As we have seen, strategic thinking was not one of his strong points. He was left alone to get on with other readjustments in the region. At the San Remo Conference in 1920, at which the former Ottoman territories were divided up, the French had been handed Syria, while the rest went to Britain. First on Churchill's list was Mesopotamia: Palestine and Trans-Jordan. Not even the notables were to be summoned for a meeting, let alone a negotiation.

Gertrude Bell, an able imperial civil servant, was assigned to 'draw the lines in the sand' that were to become the frontiers of the new states. Her hope was that the new monarchs put on hastily constructed thrones, flanked by compliant elites, would form a protective dam against the rising nationalism as well as, in her own words, 'the syndicalist and socialistic ideas seeping out of Europe'.

Churchill fully agreed. He would no doubt have been tickled had he read her letters home to her father and stepmother, in which she moved with startling ease from the new frocks in the Harvey Nichols catalogue to the necessity of deploying chemical weapons against the recalcitrant Kurds. At the foundation of the new state of Iraq, three old Ottoman provinces – Baghdad, Basra and Mosul (this latter in total breach of the armistice agreements) – were crudely pinned together, with Kuwait split off as a detached principality. Curzon gave his strong backing to Bell's plan for total British control with an Arab smokescreen.[5]

Churchill was keen to reduce the number of British troops stationed in Iraq. They needed a rest, given the casualties of the world war. He was not prepared for the Kurdish uprising that was the trigger for a generalised rebellion against British rule in 1920. Indian troops had to be sent for, and the RAF encouraged and backed to wage chemical warfare. For most of his life, Churchill was an enthusiast for new developments in the war industries that could help rapidly annihilate the enemy:

> I do not understand this squeamishness about the use of gas ... I am strongly in favour of using poisoned gases against uncivilised tribes. The moral effect should be so good that the loss of life should be reduced to a minimum ... Gases can be used which cause great inconvenience and would leave a lively terror and would leave no serious permanent effect on most of those affected.[6]

Churchill impatiently brushed aside India Office criticisms of chemical warfare, arguing that 'Gas is a more merciful weapon than high explosive shell and compels an enemy to accept a decision with less loss of life.' The Porton Down Lab in Wiltshire had been set up in 1916 precisely for the purpose of experimenting in germ and chemical warfare.

If not the father of this type of warfare, Churchill was definitely its father-in-law and undoubtedly its most effective proponent, keeping a close watch on its development, and sending congratulations to Worthington-Evans, then Secretary of State for War, for the prompt despatch of gas weapons in 1927 for use against the Chinese Communist resistance in Shanghai. Chemical warfare against the Mesopotamians led in a straight line to the terror bombing of Dresden and the obliteration of Hiroshima and Nagasaki. Churchill was not alone in this regard – Labour

---

5 See Tariq Ali, *Bush in Babylon: The Recolonisation of Iraq*, London, 2003, Chapter 3, 'An Oligarchy of Racketeers'.
6 Ponting, *Churchill*, pp. 256–8.

ministers in the war cabinet supported him, some more whole-heartedly than others.

Foreign Office squabbling over the shape and structure of the new states could not be sorted out on a departmental level. Churchill, now colonial secretary, convened a conference in Cairo in 1921 at which firm decisions were made. The more important and larger of the two rival clans in the Peninsula was led by Sharif Hussein, christened by Churchill as 'Hussein and Sons, Ltd'. This was the firm he preferred as the managing agency for the British Empire, and felt that the two sons, Abdullah and Feisal, should be provided with a state each. Abdullah got Trans-Jordan, Feisal was gifted Iraq. This was, as Churchill confided to Lloyd George, the 'best and cheapest solution' and 'no local interest could be allowed to get in the way'. It wasn't that easy.

What would happen to the rival Al-Saud outfit? A senior intelligence asset, H. S. Philby, had, during the long collaboration between the British and the Wahhabi clan, promised that their reward for siding with the British and defeating the Ottomans in the region would be the entire Peninsula. Britain had armed the Al-Saud family for years, and the older firm was completely opposed to the threat to their monopoly from the Hashemites.

Ignored in Cairo, Ibn Saud became more and more impatient. In 1924 he launched an unprovoked attacked and defeated Sharif Hussein and the Hashemites. Hussein was booted out of the country by force and died in exile seven years later. The Al-Sauds, now backed by the British, became the new Guardians of the Holy Cities in what would soon become Saudi Arabia. One of Islam's many ironies is that a demented literalist sect which targeted all Muslims who did not agree with its teachings (at that time about 99 per cent of the global community) henceforth controlled the Holy Cities, symbols of Muslim unity.

'I'll never engage in creating kings again; it's too great a strain', Gertrude Bell would later boast. Imperial vanity had got the better of her. The decision to hand Hussein's boys their thrones was, in fact, made by Churchill. Nor was there any attempt to consult groups or individuals who might be opposed to all this and who were closer to the local populations. The region re-named Iraq exploded.

Kurdish leaders had initially welcomed the British, till they real-ised there was no sympathy whatsoever in Whitehall for an inde-pendent Kurdish state, a pattern that was to be repeated later in the epoch of US global dominance.[7] They had demonstrated their alienation in 1919–20 by unleashing a rebellion in Sulaymaniyah, calmed down through the combined use of ground troops, air power, mustard gas and promised autonomy, which never arrived. Essentially to enforce a tax rise, the RAF machine-gunned peas-ants, including women and children.

Unsurprisingly, the anti-British mood spread to other regions in the country. Gertrude Bell's boss, Sir Percy Cox, had promised the citizens of Basra in 1914 that the British came 'as liberators not conquerors'. Most people, whatever their religious denomination, regarded the British as interlopers, and secret anti-colonial socie-ties, both Sunni and Shia, received a huge boost in membership after the imposition of a monarchy.

The uprising lasted over six months. During this period, armed groups raided prisons and released their leaders, then proceeded to destroy bridges and railway lines to delay the arrival of British reinforcements. British officers surrendered in both Sunni and Shia towns. The British governor, wisely in the circumstances, fled Najaf. Shia clerics called for a holy war against the infidel occupa-tion. The British Army lost 2,000 men. The resistance at least four times that number. Verses written by the popular nationalist poet, Muhammad al-Obeidi were recited wherever people gathered in public and in private:

> Set fire noble Iraqis
> Wash our shame with blood
> We are not slaves
> To adorn our necks with collars
> We are not prisoners
> To submit ourselves to be manacled . . .

---

7 Kurdish support for the invasion and occupation of Iraq in 2003 was fuelled by the same desire. In a talk in Diyarbekir that year, I suggested that 'all that will be betrayed is your illusions'.

> We are not orphans that seek a Mandate for Iraq
> And if we bow before oppression
> We shall forfeit the pleasures of the Tigris.

The new state was artificial. Power was handed to a tiny portion of the minority Sunni population, through which the British would retain control. Iraq was not destined to be stable under an imperialist occupation. Even the puppet king objected a tiny bit, which annoyed the chief representative of the master race. Irritated by this minor breach of subservience, Churchill asked his officials: 'Six months ago we were paying his hotel bill in London ... Has he not got some wives to keep him quiet?'

Feisal soon capitulated totally. Iraq's founder, satisfied with his achievement, now moved on to Trans-Jordan, where another disaster was being plotted. The League of Nations' Mandate on Palestine was about to be split between Palestinians and the 'New Jewish Home' promised to the Zionists by the British government during the First World War.

Churchill, Palestine and the Jews

In the post–First World War period, the states to be carved out of former German, Ottoman and Austro-Hungarian possessions were characterised by the newly created League of Nations as being either 'advanced nations' (white populations) or nations 'that could not yet stand up for themselves' (non-white populations) and so required imperialist tutelage. Within the latter category a further distinction was made between those closest to self-rule and those furthest away. In the Middle East, the 'top' category included Palestine, Syria, Lebanon and Iraq, hence these were listed as states that would ultimately be granted self-rule. Palestine, on this description, was not 'empty land', but a functioning province. Until self-rule was granted, these states would be governed by Mandates from the League awarded to Britain and France.

The British had already created Iraq. To this day Lebanon remains what it was at the time of its birth: the artificial creation of French colonialism – a coastal band of Greater Syria sliced off from its hinterland by Paris, once it became clear that Syrian independence was inevitable. The French wanted a colony of their own, a regional client dominated by a Maronite minority that had long been France's catspaw in the Eastern Mediterranean. Lebanon's confessional chequerboard has never been permitted an accurate census, for fear of revealing that a substantial Muslim – today perhaps even a Shia – majority is denied due representation in the political system. Sectarian tensions have never disappeared.

The British demanded and obtained a division of the Palestinian Mandate into two parts: the 'New Jewish Home' and Palestine. Here was the first example of a colonial partition via an influx of white settlers (Ashkenazi Jews). The 'War of Independence', used by most official Israeli historians to describe the 1947–9 conflict, is a misnomer. At best it could be applied to the three years (1946–8) when Zionist interests clashed with the strategic needs of the British Empire in the region. Jewish terrorist attacks on the King David Hotel and the British casualties brought Churchill close to a break with Zionism, but he hung on.

The official declarations of independence were the Balfour Declaration (1917) and the Mandate of the League of Nations (1919). Without the consistent political, economic and ideological support of the British Empire for a Zionist Jewish homeland over fifty years it is unlikely that the foundations of Israel would have been laid and a state *as exists at the present* would have come into being, regardless of the Judeocide.

Churchill was strongly in favour of a Jewish homeland, but even before he was born, the seventh Earl of Shaftesbury (an Evangelical Christian) had in 1838 taken it upon himself to kickstart the process of sending European Jews off to Palestine, and suggested as much to Palmerston, then foreign secretary, asking him to ensure Great Power protection. Old Testament pieties were mixed in with Britain's own strategic needs. Addressing Parliament a few decades later, Shaftesbury, helping to create the myth that the lands were depopulated, explained in further detail why a new British colony was almost a necessity for the Empire:

Syria and Palestine will before long become very important . . . The country needs capital and population. The Jews can give it both. And has not England a special interest in promoting such restoration? It would be a blow to England if either of her two rivals should get hold of Syria . . . Does not policy there . . . exhort England to foster the nationality of the Jews and aid them to return . . . To England then naturally belongs the role of favouring the settlement of Jews in Palestine.

As early as 1891, the Zionist pioneer Asher Ginsburg, visiting Jerusalem at a time when Jewish people, as individuals, owned less than 1 per cent of the land, reported that 'throughout the country it is difficult to find fields that are not sowed. Only sand dunes and stony mountains that are not fit to grow anything but fruit trees – and this only after hard labour and great expense of clearing and reclamation – only these are not cultivated'.[8]

Ginzburg provided a vivid description of settler racism and was far-sighted in predicting its likely outcome:

They treat the Arabs with hostility and cruelty, unscrupulously deprive them of their rights, insult them without cause, and even boast of such deeds; and none opposes this despicable and dangerous inclination.

We who live abroad are accustomed to believe that almost all Eretz Yisrael is now uninhabited desert and whoever wishes can buy land there as he pleases. But this is not true. It is very difficult to find in the land cultivated fields that are not used for planting . . . The Arab, like all the Semites, is sharp minded and shrewd . . . For now, they do not consider our actions as presenting a future danger to them . . . But, if the time comes that our people's life in Eretz Yisrael will develop to a point where we are taking their place, either slightly or significantly, the natives are not going to just step aside so easily.

---

8 Edward Said and Christopher Hitchens, *Blaming the Victims*, London, 1988, p. 216.

Compare this to Theodor Herzl's diary entry four years later (12 June 1895), where he fantasises on how the future Zionist state will be created: 'We shall have to spirit the penniless population across the border by procuring employment for it in the transit countries, while denying it any employment in our own country. Both the process of expropriation and the removal of the poor must be carried out discreetly and circumspectly.'[9]

At a Cabinet meeting in 1919, Balfour informed his colleagues that in implementing the declaration that bore his name, there was no need to waste too much time: 'in Palestine we do not propose even to go through the form of consulting the wishes of the present inhabitants'. There was no need for this since 'all the four Great powers are committed to Zionism'. This was of far greater 'import than the desire and prejudices of the 700,000 Arabs'. Churchill amplified this further, comparing the Palestinian Arabs to Aboriginals in Australia and Native Americans.

The intentions of Western imperialism were implicitly genocidal from the very beginning of the process. It was the Palestinian resistance prior to and post the *Nakba* that prevented such an occurrence.

Racism was always an integral part of Churchill's political make-up. He made no bones about it, unlike some of his colleagues in all three parties who preferred to wear a mask. He viewed Arabs as an inferior race compared to Europeans of any stripe. In the case of Palestine he accused the Arabs of behaving like a 'dog in the manger', a view he spelt out in his evidence to the Peel Commission, set up in 1936 to report on the Palestinian uprising then in motion and which had paralysed the country:

> I do not agree that the dog in the manger has the final right to the manger, even though he may have lain there for a very long time. I do not admit that right. I do not admit, for instance, that a great wrong has been done to the Red Indians of America, or the black people of Australia. I do not admit that a wrong has been done to these people by the fact that a stronger race, a higher-grade race, or

9 Theodore Herzl, *The Complete Diaries of Theodor Herzl*, Vol. I, New York, 1960, p. 88.

at any rate, a more worldly-wise race, to put it that way, has come in and taken their place.[10]

This is the voice of white supremacy, a view that was reiterated with remarkable clarity by Israel's foremost revisionist historian, the former paratrooper Benny Morris, over half a century later. Churchill would have been delighted by such a display of candour, which admitted the long-denied crimes and atrocities committed against the Palestinians in 1948 during the 'War of Independence'. Today, this is the common sense of Jewish Israel from top to bottom, the ultimate logic of the Balfour Declaration and a distillation of Churchill's own views.

Detaching myths from realities in Palestine became more and more difficult after the Balfour Declaration. The Palestinian Arabs paid an exorbitant price and are continuing to do so. The myth still persists that Palestine was almost uninhabited, that vast tracts of the promised land were thirsting for new Jewish settlers. The principal propagators of this lie were the Zionist leaders of the Yishuv and their English backers. The fact that Palestinian historians continue to produce books demonstrating that this was not the case is in itself an indication of how deep Zionist ideology remains within Israel and the diaspora.[11]

Churchill did not write a great deal on his own attitudes to Zionism and Jewish people in general. But from what he did write it is clear that his views on the creation of Israel were not always consistent. His reasoning veered from pure instrumentalism (it would be of use to the British Empire in a region filled with enemies, i.e. Arabs)

---

10 Quoted in Ponting, *Churchill*, p. 254.

11 '[D]espite archival absences, scholars have provided intriguing portrayals of early 20th-century Palestine as a dynamic time ... Yet the picture of Palestinian social life peopled by poor, illiterate masses of peasants and workers, alongside a small group of venal notables fraught with internecine competition, continues to run rampant in most historical portrayals and contemporary imaginings.' Sherene Seikaly, *Men of Capital: Scarcity and Economy in Mandate Palestine*, Stanford, 2016, p. 9.

to civilisational racism, with anti-Bolshevism playing its part as well.

The Jews were an ancient race, the 'chosen people' and *ipso facto* superior to the Arabs. This view was spelt out in what appears to be Churchill's lengthiest pronouncement on the subject: an article published on page five of the *Illustrated Sunday Herald* on 8 February 1920. The title spelt out the programmatic priorities enshrined in the text: 'Zionism versus Bolshevism: A Struggle for the Soul of the Jewish People'. 'Some people like Jews and some do not,' Churchill informs the reader, 'but no thoughtful man can doubt the fact that they are beyond all question the most formidable and the most remarkable race which has ever appeared in the world.'

On one level this was surprisingly generous, since he did not add a qualifier that specified 'after the English, of course', or words to that effect. More importantly, the notion itself is nonsensical and a throwback to Old Testament literalism.

Surely, Churchill knew English history well enough. Why then no mention of the fact that the worst pogroms and persecution of the Jews in old Europe had begun in England? German fascists would have been pleased by the fact that, in 1218, Henry III had announced a royal decree, 'The Edict of the Badge', which made it compulsory for Jews to wear a 'marking badge'. Sixty years later pogroms carried out by thieving barons led to the killing of over a thousand Jews, five hundred in London alone. The 'Edict of Expulsion' was issued by Edward I in 1290. All Jews were rounded up and expelled, their property looted and the blood-libel charge spread with a zeal that Goebbels would have envied. A classic case here of 'what's past is prologue'. Some of the Jews fled to France. Others found a haven in Muslim Spain, where there were large and free Jewish communities, participating on every level of the state.

The Jews were invited back to England by Oliver Cromwell 350 years later. Ironically, the enlightened Rabbi negotiating the return with the Protector was Menasseh ben Israel, who had tutored the young Spinoza. He was busy in London while his pupil was being expelled from the Jewish community in Amsterdam. None of this found a place in Churchill's *History of the English-Speaking Peoples*. In his 1920 article, after a few anodyne remarks about the wit and wisdom of Disraeli, the first and last Jewish-born prime minister of Britain, Churchill moves on to his next theme, helpfully subtitled 'Good and Bad Jews':

> The conflict between good and evil which proceeds unceasingly in the breast of man nowhere reaches such an intensity as in the Jewish race. The dual nature of mankind is nowhere more strongly or more terribly exemplified. We owe to the Jews in the Christian revelation a system of ethics which, even if it were entirely separated from the supernatural, would be incomparably the most precious possession of mankind, worth in fact the fruits of all other wisdom and learning put together. On that system and by that faith there has been built out of the wreck of the Roman Empire the whole of our existing civilisation.
>
> And it may well be that this same astounding race may at the present time be in the actual process of producing another system of morals and philosophy, as malevolent as Christianity was benevolent, which, if not arrested, would shatter irretrievably all that Christianity has rendered possible. It would almost seem as if the gospel of Christ and the gospel of Antichrist were destined to originate among the same people; and that this mystic and mysterious race had been chosen for the supreme manifestations, both of the divine and the diabolical.

The 'diabolical' Jews are what Hitler and his colleagues would describe a few years later as the 'Jewish-Bolshevik' conspiracy. Churchill, seething at the collapse of the Allied intervention in Russia, allows his hatred of the Bolshevik leaders of Jewish origin to cloud his rationality and resort to outrageous fibs, such as whitewashing General Denikin and his cohort of anti-Semites. It would be difficult to find even a Russian conservative historian of that period or later producing rubbish of this sort. Churchill continues, stressing that there are many good Jews in Russia, who 'as bankers and industrialists' have backed England and France, but:

In violent opposition to all this sphere of Jewish effort rise the schemes of the International Jews. The adherents of this sinister confederacy are mostly men reared up among the unhappy populations of countries where Jews are persecuted on account of their race. Most, if not all, of them have forsaken the faith of their forefathers, and divorced from their minds all spiritual hopes of the next world. This movement among the Jews is not new. From the days of Spartacus-Weishaupt to those of Karl Marx, and down to Trotsky (Russia), Bela Kun (Hungary), Rosa Luxemburg (Germany), and Emma Goldman (United States), this world-wide conspiracy for the overthrow of civilisation and for the reconstitution of society on the basis of arrested development, of envious malevolence, and impossible equality, has been steadily growing. It played ... a definitely recognisable part in the tragedy of the French Revolution. It has been the mainspring of every subversive movement during the Nineteenth Century; and now at last this band of extraordinary personalities from the underworld of the great cities of Europe and America have gripped the Russian people by the hair of their heads and have become practically the undisputed masters of that enormous empire.

What is entertaining here is that Churchill, never a votary of any religion, resorts to invoking the Jewish 'faith', the faith of those good Jews who retain 'spiritual hopes of the next world', etc., as opposed to the 'international Jew' who represents all the worst traits of the stereotype. The cynicism is breath-taking. After this preamble to describing the horrors of internationalist Jews we come to the core of his article, the subtitle of which is 'Terrorist Jews':

There is no need to exaggerate the part played in the creation of Bolshevism and in the actual bringing about of the Russian Revolution by these international and for the most part atheistical Jews. It is certainly a very great one; it probably outweighs all others. With the notable exception of Lenin, the majority of the leading figures are Jews. Moreover, the principal inspiration and driving power comes from the Jewish leaders. Thus Tchitcherin, a pure Russian, is eclipsed by his nominal subordinate Litvinoff, and the influence of Russians like Bukharin or Lunacharski cannot be compared with the power of Trotsky, or of Zinovieff, the Dictator of the Red Citadel (Petrograd), or of Krassin or Radek – all Jews. In the Soviet institutions the predominance of Jews is even more astonishing. And the prominent, if not indeed the principal, part in the system of terrorism applied by the Extraordinary Commissions for Combating Counter-Revolution has been taken by Jews, and in some notable cases by Jewesses. The same evil prominence was obtained by Jews in the brief period of terror during which Bela Kun ruled in Hungary. The same phenomenon has been presented in Germany (especially in Bavaria), so far as this madness has been allowed to prey upon the temporary prostration of the German people. Although in all these countries there are many non-Jews every whit as bad as the worst of the Jewish revolutionaries, the part played by the latter in proportion to their numbers in the population is astonishing.

Inaccurate and crass this might be, but viewed from two decades later, the implication is clear: If Hitler had only concentrated on the 'international Jews' and the 'Terrorists', he would have done Western civilisation a huge favour.

The introduction to the Nuremberg Laws of 15 September 1935 states: 'If the Jews had a state of their own in which the bulk of the people were at home, the Jewish question could already be considered solved today, even for the Jews themselves. The ardent Zionists of all people have objected least to the basic ideas of the Nuremberg Laws, because they know that these laws are the only correct solution for the Jewish people.' Many years later, Haim Cohen, a former judge in the Supreme Court of Israel, stated: 'The bitter irony of fate decreed that the same biological and racist argument extended by the Nazis, and which inspired the inflammatory laws of Nuremberg, serve as the basis for the official definition of Jewishness in the bosom of the state of Israel.'[12]

---

12   Quoted in Joseph Badi, *Fundamental Laws of the State of Israel*, New York, 1960, p. 156.

Anti-Semitism was and remains a racist ideology directed against the Jews and has old roots. In his classic work, *The Jewish Question*, published posthumously in France in 1946, the Belgian Marxist Abram Leon (a 'bad Jew', on Churchill's definition, who fought in the Resistance and was executed by the Gestapo in 1944) invented the category of a 'people-class', describing the sociological location of the Jews who managed to preserve their linguistic, ethnic and religious characteristics through many centuries without becoming assimilated.

This was not unique to the Jews, argued Leon, but could apply just as strongly to many ethnic minorities: diaspora Armenians, Copts, Chinese merchants in South-East Asia, Muslims in China, etc. The defining characteristic common to these groups was that they became middlemen in a pre-capitalist world, resented alike by rich and poor. All were subjected to repression and pogroms when times were bad.

Twentieth-century genocides included the massacres of the Congolese by Belgian imperialists and of the Armenians during the First World War, and the industrialised Judeocide of the Second World War, which played on the fears and insecurities of a deprived population. Hence August Bebel's reference to anti-Semitism as 'the socialism of fools'. The roots of anti-Semitism, like other forms of racism, are social, political, ideological and economic. The uniqueness of the Judeocide was that it took place in Europe (the heart of Christian civilisation) and was carried out systematically – by Germans, Poles, Ukrainians, Lithuanians, French and Italians (and had Hitler occupied Britain it would have been the same there as well) – as if it were the most normal thing in the world. Hence Hannah Arendt's phrase, 'the banality of evil'.

Non-Jewish Zionism, too, has an old pedigree and permeates European culture. It dates back to the birth of Christian fundamentalist sects in the sixteenth and seventeenth centuries who took the Old Testament literally. Individuals subscribing to the belief included Oliver Cromwell and John Milton. Later, for other reasons, Locke, Pascal and Rousseau joined the Zionist bandwagon. Robespierre and Napoleon insisted on the removal of all restrictions against the Jews. The former favoured the abolition of slavery as well (but not Napoleon, whose role in the reconquest of Haiti should never be forgotten). And, for vile reasons, the Third Reich, too, supported a Jewish homeland, as seen in the Nuremberg Laws.

Zionist leaders often negotiated with anti-Semites to attain their objectives: Herzl talked openly with Von Plehve, the chief organiser of pogroms in Tsarist Russia; Jabotinsky collaborated with Petlura, the Ukrainian hangman of the Jews; 'revisionist' Zionists were friendly with Mussolini and Pilsudski; the Haavara Agreement between Zionist organisations and the Third Reich arranged for the sale of German-Jewish assets and the migration of some Jews to Palestine.

Modern Zionism is the ideology of secular Jewish nationalism. It has little to do with Judaism as a religion, and many orthodox Jews to this day remain hostile to Zionism, like the Hassidic sect that regularly joins Palestinian marches against the settlements and the occupation. The Zionist movement was born in the nineteenth century, a direct response to the vicious anti-Semitism that pervaded Austria. The first Jewish immigrants to Palestine arrived in 1882, and many of them were interested only in maintaining a cultural presence.

The movement was based upon the bogus idea of a people without land, and a land without people. But there is no such thing as the 'historical right' of Jews to Palestine. Long before the Roman conquest of Judea in 70 AD, a large majority of the Jewish population lived outside Palestine. The native Jews were gradually assimilated into neighbouring groups such as the Phoenicians and Philistines, etc. Palestinians are, in most cases, descended from old Hebrew tribes, as has been recently confirmed by genetic science, much to the annoyance of Zionists. In 1979, Nathan Weinstock (followed more recently by Shlomo Sand) demolished many myths that were and still are utilised to defend the creation of a Jewish state in Palestine. In *Zionism: False Messiah*, Weinstock wrote:

In any case the progressive spread of the Hebrew population outside Palestine is an established fact. Furthermore this diaspora was formed peacefully, independently of any foreign conquest. 'As early as the period of the Assyrian and Babylonian campaigns in Palestine [that is to say before the fifth century BCE]', writes Roth, 'the fore-fathers of the Jewish people first came into touch with Europe and the Europeans. Even before the close of the Biblical Age, Hebrews were settled within the periphery of the Hellenic world.'[13]

Nevertheless Israel was created in 1948 by London, as one of the last imperial acts of an empire in serious decline, but still with sufficient colonial clout. British power was an absolute condition for Zionist colonisation. Without the violence of British police and army it would have been near impossible. The Arab majority (90 per cent) would have stopped the post–First World War build up without too many difficulties: in 1918 there were 700,000 Palestinian Arabs and 60,000 Jews. The latter were totally dependent on the protection of the British imperial state. Zionism, an ethnic nationalist movement of European-Jewish extraction, now became a form of European colonisation.

Of the two Zionist rivals for the leadership, Chaim Weizmann, based in Manchester and tapped by Churchill in 1915 for his industrial-chemistry expertise, realised early on that Britain would be the key player and said as much. His competitor for the title of Grand Patriarch of Israel, David Ben-Gurion, had wasted time and blotted his copybook by hanging on to the long coats of Ottoman officials in Istanbul, a city he loved, for far too long. He wanted to negotiate the creation of a Jewish state as an Ottoman province with Ottoman help.

A new biography, *A State at Any Cost: The Life of David Ben-Gurion*, by the Israeli historian Tom Segev, systematically confounds the myth of Ben-Gurion as the romantic young socialist–Zionist pioneer, the architect of labour unity and eternally canny father of the nation, guiding his people from one miraculous military triumph to the next.[14] In Segev's telling, his subject was never an

---

13 Nathan Weinstock, *Zionism: False Messiah*, London, 1979, p. 137, quoting Cecil Roth, *A Short History of the Jewish People*, London, 1969.

14 Tom Segev, *A State at Any Cost: The Life of David Ben-Gurion*, London, 2019.

original thinker; he acquired his Zionism from his father, a small-town notary in the Tsarist Pale. He set out for Palestine in 1906, aged twenty, 'out of despair', having failed to get a place at a Warsaw engineering institute, and thinking himself not commercially minded enough to make it in America.

Jaffa, with its oriental alleyways, was 'worse than Plonsk'; he disliked farm work and was disappointed that Jewish farmers preferred to employ cheap and highly skilled Arab labour. Ill at ease in Ottoman Jerusalem, he much preferred Thessaloniki and Istanbul (Constantinople as it then was), where he pursued legal training at the university, hoping to go on to represent the Jewish public as an Ottoman Cabinet minister.

Far from being politically far-sighted, Ben-Gurion was blind-sided by the course of the First World War and the Balfour Declaration, at which time he was fundraising for the Zionist cause in New York. He belatedly switched sides, now seeking to realise the national home under British rather than Ottoman protection. Volunteering for the US unit of the Jewish Legion, he arrived back in the Middle East in August 1918, but was hospitalised with dysentery.

Meanwhile Weizmann was cruising round Jerusalem in General Allenby's Rolls-Royce. Ben-Gurion never got over his jealousy of Weizmann's intimacy with London's power brokers, forged by the latter's work in synthetic-chemical supplies during the war and sealed through his close relations with C. P. Scott, the editor of the *Manchester Guardian*. The bulk of Ben-Gurion's time was spent outside Palestine, manoeuvring with the Brits or fundraising in America ('I don't wish on anyone to speak before an American audience sitting round dinner tables in evening dress'). On both fronts, Weizmann had already established close personal relations with the powers that be, and effortlessly outshone Ben-Gurion, who was therefore obliged to build an alternative power base for himself.

According to Segev, it was the work of the Zionist labour organiser Bert Katznelson among farm labourers that laid the groundwork for what became the Histadrut, the General Organisation of Workers, which offered Ben-Gurion a base from which to forge three tiny labour groups into a political party, Ahdut HaAvoda (the precursor to Mapai, the Workers' Party of the Land of Israel). Thanks to his efforts, the party won a plurality – 70 out of 314 seats – in the 1920 election to the quasi-parliamentary Jewish Assembly of Representatives. The foundations of Israeli apartheid were laid in the interwar years. The Histadrut did not permit Arab workers to join its ranks. The kibbutzim were for Jews only. For Ben-Gurion, separatism, based on ethnicity and ideological beliefs that helped eliminate class divisions, was necessary for creating a Zionist state.

Ben-Gurion's key assets were an indefatigable energy and an obsessive attention to detail, amassing data on every voter, bringing to mind 'the dictator's centralization of information and the addiction of a collector'. As party secretary he became 'the most powerful person in the apparatus'. Borrowing from Menachem Ussishkin's 'dictatorship of the Zionist proletariat', Ben-Gurion set out to run the Histadrut not so much as a labour union but as the proto-government of a state-in-waiting: a single bureaucracy responsible for jobs, health, education and the armed defence of settlements (the Haganah), linked to an Office of Public Works.

If the Histadrut became Ben-Gurion's personal fiefdom, Segev argues, it was also true that no one else worked as hard: he made frequent visits to workplaces and construction sites, talking to workers and obsessively jotting down what they told him in his little notebooks. According to a Haifa foreman, 'to them, he was the Histadrut'. If he now had a power base from which to outmanoeuvre his more glamorous and well-connected rivals like Weizmann and Jabotinsky, his main enemies were on the left: the Hashomer veterans were hounded as communists, the Trumpeldor Labour Battalion excoriated for its Bolshevik tendencies.

It was on this basis that Ben-Gurion mounted his bid for leadership of the Jewish Agency, the international executive body established by the Zionist Congress in 1929, headed by Weizmann. Segev gives a riveting account of Ben-Gurion's victorious leadership campaign in 1933, which involved 'closely tracking what was being done in each cell of the political hive he sought to conquer', and crisscrossing Poland (he had 800 towns on his list) to recruit members who would vote for 'a labour victory to save Zionism' from Jabotinsky's Revisionists.

While remaining head of the Histadrut, he took command of the Jewish Agency office in Jerusalem, becoming de facto prime minister in waiting. Ben-Gurion immediately grasped the 1936 UK partition proposal as an opportunity, drawing up a list of Arab villages in the Jewish zone and their number of inhabitants. Following Herzl, population transfer was always part of Zionist strategy, though Ben-Gurion recognised 'the horrible difficulty of a foreign force uprooting some hundred thousand Arabs from the villages they have lived in for hundreds of years'.

Segev gives a chilling account of Ben-Gurion's ruthless attitude towards wartime rescue operations of European Jews: 'I would rather save half the children in Palestine than all of them in England.' The Zionist enterprise was more important than any community of diaspora Jews. 'The persecutions in each country affect only the Jews in that country. What happens here strikes at the heart of the nation' was his response to the first reports of systematic extermination. Ben-Gurion himself spent most of the war years in London or fundraising in the United Sates, engaging in a showdown with Weizmann in New York, enraged at his refusal to offer an introduction to Roosevelt. Snobbishly perhaps, Weizmann described him as 'morally stunted', 'reminiscent of a petty dictator': 'nothing is more dangerous than a small man nursing his grievances'.

While the post-war political reverberations helped further the Zionist movement's diplomatic campaigns, there was no basis for claiming that the state of Israel was founded as a result of the Holocaust. As Segev argues, it was an imperial exercise: 'the British played a much larger role', having overseen pre-war the establishment of a solid political, economic and military infrastructure for the state-to-be. In fact, Segev contends that, after the war, Ben-Gurion tried to persuade the Brits to extend the Mandate, even if that meant working under the ferociously anti-Semitic Ernest Bevin, to allow him time to build the Haganah into a force capable of fighting the Arab states.

His direction of the 'War of Independence' was guided by the strategic aspiration 'maximum territory, minimum Arabs'. He pocketed the 1947 UNSCOP partition plan (twice as generous as the Peel proposal that had triggered the Arab Revolt) as a tactical step forward, while telling Haganah commanders to prepare for war and embracing the policy of 'offensive defence'. In other words, he had planned the pre-emptive attack on Palestinian villages, capturing or destroying them and driving out their inhabitants, from the outset. 'There was no need to issue an explicit order' – 'the spirit of the message' conveyed by Ben-Gurion as commander-in-chief was clear enough.

In the case of Plan Dalet, formal written orders were drafted by Yiguel Yadin, in line with Ben-Gurion's general direction – the destruction or eradication of villages and the expulsion of the Palestinian population beyond the Jewish state's borders. Local Haganah commanders could decide whether villages should be 'captured, cleared out or destroyed', while exemplary atrocities – such as Deir Yassin – combined with a 'whispering campaign' spreading rumours of worse, would help speed population flight.

Segev underlines Ben-Gurion's narrowly political imposition of Mapai commanders and sacking of the more left-wing Galili in May 1948, at the height of the war (again, though Segev doesn't say this, bringing to mind a miniature Stalinist purge in his battle against the Mapam left), which provoked the Generals' Revolt. Ben-Gurion's unilateral Declaration of Independence on 14 May 1948 – contra the Truman administration's call for a three-month ceasefire – was aimed not only to block Arab return but also to restore his own political prestige, damaged by Haganah's failures and his besting by the generals. Officers complained bitterly about his poor grasp of military strategy, especially his obsession with taking the well-defended Arab position at Latrun, at a cost of hundreds of Haganah lives, and his pursuit of vendettas against the left and military leaders in the midst of the war.

Ben-Gurion was 'entirely at peace' with the displacement of 500,000–750,000 Palestinians as the price of Israel's independence. He denied that they had been forced to flee, claiming all who left did so under British rule. In fact, half left after the Declaration of Independence. Ben-Gurion claimed these were 'not refugees, but enemies', gloating that '[t]here may well have been cases where they were helped a bit to flee but fundamentally, this really was an inexplicable phenomenon' – it 'showed that the Arab national movement wasn't based on positive ideas, only on religious hatred, xenophobia, the leaders' ambitions'. 'History has proven who is really connected to this land and for whom it is nothing but a luxury that can easily be done without.'

Only later did Ben-Gurion claim that the Grand Mufti had ordered the Palestinians to flee, elaborating on the myths of David versus Goliath ('700,000 Jews vs 30 million Arabs') and ethnic superiority ('Our human material has much greater moral and intellectual capacity than that of our neighbours'). In fact, both the Haganah/IDF and the Arab armies fielded around 100,000 troops, but the IDF was also armed from overseas: US donations provided $50 million for arms purchases – including artillery and combat aircraft – without which, and without the deal brokered with Abdullah of Jordan, victory would have been unlikely, as Golda Meir later admitted. In addition, the Palestinians had barely recovered from the brutal suppression of the Arab Revolt by the British occupiers, who in thirty years had neglected to institute mandatory education; less than a third of Palestinian children went to school or were in any way prepared for modern national life. The fact that those who rehearse this history are denounced as anti-Semites (a recent example being the filmmaker Ken Loach) and expelled from political parties is an indication, among numerous others, that the colonial Zionist state created in 1948, under attack by global movements in solidarity with the Palestinians, is still heavily dependent on the United States and Germany for subsidies and on the rest of the West for ideological support.

Such genesis stories suggest that while Israel is a *sui generis* European settler-state, it is not simply that. When the interests of Zionist nationalism clashed with those of the British, the Stern Gang, led by Menachem Begin, were not easily scared. The worst terrorist attack during the Mandate was the explosion that destroyed the King David Hotel in 1946. The ninety-three dead included British civil servants and officers and many Arabs. Begin had the last laugh when in 1978, as prime minister of Israel, he was awarded the Nobel Peace Prize.

Moderate and right-wing Zionists disagreed on the means. They were always in agreement on the ends. Weizmann, Ben-Gurion, Begin, Dayan and so on, up to Netanyahu, belonged to different political outfits, but each of them believed in a greater Israel. The only difference was over where the final line in the sand should be drawn, and here too the dispute was largely cosmetic. Early Zionists, implacable and determined to create a separate state, were tougher than Ben-Gurion in treating non-Zionist or/and integrationist Jews with the utmost contempt.

Which brings one back to Benny Morris, and in particular his startling interview published in the liberal daily *Haaretz* on 8 January 2004, under the title 'Survival of the Fittest' – a document of unusual significance in the modern history of Zionism. To his shocked interlocutor, Morris lays out two unpalatable truths: that the Zionist project could only be realised by deliberate ethnic cleansing; and that, once it was embarked upon, the only reasons for stopping short of completely removing the Arab population from Palestine were purely temporary and tactical ones. It was letting the second of these cats out of the bag that generated the most uproar among conventional opponents of the Likud and Labour establishments.

Arguments for the wholesale ejection of the Palestinians from the promised land have long been openly expressed on the right of the Israeli spectrum, and have freely circulated in labour and liberal circles, in Israel and the diaspora. But Morris's forthright judgement that Ben-Gurion made a fatal mistake in not clearing the future West Bank of its Arab inhabitants comes with the unique authority of one still at work revealing hidden atrocities from the 'War of Independence'. The same rigour he has brought to Zionist war crimes he also brings to the underlying logic of Zionism – left or right. In doing so, Morris – invoking Camus – places himself squarely on the side of his community, whatever the disasters it has inflicted on the Palestinians, disasters he has unsparingly recorded.

The daily suffering of the Palestinians fails to excite the liberal conscience of Europe, guilt-ridden (for good reason) by its past inability to defend the Jews of Europe against extinction. But the Judeocide should not be used as a cover for committing crimes against the Palestinian people. To be intimidated by Zionist black-mail is to become an accomplice of war crimes. As the Hebrew poet Aharon Shabtai wrote in his poem 'Nostalgia' in 2003:

> And when it's all over,
> My dear, dear reader,
> On which benches will we have to sit,
> Those of us who shouted 'Death to the Arabs!'
> And those who claimed they 'didn't know'?[15]

Churchill and the 1953 Regime Change in Iran

In Iran, the Anglo-American coup of 1953, which brought about regime change by toppling the popular nationalist, liberal-demo-cratic prime minister Mohammed Mossadegh ('Messy Duck' in Churchill's pathetic coinage), had a pre-history stretching back to the First World War.

For many years prior to the war, Iran had been a football kicked around by Tsarist Russia and the British Empire, with a few German linesmen watching from the side. In 1907, the two powers had signed a secret agreement to dismantle the country and divide it between themselves. After the Bolshevik Revolution, Lenin and Trotsky, as they had pledged, made public all the secret imperialist treaties they could find in the archives, including this one. When news of this reached Tehran, there was political mayhem. Virtually every sector of Iranian society, from landlords to peasants and the bazaars, was shocked. With the collapse of Tsarist Russia, the British, and Lord Curzon in particular, attempted to sort out the chaos by pushing their agents and payroll buddies among the Tehran notables to rapidly form a government. This was how Vosuq al-Dawleh came to be appointed prime minister in August 1918, and that is why his name became the equivalent of the Norwegian Nazi, Quisling, who established a similar reputation

---

15 Aharon Shabtai, *J'Accuse*, trans. Peter Cole, New York, 2003.

during the next world war. With this difference: few outside Iran were aware of Vosuq's knavery.

Soon after the infamous Treaty of Versailles gave the green light for the continuation of European colonialism by rejecting any demand for national self-determination from colonised peoples, Sir Percy Cox, the British minister in Tehran, acting on Curzon's orders, entered into secret negotiations with Vosuq and two of his close colleagues. The aim was to secure a new secret treaty that effectively made Iran a British protectorate.[16] Vosuq agreed to the deal provided the British paid the three of them a consultancy fee and expenses: 500,000 tomans were demanded in a verbal invoice. A dissident member of the Majlis (Parliament), Mohammed Mossadegh, computed the figures as being the equivalent of £131,000 at the time. The money was paid and in 1919 the deal was done, with British 'advisers' appointed to supervise the treasury and the army.

Hostility to the deal united Iran, with poets in the vanguard of the nationalist upheavals to come. Aref addressed a public poem to Vosuq with an angry opening line: 'Thou, the doors of whose home are open to whores'. A fellow-poet versified: 'O, Vosuq al-Dawleh, Iran was not your daddy's estate ...'. Farrokhi Yazdi targeted another member of the treacherous trio:

> Nosrat al-Dawleh is busy in Europe
> Annihilating the motherland – look and see,
> Like a dealer for the sale of the motherland
> Constantly finding customers – look and see
> To deliver the motherland to Britain
> He is even keener than her – look and see.

---

16 Homa Katouzian's *Iranian History and Politics*, London, 2002, is a valuable survey, though, ironically, published in the 'Routledge Curzon/BIPS Persian Study Series'. Did some section of Curzon's family leave a bequest with a regular stipend? We should be told. Whatever the motive, the money is being well spent. See Chapter 9 for further details on the 1919 agreement as well as later developments. The poems quoted are from this volume.

Others were busy in London as well. Churchill as minister of war was in this instance hostile to Curzon's adventures, and joined with the India Office to demand a halt to proceedings (even insisting that, as a naval fleet led by the veteran Bolshevik Raskolnikov appeared at the Caspian port of Enzili to demand a return of Russian vessels moored there, there should be no resistance whatsoever). Both Churchill and Lord Hardinge, the Viceroy of India, were extremely nervous that any huge setback for Britain in Iran would have serious repercussions in India. Hardinge made it clear that no Indian troops would be supplied to help Curzon.

Weeks before the treaty was announced, the Soviet Commissar for Foreign Affairs, Georgi Chicherin, announced that the Soviet Union had unilaterally cancelled all Iran's debts to Russia and declared an end to all Russian privileges and concessions. This position did not change.

The United States, for its own reasons, was not pleased by the 1919 treaty, and though Curzon insisted he had cleared it with Woodrow Wilson via his chief of staff, the State Department issued a statement that contradicted Curzon, who then went into a sulk, noting that he was disinclined to continue 'polemics on a question on which the US government have gone out of their way to be nasty'. The French were being unpleasant as well, with *Le Figaro* mocking that 'a midget Shah had sold his country for a centime'.

It was obvious that the agreement was untenable. The whole of Iran opposed it and, for differing reasons, three big powers – the United States, France and the Soviet Union – refused to accept the outcome. The British establishment itself was divided, and Curzon's inflexibility on a number of important tactical questions brought the business to an end.

Undeterred, Curzon and cronies organised a coup by a British-created Cossack regiment, commanded by General Ironside, who handed over the reins to an ambitious sergeant promoted to officer rank. This was Reza Khan, who appointed a civilian prime minister and, only too aware of national sentiment, declared the 1919 treaty null and void. The coup had been bloodless, but it triggered a movement that finally led to the Constitutional Revolution. Many liberal intellectuals in Iran, as well as the more radical additions inspired by the Russian Revolution, and some clerical leaders, favoured a republic, an elected parliament and a democratic constitution. The rule of law became a central demand, with the movement describing itself as 'against all forms of arbitrary rule'.

By 1926, Reza Khan, who had toyed with the idea of a republic, had acceded to the throne after successfully persuading the Majlis to remove the last Shah of the Qajar dynasty. Reza was an odd mixture. He copied Kemal Ataturk to a certain extent, introducing some modernist measures, but left the countryside intact. He attempted to create a new Iranian identity on the Turkish model, but succeeded only in antagonising ethnic groups.

During the Second World War, Reza's pro-Axis stance began to worry the Allies. In 1941, the British removed him from power and replaced him with his son. Reza was sent into exile in South Africa, where he died a few years later. Churchill and Stalin temporarily divided the country to secure the oil, considered necessary for the war, but the Red Army withdrew soon after the Allied victory in 1945.

British influence was maintained via trade, military aid and the Anglo-Iranian Oil Company, whose managers behaved like colonial officers, treating Iranian leaders with total contempt. As royalties fluctuated, the Iranians felt they were getting a raw deal. They demanded a 50–50 division of the oil shares, as the US had agreed with the Saudis. The British refused, insisting on keeping a majority holding. Both Islamic and secular political groupings protested strongly. On 7 March 1951, the pro-British prime minister, General Razmara, was assassinated by the Fedayeen-i-Islam. The Majlis soon passed a resolution demanding nationalisation of the oil company. A secular constitutionalist party, the National Front, grew in popularity, and street demonstrations pressured the Shah into appointing the party's leader, Mohammed Mossadegh, as prime minister.

On 1 May 1951, Mossadegh signed the bill nationalising the oil industry. The worn-out and by now totally visionless Labour government in Britain regarded this as a body blow to British influence in the region as well as an economic disaster. They were correct on both counts. Foreign Secretary Herbert Morrison favoured a rapid military intervention, but the White House was uneasy and advised Attlee to tread carefully. The Labour minister for war, Emanuel 'Manny' Shinwell, cursed his fate. He too favoured a short, sharp war, but if that was not possible then the British would have to put on a tough act:

> We must in no circumstances throw up the sponge not only because of the direct consequences of the loss of Persian oil, but because of the effect which a diplomatic defeat in Persia would have on our prestige and our whole position throughout the Middle East. If Persia was allowed to get away with it, Egypt and other Middle Eastern countries would be encouraged to think they could try things on; the next thing might be an attempt to nationalise the Suez Canal.[17]

This was, of course, Churchill's own view, but neither he nor the Labour imperialists were prepared to countenance the thought that the British Empire was over.

Back in office after Labour's defeat in 1951, Churchill secured Truman's support for a coup against Mossadegh. The SIS (MI6) and the CIA were assigned the task. Until recently it was widely believed that the CIA played the major role. On paper, perhaps. But Churchill was determined to teach Mossadegh a lesson for having dared to nationalise British assets.

In late 2020, the British filmmaker Taghi Amirani (of Iranian origin) finished his documentary film, *Coup '53*, a powerful account of Western intervention in Iran, revisiting the historical milestones. The remarkable footage, skilfully blended with the new material by the film editor, Walter Murch, would have created a strong impact on its own had there been nothing else. Astonishingly, during his research, Amirani was informed by Mossadegh's grandson of a document that very few people knew existed: the transcript of an interview with the senior British agent in Iran at the time, Norman Darbyshire. It was he who planned the details of the coup at ground level, and successfully

---

17   Ervand Abrahamian, *The Coup: 1953, the CIA, and the Roots of Modern U.S.–Iranian Relations*, New York, 2013.

removed Mossadegh from power by kidnapping him on 19 August 1953.

Darbyshire first made the disclosure in an interview for the Granada Television series *End of Empire* that aired in 1985. But his account never made it into that series. At first the producers insisted they had never interviewed him. Technicians who were recorded saying the contrary suddenly changed their minds. The latest version appears to be that the interview was conducted, but Darbyshire withdrew permission. The secretiveness of MI6 is not a secret, and whatever happened then or since has their pawprint on it. In fact most of the documents dealing with Britain's role in the coup have been destroyed.

The existence of this transcript (what happened to the videotape?) must have been irritating. It confirms beyond all doubt the role Britain played. The CIA agent Kermit 'Kim' Roosevelt came to report the success directly to Churchill over a boozy lunch at the Connaught. The old man was delighted, revelling in the details despite falling asleep throughout the lunch. Darbyshire's presence might have enhanced the occasion by curbing Roosevelt's self-praise.

The interview transcript, disappeared for more than three decades, reveals that the kidnapping and execution of Tehran's pro-Mossadegh police chief, General Mahmood Afshartous, was organised by Darbyshire himself.

The interviewer asks: 'Were you involved in [the] Afshartous assassination?' Darbyshire replies 'Yes', then tries to explain that the intention was not to kill him: 'something went wrong; he was kidnapped and held in a cave'. His guard was a 'young army officer'. Supposedly, Afshartous 'was unwise enough to make derogatory comments about the Shah . . . and the young officer pulled out a gun and shot him'. Darbyshire (his words spoken and acted in the documentary by Ralph Fiennes) insisted the point of the abduction was 'to boost the morale of the opposition' to Mosaddegh, and that Afshartous's death 'didn't help'. This is unconvincing. Given the character of the opposition, only death would have helped. Since the former agent is long dead, we may never know the whole truth.

Mossadegh had refused to accept the authority of the Shah, who had sacked him in August 1953, and informed the public that this was illegal. The Shah, who was simply carrying out CIA/MI6 instructions, became panicked by the support for Mossadegh, fled the country and was given refuge in Rome. He had to be persuaded forcefully to return by his sister, Ashraf (who Darbyshire reveals was heavily bribed before she accepted the job of bringing her twin brother back).

The coup was a Western success in the short term. It had got rid of a popular prime minister, the nationalist government and the (communist) Tudeh Party. The trade union movement was crushed by the Shah's supporters and his conniving, greedy, shameless twin sister. There was a very weak public demonstration in support of the Shah. The pimps, prostitutes and thugs of downtown Tehran lent a hand by gathering a few like themselves, to swell the crowd, and a two-bit general, Fazlollah Zahedi, became the new prime minister. At least two major ayatollahs, Kashani and Behbehani, were prevailed upon to give their blessings.

The stage was now set for returning Iran to safe hands with the United States firmly in control. Having disrupted the organic flow of Iranian democracy, the Americans backed the Shah to the hilt, defended his regime (including the secret police SAVAK, whose contribution to the torture industry was a grill on which political prisoners could be slowly roasted), armed him to the teeth, indulged all his foolish fantasies and then acted surprised when he was overthrown by a popular revolution in 1979. Having helped destroy the nationalists and the left, they were even more surprised that the clerics had taken over.

Regime change in Iran was to be Churchill's last contribution to the cause of 'freedom and 'democracy' before resigning in 1955 as prime minister. His own party emitted a loud sigh of relief. It was slightly premature. Churchill's successor Anthony Eden failed to learn the key lesson of the coup in Iran, namely that such operations could only be successful with US support. He immediately began plotting with France and Israel to effect a regime change in Egypt. The Suez war of 1956 was not greenlighted by the United States. Washington was livid and ordered an immediate withdrawal. Gamal Abdel Nasser had already electrified the Arab world when he nationalised the Suez Canal. His standing in the

Arab world skyrocketed after the Zionist entity and its imperialist allies were sent packing by Washington.

Eden too did not last long. What of the ghost in the attic? Churchill did not say much but wrote to President Eisenhower expressing great regret that relations between the two countries had reached such a low and the hope they would be repaired soon. But the Suez disaster had only made public what most Anglo-American diplomats and politicians already knew. Churchill's empire was finished. The funeral rites would have to wait for another decade, but the game was up.

15

War Crimes in Kenya

> *A wind is ruffling the tawny pelt*
> *Of Africa. Kikuyu, quick as flies*
> *Batten upon the bloodstreams of the veldt,*
> *Corpses are littered through a paradise.*

Derek Walcott, 'A Far Cry from Africa' (1956)

The death spasms of the British Empire parallel Churchill's final decade, playing out across the global south. Kenya was a case in point. Conquered by the British in 1895, its land was handed over to European settlers. The most fertile soil was in the highlands, which is where the whites were settled in 1905. Protesting Africans had their cattle seized and sold. By 1910, 600 acres a year were being handed over to Europeans. They rented the farms and land on 999-year leases, paying just £10 a year for a 5,000-acre holding. By 1930, just over 2,000 settlers owned over 5 million acres of Kenya. The British government decided on the crops to be grown to reduce the import bill in London: maize, sisal, coffee. Africans were bludgeoned into forced labour for sixty days a year. They were moved from ancestral lands and put into huts on reservations attached to the farms. It was a form of paid slavery, the most extreme form of exploitation of blacks by whites.

At the end of the Second World War the European colonial powers were confronted with a severe crisis. The global conflict had exposed their shortcomings and they knew that nothing much could be done without US military and political support. Churchill was only too aware that the British Empire had run out of cash and was living off US largesse.

After they won the election in 1945 even the most diehard Labour imperialists knew that it was impossible to keep India any longer. Most Conservatives, barring Churchill, were of a similar opinion. In India itself, the end of the war had resulted in a new mood. Naval ratings in Mumbai had mutinied in February 1946, taking charge of battleships. Hindu and Muslim sailors, acting in unison, refused to negotiate with the British. Karachi followed suit. Admiral Godfrey, in full Churchillian mode, fumed and threatened retribution.

Gandhi was equally perturbed. On 7 April, after Hindu and Muslim workers engaged in strikes, he wrote in his paper *Harijan* that to accept this 'unholy combination' would mean 'delivering India over to the rabble. I would not wish to live up to 125 to witness that consummation. I would rather perish in flames.' His leading lieutenant and Congress Party colleague, Jawaharlal Nehru, indulged in his characteristic hand-wringing and came down on Gandhi's side, explaining in a letter to another Congress colleague that 'the situation is volcanic and definite choices have to be made ... the choice is often a very difficult one'.

Mohammed Ali Jinnah, the leader of the Muslim League, joined the bandwagon, but restricted his appeal to the Muslims involved in the strike: 'I call upon all the Muslims to stop and create no further trouble until we are in a position to handle this very serious situation.' Abandoned by the national-communalist parties, the strike committee gave up, but insisted they were surrendering to the Indian parties and not the British.

There was nothing else for it but to divide and quit, the hallmark of British rule in most of its colonies. These were the instructions given by Attlee to Lord Mountbatten, who did as he was told. A couple of lines were drawn and one became two. Almost 2 million people would die as a result of the Partition. Ironically, the only people who could walk the streets safely were the departing whiteskins.

The deed done, the British moved on to fight in Malaysia. Labour MPs who went to visit, including John Strachey, were photographed posing for the cameras with the decapitated heads of the predominantly Chinese Malaysian freedom-fighters laid out neatly on the ground in front of them. Labour's colonial record was appalling – an early proof that they were a responsible party. Reforms at home were not extended to the colonies. African countries remained under the iron heel.

The Conservatives won the 1951 general election even though Labour had a numerical majority of the votes cast. Like Donald Trump sixty-five years later, Churchill could not win a majority of the electorate. He looked frail as he re-entered Downing Street, a replica of the Empire he did not want to lose. Britain was broke and rearmament was not possible. Truman's successor, General Eisenhower, knew Churchill well and made no secret of his opinion that a younger man should have been put in charge. Many Tory MPs agreed, but Eden was too weak to wield the knife and the palace was extremely reluctant to endorse an in-house coup. Churchill was left to his own devices, including a whinge or two in the House of Commons:

> Tragic indeed is the spectacle of the might, majesty, dominion and power of the once magnificent and still considerable British Empire having to worry and wonder how we can pay our monthly bills. I fully admit I am tortured by this thought and by the processes which I see around me, and I shall do everything in my power (shouts of 'Resign, resign') to bring home to the mass of our race and nation the sense of peril and the need for grave and far-reaching exertions.[1]

It was empty rhetoric. Nationalism was on the rise. The corrupt and useless monarchs preferred by Churchill were under serious threat in Egypt, Iraq and Iran. British colonies in Africa were bubbling beneath the surface, and names like Kenyatta, Nkrumah, Mboya, Mandela, Nyerere, Nasser and Ben Bella were beginning to appear in the Anglo-American press. The revolutionary victory in China (1949), the French defeat at Dien Bien Phu (1954), the

---

1 Quoted in Richard Toye, *Churchill's Empire*, London, 2010, p. 284.

independence of India (1947), all this had a huge impact on the liberation movements developing throughout Africa.

The continent had long been treated by white settlers as their domain. Racism grew as a conscious and well-oiled weapon of domination and exploitation. It was never a mistake, a terrible misunderstanding, or a regrettable reversion to barbarism, as many well-meaning white people thought at the time. It was designed as a moral justification for the state and its church to treat black people with methods that could no longer be used against white people. It justified slavery and its successor, imperialist colonialism. Throughout Africa, the same arguments were used to justify white settlements. South Africa became the template for the rest of the continent. Europeans were taught that before the white settlers arrived Africa was a sea of nothingness. A swamp of ignorance and barbarism.

In 1922 Colonel Richard Meinertzhagen, a nephew of the Fabian intellectual Beatrice Webb, visited Nairobi. Utilising his aunt's name and connections to meet people, he was invited to dinner by the high commissioner in Kenya, Charles Eliot. In his diary, Meinertzhagen describes Eliot as a philosopher, a don, a man of vision, but:

> He amazed me with his views on the future of East Africa. He envisaged a thriving colony of thousands of Europeans with their families, the whole of the country from the Aberdares and Mount Kenya to the German border [Tanganyika, now Tanzania] divided up into farms; the whole of the Rift Valley cultivated or grazed and the whole country of Lumbwa, Nandi to Elgon and almost to Baringo under white settlement. He intends to confine the natives to reserves and use them as cheap labour on farms. I suggested that the country belonged to Africans and their interests must prevail over the interests of strangers. He would not have it; he kept on using the word 'paramount' with reference to the claims of Europeans. I said that some day the African would be educated and armed; that would lead to a clash. Eliot thought that that day was so distant as not to matter and that by the time the European element would be strong enough to look after themselves.

This was the colonial mind at work. Churchill would have endorsed every single sentiment expressed by Eliot. Both men believed in what they referred to as a 'protective civilisation'. In 1921 Churchill embroiled himself, as was his wont, in the clashes between white settlers in Kenya and the more recent Indian settlers who were demanding an end to racial segregation. He put on a show of moderation by explaining to a fellow member of the Cabinet, Edwin Montagu, whose job it was to arbitrate the dispute, that he was not on principle against desegregation, but that the sanitary regulations must be so stringent that few Indians would be able to meet European standards. (I'll resist a digression on sanitary conditions in Britain during the first decades of the twentieth century.)

The following conversation between Churchill and S. S. Varma, one of the Indian Kenyan delegates – a pathetic figure as his words testify – is revealing:

CHURCHILL: Broadly speaking, would you subscribe to Mr Rhodes' formula – Equal Rights for Civilised Men?
VARMA: I say exactly in those words, for civilised men, even including Indians.
CHURCHILL: Certainly, if the individual becomes civilised and lives in a civilised way, in a civilised house, and observes civilised behaviour in his goings on, and in his family life, and he is also educated sufficiently – that principle seems to be a very valuable principle, and it is very practical. It is absurd to go and give the naked savages of the Kikuyu and the Kavirondo equal electoral rights, although they are human beings – you cannot do that.
VARMA: No.

What makes this ironical is that white 'civilisation' in Kenya was particularly notorious for its criminality both within and outside the white bubble. Rape, murders, alcoholism, theft and corruption were not as uncommon as some liked to believe. Rotten apples were a staple product on the white-owned highland plantations. Had Varma not been so spineless and sycophantic he might have asked Churchill which of these traits he would like Indians or Africans to mimic. In South Africa, Gandhi's first campaign was to demand separate lavatories for Indians. Sharing them with Africans was unacceptable. The caste mentality ever present.

Here and on numerous other occasions, Churchill debases the colonised to exalt the coloniser. Its not enough to steal their lands. Their very humanity must be questioned, so that some of them come to believe in their own inferiority. They must be oppressed to such an extent that the force used, the terror employed, the exploitation permanently embedded in the colonial situation, comes to appear normal to them. That is what colonisers always wish to achieve: a calm acceptance of colonial destructiveness. But they always fail.

Africans were regarded as talking beasts who could not think like Europeans. The fear of the native that white society inculcated in its everyday life was born out of the situation *it* had imposed on black Africans. The emancipation of the slaves in the United States created a tiny window that permitted some degree of equality – the period known as the Reconstruction – but the iron shutters were rapidly brought down. White supremacy flourished, the Ku Klux Klan became the largest political organisation in US history, and the police force and the judiciary implemented the supremacy that led to the incarceration levels for black people today.

Many of the post-colonial African states produced black elites who enforced laws that were variants of what existed in the United States and South Africa. They were not racial, but in essence they were not too dissimilar. When some Western politicians attempt to justify colonialism by pointing to the excesses of a Mobutu or a Bokassa or an Arap Moi, there is only one possible reply: *De te fabula narratur!* This story is about you.

It needs to be stressed in relation to Britain's African colonies. The Labour government of 1945–51 should have started the decolonisation process, but ideologically (one has only to read the pronouncements of the Fabians), and above all in the bloated personage of the foreign secretary Ernest Bevin, a majority of Labour parliamentarians were staunch empire loyalists, as they are US/NATO loyalists today. They had been driven out of India, but they refused to learn the lessons. The diarist Chips Channon observed from the opposition benches how pleasing it was listening to Bevin, who sounded just like a Tory, so much so that the cringing Anthony Eden, his opposite number, found it difficult to reply. The continuities in foreign policy between Labour and the Conservatives were such that, on his return to Downing Street in 1951, Churchill simply carried on as before. No changes were needed.

The Kenyan people could not afford to carry on in the same old way. They knew what was really going on behind the facade of 'normality' and launched a rebellion against British rule in 1950. The Mau Mau mobilisations were a direct response to the shameless expropriation of African lands, repeating what had already happened in white-settler-controlled Rhodesia (Zimbabwe). The number of white settlers in Kenya had shot up from 21,000 in 1938 to 40,000 by 1953.

Churchill and his successive appointees in the Colonial Office – Oliver Lyttleton, Alan Lennox-Boyd and the much-loathed proconsul Evelyn ('Over-')Baring – were all agreed that the core of imperial policy in Kenya was the creation of another white settler state. The Rhodesian model had been a huge success and could easily be repeated. They reckoned without the growing anger of the group most affected, the Kikuyu, who numbered 1.5 million by the mid-1950s.

Despite the concerted efforts made by officialdom and conservative historians to cover up British atrocities in Kenya, they have failed. A persistent, determined and gifted American scholar at Harvard, Caroline Elkins, managed to uncover most of the truth. Her book *Britain's Gulag: The Brutal End of Empire in Kenya* charts the course of the vicious repression inflicted on the Kikuyu, and of the camps in which tens of thousands were detained between 1952 and 1960.

The Agathi camp gate slogan was: 'He Who Helps Himself Will Also Be Helped'. What this really meant was that he who helped the British would be treated better than the hardcore rebels. Churchill was fully aware of and supported the crimes being committed. He was, after all, prime minister at the time, and his involvement with and support for the white settlers is hardly a secret. What neither Churchill nor the settlers could have foreseen was that one of the 150,000 Mau Mau rebels they arrested, Hussein Onyango Obama, begat a son, who begat a son, who became president of the United States, creating academic interest in the country.

As John Newsinger explained in reviewing Elkin's book, the Kikuyu had

> increasingly been subjected to land hunger and wage squeezes as white settlement displaced them from their fertile highlands. Prevented from owning land outside the Native Reserves, as of the early 1930s most Kikuyu faced a choice of three forms of destitution: to return to the depleted soils and land shortages of the Reserves; work Europeans' land outside the Reserves as insecure tenants; or join those flooding into Nairobi's Eastland slums in search of employment.[2]

Meanwhile, the settlers grew fat on the wartime boom in commodities and refused any suggestion of a deal with 'moderate African nationalists' (such as Jomo Kenyatta), people they openly referred to as 'monkeys'. Under Churchill, Kenya was a white-settler dictatorship backed by British arms. The Kikuyu-led movement – Mau Mau was the appellation given them by the oppressors – decided on an armed revolution to drive the British and their progeny out of the country, and swore oaths to that effect. Settlers were attacked, their cattle stolen or destroyed, and African collaborators were dealt with severely.

Outside the Churchill government, the Labour front bench continued their support, but left-wing Labour figures such as Barbara Castle, Fenner Brockway and others in the Movement for Colonial Freedom began to protest in strong terms. At an official pre-coronation reception in 1953, Lady Edwina Mountbatten taunted and verbally abused the racist colonial secretary Oliver Lyttleton on the atrocities in Kenya. Her lover, the Indian prime minister Jawaharlal Nehru, also present, turned his back on

---

2   John Newsinger, 'English Atrocities', *New Left Review* 32, March–April 2005.

Lyttleton and left the room. When Lyttleton complained to Churchill, he instructed the Foreign Office to ban Edwina Mountbatten from accompanying her husband on an official visit to Turkey. Mountbatten ignored the request.

As the atrocities grew so did the resistance, until a decisive point was reached: the movement had lost its fear of death. Mau Mau guerrillas were led by men with a political culture. One of them, Waruhiu Itote, better known by his *nom de guerre* 'General China', recalled in his memoirs that he had also been influenced by the Haitian Revolution, recounted to him by an African-American soldier. History travels, and relevant history does so at a brisk pace.

In contrast, the British propaganda campaign portrayed the Mau Mau as brutal and uncaring savages, a view taken up and promoted uncritically by many US magazines and papers, with *Life* publishing gory photographs of 'Mau Mau atrocities' and ignoring the causes of the rebellion. The picture painted by David Anderson, in his *Histories of the Hanged: Britain's Dirty War in Kenya and the End of Empire*, provides the most detailed account of the rebellion, the composition of the movement's armed fighters, and the strategy and tactics deployed by their British enemies. More importantly, he details how, after the defeat of the Mau Mau (11,000 were killed to prolong British rule for a few more years), Britain set about putting in place the African loyalists who had supported them. Many of them were encouraged to buy the white-settler lands that were being sold. This was a loyalty reward, designed to ensure continued collaboration after formal independence. It worked.

Economically and politically, the limits of independence were being delineated. Decolonisation in Kenya and other colonies meant a neo-colonisation. Where African leaders refused to comply, the former colonial powers either killed them (Patrice Lumumba in the Congo) or removed them from office (Nkrumah in Ghana, Obote in Uganda). Jomo Kenyatta, one of the Mau Mau leaders, alas agreed to play the game and was lionised by the British establishment soon afterwards when he visited Britain. The 'terrorist' was invited to dinner at the palace, and offered numerous teas and cucumber sandwiches in the gardens of returning settler families, now safely ensconced in their native habitat.

Even when in prison, Kenyatta had fallen out with a majority of the Mau Mau leadership. The British had provided him with separate accommodation because the political differences were so acute that they feared violence. More likely he had been identified as a potential recruit to the loyalist faction of elite Kenyans. One of the other Mau Mau prisoners explained that Kenyatta had never been in total sympathy with the movement's programme in the first place. He had refused to join the political party created by activists at the Lokitaung prison camp, a party whose programme was based on the motto 'Liberty, Equality and Justice'. This was too extreme for Kenyatta. One of the founders, Kaggia, explained: 'Kenyatta was not one of us in prison. He had married a woman whose father was a chief, and because of that when we went to prison, he was often on the side of the conservatives and the government. I became the leader of the group in his place, though we were all disappointed.'[3]

Churchill, Alan Lennox-Boyd (a personal favourite, hand-picked for the Colonial Office after he had also opposed Indian independence) and the governor of Kenya, Evelyn Baring, were core racists. Baring would have easily slotted in as a Third Reich bureaucrat. He was a vicious brute as far as Kenyan Africans were concerned, not simply obeying orders from London, but pre-empting them. Political resistance to the British had grown in the 1950s and the people who created the Mau Mau were no longer prepared to tolerate the degree of violence inflicted on their people. In response Baring, with Churchill's backing, created a network of prison camps much, much worse than anything Churchill had himself witnessed during the Boer War in South Africa. Prisoners' descriptions of how they were treated read like slave diaries. 'It was like Hell on Earth' said one survivor. Elkins summarises what occurred both inside and outside the camps: 'Violence and torture had for years dominated life in Kenya's camps. A pornography of terror, including public brutality, rape,

---

3 Quoted in Caroline Elkins, *Britain's Gulag: The Brutal End of Empire in Kenya*, London, 2005, p. 197.

and starvation, swept through the villages as well, and thousands died there.'[4]

The massacre at Hola camp in which eleven prisoners were beaten to death – Parliament was told they died from drinking contaminated water – finally did for the British. It was no worse than other atrocities, but turned out to be the last straw. The cover-up failed because a left-wing, anti-colonial QC, D. N. Pritt, was in Kenya at the time and used his connections to uncover the truth. Anglican churches stirred into action, together with many Labour MPs. Conservative MPs, too, were becoming uneasy. One of them, Enoch Powell, found the events at Hola deplorable. Finally, the excruciating prolongation of colonial rule in Kenya came to an end. Kenyatta became the official leader, had lots of children (like Boris Johnson), and was feted by the Queen.

One of the strongest myths about the British Empire concerns its demise: 'How good we were about it', apologists still say to each other and to us. 'We beat such a dignified retreat unlike the awful French in Vietnam and Algeria.' Hidden from the public gaze are the catastrophe of Partition in India, portrayed as unpleasant religions fighting each other; the brutal repression of the Malayan insurgency; and the vicious campaign against the liberation movement in Kenya. All this is under challenge as African and Asian historians, together with some of their US and British counterparts, demystify the mythologies peddled by neo-imperial historians by exposing the price in human lives that was paid to accelerate decolonisation.

What happened in Kenya was a set of systematic crimes. Churchill, Lennox-Boyd and Baring went unpunished.

---

4   Ibid., p. 313.

Derek Walcott, 'A Far Cry from Africa' (1956)

A wind is ruffling the tawny pelt
Of Africa. Kikuyu, quick as flies,
Batten upon the bloodstreams of the veldt,
Corpses are scattered through a paradise.
Only the worm, colonel of carrion, cries:
'Waste no compassion on these separate dead!'
Statistics justify and scholars seize
The salients of colonial policy.
What is that to the white child hacked in bed?
To savages, expendable as Jews?

Threshed out by beaters, the long rushes break
In a white dust of ibises whose cries
Have wheeled since civilization's dawn
From the parched river or beast-teeming plain.
The violence of beast on beast is read
As natural law, but upright man
Seeks his divinity by inflicting pain.
Delirious as these worried beasts, his wars
Dance to the tightened carcass of a drum,
While he calls courage still that native dread
Of the white peace contracted by the dead.

Again brutish necessity wipes its hands
Upon the napkin of a dirty cause, again
A waste of our compassion, as with Spain,
The gorilla wrestles with the superman.
I who am poisoned with the blood of both,
Where shall I turn, divided to the vein?
I who have cursed
The drunken officer of British rule, how choose
Between this Africa and the English tongue I love?
Betray them both, or give back what they give?
How can I face such slaughter and be cool?
How can I turn from Africa and live?

16

What's Past Is Prologue:
Churchill's Legacies

It was here that the Sioux had a camp on the long trail
Cutting the loops of the rivers from beyond the Missouri and
　　Mandan
East: towards Big Stone Lake and beyond to the Pipestone Quarry,
The place of peace . . .

A confusion of waters, surely, and pollution at the head of the river!
Our history begins with the first wound: with Indian blood
Coloring the water of the original springs – earlier even:
Europe: the indentured . . .

Thomas McGrath, extract from
Letter to an Imaginary Friend (1997)

The causes of events in which we remain entangled can only be interpreted by our own lights. And these come in different colours. The American poet Thomas McGrath's epic poem is his take on the empires of recent centuries. Most pro-Churchill historians and politicians, on the other hand, admire the British Empire and the even larger one that took its place, and those of other European colonisers. Some even suggested after 9/11 – twenty years ago, as the US launched its wars for global hegemony (backed initially by Russia and China) – that the British Empire model remained the best on offer. Ivy League campuses hired pro-imperialist British historians to drive the lesson home. In their instrumentalist books, they argued for a more solid British-style frame than the more indirect US version. All supported the war in Afghanistan, even though Britain's own past in that region had been an unmitigated disaster.

Most defended the 2003 war in Iraq, and the UK prime minister Tony Blair presented his leader in the White House with a bust of Churchill. The US defense secretary and recently deceased war criminal Donald Rumsfeld, in preparing to launch the war, compared George W. Bush to Churchill in 1939. Both were isolated – hardly the case as far as Bush was concerned – on the eve of taking on evil dictators. Both were determined to push ahead. Rumsfeld was off-mark as usual; some adviser should have informed him that while Bush was certainly following in Churchill's footsteps, the correct analogy was not Europe, but post–First World War Iraq.

A nimble-minded adviser might even have done a tiny bit of research and pointed out that, as secretary of state for war in 1920, Churchill had enthusiastically supported the terror bombing of civilians: Kurds and Arabs were pelted with bombs and chemical weapons when they resisted the British plans for their country. Kurdish tribal chiefs were bought and the size of pliant tribes increased by labelling individuals as 'tribesmen' and placing them under a 'tribal leader'. The process was known as 're-tribalising'. A senior British civil servant in the field explained: 'Every man who could be labelled a tribesman was placed under a tribal leader. The idea was to divide South Kurdistan [Iraqi Kurdistan] into tribal areas under a tribal leader. Petty village headmen were unearthed and discovered as leaders of long dead tribes.'[1]

Two RAF officers were not shy in explaining how British rule in Iraq would be accomplished. Wing Commander Gale of 30 Squadron pointed out: 'If the Kurds hadn't learned by our example to behave themselves in a civilised way then we had to spank their bottoms. This was done by bombs and guns.' His colleague, Arthur Harris – who, twenty-two years later, would mastermind the destruction of Dresden and the bombing of civilians in other

---

1   Major E. B. Soane, British Political Officer, 1919, quoted in David McDowall, *A Modern History of the Kurds*, London, 1997, pp. 120–1.

German cities, proudly accepting the sobriquet attached to his name ('Bomber' Harris) – was far more explicit, as was his wont: 'The Arab and Kurd now know what real bombing means in casualties and damage. Within forty-five minutes a full-size village can be practically wiped out and a third of its inhabitants killed or injured.'

A year later, a third Wing Commander, J. A. Chamier, explained that the best way to demoralise the Arabs was to pulverise them by concentrating on the 'most inaccessible village of the most prominent tribe which it is desired to punish. All available aircraft must be collected, the attack with bombs and machine guns must be relentless and unremitting and carried on continuously by day and night, on houses, inhabitants, crops and cattle.'[2]

Even this was not enough for some. The narcissist and vainglorious idol of the British Empire, T. E. Lawrence, wrote to the *Observer* and complained: 'It is odd that we do not use poison gas on these occasions.' Any bombing was justified if it saved the lives of British and colonial soldiers who shouldn't have been there in the first place. On this level the terror bombing was a success:

> Winston Churchill, secretary of state for war and air, estimated that without the RAF, somewhere between 25,000 British and 80,000 Indian troops would be needed to control Iraq. Reliance on the airforce promised to cut these numbers to just 4,000 and 10,000. Churchill's confidence was soon repaid ... the RAF flew missions totalling 4,008 hours, dropped 97 tons of bombs and fired 183,861 rounds for the loss of nine men killed, seven wounded and 11 aircraft destroyed behind rebel lines.[3]

This was the legacy that Bush accepted in relation to Iraq and Afghanistan, and Obama when it came to Libya and Syria. As the Second World War ended, Churchill was only too aware of British decline. He wanted an umbilical cord made of piano

---

2 Quoted in Jonathan Glancey, 'Our Last Occupation', *Guardian*, 19 April 2003.
3 Ibid.

wire that would tie Britain to the United States in perpetuity. The master-races had to remain united. The architecture of white supremacy must be preserved. Trump was not so different from Churchill in this regard. During the Second World War, however, some Democrat politicians found the blatant racism a bit difficult to swallow. The US vice-president, Henry Wallace, a progressive Democrat, was taken aback by Churchill's views, writing in his May 1943 diary:

> I said bluntly that I thought the notion of Anglo-Saxon superiority, inherent in Churchill's approach, would be offensive to many of the nations of the world as well as to a number of people in the United States. Churchill had had quite a bit of whisky, which, however, did not affect the clarity of his thinking process, but did perhaps increase his frankness. He said why be apologetic about Anglo-Saxon superiority, that we were superior, that we had the common heritage which had been worked out over the centuries in England and had been perfected by our constitution. He himself was half American, he felt that he was called on as a result to serve the function of uniting the two great Anglo-Saxon civilizations in order to confer the benefit of freedom on the rest of the world.

British denialism since the war, refusing to fully accept the fact that the UK is little more than a US satrapy, continues half-heartedly to this day. Officialdom boasts that there are British troops in forty-six countries, but underplays their total logistical dependence on the United States. British politicians who refuse to declare that, as prime minister, they would use nuclear weapons, are pilloried in the media and by their own loyalist colleagues. Few ever ask whether it is possible for any British prime minister to use nuclear missiles stationed in Scotland without the permission of the Pentagon. Every politician, military officer and intelligence operative, not to mention the British royal family, is aware of this fact. But they prefer to mask the truth.

A veil has usually been cast over the more unsavoury aspects of British imperialism. Greece and Kenya are two examples of evasions, cover-ups and downright falsehoods. It took a couple of

US historians, cited earlier in this book, to expose British colonial atrocities in Kenya. Their shamefaced British colleagues at Harvard and elsewhere had either denied the scale of these or ignored them altogether. They now appear to have fallen into line. But secrecy, hiding facts from the electorate, remains firmly in place. A recent book, mildly critical of the British Army's role in the wars 'east of Suez' over the last two decades, was pulped by Penguin Random House on the no doubt ultra-friendly 'advice' of the Ministry of Defence.[4]

Britain and its European counterparts accumulated a great deal of ideological garbage over two centuries. The subjugated populations of empire (the Irish a stand-alone exception) were all people of colour. Their destinies were dictated by the stirring of a white imperialist finger. Notions of racial superiority were so deeply embedded that racism was the common sense of the imperial age. Colonialism, the slave trade and the extermination of indigenous populations were first cousins.

That Churchill was a racist is indisputable. Imperialist historians invariably coated events in black and white. Chisellers of stone carved statues to celebrate the military and political leaders of imperial triumphs at home and abroad. Colonised peoples were exhorted to admire these statues, symbols of incontestable power, effigies that had suppressed other histories. Perpetual endurance and perpetual resistance (political and armed) have remained close to each other, historically. Deployed to maintain imperial hegemony on political, cultural and military levels, notions of racial superiority and white supremacy are more recent, linked to Puritanism and its offshoots as well as the Catholic Church, but generalised in the eighteenth and nineteenth centuries.

All the European powers used colonial soldiers to fight in their wars. Indians and Africans were cannon-fodder but were permitted to use the latest weapons. Black South Africans were recruited

---

4 For a judicious review of the book – Simon Akam's *The Changing of the Guard: The British Army since 9/11*, published by Scribe in 2021 – see Tom Stevenson, 'The Most Corrupt Idea of Modern Times', *London Review of Books*, 1 July 2021.

but not given military training or allowed to bear arms. The US Army was segregated in both world wars.

The British imperial legacy was handed to the United States during and after the Second World War. Churchill knew there was no other option. By the early 1960s, the United States had become a key player in large parts of Africa, Asia and the Greater Middle East. It operated in a different style but destroyed countries with ease, and was not at all squeamish about toppling regimes that refused to kow-tow, using nuclear weapons, chemical warfare and B-52 bombers.

The British imperial past refused to die. Churchill and Attlee had not foreseen that Lazarus would emerge in the shape of thousands of migrants from the old colonies: South Asians and West Indians led the field. A wrecked British economy was short of labour. Enoch Powell, a Conservative politician in Churchill's post-war cabinet, realised that the cheapest source of labour was the colonial and post-colonial world. As Secretary of State for Health, he authorised NHS posters advertising jobs to be distributed widely in Jamaica, Trinidad, Barbados and the smaller islands.[5] The descendants of African slaves were being encouraged to shift voluntarily to get jobs in Blighty. They did so. Visas were not needed. Commonwealth and colonial citizens entered and departed freely. The *Empire Windrush* passengers of 1948 were legally UK citizens with all their rights intact.[6] News of

---

5 See Paul Foot, *Immigration and Race in British Politics*, London, 1965.

6 The Caribbean novelist Mike Phillips explained the situation thus: 'When the Windrush stopped in Jamaica to pick up servicemen who were on leave from their units, many of their former comrades decided to make the trip in order to rejoin the RAF. More adventurous spirits, mostly young men, who had heard about the voyage and simply fancied coming to see England, "the mother country", doubled their numbers' ('Windrush – the Passengers', at bbc.co.uk/history). Two female Conservative home secretaries, Theresa May and Priti Patel, unleashed and defended the blatantly racist campaign to deport 'illegal' immigrants, resulting in the 2018 political storm. The Windrush scandal was a racist own goal.

several hundred Jamaicans on their way to Tilbury created panic. The Labour prime minister, Attlee, inquired politely whether the ship might not be diverted to East Africa. Churchill thoughtfully suggested that the Tory election slogan for the 1955 general elections could be 'Keep England White'.

Churchill had few problems with Labour's foreign policy. Even his irrationality regarding India's independence was soon tempered by historical realities. Labour maintained the decaying Empire in Africa and the Middle East as long as possible. African independence was ultimately granted by a Conservative government. Churchill's main concern was to make sure the United States was given all possible help by the dying, but experienced, British Empire. Usually this consisted of little more than advice. The 'special relationship' that Churchill had set in place did not amount to very much. Roosevelt and his inner circle did not treat it too seriously, even during the war. The United States would have done a deal with Hitler had Britain fallen. It maintained diplomatic relations with the Vichy government till 1944.

Like the 'Dunkirk spirit', the 'special relationship' was essentially a propaganda device, designed for the population at home to justify satrapy status after the war. This became much easier after the communist cells in British intelligence were exposed and the key leaders (Philby, Burgess and MacLean) sought refuge in Moscow. Trust between the US and British security services – stern monitors of the 'special relationship' – was restored. Philby was honoured by the Soviets with a medal and a stamp to celebrate his achievements.

Churchill had always believed that the only way to defeat the 1917 Russian Revolution and its variegated offspring was by deploying brute force, a view shared at State, Defense and the White House during the last century. He never abandoned this position even during the Second World War, when the Red Army was engaged in ferocious battles to defend not only the Soviet Union but also European bourgeois democracy. Churchill and, more importantly, the United States, got it wrong. Churchill had hoped for better things from European fascism. He had befriended Mussolini and Franco and was prepared to take the same approach with Hitler. It was the German who refused to play. He had his own plans.

A few millions died during the 'Cold' War, 2 million in Vietnam alone. The Cold War came to an end not with a bang but with a quiet implosion: the Soviet bureaucracy ran out of intellectual fuel. Henry Kissinger had been waiting for a long time. He had thought that a Russian Pinochet might be the result of a Soviet collapse, but that this would be preferable to any continuation of the old Bolshevik state. Kissinger could not forget his fellow-murderer General Pinochet and the politicide they had carried out in Chile in September 1973.

This prediction too was proved wrong. In both the Soviet Union and China, reform currents emerged from within the communist parties, leading to very different outcomes in each regime. The last two leaders of the Soviet Union, Gorbachev and Yeltsin, put their entire trust in Washington. The rise of the oligarchs and the breakup of the Soviet Union was the immediate result. The first Gulf War and the destruction of Yugoslavia followed soon afterwards.

The leadership of the Chinese Communist Party (marking its centenary as I write) followed a different course. They allowed themselves to be used by the United States to cripple the Soviet Union. The most disgraceful action that followed was Deng Xiaoping's attempt to curry even more favour with Washington by unleashing a war against Vietnam in 1979. He wanted to 'pierce the myth of Vietnamese invincibility' and punish the Vietnamese for removing Pol Pot (supported by China as well as the West) and the Khmer Rouge from power in Cambodia, but his troops came back bleeding. One can only hope that one day a courageous Chinese historian will reveal the whole truth regarding this ugly adventure. US motives in giving China an almost free pass to capitalism were premised on weakening their old Soviet rival and gaining entry to a hitherto closed market. Three decades ago, the collapse of the Soviet Union was more than they had hoped for, and the market opening in China, too, appeared pregnant with promise.

With the end of the Cold War and the dismantling of the South American dictatorships, many hoped that the much talked about 'peace dividend' promised by Bush senior and Thatcher would actually materialise. No such luck. Instead, we have experienced continuous wars, upheavals, intolerance and fundamentalisms of every sort – religious, ethnic and imperial. The exposure of the Western world's surveillance networks has heightened the feeling that democratic institutions aren't functioning as they should; that, like it or not, we are living in the twilight period of democracy itself. Churchill was always opposed to any press criticism during critical periods in Britain. The media conformity today would have pleased him enormously. It is beyond his wildest dreams.

Over recent decades there has been an ongoing debate around the world on the question of whether the American Empire is on the way out, like Britain's was after the last world war. There is a vast literature on the subject, with many historians and others insisting that the decline has begun and is irreversible. I doubt whether Churchill would have agreed with this assessment. The American Empire has suffered serious setbacks – but which past empire didn't?

In the 1970s and '80s, many thought that the defeat US imperialism suffered in Vietnam in 1975 was definitive. It wasn't, and the United States has not suffered another setback on that scale since. The debacle in Afghanistan in August 2021 was – leaving aside the images of helicopters packed with US retainers fleeing from embassy to airport – different in character. It was a political-ideological defeat but not a military disaster. A short time after the defeat in Vietnam, the US was back in action against the Sandinistas in Nicaragua and supporting the South Africans in Angola. This time they're simply moving on with a new offensive against China, with two testicle-states in tow: Australia and Britain. But unless we know and understand how this empire functions globally, it is very difficult to propose any set of strategies to combat or contain it. Realist theorists such as Chalmers Johnson, John Mearsheimer and Andrew Bacevich have argued that to humanise their country it is essential to demand that the United States dismantle its bases throughout the world and operate at a global level only if it is actually threatened as a country.

Many realists in the United States argue that such a withdrawal is necessary, but they are arguing from a position of weakness in the sense that the setbacks which they regard as irreversible, aren't. There are very few reversals from which imperial states can't recover, unless there is a stronger rival waiting in the wings. Some of the declinist arguments are simplistic – that, for example, all empires have eventually collapsed. This is of course true, but there were contingent reasons for those collapses, and at the present time the United States remains unassailable: it exerts its soft power globally, including in the heartlands of its economic rivals; its hard power is still dominant, enabling it to occupy countries it sees as its enemies; and its ideological power is still overwhelming in Europe and beyond. Its punitive capacities are not simply military, but economic. It imposes sanctions (usually backed by its NATO allies) against countries that refuse to tow the line: Venezuela, Russia, Iran and now China, whose astonishing economic advances have shaken its rivals in the West.

The United States continues to suffer at least temporary blows on a semi-continental scale in South America. The 2021 referendum in Chile for a new constitution, and the victory of a left-wing socialist teacher in the Peruvian presidential elections the same year, are an indication that the pink tide is resisting the imperial order. These political setbacks have been ideological rather than economic. They can't be too controversial now, given that the global nature of the Covid-19 pandemic has delivered such a hit to neoliberal capitalism. A diluted Keynesianism is back in the market, but to be effective it will need to amount to more than the single-jab vaccine proposed by Biden's recovery plans. On 23 March 2020, for the first time since the 1930s, the Federal Reserve prefigured Biden by announcing that in response to the global virus it would provide loans to non-financial institutions and services. The pandemic demonstrated that the market was incapable of helping the majority of those afflicted. It forced the US and the EU into recovery programmes on a large scale. In February 2021, the Next Generation EU Programme offered a modest 750 billion-euro deal to help its members restructure: digitalisation plus a bit of greening. The precedent, however, is much more important than the cash offered. The United States followed suit on a grander scale, hailed in the mainstream media as a historic shift, as tartly noted by *New Left Review*:

A month later, on 11 March, Biden signed the $1.9 trillion American Rescue Plan into law, giving $1,400 to all Americans earning under $75,000 a year, as well as a monthly child allowance, emergency health insurance and a weekly $300 unemployment benefit. An additional $750 billion went towards vaccinations and state/city support. In late March, Biden unveiled a $2 trillion American Jobs Plan, a 'paradigm shift' in infrastructural investment – transport, power grid, rural broadband, clean energy, electric vehicles, R&D, 'to win the competition with China' – and promised a Climate Plan and an American Families Plan to follow. Comparisons with FDR and Eisenhower proliferated. Biden's rescue programme was 'almost as historic as the pandemic it seeks to mitigate', according to the *Financial Times*. Not simply 'the biggest anti-poverty effort in a generation' (*New York Times*) and a 'seismic shift in US politics' (*Washington Post*), but the dawn of a new economic era – a structural break with the neoliberal consensus.[7]

State-sponsored economic stimuli, once considered intolerable within the neoliberal variant of the economic system imposed by global capital, are back in fashion. If one argues, as those in power do (if not explicitly then implicitly), that it is necessary to have a political structure in which no challenge to the system is permitted from below, then we are living in dangerous times. Elevating terrorism into a threat equivalent to the communist threat of old is bizarre. De-linking terrorist acts from Euro-America's wars in the world of Islam is shortsighted. The use of the very word 'terrorism', the bills pushed through Parliament and Congress to stop people speaking up, the vetting of people invited to give talks at universities, the idea that outside speakers have to be asked what they are going to say before they are allowed into the country: all these seem minor things, but they are emblematic of the age in which we live.

---

7 See Susan Watkins, 'Paradigm Shifts, *New Left Review*, 128, March–April 2021.

And the ease with which all this is accepted is frightening. If what we're being told is that change isn't possible, that the only conceivable system is the present one, then we're going to be in trouble. Ultimately, it won't be accepted. If you prevent people from speaking or thinking or developing political alternatives, it won't just be Marx's work that is relegated to the graveyard. Karl Polanyi, the most gifted of the social-democratic theorists, will suffer the same fate if he hasn't already.

We have seen the development of a form of government I call the extreme centre, which currently rules over large tracts of Europe and includes left, centre-left, centre-right and centre parties. A whole swathe of the electorate, young people in particular, feels that voting makes no difference at all, given the political parties we have. The extreme centre wages wars, either on its own account or on behalf of the United States; it backs austerity measures; it defends surveillance as absolutely necessary to defeat terrorism, but without ever asking why this terrorism is happening – to ask that question is almost to be a terrorist oneself.

Why do the terrorists do it? Are they unhinged? Is it something that emerges from deep inside their religion? These questions are counterproductive and useless. If you ask whether American imperial policy or British or French foreign policy is in any way responsible for the terrorism, you're attacked. But of course the intelligence agencies and security services know perfectly well that the reason for people going crazy – and it is a form of craziness – is that they are driven not by religion but by what they see.

Hussain Osman, one of the men who failed to bomb the London Underground on 21 July 2005, was arrested in Rome a week later. 'More than praying we discussed work, politics, the war in Iraq', he told the Italian interrogators. 'We always had new films of the war in Iraq . . . those in which you could see Iraqi women and children who had been killed by US and UK soldiers.' As Eliza Manningham-Buller, who resigned as head of MI5 in 2007, observed: 'Our involvement in Iraq has radicalised, for want of a better word, a whole generation of young people.'

Before the 2003 war, Iraq, under the authoritarian dictatorship of Saddam and his predecessor, had the highest level of education in the Middle East. When you point this out you're accused of being a Saddam apologist, but Baghdad University in the 1980s had more female professors than Princeton did in 2009. There were crèches to make it easier for women to teach at schools and universities. In Baghdad and Mosul there were libraries dating back centuries. The Mosul library was functioning in the eighth century, and had manuscripts from ancient Greece in its vaults. The Baghdad library, as we know, was looted after the US occupation, and under Islamic State thousands of books and manuscripts were destroyed in the libraries of Mosul. Civilisation? Barbarism?

Everything that happened in post-2003 Iraq (including the emergence of jihadi terrorism, first al-Qaeda and later ISIS) was a consequence of the disastrous imperialist war, which assumed genocidal proportions. The numbers who died are disputed, because the 'Coalition of the Willing' did not count the civilian casualties in the country it was occupying. Why should it bother? But others have estimated that up to half a million Iraqis were killed, mainly civilians. The puppet government installed by the occupation confirmed these figures obliquely in 2006, by officially admitting that there were 5 million orphans in Iraq.

The occupation of Iraq was one of the most destructive acts in modern history. Even though Hiroshima and Nagasaki were nuked, the social and political structure of the Japanese state was maintained; although the Germans and Italians were defeated in the Second World War, most of their military structures, intelligence structures, police structures and judicial structures were kept in place, because there was another enemy already in the offing – communism. But Iraq was treated as no other country has been treated before. The reason people don't quite see this is that once the occupation began most of the correspondents came back home. You can count the exceptions on the fingers of one hand: Patrick Cockburn, Robert Fisk, one or two others.

Iraq's social infrastructure still isn't working, years after the occupation ended; it's been wrecked. The country has been de-modernised. The West destroyed Iraq's education services and medical services, and handed over power to a group of clerical Shia parties which immediately embarked on bloodbaths of revenge. Several hundred university professors were killed. If this isn't disorder, what is? I have argued elsewhere that what we are witnessing is a form of re-colonisation. It's being carried out in different times and different circumstances, but its aim is no different from that of Churchill's Empire: the establishment and preservation of US global hegemony.

In the case of Afghanistan, most commentators acknowledge that the intervention there was not – as Cherie Blair and Laura Bush, the wives of the two instigators, were wheeled into TV studios to declare – a war for women's liberation. If it had been, it would have been the first in history. We now know what it really was: a crude war of revenge which failed because the occupation strengthened those it sought to destroy. I have discussed this war in great detail over the last forty years, arguing that countries in which a large segment of the population do not wish to be occupied by an imperialist power usually mount a resistance, and the cycle of war-occupation-resistance – more bombing attacks, more civilian deaths, more support for the resistance – continues regardless of its political complexion. The Taliban were the sole victors because *nobody* else fought against the US/NATO occupation.[8]

These two wars have not done anyone any good, but they have succeeded in dividing the Muslim and Arab world, whether or not this was the intention. The US decision to hand over power to clerical Shia parties in Iraq deepened the Sunni–Shia divide: there was ethnic cleansing in Baghdad, which used to be a mixed city in a country where intermarriage between Sunni and Shia was common. The Americans acted as if all Sunnis were Saddam supporters, yet many Sunnis suffered arbitrary jail sentences under him. But the creation of this divide has ended Arab nationalism for a long time to come. The battles now are to do with which side the US backs in which conflict. In Iraq, it backs the Shia.

The demonisation of Iran is deeply ironic, because without the tacit support of the Iranians the Americans could not have taken or held Iraq. The Iraqi resistance against the occupation was

8   See Tariq Ali, *The Forty-Year War in Afghanistan: A Chronicle Foretold*, London, 2021.

making headway until the Iranians told the Shia leader Muqtada al-Sadr, who'd been collaborating with Sunni opponents of the regime, to call it off. He was taken to Tehran and given a 'holiday' there for a year. Without Iranian support in both Iraq and Afghanistan, it would have been very difficult for the United States to sustain its occupations. Iran was thanked with sanctions, further demonisation and double standards – Israel can have nuclear weapons, you can't. Iran's decision to mend its fences with the Taliban is hardly a surprise.

The Middle East is now in a total mess: the central, most important power in the region is Israel, expanding away; the Palestinians have been defeated and will remain defeated for a very long time to come; all the principal Arab countries are wrecked, first Iraq, now Syria; Egypt, with a brutal military dictatorship in power, is torturing and killing as if the Arab Spring had never happened – and for the military leaders, it hasn't.

As for Israel, the blind support it gets from the US is an old story. And to question it, nowadays, is to be labelled an anti-Semite. The danger with this strategy is that if you say to a generation which had no experience of the Holocaust outside of movies that to attack Israel is anti-Semitic, the reply will be: so what? 'Call us anti-Semitic if you want', young people will say. 'If that means opposing you, we are.' So it hasn't helped anyone. It's inconceivable now that any Israeli government is going to grant the Palestinians a state. As the late Edward Said warned us, the Oslo Accords were a Palestinian Treaty of Versailles. They turned out to be much worse than that.

So the disintegration of the Middle East that began after the First World War continues. Whether Iraq will be divided into three countries (two US protectorates and one Iranian), whether Syria will be divided into two or three countries, whether Libya will ever be united again, we don't know. But it would hardly be surprising if all the states in the region, barring Egypt, which is too large to dismantle, ended up as Bantustans, or principalities, on the model of Qatar and the other Gulf States, funded and kept going by the Saudis on the one hand, and the Iranians on the other.

All the hopes raised by the Arab Spring went under, and it's important to understand why. Too many of those who took part didn't see – for generational reasons, largely – that to hit home you have to have some form of political movement. It wasn't surprising that the Muslim Brotherhood, which had participated in the protests in Egypt at a late stage, took power: it was the only real political party in Egypt. But then the Brotherhood played straight into the hands of the military by behaving like Mubarak – offering deals to the security services, offering deals to the Israelis – so people began to wonder what the point was of having them in power. The military was thus able to mobilise support and get rid of the Brotherhood. All this has demoralised an entire generation in the Middle East.

What is the situation in Europe? The first point to be made is that there isn't a single country in the European Union that enjoys proper sovereignty. Since the end of the Cold War and reunification, Germany has become the strongest and strategically the most important state in Europe, but even it doesn't have total sovereignty: the United States is still dominant on many levels, especially as far as the military is concerned.

Britain became a semi-vassal state after the Second World War, and its power to act on its own, after the Suez debacle of 1956, has long gone. Churchill himself was critical that the permission of the United States had not been obtained for that intervention. Since then, Britain has invariably done the Americans' bidding even when large parts of the British establishment were against it. There was a great deal of anger in the Foreign Office during the Iraq War among those who felt there was no need for Britain to be involved.

In 2003, when the war was underway, I was invited to give a lecture in Damascus. I got a phone call from the British embassy there asking me to come to lunch. I thought this was odd. When I arrived I was greeted by the ambassador, who said: 'Just to reassure you, we won't just be eating, we'll be talking politics.' At the lunch, he said: 'Now it's time for questions – I'll start off. Tariq Ali, I read the piece you wrote in the *Guardian* arguing that Tony Blair should be charged for war crimes in the International Criminal Court. Do you mind explaining why?' I spent about ten minutes explaining, to the bemusement of the Syrian guests. At the end the ambassador said: 'Well, I agree totally with that – I don't know about the rest of you.' After the guests had left, I said: 'That was very courageous of you.' And the MI6 man who was also at the lunch said: 'Yeah, he can do that, because he's retiring in December.' But a similar thing happened at the embassy in Vienna, where I gave a press conference, in the British ambassador's living room, attacking the Iraq War. These people aren't fools – they knew exactly what they were doing. And they acted as they did as a result of the humiliation they felt at having a government that, even though the Americans had said they could manage without the UK, insisted on joining in anyway.

The Germans know they don't have full sovereignty, but when you raise it with them they shrug. Many of them don't want it, because they are obsessed with their past, with the notion that Germans are almost genetically predisposed to like fighting wars – a ludicrous view, which some people who should know better have expressed again in marking the anniversaries of the First World War. The fact is that – politically, ideologically, militarily and even economically – the European Union is largely under the thumb of the global imperial power. When the Euro elite was offering a pitiful sum of money to the Greeks, Timothy Geithner, then US Secretary of the Treasury, had to intervene, and tell the EU to increase its rescue fund to €500 billion. They hummed and hawed, but finally did what the Americans wanted.

All the hopes that had been raised, from the time the European idea was first mooted, of a continent independent of the other major powers charting its own way in the world, disappeared once the Cold War ended. Just when you felt it might be able to achieve that goal, Europe instead became a continent devoted to the interests of bankers – a Europe of money, a place without a social vision, leaving the neoliberal order unchallenged.

The Greeks were punished not so much for the debt as for their failure to make the reforms demanded by the EU. The right-wing government Syriza defeated only managed to push through three of the fourteen reforms the EU insisted on. They couldn't do more because what they did push through helped create a situation in

Greece which has some similarities with Iraq: de-modernisation; totally unnecessary privatisations, linked to political corruption; the immiseration of ordinary people. So the Greeks elected a government that offered to change things, and then they were told that it couldn't. The EU was frightened of a domino effect: if the Greeks were rewarded for electing Syriza other countries might elect similar governments, so Greece had to be crushed.

The Greeks can't be kicked out of the European Union – that isn't permitted by the constitution – or out of the eurozone, but life can be made so difficult for them that they have to leave the euro and set up a Greek euro, or a euro drachma, so that the country keeps going. But were that to happen conditions would, at least temporarily, get even worse – which is why the Greeks have no choice but to resist it. The danger now is that, in this volatile atmosphere, people could shift very rapidly to the right. That is the scale of the problem, and for the Euro elite to behave as it's doing – as the extreme centre, in other words – is short-sighted and often foolish.

And, most importantly, there's the rise of China. The huge improvement in living standards in that country, and the transformation of its infrastructure that has made it the 'workshop of the world', have helped shift the centre of the world market eastwards. There's no doubt that enormous gains have been made by capitalism in China, and the Chinese and American economies are remarkably interdependent. When a veteran of the labour movement in the United States recently asked me what had happened to the American working class the answer was plain: the American working class is in China now. But it's also the case that China isn't even remotely close to replacing the United States. All the figures produced by economists over the last decade or so show that, where it counts, the Chinese are still behind.

Consider the national shares of world millionaire households in 2012: the United States, 42.5 per cent; Japan, 10.6 per cent; China, 9.4 per cent; Britain, 3.7 per cent; Switzerland, 2.9 per cent; Germany, 2.7 per cent; Taiwan, 2.3 per cent; Italy, 2 per cent; France, 1.9 per cent. So in terms of economic strength the United States is still doing well. In many crucial markets – pharmaceuticals, aerospace, computer software, medical equipment – the US is dominant; the Chinese are nowhere. The figures in 2010 showed that three-quarters of China's top 200 exporting companies – and these are Chinese statistics – are foreign-owned. There is a great deal of foreign investment in China, often from neighbouring countries like Taiwan. Foxconn, which produces computers for Apple in China, is a Taiwanese company. The last decade has seen a catch-up by China, but they are still far from overtaking the US.

The notion that the Chinese are suddenly going to rise to power and replace the United States is baloney. The current campaigns being waged against China are largely designed to reassert US economic hegemony by clipping the dragon's wings. The imminent ascendancy of China is implausible militarily, economically, politically and ideologically; it's obvious that it's not the case. When the British Empire began its decline, decades before it collapsed, people knew what was happening. Both Lenin and Trotsky realised that the British were going down. There's a wonderful speech of Trotsky's, delivered in 1924 at the Communist International, where, in inimitable fashion, the Jewish Bolshevik enraged Churchill by his reflections on the English bourgeoisie:

> Their character has been moulded in the course of centuries. Class self-esteem has entered into their blood and marrow, their nerves and bones. It will be much harder to knock the self-confidence of world rulers out of them. But the American will knock it out just the same, when he gets seriously down to business. In vain does the British bourgeois console himself that he will serve as a guide for the inexperienced American. Yes, there will be a transitional period. But the crux of the matter does not lie in the habits of diplomatic leadership but in actual power, existing capital and industry. And the United States, if we take its economy, from oats to big battleships of the latest type, occupies the first place. They produce all the living necessities to the extent of one-half to two-thirds of what is produced by all mankind.

If we were to change the text, and instead of the 'English bourgeois character' say the 'American bourgeois character has been moulded in the course of centuries ... but the Chinese will knock it out just the same', it wouldn't make sense. And for good reason. Global hegemony is not a strategy adopted by China, whose aims so far have been largely defensive, despite the US provocation in September 2021 when it overrode a French nuclear submarine deal with Australia, replaced it with its own, and drew the Australian politico-military elite into a new security pact targeting China. There is also a US–EU operation being prepared, intended to use the Uighurs as pawns in furthering internal destabilisation. There are, reportedly, several thousand Uighurs in Turkey being trained in live wars (such as in Syria) and prepared for a journey home. What is taking place is more than rocket-rattling.

Where are we going to be at the end of this century? Where is China going to be? Is Western democracy going to flourish? One thing that has become clear over the last few decades is that nothing happens unless people want it to happen; and if people want it to happen, they start moving. You would have thought that the Europeans would have learned some lessons from the 2007–8 crash and the recession that followed, and would have acted. But they didn't. They just put a sticking plaster on the wounds and hoped that the blood would be stemmed. So where should we look for a solution? One of the more creative thinkers today is the German sociologist Wolfgang Streeck, who makes it clear that an alternative structure for the European Union is desperately needed and that it will necessitate more democracy at every level – at a provincial and city level as well as at a national and European level. There needs to be a concerted effort to find an alternative to the neoliberal system.

Many people in Eastern Europe feel a nostalgia for the societies that existed before the fall of the Soviet Union. The communist regimes that governed the Soviet bloc after the arrival of Khrushchev could be described as social dictatorships: essentially weak regimes with an authoritarian political structure, but also an economic structure that offered people a threadbare version of Swedish or British social democracy. In a poll taken in January 2018, 82 per cent of respondents in the old East Germany said that life was better before unification. When asked to give reasons, they said that there was more sense of community, there were more facilities, money wasn't the dominant thing, cultural life was better and they weren't treated, as they are now, like second-class citizens.

The attitude of West Germans to those from the East quickly became a serious problem – so serious that, in the second year after reunification, Helmut Schmidt, the former German chancellor and not a great radical, told the Social Democratic Party conference that the way East Germans were being treated was completely wrong. He said East German culture should no longer be ignored; if he had to choose the three greatest German writers, he said, he would pick Goethe, Heine and Brecht. The audience gasped when he mentioned Brecht.

The prejudice against the East is deeply ingrained. The reason the Germans were so shocked by the Edward Snowden revelations is that it suddenly became clear to them they were living under permanent surveillance – after one of the big ideological campaigns in West Germany had been to do with the evils of the Stasi in the East, who, it was said, spied on everyone all the time. Well, the Stasi didn't have the technical capacity for ubiquitous spying. On the scale of surveillance, the United States is far ahead of West Germany's old enemy.

Not only do many former East Germans prefer the old political system, they also come at the top of the atheism charts: 52.1 per cent of them don't believe in God; the Czech Republic is second with 39.9 per cent; secular France is down at 23.3 per cent (secularism in France really means anything that's not Islamic). If you look at the other side, the country with the highest proportion of believers is the Philippines at 83.6 per cent; followed by Chile, 79.4 per cent; Israel, 65.5 per cent; Poland, 62 per cent; the US, 60.6 per cent; compared to which Ireland is a bastion of moderation at only 43.2 per cent. If the pollsters had visited the Islamic world and asked these questions they might have been surprised at the answers given in Turkey, for instance, or even in Indonesia. Religious belief is not confined to any single part of the globe.

It's a mixed and confused world. But its problems don't change – they just take new forms. One thing alone remains permanent. The refusal of the threatened and underprivileged to remain passive for too long. And this politico-anthropological-historical element in world politics began in the ancient world. I will quote two examples. The first from Greece, the second from China.

In Sparta in the third century BCE, a fissure developed between the ruling elite and the ordinary people following the Peloponnesian Wars. Those who were ruled demanded change because the gap between rich and poor had become so huge it couldn't be tolerated. A succession of radical monarchs – Agis IV, Cleomenes III and Nabis – created a structure to help revive the state. Nobles were sent into exile, the magistrates' dictatorship was abolished, slaves were given their freedom, all citizens were allowed to vote and land confiscated from the rich was distributed to the poor (something the EU or Britain wouldn't tolerate today).

The early Roman Republic, threatened by this example, sent its legions under Titus Quinctius Flamininus to crush Sparta. According to Livy, the following was the response from Nabis, the king of Sparta, full of cold anger and dignity:

> Do not demand that Sparta conform to your own laws and institutions … You select your cavalry and infantry by their property qualifications and desire that a few should excel in wealth and the common people be subject to them. Our law-giver did not want the state to be in the hands of a few, whom you call the Senate, nor that any one class should have supremacy in the state. He believed that by equality of fortune and dignity there would be many to bear arms for their country.

In 9 CE, the Chinese high official who had usurped the throne and become a temporary emperor was quoted in the *Han History* as arguing for a 'True Way' forward:

> The Chin dynasty was without the True Way. It increased taxation to supply itself with services. It exhausted the people's strength in order to take its desires to the extreme. It destroyed the system of the sages and abolished the well-fields. In consequence the accumulation of property began. Greed and vice came into being. The powerful counted their fields in thousands, while the weak had not even the space in which to insert the point of an awl … Fathers and

sons, husbands and wives, worked all the year long at ploughing and hoeing without gaining enough to live on. So the rich had dogs and horses fed on more grain and vegetables than they could eat, and acted in a manner that was haughty and depraved. The poor could not get their fill of dregs . . .[9]

Far from being 'squeamish' (one of Churchill's favourite words to justify atrocities) about today's military-technological developments – missiles carrying depleted uranium, drones able to target individuals and facilities without incurring any Western casualties, watched by the offending president or prime minister – Churchill would have been delighted by them. Better, then, to forget about him. Obama and Biden had Churchill's bust removed from the Oval Office ostensibly because of Kenya and Ireland respectively, but in reality because they don't need Blair's gift to Bush. The imperialist record of many US presidents, especially their kill ratio, leaves Churchill way behind. Britain is destined, unless there is a determined change of course, to live in the capacious posterior of the White House together with the Saudis and Israel, both creations of Churchill's beloved Empire. The ship of state that Churchill left behind drifted half waterlogged into the twenty-first century. It is still foundering under old habits, rotting institutions and a set of visionless political parties. The Scottish lifeboat might cut the rope and drift in a different direction. Meanwhile *HMS Britain*'s hull remains encrusted with a nostalgia of which Churchill forms a huge part. Best to scrub him off.

---

9   Quoted in Mark Elvin, *The Pattern of the Chinese Past*, Stanford, 1973, p. 31. For any reader interested in Chinese history and its distinct shapes over two millennia, this book has no peer in the field.

EPILOGUE

Gerald Scarfe.

This is our lot if we live so long and labour unto the end –
That we outlive the impatient years and the much too patient friend:
And because we know we have breath in our mouth and think we have
thoughts in our head,
We shall assume that we are alive, whereas we are really dead.

Rudyard Kipling, 'The Old Men' (1902)

This cartoon ('Churchill's Last Day in Parliament') by Gerald Scarfe was commissioned by the (pre-Murdoch) *Sunday Times*. They refused to publish it. Scarfe sent it to Richard Ingrams at *Private Eye*, who made it their cover. It is reprinted here with the kind permission of the artist.

SELECT BIBLIOGRAPHY

Too many pages would be required were I to list every book I read to write this one. Most of them are mentioned in the footnotes. But some need more prominence. They were the necessary crutches that kept me going during the lockdown when libraries were closed, and are offered here as a reading list for those who wish to explore further. In terms of journals, there are several very stimulating essays on Churchill by various essayists in the *London Review of Books*, and discussions on British history, politics and culture in *New Left Review*. To these should be added the early *History Workshop Journal* and *Past and Present*.

Of all the existing biographies, I would strongly recommend Clive Ponting's work. A senior mandarin at the ministry of defence, Ponting turned whistle-blower during the Falklands War and subsequently devoted himself to writing history, with remarkable success. His fine mind was a loss to the English civil service, but an important gain for history. Geoffrey Wheatcroft's book arrived too late for me to read for this one, but the US reviews suggest it is of high quality.

Acheson, D. *Present at the Creation: My Years in the State Department*, W. W. Norton, 1988.

Anderson, P. *American Foreign Policy and Its Thinkers*, Verso, 2014.

Anderson, P. *Ever Closer Union: Europe in the West*, Verso, 2021.

Barnett, A. *Iron Britannia: Why Parliament Waged Its Falklands War*, Allison & Busby, 1982.

Dangerfield, G. *The Strange Death of Liberal England 1910–1914*, McGibbon & Kee, 1966.

Davis, M. *Late Victorian Holocausts*, Verso, 2017.

Dower, J. W. *War Without Mercy: Race and Power in the Pacific War*, Random House, 1988.

Elkins, C. *Britain's Gulag: The Brutal End of Empire in Kenya*, Jonathan Cape, 2005.

Elvin, M. *The Pattern of the Chinese Past*, Stanford University Press, 1973.

Erickson, J. *The Road to Stalingrad*, Cassell, 2003.

Gopal, P. *Insurgent Empire: Anticolonial Resistance and British Dissent*, Verso, 2019.

Gott, R. *Britain's Empire: Resistance, Repression and Revolt*, Verso, 2011.

Gott, R. and Gilbert, M. *The Appeasers*, Weidenfeld and Nicolson, 1967.

Jackson, J. *A Certain Idea of France: The Life of Charles de Gaulle*, Allen Lane, 2018.

Jenkins, R. *Churchill: A Biography*, Macmillan, 2001.

Johnson, B. *The Churchill Factor: How One Man Made History*, Hodder & Stoughton, 2014.

Mukerji, M. *Churchill's Secret War: The British Empire and the Forgotten Indian Famine of the Second World War*, Basic Books, 2010.

Nairn, T. *The Break-Up of Britain*, Verso, 1977.

Pankhurst, S. *The Suffragette: A History of the Women's Militant Suffrage Movement, 1905–1910*, Dover, 2015.

Ponting, C. *1940: The Myth and Reality*, Ivan R. Dee, 1991.

Ponting, C. *Churchill*, Sinclair Stevenson, 1994.

Preston, P. *The Spanish Holocaust: Inquisition and Extermination in Twentieth-Century Spain*, Harper, 2012.

Saville, J. *The Politics of Continuity: British Foreign Policy and the Labour Government 1945–1949*, Verso, 1993.

Thomas, H. *Cuba: A History*, Penguin, 1971.

Thomas, H. *The Spanish Civil War*, Penguin, 2012.

Thompson, E. P. *The Making of the English Working Class*, Penguin, 2013.

Toye, R. *Churchill's Empire: The World That Made Him and the World He Made*, Henry Holt, 2010.

Wigg, R. *Churchill and Spain: The Survival of the Franco Regime, 1940–45*, Routledge, 2005.

Wheatcroft, G. *Churchill's Shadow: The Life and Afterlife of Winston Churchill*. W. W. Norton, 2021.

INDEX